REDISCOVERING FORT SANDERS

EAST TENNESSEE AND V
BATY WILTSEE
FT COMSTOCK
BATY BILLINGSLEY
BATY GALPIN
BATY ZOELLNER
ORT SANDERS
198
KNOXVILLE
FT BYINGTON
BATY NOBLE
Military Bridge
Pontoon Bridge
BARRACKS
FT STANLEY
(UNFINISHED)
FT DICKERSON
325
310

REDISCOVERING FORT SANDERS

THE AMERICAN CIVIL WAR AND ITS IMPACT ON KNOXVILLE'S CULTURAL LANDSCAPE

TERRY FAULKNER AND
CHARLES H. FAULKNER

THE UNIVERSITY OF TENNESSEE PRESS / KNOXVILLE

FIRST EDITION.

A portion of this project was funded by the Tennessee Civil War National Heritage Area, a partnership unit of the National Park Service and administered by the Center for Historic Preservation at MTSU.

Library of Congress Cataloging-in-Publication Data

Names: Faulkner, Terry (Historian), author. | Faulkner, Charles H., author.

Title: Rediscovering Fort Sanders : the American Civil War and its impact on Knoxville's cultural landscape / Terry Faulkner and Charles H. Faulkner.

Description: First. | Knoxville : The University of Tennessee Press, [2020] | Includes bibliographical references and index. | Summary: "What begins here as a scholarly investigation into a Civil War-era fort opens onto a new view of present-day Knoxville, the historic Fort Sanders community adjacent to the University of Tennessee campus, and the city's commemoration and memory of the fort. Using historical-archaeological methods, Terry Faulkner and Charles H. Faulkner uncover remnants of the fort, exposing a small error in the historic location and present-day commemoration. More importantly, this book is the first scholarly treatment of Fort Sanders and its history since Digby Seymour's 1963 publication *Divided Loyalties*, and brings the story of Fort Sanders into the twenty-first century"—Provided by publisher.

Identifiers: LCCN 2020004451 (print) | LCCN 2020004452 (ebook) | ISBN 9781621904816 (hardcover) | ISBN 9781621904823 (pdf)

Subjects: LCSH: Fort Sanders (Knoxville, Tenn.)—History. | Knoxville (Tenn.)—History.

Classification: LCC F444.K7 F39 2020 (print) | LCC F444.K7 (ebook) | DDC 976.8/85—dc23

LC record available at https://lccn.loc.gov/2020004451

LC ebook record available at https://lccn.loc.gov/2020004452

To our best friends, the members of our family:
Kelly, Stephanie, Andrew, Matthew, and Michael

CONTENTS

★★★★

ILLUSTRATIONS

★★★★

PREFACE

★★★★

While serving as president of Keep Knoxville Beautiful (KKB) in 2008, I was also privileged to be a member of the Knoxville City Tree Board. At that time one of the goals of the KKB Board was to select and beautify a major entrance into Knoxville, and one of the goals of the Tree Board was to help provide trees for the city. As the 150th year commemoration of the Civil War, a Sesquicentennial, was to begin in 2011, KKB Board members suggested that 17th Street, a critical north–south connection through the neighborhood of Fort Sanders to the University of Tennessee campus and the city of Knoxville, be chosen. This street was first called Fort Sanders Avenue because it accessed a massive Civil War fortification called Fort Sanders, for which this historic neighborhood was named. City Tree Board members and Knoxville's mayor at that time, Bill Haslam, agreed this would be an excellent and timely beautification project for KKB members to undertake. The Tennessee Department of Transportation joined the effort, providing a grant for landscaping along I-40, and the Knoxville City Council members matched a grant from the State of Tennessee to fund a Tennessee Civil War Trails Marker. With the approval of the staff and members of Fort Sanders's Redeemer Church, we were able to complete the partnership, as the church members graciously agreed to have a Tennessee Sesquicentennial Civil War Trails educational marker placed on their property on 17th Street. Civil War tourists and local visitors were also welcomed to park in their church lot so they could read the trails signage about Fort Sanders and then walk the area where the fort had been located.

While working on this project, an idea came to me: why not try to create a walking tour for Sesquicentennial tourists in the area of the Fort Sanders neighborhood where the Civil War fort had been located? As the unofficial Bearden historian, I had previously worked with city engineers in the late 1990s to install markers documenting Bearden history in new greenways and sidewalks in the Bearden community. Why not suggest that the city consider funding a similar project to document Civil War Fort Sanders?

During the time before the Sesquicentennial began in 2011, Civil War sites in South Knoxville were being preserved and prepared by the Legacy Parks Foundation, local Civil War Roundtable members, and the City of Knoxville for future Civil War tourism. It seemed likely that an educational walking tour on the north side of the river, where the major battle for Knoxville took place, would increase tourism in the Fort Sanders neighborhood and help to preserve this historic area that had been named after the fort. I talked with Mayor Haslam about the possibility of completing such a project before the Sesquicentennial began and was referred to city engineers Karen McKeehan and Shawn Fitzpatrick, so that a budget could be prepared for his consideration. A proposal was presented to the engineers for a walking tour around the traditional location of the fort based on the illustration in Digby Gordon Seymour's signature book, *Divided Loyalties: Fort Sanders and the Civil War in East Tennessee,* first published in 1963. Seymour's book was published by the University of Tennessee Press to commemorate the 100th anniversary of the Battle of Fort Sanders in 1863. Included in the packet of information prepared for the engineers were photos of the historic markers documenting the battle in the area of the fort, Union army contour maps, current KGIS contour maps, eyewitness accounts of the battle, and Seymour's map from *Divided Loyalties,* which shows the location of the fort with the west wall on 17th Street and the northwest bastion, the site of the 1863 attack by Confederate troops, at the corner of 17th Street and Laurel Avenue. All editions of Seymour's book (2nd, 1982, and 3rd, 2002) contain maps showing the site of Fort Sanders at this same location, and this placement of the fort has been accepted without question by local Civil War historians as the correct location since 1963 and perhaps even as early as 1957.

The budget prepared by city engineers for the installation of 30 granite educational markers into new panels of sidewalk to create a walking tour around the traditional fort location was $80,000; this amount was good news. The bad news was that the engineers said they could not recommend that this amount of city funds be spent on the project because they felt the information provided them was not sufficient to prove that the traditional location for the fort was accurate.

It was understandable that city engineers would not recommend any expenditures by the city for a walking tour until it was proved beyond any doubt that the correct location of the fort had been identified. So I began to do additional research on Fort Sanders at the Calvin M. McClung Historical Collection at the East Tennessee History Center to produce totally convincing evidence that the information I had originally provided them was correct.

The result of the research was the discovery that Ms. McKeehan and Mr. Fitzpatrick were right to question the traditional location. After several months of research at the McClung Collection, the correct location of Fort Sanders had been identified for the first time in decades. Realizing the importance of this discovery, I continued the archival research and soon my husband, Charlie, joined me. Over the next several years he directed the geological and archaeological testing on the fort site and areas surrounding the fort and has been an equal partner in writing this book.

We arranged early in the project to visit with the late Digby Seymour to talk about why he had located the western wall of the fort on 17th Street and the northwest bastion at 17th Street and Laurel Avenue. Digby, who was 94 at this time, was happy to discuss the reasons he had written the book, but he had no memory of why he had placed the fort at that location. He told us that he was sure "that he had placed it according to the best information available at the time" (personal communication, 2008). Seymour's location places the interior of the fort between 17th and 16th Streets on the topographical crest of White's Hill. We believe that we have discovered while researching this book why Seymour inaccurately located the fort between 17th and 16th streets on the topographical crest instead of the military crest.

After compiling and reviewing our initial evidence for this location, we met with the supervisor of the McClung Collection, Steve Cotham, to show him our research, which proved our new location of the fort was correct. Mr. Cotham carefully considered our research and agreed that we had indeed discovered the actual location of Civil War Fort

Sanders. We then contacted engineers and the officers of the Historic Fort Sanders Neighborhood Association, Randall De Ford and Cathy Irwin, who joined us in requesting that the East Tennessee Community Design Center create a walking tour around the location of the interior of the fort, the area between Clinch and Laurel Avenues and 17th and 18th Streets. The excellent plan produced by the Design Center includes a walking tour around that block with historic markers set into the sidewalks that document the siege of Knoxville, the battle of Fort Sanders, Civil War weaponry, Union and Confederate commanders, and so on. In the years following the completion of that plan in 2010, we have intermittently joined with the leaders of the Historic Fort Sanders Neighborhood Association in searching for funding for this important educational project about the history of the Civil War in Knoxville.

We also have participated in efforts to preserve the only existing original topography in the area of the fort, the remains of a sinkhole located immediately west of 18th Street between Laurel and Highland Avenues described by Confederate General Porter Alexander in his account of the battle of Fort Sanders. Research continued into June 2012 when an archaeological excavation was completed by the authors during withering 105-degree heat. Our findings verified the results of earlier geological testing in the area that indicated the interior of the fort was located between 17th and 18th Streets and Clinch and Laurel Avenues.

We have continued to verify our location with information found in newly discovered historical sources and with evidence produced by remote sensing in critical areas, even as we were completing this book. We have found nothing whatsoever in relevant archival material that successfully disputes our location of the fort on the western military crest of White's Hill between of 17th and 18th Streets and the northwest bastion at the corner of 18th and Laurel Avenue. We discovered and have documented here additional information about the almost total destruction of this immense earthwork completed by Union forces in 1865 under the direction of General Davis Tillson.

All structures built by humans, including those built mainly of soil, such as Civil War Fort Sanders, have a life cycle that can be examined either piecemeal or in totality; this cycle includes four potential stages of human and natural impacts on the structure. Initially, there is a close interplay between humans and the environment as a building site is prepared for construction. The second stage is completion of the structure and an evaluation of how well it serves the purpose for which it was built. A third stage can either take place or not; the structure might be added to or renovated to provide for a change in function, or it might be restored to its original condition if it has fallen into disrepair. In the final, fourth stage, the structure can be abandoned and physically disappear due to environmental causes, human neglect, or deliberate destruction.

After identifying the exact location of the fort on White's Hill, explaining why that location was chosen, describing the battle, detailing the history of the construction to completion, and documenting the remnants of the old fort, we were called to continue our research by one of the many voices of Confederate soldiers who spoke to us from their diaries, articles, and books.

Twenty-one-year-old Private Edward M. Burruss of the 21st Mississippi Infantry was awed by the partially completed fort in 1863 and called it "the most immense work" he had ever seen (Burruss 1863). We became determined to document the fourth stage of the life cycle of this structure, which more than doubled in size by the time it was completed in 1865. How and why did this enormous earthwork almost completely vanish after being abandoned in 1866? How had the slow, relentless impacts of environmental factors and human "progress" reduced this immense fortification to a few, almost unrecognizable remnants?

We chose to employ a holistic scientific method called historical ecology to complete a study of the impact of fort construction on the landscape up until the time of abandonment (Troll 2007). Historical ecology focuses on the interactions of humans with their environment over long periods of time and on a wide scale which result in significant changes in the landscape on which they live (Crumley and Marquart 1978). We continued to apply this method, establishing a timeline for the cultural and environmental impacts. We documented why and how both the fort and landscape in the vicinity of the fort were altered through the decades after the fort was abandoned. We recorded the scientific evidence of those transformations that took place and explained why existing remains were unintentionally preserved. We described how the enormous earthwork that had challenged Confederate attackers in the 19th century had again challenged in the 20th century the developers of Knoxville's first western suburb, West Knoxville. We note the effects that new development in the late 20th and early 21st century has had on this area and why continuing development threatens to affect not only the integrity of the existing historic overlay protecting the location of Fort Sanders, but also those areas of the neighborhood outside the overlay.

Preserved Civil War fortifications are among the most visible, significant, and stirring structural memorials to the brave men who fought on both sides during the war; many still stand today as impressive reminders of the laborious efforts of the myriad of dedicated soldiers, civilians, and enslaved people who built, maintained, and protected them until the conflict ended.

We hope that our in-depth study will help the reader understand how Fort Sanders was transformed in time from a dynamic place of life, death, bravery, and folly to a place that was visited and revered, then robbed of its artifacts and the material of which it was constructed, as well as why in the mid-20th century the location of the fort was unintentionally misplaced on the landscape and Fort Sanders was finally declared to be "only a memory."

ACKNOWLEDGMENTS

★★★★

Since we began this project 10 years ago we have met and worked with countless people who were very interested and excited about our research on Civil War Fort Sanders. Most were eager to assist us in every way possible in finishing the research and the writing of this book so that we could share our discoveries about this important fortification with others. In 2017, after eight years of continuing archival research, geological and archaeological testing, and intermittent writing, we submitted our manuscript to Thomas Wells, acquisitions editor for the University of Tennessee Press. We are grateful to Thomas for encouraging us to submit the manuscript to the members of the board of UT Press, to Jon Boggs, assistant editor, and the peer reviewers who supported publication of this book.

The first person we spoke with about the actual location of Civil War Fort Sanders was Digby Seymour, author of the classic book *Divided Loyalties: Fort Sanders and the Civil War in East Tennessee,* which was first published in 1963. Dr. Seymour (1923–2017) died recently, but he will not be forgotten. He left us with an amazing book, one that is well researched, documented, and illustrated, as well as being so well written that it is revered by every local Civil War enthusiast. It is the premier authority on the war in Knoxville and East Tennessee. A second, living authority, Steve Cotham, is not only an expert on the history of the Civil War in Knoxville but also on the entire history of Knox County. Steve is the Knox County Historian and the executive director of the Calvin M. McClung Historical Collection, and he is still very much doing what he loves, caring for and adding to the historic collection and supporting those interested in researching area history or the history of their ancestors.

We first described and interpreted our archival and photographic proof of the actual location of Fort Sanders to Steve for his opinion. After studying the material he said, "you have nailed the location of the fort." Steve encouraged us continuously as we proceeded to record our findings in this book. He directed our attention to additional pertinent information in the McClung Collection and Tennessee State archives and helped with various other requests during the years it took to complete the manuscript. We are sincerely grateful for his help.

After Steve's endorsement of our location of the fort, we shared our information with many others whose thoughts and opinions we respected. First among these was Jim Tumblin, Fountain City historian, and Jim Bletner, each an expert on the Civil War in Knoxville. Next came Randall De Ford, Wes Goddard, Cathy Irwin, Charlie Thomas, and R. B. Morris, all present or past residents of the Fort Sanders neighborhood, who have studied the history of Fort Sanders and searched the terrain for clues as to the exact location of the fort.

Many others were fascinated with our research and wanted to review our proof, maps, photographs, and so on. They asked questions that initiated more research, and they wanted to be shown remains of the fort. Some periodically read or edited the manuscript for grammar, punctuation, readability, and scholarship. These contributors to the project were Sara Bryant, Cindy Estes, Nancy and John Rennie, Christine Griffin, Joe Finecane, Cindy Spangler, and Marsha Grieve. Our grandson, Matthew McGill, was an excellent editor and advisor, along with his mother, Kelly McGill; and our younger daughter, Stephanie Faulkner, a librarian, provided us with books we needed, encouragement, and food sometimes, too.

Many professionals and professors helped with the research, and we are especially grateful to them for their expertise and for being as obsessed and curious as we were about the geology, archaeology, soils analysis, human interaction with the landscape, and plain old sinkholes. Thank you, Dr. John Foss, UT earth science professor, who did the soil coring on the Ronald McDonald House site to determine the presence and location of those soil strata associated with the fort and who also cored at the Scarlett house site and Monday Apartments. We are greatly indebted to Dr. Robert Hatcher, a Distinguished Scientist in the Department of Planetary and Earth Sciences at the university, who performed the XRD refraction analysis that identified the silica sand excavated at the fort, which we believe filled the sand bags used in the embrasures of the fort. Retired geologist Harry Moore and Dr. David Leiske examined the sink hole between Laurel and Highland at 18th Street that played such an important role in locating the fort. Pat Garrow, Dr. Tim Bauman, Valerie Alzheimer, and Paul Avery are historic archaeologists who advised us on stratigraphy and the archaeological features we uncovered during our excavation. Two other excellent archaeologists, Dan Brock and Howard Cyr, did the remote sensing; Dan created the graphics for this book. We are grateful that these respected volunteer scholars were a joy to work with; they helped prove time and again that it's fun to get dirty.

We thank Gerald Green, director of the Knoxville–Knox County Metropolitan Planning Commission (MPC) and Kaye Graybeal, the MPC historic preservation planner, who studied the new location of the fort site and prepared a file at MPC that contains important information and photographs about the fort site and the area where the sinkhole is located. These properties are included in the Fort Sanders MPC H-1 Historic Overlay District for the Fort Sanders neighborhood. Two talented and competent staff members of the East Tennessee Community Design Center, Leslie Fawaz and Perry Childress, created the design for the Civil War walking tour at the fort site, and we thank them and all of the staff of this nonprofit organization, which provides pro bono design services for community projects throughout East Tennessee.

The ability to easily access books, journals, photographs, letters, and volumes of the minutes of West Knoxville Council meetings was critical for completing our research. We are very grateful to Melissa Peters, Cindy Mitchell, and Susan Wilson, who climbed up and down the ladder in the Knoxville City Council document storage vault, extracting and replacing the heavy tomes of West Knoxville minutes for us; most important, they always offered us coffee so we could stay awake and finish our research by the end of their work day. Sally Polhemus and Danette Welch, stellar members of the McClung Collection staff, happily provided us with information and lots of photographs. We are indebted to Gerald Augustus and Brent Cantrell, who shared relevant letters from soldiers who fought at Fort Sanders from their personal collections for us. Tamara Kennelly, archivist at Virginia Tech University, obtained permission for us to publish photographs of Fort Sanders from their collection, and Steve Cotham has permitted us to use photographs from the Calvin M. McClung Collection.

We are also very grateful to the people who allowed us to do "boots on the ground" research. Many residents and property owners in the fort area willingly gave us access so that we could examine and test sites that were especially critical to our research. Sue Beverly, director of the Ronald McDonald House, and her board members allowed us to undertake a major archaeological excavation that resulted in the discovery of buried remnants of the fort; Rebecca Scarlet allowed us access to a construction excavation adjacent to her front porch, and the late Glenn Shinaberry, a law student with a physically challenging summer job, helped by exposing areas that we needed to photograph and measure. Gene Monday and his son Will gave us permission to shovel-test their property next to the Pickle house and access the crawlspace under Fort Sanders Manor to study the geology of the ridge top. Andrew and Alice Brasler, who were building a house at the corner of Clinch Avenue and 17th Street, allowed us to examine the stratigraphy exposed in the newly excavated basement walls. After the Pickle house on Clinch Avenue burned and its remnants were razed, owners Jon Clark and Ron Turner gave us permission to test for traces of the fort in exposed areas on the property.

There was a constant need for technical help, and friends were eager to provide it. We thank Brad Hedge and acknowledge Jim Bletner for their technical support. We are sad that Jim didn't live to see this book finished. He taught us how to use the KGIS maps, and his enthusiasm for this research kept us going through some rough times. Brad saved us from living in constant fear that we would somehow delete our manuscript and kept our computer functioning for six years. Caroline Miller, Steven Mancuyas, and Josh DeMotte graciously advised and helped us with the printing of numerous manuscripts. Our good friends in the Anthropology Department, Pam Poe and Charlene Weaver, were always calm and competent when we needed them to be. And to Mark Barnes at Thompson Photo Products: we can never thank you enough for all you have done to prepare the photographs for this book. Finally, we must thank city engineers Karen McKeehan and Shawn Fitzpatrick, who are, in fact, responsible for the discovery of the correct location of Fort Sanders and for this book.

We also express our sincere thanks to Steve Cotham and the Friends of the Library for a grant that is enabling producers Melissa and Bill Sykes to film the present remains of Civil War Fort Sanders and complete a documentary around the archival, archaeological, and geological research which authenticates the correct location of the fort. We are also grateful to the Sykeses for including filmed interviews with professionals who participated in this research. The documentary will be available to the public in the Calvin M. McClung Historical Collection.

Charlie and I hope that all of you are as proud of this book as we are, and are as happy as we are, that we have remained a couple after 53 years of marriage and this experience of researching and writing a book together.

INTRODUCTION: LOST IN TIME

Eighty-five years after the founding of America, the first nation in history to be based on the principles of liberty and "dedicated to the belief that all men are created equal" was engaged in a great civil war that would threaten its continued existence. The victory of the Federal forces in that war ensured the survival of the union of the United States, and American citizens today continue to enjoy the benefits of freedom and equal treatment under the law. Because of that momentous conflict that took place between 1861 and 1865, hundreds of thousands of people between 2011 and 2015 attended or participated in local and national events during the Sesquicentennial commemorating the 150th anniversary of the Civil War.

Thousands of Civil War sites and historical figures associated with the war were honored in some way during this period. Many of the battlefield sites, historic structures, Civil War leaders, and notable civilians of that time are well known to the public here and abroad. Presently many battlefields, military artifacts, and personal artifacts are reverently preserved by museums and state, local, and federal agencies. Because of the Sesquicentennial commemoration, many other sites and objects related to the war that had been lost in time have been rediscovered, documented, preserved, and readied for public viewing and research.

In Knoxville, Tennessee, in 2008, as citizens prepared to commemorate the Civil War Sesquicentennial, the authors began an effort to discover and document the exact location of Fort Sanders, a large Union earthwork where the major battle for the town took place. We hoped that funding could be found to create an educational walking tour in the area of this well-known Civil War fortification for the 150th commemoration of the war. This quest resulted in two major discoveries of historic significance: that the fort was located a block farther to the west than previously recognized, and that there are still identifiable remnants of the fortification where none were believed to exist. Local historians had long believed that all evidence of the fort had been lost during the development of the first west Knoxville suburb, which began in the late 19th century and continued into the early 20th century. This area, initially called the town of "West Knoxville," has since assumed the name of the very fort that it almost completely destroyed.

The Civil War is often called the first modern war by military historians. It is the first war in human history to be extensively documented by first-person observation and personal mail, and by newspaper reporters, photographers, and artists who were present on the fields of battle. Their observations, thoughts, and feelings have been a source for thousands of books and articles; their descriptions of war have been brought to life in movies, on television, in outdoor dramas, and in reenactments. The momentous and traumatic impact of this horrendous conflict resulted in different eyewitness accounts of the same battle. These could be brief or embellished, and even myths can appear in the records. This is one reason why professional historians and other students of history continue to sift through the literature and study photographs and engravings in an effort to discover and document new facts that might provide insight as to why and how this war was fought.

In both the written word and on the landscape of actual battlefields, much documentation revolves around the end result of the event itself and the effects or consequences of that event. Understandably, the physical landscape, battle sites, and construction techniques used in building fortifications were often not adequately described or even documented at all. So the earthworks that are still preserved today remain our most visible evidence of the conflict that consumed this country for four years.

During the war, millions of cubic feet of earth were excavated using shovels, picks, axes, sticks, and even knife blades, tin cups, and spoons. This earth was loaded into buckets, wheelbarrows, and wagons, or into whatever containers might be available at the time, and then moved to an appropriate place to create a defensive earthworks for the soldiers.

Forests surrounding these sites were often denuded of trees to build stockades, gun platforms, and supporting walls for embankments of earth, and also to provide firewood and shelter for the troops. Not only did forts built in this manner effectively absorb and disperse the energy of enemy cannon fire, but the material to build them was usually readily available at the site to be fortified. Earth, inside and outside of the area to be fortified, was removed and added to the earthworks. Interior removal of soil produced level areas for parade grounds and movements of forces within the fort. Defensive trenches like "rabbit warrens" were dug outside the fortification to provide additional protection by blocking and entrapping attacking foot soldiers and cavalry. Many of these works were so formidable that 150 years of erosion, construction, and landscaping have not erased the magnitude and vestiges of the earthworks nor diminished the respect one feels for the soldiers who built them.

While the construction and plans for many of these fortifications are sometimes presented in detail, often only a map, sketch, or photograph remains to illustrate what they looked like during their use and after their abandonment. However, like any built structure, these works went through an evolution of phases, including initial construction, remodeling or modification, removal or reuse of earth, eventual abandonment and erosion, or complete destruction. These aspects of a transformation of earthen fortifications through time are seldom discussed. A case in point is the Civil War earthwork now called Fort Sanders, which was built and maintained on a ridge located just west of Knoxville, Tennessee, during the years 1863–65. Although one can find photographs and many eyewitness descriptions of the fort in various archives, only a small amount of archival evidence indicates exactly where the fort was located and very little is to be found that documents the process of the fort's construction.

During our eight years of research, we carefully examined historic maps, photographs, and archival records, conducted archaeological surveys and testing, and excavated both in the fort and the area surrounding it. We discovered how the original fort was built, the ways in which it was modified during additional construction, and how it looked in 1865 at the war's end. We learned that the actual site of the fortification did not correspond exactly to the traditional location and that historic markers present in the area today are inaccurate. Most important, we found that, contrary to the widespread belief that the fort had been completely destroyed by development, remnants of the earthworks can still be seen. We saw how the fort, like any feature on an urban landscape, whether natural or manmade, can be transformed by environmental processes and human activity over time. We learned how this large fortification affected the original topography of the ridge upon which it was located and impeded the development of the town of West Knoxville between 1888 and 1897 and the neighborhood of Fort Sanders that succeeded it. The following account tells of this exciting journey of discovery, and provides a complete and accurate record of this historically significant site.

1

THE WAR THAT CHANGED ALL WARS

Depending on which historian you read, the American Civil War was either the last of the old-fashioned wars or the first of the modern wars in human history. Because of increasingly deadly firepower, by 1861 the manner in which battles were fought began to change. The historic tactics of armies initially facing each other at close range in the field and then maneuvering during the battle for the best field position transitioned into a strategy of creating cover on the battlefield to increase protection for ground troops.

Before the Civil War, infantry units were largely armed with smoothbore muskets, which had an effective range of about 100 yards. The foot soldier was supported by smoothbore artillery that could reach an enemy's position with accuracy at a distance of only about 1,000 yards. During the American Civil War, the prototypes that preceded the development of modern firearms became standard; rifled muskets could now hit an enemy soldier at 500 yards, repeating rifles could fire as many as 20 rounds per minute, and rifled cannons had an effective range of over a mile. Battles eventually ceased to be an eyeball-to-eyeball encounter of shoulder-to-shoulder, opposing ranks of men as occurred in Napoleonic times (Nosworthy 2003).

By the end of the first year of the war, smoothbore muskets were rapidly being replaced by the Springfield Model 1861 rifled musket, used by the Union army, and the British Pattern 1853 Enfield rifle musket, favored by the Confederate forces (Bilby 2005). These weapons fired a .57- to .58-caliber conical ball, which caused massive injuries such as shattered limb bones, usually requiring amputation, or irreparable gaping wounds in other parts of the body, which meant certain death. And even if a wounded soldier did make it to a hospital, there was a good chance he would not survive because of primitive surgical techniques and unsanitary conditions.

As was common throughout the history of warfare, military tactics lagged woefully behind advances in firepower. Early in the Civil War, shoulder-to-shoulder lines of infantry continued to march within 100 yards of each other before opening a mass volley, which was often followed by a bayonet charge. The result of such outmoded infantry tactics was painfully evident when General Ambrose Burnside's Union troops took 12,000 casualties during repeated attacks on Confederate infantry entrenched behind a stone wall at Fredericksburg, Virginia, on December 13, 1862 (Marvel 1991), and when General Robert E. Lee on a hot and bloody July afternoon sent 15,000 men on Pickett's Charge against Union forces dug in on Gettysburg's Cemetery Ridge (Gallagher, editor 1999). One thousand, gray-clad infantrymen died in that attack and 4,000 were wounded, most of whom later languished in prisoner-of-war camps (Gallagher, editor 1999). As late as the First World War, the 1916 clash of British and German forces at Verdun in France resulted in over 750,000 casualties from infantry attacks and counterattacks by soldiers storming an elaborate system of machine-gun-protected trenches (Jankoski 2014; Mason 2000). The reasons for these disastrous decisions of the high command to continue mass frontal assaults in battle can probably be attributed to the commanding officers' reluctance to change tactics still being taught in military schools of the day and the tactics they believed would guarantee success on the battlefield.

One of the most notable and popular military theorists of the 19th century was the Swiss-born Baron Antoine-Henri de Jomini, (1779–1869), who served with Napoleon I and later became an aide-de-camp to Czar Alexander of Russia. His book *The Art of War* was published in French in 1836 and translated into English in 1862. Jomini began his book focusing on the necessity for the leaders of a state or country to develop an overall strategic tactical plan to fight a war and subsequently his focus narrows to address such specifics of battle as detailed as how individual battalions should be deployed on the battle line. Every aspect of military policy was described in a way that was all-inclusive and easily understood. Jomini's book became a pre–Civil War West Point bible; however, because of the over-simplification of his thinking by Union commanders during the Civil War, his reputation began to suffer (Crocroft 2007). Jomini believed that the best offensive strategy was to line up the troops for battle, then blast away at each other with cannons, followed by a massed infantry charge (Jomini 2007 [1836]). The victims of this type of slaughter were usually brave men who obeyed orders and did not hide from but boldly confronted the enemy. However, by 1863 Civil War infantrymen had become acutely aware that they were being shot at by an enemy they could not even see, and they began to hunker down and dig in.

Many officers objected to their soldiers "digging in," a practice they felt impeded offensive action against the enemy. One of Jomini's maxims was that employing the shelter of earthworks and fortifications was to be scorned. He firmly believed that burying an army in entrenchments that could possibly be forced in front, or outflanked and surrounded was absolute folly (ibid.).

The Union army almost lost the Battle of Shiloh early in the war because they did not fortify their camp (Groom 2012). General William T. Sherman explained that he did not fortify against an attack because he believed it would have made his inexperienced soldiers timid (Sherman 1875). Before the battle of Murfreesboro, Confederate general Braxton Bragg remarked that he would never use the shovel again as digging in did not convey the "genius" of the Southern population (Lindsley 1886).

Robert E. Lee assumed command of the Army of Northern Virginia, on June 1, 1862, after General Joseph E. Johnston was critically wounded during the Peninsular Campaign. Lee had graduated first in his class from West Point in 1829. He had studied as a cadet with another outstanding West Point graduate, Dennis Hart Mahan, who began teaching as a third-year cadet in the military academy in 1823. Mahan would later become a professor of civil and military engineering, and in 1832 he was appointed chair of the Engineering Department at West Point. Mahan was still serving in this capacity during Lee's three-year tenure (1852–55) as superintendent of the academy. By the time Lee left West Point, Mahan had published five books on civil engineering and military works in the field. It is likely that his detailed specifications on defensive-field earthworks and defensive tactics played a significant role in Robert E. Lee's military career.

Despite Lee's competence for command as demonstrated in the Mexican War, the *Richmond Examiner* proclaimed that with Lee as commander, the soldiers would never be permitted to fight. The author added to that insult, writing that shovels and spades were the only tools of war which were familiar to Lee. Lee was derisively labelled by many as the "King of Spades"(Thomas 1995; Gallagher 2001). But there were those who supported Lee in his efforts to carefully prepare defensive positions for his men. And in spite of the initial condemnation, he persisted in protecting his troops with earthworks until the end of the war, as witnessed by the elaborate trenches at Spotsylvania and Cold Harbor which stopped General Ulysses Grant dead in his tracks for weeks in 1864–65 during his Overland Campaign to capture Richmond (Catton 1953).

As the Civil War progressed, both sides placed an increasing emphasis on the importance of individual soldiers taking defensive measures in the field. The infantry began taking precautions on the battlefield by throwing up temporary barricades to impede an expected attack or counterattack at such battles as Chickamauga in August 1863 and the Wilderness in the spring of 1864. These tactics included chopping down trees, piling up brush and fence rails, and digging in. Because soldiers in the Civil War had few entrenching tools, they were often forced to dig shallow pits or trenches with their tin mess plates, cups, knives, or a musket butt. A folding shovel for digging in would become standard equipment for members of the United States infantry serving in World Wars I and II. It became increasingly clear during the Civil War that this defensive measure was essential for any chance of survival against the awesome killing power of the rifled musket.

Elaborate permanent defenses began to be constructed for the protection of occupying armies in towns and cities, and at vital centers of troop concentrations such as commercial and industrial areas and transportation centers. Early in the war, key cities such as Washington,

Fig. 1. Gen. Robert E. Lee.
Library of Congress.

D.C., and Richmond, Virginia, were encircled by miles of interconnected trenches and earthen ramparts. Washington became one of the most heavily defended capitals in the world, surrounded by 37 miles of fortifications that included 68 forts (National Park Service n.d.). Counter-defensive works reached their zenith at Petersburg, Virginia, outside the Confederate capital, when from June 15, 1864 to April 3, 1865, General Ulysses S. Grant was forced to repeatedly attack the city from offensive trench lines that eventually extended over 30 miles. The Confederates dug an opposing system of reinforced defensive trenches and bombproofs, and both sides used these fortifications for defensive and offensive operations. When Union forces left their trenches to seize rail lines around Richmond, they were countered by Confederate infantry emerging from their trenches to protect these vital supply links (Trudeau 1993).

Smaller towns were also fortified with the scope of construction and placement of defenses determined by the topography, the direction in which the enemy army was moving, and the real or perceived points of attack. One of these fortified towns was Knoxville, Tennessee, which was occupied by Confederate forces during the first two years of the war. After the Union army captured Knoxville in September 1863, extensive defensive fortifications were built and existing ones improved. The town remained strongly fortified until the war ended (Smith and Nance 2003).

Construction on the principal earthwork was begun during the Confederate occupation of Knoxville and was first called Fort Buckner, and later Fort Loudon, by the Confederates. When Federal forces occupied the town in September 1863, they immediately began to improve this earthwork, which was situated on an imposing ridge located about one mile west of the town along the Kingston Road (now Cumberland Avenue). This earthwork was then linked to other fortifications placed north and east of town and to other entrenched artillery posts located on several other high points surrounding the town. Bluffs on the south side of the river across from the town were also well fortified by Union troops. In December 1863, a Union soldier stationed in Knoxville wrote his family that "Knoxville was one of the strongest positions I have ever seen" (Huddart, William A. Letter to parents 1863).

2

A NATION AND STATE DIVIDED

After the election of President Abraham Lincoln on November 6, 1860, secession of the southern states began, with South Carolina officially seceding from the Union on December 20, two and a half months before Lincoln took office. By February 1861, six more states had followed the Palmetto State's lead and seceded (the total would eventually be eleven), and representatives of those states met together in Montgomery, Alabama, to form a separate government called the Confederate States of America. In that same month, Tennessee voters rejected a state referendum calling for secession by a 54–46 percent margin with East Tennesseans expressing the strongest opposition to leaving the Union. But this victory for Unionists would be short lived. In April 1861, President Lincoln called for 75,000 troops to put down the rebellion after the fall of Fort Sumter in Charleston Harbor. Tennessee governor Isham Harris, a staunch Confederate supporter, countered in May and led the Tennessee assembly into joining a military league formed by the Confederate states. By May 25, 15 companies of Confederate troops of the Provisional Army of Tennessee were in Knoxville (U.S. War Department, *Official Records* [hereafter cited as *OR*] 1898:pt. 2, 108). A defiant and angry Harris had responded to Lincoln's call by saying, "Tennessee will not furnish a single man for coercion, but fifty thousand, if necessary for the defense of our rights and those of our Southern brothers." In July 1861, the Tennessee State Army was released to the Confederate government, and it became the core of the Army of Tennessee (Brewer and Brewer 1975).

Prior to the second referendum on secession scheduled for early June 1861, thousands of East Tennesseans attended meetings to listen

Fig. 2. President Abraham Lincoln. Library of Congress.

to advocates for both sides, who sought to rally their supporters and keep them firm in their beliefs. Notable dignitaries, both for and against secession, traveled all over the state to express their views. In East Tennessee, secessionist newspapers made efforts to frighten those loyal to the Federal government. Trains running on the East Tennessee railroads connecting Georgia to Virginia provided the means of travel for fiery secessionists in their efforts to drum up support for the Southern cause. These dedicated advocates for secession stopped in the major villages and towns along the line to lead heated rallies against the "disunionists." Oliver P. Temple, a Knoxville attorney, judge, historian, and avid Federalist, wrote that all "the towns along the railroad line, except Knoxville, became disloyal in sentiment"(Temple 1899:187). He also noted that another important means of adding to Confederate troop strength was the influence of Southern women over their sons, husbands, boyfriends, and fathers.

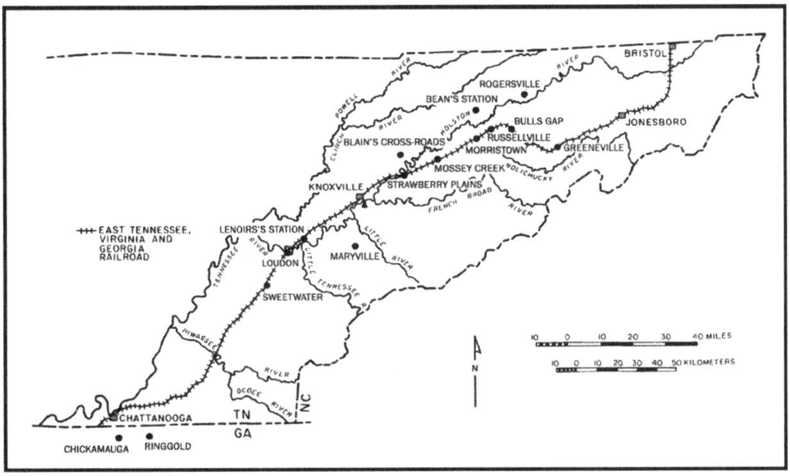

Fig. 3. Details of the East Tennessee, Virginia, and Georgia Railway.

A major pro-Union rally held in Greeneville, Tennessee, led by Senator Andrew Johnson (Lincoln's vice-presidential choice in 1864), was attended by over 4,000 citizens. Although Johnson had voted against Lincoln in 1860, he strongly supported the Constitution and its guarantees, calling for patriots to rally for the republic so that the Union could be preserved (ibid.). Joining Temple and Johnson in their efforts to convince voters that Tennessee should remain in the Union was the vituperative William G. "Parson" Brownlow, editor of the *Knoxville Whig,* who derided South Carolina's secessionism and also their state flag which featured a palmetto leaf. Brownlow insulted the depiction of the palmetto leaf likening it to a miserable looking cabbage leaf (Coulter 1999). Foreshadowing Churchill's famous words during World War II, Brownlow resolved that he would wage continuous war against the secessionists until the fires of hades turned to ice (McKenzie 2006).

Temple documented the deep division among East Tennesseans in the lead-up to the war. He also described his personal efforts to win the citizenry over to the Union cause in his book *East Tennessee and the Civil War,* published in 1899. Brave and outspoken, even at rallies that slaveholders attended, he passionately urged citizens in East Tennessee to support the preservation of the Union, often ending his

Fig. 4. William G. Brownlow. Library of Congress.

speeches with the words "let slavery perish and the Union survive" (Temple 1899:197).

On June 8, 1861, a majority of Tennesseans voted for secession, but voters in East Tennessee remained opposed to leaving the Union by a margin of two to one. Two-thirds of the population living in the rural areas remained loyal in varying degrees to the Union cause, and they surrounded the majority of Confederate supporters, who lived in Knoxville, the designated capital of East Tennessee. O. P. Temple believed that the June triumph of the secessionists and the fact that Southern troops already occupied several important places had created so much confidence in the secessionists that they felt entitled and safe in demeaning and denouncing Union supporters, whom they called cowards, Lincolnites, and Tories. Temple noted with sadness that at times long term friendships ended, and that even the most upstanding

Fig. 5. Oliver P. Temple. From John Trotwood Moore and Austin P. Foster, *Tennessee: The Volunteer State, 1769–1923*.

Confederate supporters felt justified when they informed on their Union friends and relatives. Temple did not understand how such intense hatred could result among his fellowmen as a consequence of war (ibid.). Both Lincoln and Davis from the beginning of the war fully understood that because of this strong and dangerous division it was critical to successfully occupy and control Knoxville and East Tennessee (ibid.).

Other members of the Confederate government also immediately recognized the importance of this area and labeled it the "Arch of the Confederacy" because of the direct rail connection that ran between their capitol in Richmond, Virginia, through Knoxville to Chattanooga, branching from there to Atlanta and the Mississippi Valley. The Confederate leaders tried to protect this lifeline, while Lincoln sought to cut it with the help of local Union supporters. Both Northern and Southern leaders were also acutely aware of the abundance of rich farmland in East Tennessee, which could produce plentiful food for their troops stationed there and also shipped by rail to feed thousands of soldiers in other areas.

"Between 1850 and 1860 [Knoxville] grew from 2,076 to 5,300, an increase of 155.3 percent. With five large commission mercantile firms and twelve dry-goods dealers in operation in 1860 it became the major distribution and merchandising center for the region" (Groce 1999:15).

For all these reasons, Confederacy president Jefferson Davis quickly stationed 10,000 Confederate troops in the region; and Union supporters began to be isolated, denounced, bullied, and spied upon, which greatly troubled President Lincoln. He began to plan for the time when he would be able to permanently ensure the safety and well-being of his brave supporters in East Tennessee. Oliver Temple described the courage of the Unionist citizens, saying that they "exhibited a heroic constitution and a sublime fortitude seldom surpassed in the history of patriotic achievement" (Temple 1899). However, many feared imprisonment and fled to Kentucky in the next months. Temple himself felt it necessary to go north, but soon returned to Knoxville and his law practice, promising authorities that he would stay neutral during the conflict. His colleague in the effort to keep Tennessee in the Union, Parson Brownlow, was jailed for treason in December 1861, and after his release by the Confederate secretary of war, Judah P. Benjamin, he was promptly escorted by Confederate troops to Union-occupied Nashville. Brownlow had become a celebrity in several states in the North and Midwest, and he left Nashville for Ohio, where he began a series of speaking tours. He published a best-selling book on secession before returning to Knoxville with Burnside's troops in September 1863 (Coulter 1999 [1937]).

As Brownlow was traveling in the Midwest and Northeast, loyal Unionists, initially single young men, were traveling to Kentucky. As Confederate harassment increased, married men began to leave their families and make the dangerous journey through little-known gaps and trails in the mountains to the Kentucky recruiting camps (Brewer and Brewer 1975). To avoid Confederate soldiers and home guards patrolling the roads, Unionist recruiters, called "scouts" or "pilots,"

Fig. 6. Jefferson Davis. Library of Congress.

led loyal citizens on these secret byways at night. One of the most dangerous areas was the border between Hancock and Hawkins Counties in Tennessee and Lee County, Virginia (Bible 2011; Ellis 1867).

The Confederates had first garrisoned Knoxville and the nearby towns as early as February 1861. Additional men were mustered into service from Knoxville and surrounding areas. Soon Southern troops were encamped atop College Hill, the hilltop campus of East Tennessee University, which was located just east of Melrose Hall, the elegant, Italianate home owned by Union supporter Thomas Powell.

By the end of February, approximately 800 raw recruits were being organized and trained in Knoxville at Camp Cummings. The camp was named after D. H. Cummings, who commanded Company E of the 19th Tennessee infantry. According to Dr. W. J. Worsham, the organization of the 19th Tennessee Regiment took place at the fairgrounds located east of the town (Sealy et al., n.d.). By April 1861, academic life at East Tennessee University (the present-day University of Tennessee) had all but disappeared. The majority of eligible students and faculty enlisted in the Confederate army, and the school finally closed in early 1862 (Purcell 2007).

Todd Groce, in his book *Mountain Rebels: East Tennessee and the Civil War,* stated that about 24,000—less than 14 percent—of the 186,652 volunteers who served in the Southern army from Tennessee were from East Tennessee. They never gained the trust of the Richmond command and were derided by fellow Confederates from other areas, including Middle and West Tennessee, because they came from Unionist East Tennessee (Groce 1999).

The Union loyalists, or "Lincolnites," as they were often called, were not idle during the Southern occupation of Knoxville. They continued to publicly speak out against secession and the Confederate government. Union Home Guard companies were formed and drilled, and secret meetings were held to plan their own secession from Tennessee, just as West Virginia would later break away from its parent state on June 20, 1863 (McKenzie 2006). When the false rumor spread that 15,000 armed Lincolnites were preparing to rebel against their occupiers, the Confederate authorities were duly alarmed. Not only did they have to worry about the Federal army that had quickly occupied eastern Kentucky, but they also feared a fifth-column, guerilla war from the armed and hostile citizens surrounding them. On November 4, 1861, James Gettys McCready Ramsey, a fiery secessionist and political leader in Knoxville, wrote to Confederate president Jefferson Davis with this warning:

> The enemy intends to carry into effect the policy, long entertained and strenuously advised by Andrew Johnson and others, of invading East Tennessee. This may be attempted, not via Cumberland Gap, as generally apprehended, but via Jamestown and the several passes in Fentress County, where the mountain is much lower and the country more accessible. The inhabitants on that route are more rebellious and more disloyal to your Government. A radius of 50 miles, with Jamestown or Huntsville as a center, will embrace a population, both

> in Kentucky and Tennessee, of as anti-southern communities as can be found south of the Ohio. That population is nearer to our railroad than any other point—much more so than that contiguous to Carter and Johnson Counties, also a disloyal neighborhood. Camp McGinnis is more vulnerable than Cumberland Gap, having fewer fortifications and fewer natural defenses. We need, therefore, to guard against invasion from that quarter; and while everyone admits the bravery and vigilance of the officer in command (Captain Bledsoe, I believe), we all believe the safety of the country demands that he be reinforced (*OR* 1882: Series 1, Vol. 4, 511–512).

UNDER THE BONNY BLUE FLAG

Realizing the danger, the Confederate government established the District of East Tennessee of the Confederate Armies on June 26, 1861, and Brigadier General Felix K. Zollicoffer was placed in command on August 1. Zollicoffer was a popular prewar Tennessee politician, and Governor Harris believed that the general's political skills would help preserve the peace in East Tennessee (Stamper 2007). In the fall of 1861 Zollicoffer's headquarters in Knoxville became an armed camp. Trains rumbled through Knoxville every day filled with soldiers from the deep South bound for the Virginia front and recruits headed for the training camps located east of Knoxville (*Knoxville Whig* 1861). A strong Confederate presence in East Tennessee was made necessary by the growing resistance of Union sympathizers angered by the harsh policies of the occupying troops.

In August 1861, the "Alien Enemies Act" was passed by the Confederate Congress. One law in the act stated that all citizens of any nation hostile to the Confederacy were ordered to leave within forty days, after which time they could be arrested, imprisoned, or removed as alien enemies. Companion legislation called for the confiscation of property belonging to these real or perceived enemies. Further angered by these laws, there was a mass exodus of the so-called Lincolnite rebels, who fled to Kentucky to join the Union army there. Men who stayed at home were given the choice of incarceration in a Tuscaloosa, Alabama, prison camp or of becoming "galvanized Yankees." Galvanized Yankee was a term used to designate a Confederate prisoner who took the Union oath and joined the Union army to gain his freedom (McKenzie 2006).

When Southern troops were sent out into the countryside to disarm these "traitors" and vigilantes were posted around the region to arrest persons suspected of hostile action, the Unionists struck back. Aware that President Lincoln was prodding his generals to invade East Tennessee, and mistakenly anticipating the quick arrival of the Federal army to aid them, the Union partisans decided to help cripple their tormentors by sabotaging the vital railroad through East Tennessee. While Washington clandestinely funded the operation, it did not send troops, which left only loyal civilians to carry out the secret mission. On November 7, 1861, the "bridge burners" succeeded in destroying five wooden bridges and trestles of the East Tennessee and Virginia Railroad and the East Tennessee and Georgia Railroad between Bristol, Tennessee, and Bridgeport, Alabama. Guilty and innocent alike were quickly arrested. Because a number of men had been arrested for their possible participation in the attack on the bridges, Judah Benjamin, the Confederate Secretary of War, instructed Colonel Danville Leadbetter and the military command that all prisoners identified "as having been engaged in bridge burning are to be tried summarily by drum-head court-martial, and if found to be guilty, executed on the spot" (Humes 1888:147). Drum-head court-martial was a summary court-martial trial for offenses on the battlefield. Of seven men tried for the bridge burnings, five were found guilty and were hanged (Bible 2005; Madden 1980–81). In Greeneville, Colonel Leadbetter used his immediate authority to try Jacob Hensie and Henry Fry. He found them guilty and had them executed on the same day. Instead of exactly following Benjamin's order that the bodies of those executed should be hung near the burned bridges (Humes 1888:147), Leadbetter had Hensie and Fry "swung from the projecting limb of a tree which stood north of the railroad and the depot" (Temple 1899:393). Henry Fry was later found to be innocent (Humes 1888:147).

Leadbetter was happy to comply with Benjamin's order and afterwards said that "he would dissolve the court-martial . . . on its determination of the few military cases yet to be tried," after which he would proceed to deal with the "political offenders" as he "had done at Greenville [*sic*] (Temple 1899:396). O. P. Temple observed with sorrow that the bridge-burning attempt and its partial success were "unwise and unfortunate. It did little injury to the enemy, while it brought countless calamities and sufferings on the Union people" (Temple 1899:387). In addition to the five people who were hanged, between 1,500 and 2,000 men were sent to prisons in Mobile, Tuscaloosa, and Macon, and 5,000 to 10,000 men were forced from their homes into exile. The minds of all Union supporters were filled with fear, and they were placed in constant and extreme stress for almost two years (Temple 1899).

The Confederate troops were enraged, and Union citizens were terrified. "Then followed those . . . repressive acts on the part of the military authorities which . . . made the sufferings of the people of East Tennessee known throughout the land." Brigadier General William H. Carroll, from his command post in the Confederate headquarters of the rifle brigade, wrote to Judah Benjamin that he had placed Knoxville under martial law and the time had come for the "sternest measures of military policy." He also suspended "for a time the functions of the civil tribunals" (Temple 1899:395).

Knoxville became even more heavily occupied with troops arriving from East Tennessee and Georgia, and during the next few months fear overtook the Union men. "For the first time, they began to realize fully that they were among enemies, who counted the success of the new government, above all things else—above kinship, above old friendship, above the most sacred ties hitherto uniting them" (Temple 1899:403).

They recognized that "There was not a man so high, or one so noble, but felt that he was liable to be accused, seized and thrust into prison at any moment" (ibid.). The anticipated armed rebellion of East Tennessee Unionists never materialized, although the hostile activities of partisan guerillas were a constant nuisance. Soon the Confederate government began to realize that J. G. M. Ramsey was correct when he warned that the most serious threat to their occupation of East Tennessee was not with local Unionists but with the presence of a growing Union army located in southeastern Kentucky (Hesseltine 1954).

On December 2, 1861, orders had been issued by the Union general Don Carlos Buell to create the Army of the Ohio in Louisville, Kentucky, which comprised six divisions from the states of Ohio, Michigan, Indiana, and Kentucky (Stamper 2007). General Zollicoffer was aware that this newly created army was not yet well trained enough to be of immediate danger to the Confederate stronghold in East Tennessee, but he was gravely alarmed and decided that it was necessary to immediately employ an aggressive offense as the best way to defend the Southern position in Knoxville. Zollicoffer was not only deeply disturbed by thoughts of a new Union army being formed in Kentucky, but he was also gravely concerned about the very porous nature of the military frontier between an expanding Union occupation of "neutral" Kentucky and the Confederate state of Tennessee (ibid.).

The most critical geographical entry point that threatened the Confederate military center at Knoxville was only 60 miles to the northeast at Cumberland Gap. The "Gap" is a deep V-shaped cut in the Cumberland Mountains discovered in 1748 by Dr. Thomas Walker, who named it in honor of the English Duke of Cumberland. This remarkable north–south passage near the Kentucky-Tennessee-Virginia border had been known as the gateway to the West since early pioneer times (Luckett 1964). Wisely deciding to take control of the Gap in early September, Zollicoffer fortified it and then moved 4,000 troops north to the Cumberland River in Kentucky. While in the Gap on September 18, 1861, one of Zollicoffer's raiding parties managed to destroy Camp Andrew Johnson, a Barbourville, Kentucky, military training center for Union sympathizers who had fled north from East Tennessee (Stamper 2007).

While traveling by train to Middle Tennessee, President Jefferson Davis stopped in Knoxville on December 11 and gave a brief talk at the railroad station. Unimpressed by Burnside's operations in Kentucky, the president of the Confederacy reported that he was "confident of his capacity, in conjunction with that of Gen. Johnson, to restore the condition of things in Mississippi and Tennessee, as they had been twelve months ago." Davis added that "he had heard it reported that East Tennesseans were disloyal, but he was loth [*sic*] to believe that the land which had owned a Jackson" would give birth to men who would prove recreant to their country" (*Knoxville Daily Register*, January 12, 1862).

But in spite of General Zollicoffer's successful offensive measures to protect East Tennessee from Federal invasion, President Davis was dissatisfied with what he thought was "velvet glove" treatment by Zollicoffer for the belligerent East Tennessee Lincolnites. In early January 1862, Davis replaced him with Major General George B. Crittenden, who took command of the District of East Tennessee on November 24. Zollicoffer remained in field command and continued his efforts to fortify southern Kentucky by shifting five infantry regiments and several hundred cavalry to Somerset, Kentucky (Stamper 2007).

While inspecting Zollicoffer's position on January 18, 1862, Crittenden learned that General George Thomas, Federal commander of southeast Kentucky, was approaching Somerset with a large force. Instead of taking a defensive stand to repulse Thomas, Crittenden decided to pounce on the unsuspecting Union army along Fishing Creek near Mill Springs. However, Crittenden's surprise attack failed; General Zollicoffer was killed; and the Confederate army retreated back to Tennessee confused and dispirited (Hafendorfer 2001).

Knoxville began to fill with wounded and disillusioned Southern soldiers who realized that the Cumberland Mountain buffer between Knoxville and "Lincoln's Hessian Hordes," as the Federal army was derisively called, was illusory. On January 17, 1862, a Union spy traveling through Knoxville by train reported to Washington, "At Knoxville, stationed one regiment of infantry and four pieces of artillery. A lieutenant at Knoxville stated that they were not half armed, but well dressed. . . . Provisions in Knoxville plenty; business nothing, except tanneries" (*OR* 1882: Series I, 934).

There was increasing alarm about a possible Union invasion of East Tennessee. General Grant had successfully taken Forts Donaldson and Henry on the Cumberland River in February, and the Confederate high command was well aware that they lacked adequate fortifications and troops to defend Knoxville from an attack.

THE KENTUCKY CAMPAIGN

On March 8, 1862, Major General Edmund Kirby Smith took command in Knoxville, where only 2,000 Confederate troops were now stationed. An additional 4,000 soldiers were nearby, holding Cumberland Gap (Seymour 1963). While General Smith was attempting to recruit additional troops from East Tennessee, local Union supporters began quickly to head north in large numbers because of the new conscription laws passed by the Confederate Congress. Many joined the Union Army of the Ohio in Kentucky, and by early March, the 7th Division of the Army of the Cumberland under General George Morgan was preparing to take Cumberland Gap from the Confederates. On June 18, the Confederate garrison chose to retreat from this strategic position, which opened the gateway from Kentucky to Tennessee. Union General Morgan quickly entered the Gap and placed four infantry brigades and supporting artillery behind the abandoned Confederate earthworks; he would, however, remain there for only a short while (ibid.).

At the same time the Confederate High Command in Richmond was debating a decision to retake or totally abandon the Gap, it was hatching a plan to capture Louisville via a bold two-pronged invasion of Kentucky that would directly affect the future of the Confederate army based in Knoxville. When the Civil War had become a reality, Kentucky, a border state, tried to remain neutral. However, their neutrality was broken by both sides, and in 1861 a pro-Confederate government was formed in the Bluegrass state. The state was rapidly occupied by Federal troops and did not secede from the Union; however, Kentucky suffered from major military clashes in the early days of the war. To counter this occupation of Kentucky, the Confederate high command proposed that Confederate forces under Generals Braxton Bragg and Edmund Kirby Smith should attempt to outflank the Union Army of the Ohio in Kentucky and bring the Bluegrass State completely into the Confederate fold (Rule 1900).

In July, General Bragg, commander of the Western Department of the Confederacy, moved his Army of Mississippi to Chattanooga to link up with Kirby Smith for the upcoming invasion of Kentucky. He also ordered Smith to send cavalry commander General John Hunt

Fig. 7. Gen. Braxton Bragg. Library of Congress.

Morgan into Kentucky to pave the way for the invasion. In early June, the dashing cavalry commander had established his headquarters in Knoxville and succeeded in recruiting two companies of East Tennesseans into his band of cavalry raiders.

Despite having very little military experience, Morgan, who would become known by Northerners as "the great guerilla" and the "King of Horse Thieves," (Duke 1963:xi) was to initiate a major change in the old methods of cavalry warfare during the Civil War. His brother-in-law and second in command, Basil W. Duke, described Morgan's achievements this way: "While other cavalry officers were adhering to the traditions of former wars, and the systems of the schools, however inapplicable to the demands of their day and the nature of the struggle, he originated and perfected, not only a system of tactics, a method of fighting and handling men in the presence of the enemy, but also a strategy as effective as it was novel" (ibid.:15). He armed his men with light rifles and pistols, discarding the traditional saber. He "rejected the storied charge . . . dismounted his men and fought them as infantry," while keeping the horses nearby to pursue or flee the enemy. His

Fig. 8. Gen. John Hunt Morgan. Library of Congress.

innovation of using cavalry to raid within enemy territory—causing mayhem, disrupting communications, destroying property, and stealing goods and horses—pinned down enemy troops that could have been employed to advantage elsewhere. Other officers of both armies were soon imitating his tactics (Duke 1960).

Joining Morgan in Knoxville that month to fight for the South was the flamboyant George St. Leger Grenfell, age 54. Born in Cornwall, England, Grenfell was a soldier of fortune and a veteran of wars in Tangier, Morocco, the Crimea, India, Italy, and South America. A strong disciplinarian who always wore a scarlet British-style skull cap, Grenfell became Morgan's adjutant, drilling the new recruits in the methods of the French cavalry. He left Knoxville with Morgan's band of raiders on July 4, 1862, for a foray into Kentucky. In the next 24 days, Morgan, Grenfell and 900 Confederate soldiers rode over a thousand miles and came within 40 miles of the Ohio River, causing panic among the residents of Cincinnati. They captured 17 towns, defeated a superior Union force, and destroyed military supplies, railroad bridges, and property valued at $10 million. Morgan shared Union supplies with the local population, earning him the title of "the American Robin Hood." Lincoln became anxious and asked General Henry Halleck to attend to it (Seymour 1963:59).

A year later, General Morgan would carry out his most spectacular raid, crossing the Ohio River against General Bragg's orders and riding 1,000 miles through southern Ohio and Indiana, creating mayhem for Union troops and civilians alike. It was the farthest advance of Confederate soldiers north during the war. He was captured on July 26, 1863, but four months later he escaped from an Ohio prison and returned to duty in the Confederate army (Duke 1960).

On August 14, 1862, General Edmund Kirby Smith was ordered to move his 18,000-man army into the Blue Grass State. Union General George Morgan, recognizing that his supply line might be cut off from his base in Kentucky, retreated from the Gap north to the Ohio River on September 16 (Seymour 1963). By September 4, Smith's army had reached Lexington, Kentucky; and with the support of Morgan's raiders, he moved forward to the south bank of the Ohio River opposite Cincinnati (ibid.). During this same time, the main invasion force under the command of General Braxton Bragg had marched up the Sequatchie Valley from Chattanooga, crossed into Kentucky, and captured Mumfordville. General Bragg promptly issued a proclamation: "Kentuckians, I have entered your state with the Confederate Army of the West, and offer you an opportunity to free yourselves from the tyranny of a despotic ruler. . . . We come to guarantee to all the sanctity of their homes and altars. . . . I shall enforce a rigid discipline and shall protect all in their persons and their property" (*OR* 1886:pt. 2, 822).

Although Bragg's campaign at the beginning had seemed promising, few Kentuckians joined with the Confederates to free themselves from the "despotic ruler." Disheartened, the mercurial Bragg, who appeared to be well on his way to successfully combining his forces with Kirby Smith to attack Louisville, hesitated and then moved off to the east, never reaching Smith's army. General Don Carlos Buell, whose Union troops had entrenched to protect Louisville, went on the offensive and on October 8 attacked Bragg's army at Perryville, Kentucky. Although outnumbered, the Southerners held the field; but the timid

Bragg, as he was to do at Chickamauga a year later, failed to follow up his advantage. Both Bragg and Smith withdrew their armies; and by October 23, General Smith was again back in Knoxville, where thousands of his wounded soldiers finally received medical care (Noe 2001; Nosworthy 2003).

The Confederate offensive campaign was not rewarded with a Southern occupation of Kentucky, but it was successful in other ways. Thomas B. Van Horne, author of the *Army of the Cumberland*, acknowledges Bragg's achievements, but also informs the reader of the cost of the offensive campaign to both Kentuckians and the Confederates. "He gained territory of vast extent with its ungarnered corn, and military advantages which were only overcome by a campaign of a year's duration, a great battle, and a vast expenditure of war material. He also made a heavy draft upon the resources of Kentucky. Her granaries supplied his armies while they were in the state, and doubtless for a time after they left it. Kentucky's stores and looms supplied his needy soldiers with clothes; the farms and stables of rich Kentuckians furnished his troopers with the best horses in the land" (Van Horne 1875:199).

These were not the results that brought satisfaction or hope to the Southern people, as they had expected a successful campaign that would bring about the recognition of the Southern Confederacy "by foreign nations and even by the United States." Van Horne continued: "And when General Lee retreated from the battle-field of Antietam, General Bragg from Perryville, and General Van Dorn from Corinth, the Southern people saw plainly that the war was still to bring desolation to their section, and that the boldest strategy and the exertion of their full strength could only press back, temporarily, the national armies" (ibid.).

Although the Confederates still controlled East Tennessee in the early months of 1863 and once again occupied Cumberland Gap, this strategic region was slowly being squeezed by Federal forces. The Union army now had a strong hold on central Kentucky, and the Army of the Cumberland based in Nashville under the command of General William Rosecrans was ready to move south to capture the vital rail junction at Chattanooga.

The Confederates in East Tennessee believed that they were protected by the rugged Cumberland Mountains, a formidable natural barrier for a Federal army seeking to take East Tennessee from the west. But the Kentucky border to the north provided some access to Knoxville and East Tennessee through the mountains via the Jamestown and Jacksboro Roads. In March 1862, a small Union force led by Samuel Powhatan Carter took advantage of this access and entered Tennessee from Kentucky through the Cumberlands at Big Creek Gap and reached Jacksboro, Tennessee, before being driven back. In December of that year, Carter again led a party of Union raiders through the mountains, capturing Blountville, Tennessee; he then moved on to burn the railroad bridge over the Holston River in Watauga (Seymour 1963). It was not until the fall of 1863 that this mountainous barrier was successfully penetrated by the Army of the Ohio on their way to occupy Knoxville under the command of General Ambrose Burnside.

3

THE WAR COMES TO EAST TENNESSEE

The first few months of 1863 were fraught with tension for the Confederate leadership in Knoxville. The *Knoxville Daily Register*, local mouthpiece of the Confederate government, periodically exacerbated this tension by printing false rumors about an impending Union invasion. In March of that year, the *Register* reported that a Federal army was massing along the Kentucky border west of Cumberland Gap and that General Ambrose Burnside, commanding the Army of the Ohio since March 1863, had 30,000 men poised and ready to attack East Tennessee (*Knoxville Daily Register* 1863a).

These threats to the East Tennessee Southern army were exaggerated at the time, but Major General William Rosecrans and his Army of the Cumberland were located west in Murfreesboro ready to move on Chattanooga. There was also a possibility of a Union flanking movement from Burnside's army located in the east. Worried about their proximity to Knoxville, the Richmond High Command made a decision to send the popular Major General Simon Bolivar Buckner to Knoxville, instructing him to take command of the Department of East Tennessee and giving him the difficult task of strengthening the defenses of the town and the entire East Tennessee region. Buckner was perceived as a "true gentleman and a . . . superior soldier" and the townspeople thought him an imposing figure as he rode "without escort on a splendid charger" up and down Gay Street (Humes 1888:208). However, Buckner's tenure in Knoxville was to be short-lived: he took command on April 27, 1863, and evacuated the town in September (Rule 1900). During those four months, he and his chief engineer, Colonel Danville Leadbetter, partially completed only two earthworks of note; one, Fort Buckner, was located

Fig. 9. Gen. Simon Bolivar Buckner. From Francis Trevelyan Miller, *The Photographic History of the Civil War in Ten Volumes.*

on a ridge west of town and another was located on Summit Hill, north and east of Gay Street in town. Buckner was forced to evacuate the town when General Burnside prepared to advance upon Knoxville through the mountains with the Army of the Ohio, at the end of August 1863.

After General Burnside assumed command of the Army of the Ohio, President Lincoln immediately ordered him to prepare his army for the invasion of East Tennessee. Lincoln had been exceedingly distressed since 1861 about his "friends in East Tennessee" and gravely concerned that the Union could possibly lose "the most valuable state we have in the South" (Temple 1899:442). Burnside was to be delayed in this rescue endeavor, however, when part of his army was sent to Vicksburg, Mississippi, in June to help General Ulysses Grant break the siege there.

Making the best of the delay, General Burnside sent Colonel William P. Sanders with 1,500 mounted infantry to strike East Tennessee and disrupt Confederate communications before an invasion attempt was made. Sanders, a thirty-year-old graduate of West Point and a cousin of Jefferson Davis, moved south from Mount Vernon, Kentucky, to Williamsburg on June 14. He rode to Williamsburg and then followed the Marsh Creek Road into Tennessee, capturing the Confederate garrison at Wartburg on June 17. Unfortunately for Sanders, several Southern cavalrymen escaped capture and headed to Knoxville to warn General Buckner. General Sanders, skirmishing with Confederate troops in Wartburg, avoided the Southern garrison in Kingston and turned his attention to the railroad bridge over the Tennessee River at Loudon but found it too well guarded to attack. Planning to cripple the vital East Tennessee and Georgia Railroad, his band next headed for Lenoir's Station (now Lenoir City). Subduing a Confederate artillery unit there, Sanders's men burned the large brick railroad station filled with military stores, destroyed a cotton factory, cut the telegraph lines, and ripped up rails of the tracks every mile or so as they headed towards Knoxville (Kelly 2002).

General Buckner was aware that the Federal cavalry was on the way to Knoxville, but a feint by Union Colonel Samuel Gilbert at Big Creek Gap had convinced him that a major invasion force was headed through the gap to East Tennessee. General Buckner moved north

Fig. 10. Gen. William P. Sanders. National Archives.

toward Big Creek Gap to stop it (Seymour 1963). While Buckner and his men were away, Sanders would strike.

On Kingston Road, an early Indian trail that had become a major road connecting Knoxville west to Nashville and south to Chattanooga, stood an elegant, two-story, brick home built by a prominent Confederate doctor, James Harvey Baker. Baker's home was one of many so-called "plantation" houses owned by well–to-do Knoxville farmers located on Kingston Road between Knoxville and Campbell's Station (Faulkner 1992). Baker's house still stands west of Ten Mile Creek on the corner of Kingston Pike and South Peters Road.

On June 18, 1863, as Sanders's cavalry approached the Baker farm after leaving Lenoir's Station, they found Confederate pickets were waiting for them. There was an exchange of fire, and Dr. Baker was killed. Union troops would later defend themselves against a charge by Confederate pickets, testifying that "Baker stood in his yard and fired upon them as they advanced and they shot him in retaliation." The Confederates claimed Sanders's men murdered the doctor in his house, where he had sought shelter (*Knoxville Daily Register* 1863b). Sanders left some of his men to deal with the situation and continued with the rest of his troops to Knoxville to prepare for a surprise attack.

General Buckner had known that Sanders's cavalry was on its way to Knoxville, but he had chosen to leave, taking most of his Knoxville garrison with him. A feint by Union forces under Colonel Samuel Gilbert at Big Creek Gap had convinced Buckner that a major invasion force was headed through the gap to East Tennessee, and Buckner moved north toward Big Creek Gap to deal with the threat. Colonel R. C. Trigg was left in command of about 1,000 fit troops; after learning that Sanders was on his way, he quickly added 200 more defenders by recruiting volunteer citizens and a motley assortment of convalescent soldiers from the Asylum Hospital.

Batteries were manned at College, Summit, and McGhee Hills (Seymour 1963). Sanders moved into Knoxville via the Tazewell Road with 1,500 cavalry on June 19, and the next day he placed his two field pieces near the present-day intersection of Fifth Avenue and Broadway. Fired upon by Confederate batteries located on Summit Hill, his men sheltered in nearby houses, while sharpshooters went forward to eliminate the artillerists. The artillery fight lasted an hour, leaving four Confederate defenders killed and four wounded (Kelly 2002).

Among the mortally wounded was Captain Pleasant Miller McClung, who was hit by a Union shell as he sat watching the fight on a fence at the Deaf and Dumb Asylum located west of Summit Hill (Seymour 1963). Reverend Thomas Humes described the mutilated body that was carried to a house nearby where Pleasant McClung died. McClung was the only living male descendant of two of Knoxville's founders, James White and William Blount (Humes 1888). He was a respected member of the Home Guards, beloved in the community, and a close friend of nineteen-year-old Ellen Renshaw House. Ellen was an attractive, dangerously outspoken, Savannah-born, rabid Confederate supporter who proudly called herself "a very violent Rebel." Although she did not write in her diary about her grief at the loss of her friend, she was surely enraged by Sanders' sudden attack on her adopted town, which resulted in the death of Pleasant McClung. Ellen would begin to vociferously express her hatred of the "vile Yankees" both publicly and privately when Union troops finally occupied Knoxville in September 1863, and she would end up in a lot of trouble (Sutherland 1996).

Because the Southern defenders gave such a spirited account of themselves, Sanders quickly realized that he might capture Knoxville but would not be able to hold the town. So, he moved east to Strawberry Plains, where he destroyed the 1,600-foot-long Holston River railroad bridge. He then continued up the line to Mossy Creek (today's Jefferson City) and burned a 300-foot-long trestle. Escaping the pursuing Confederate cavalry, he made his way through the rugged Cumberlands via Chalder's Gap and reported back to Burnside in Kentucky on June 24. Sanders was ordered to immediately head north with his men to pursue John Hunt Morgan (Seymour 1963).

For two years, Confederate occupiers of Knoxville had nervously looked to the north for invading enemy forces which had now finally come close enough to shell the town. It is difficult to understand why, with the constant threat of a Union attack from the north, the Confederates did not construct substantial defensive works to protect

Knoxville, their most important base in East Tennessee. Little evidence can be found in military reports to indicate that the town was even moderately fortified during that time; however, it is possible that reports of such mundane but critical activity in 1862 and early 1863 did not reach the Confederate government in Richmond.

At times there were thousands of Southern soldiers about the town. In September 1861, the *Knoxville Whig* reported that twelve thousand troops were in Knoxville and its surroundings (*Knoxville Whig* 1861). These troops seem to have been largely transient soldiers unable to be of use to local authorities, and the Unionist public in Knoxville could definitely not be counted on to help build Confederate defenses. If enough men had been available to complete the work, Knoxville could easily have been made defensible by simply adding large earthworks on top of the naturally occurring geological and topographical features that surrounded this town in the beautiful Ridge and Valley Physiographic Province of Tennessee.

This region of Tennessee is characterized by long, steep ridges and narrow valleys trending in a northeast–southwest direction (Fenneman 1938). In Knoxville these topographical features provided obvious defensive advantages. After the war, Major Henry S. Burrage described Knoxville as follows: "For the most part the town is built on a table land" on the north bank of the Holston (Tennessee) River, which is "nearly a mile square and about one hundred and fifty feet above the river" (Burrage 1866). For purposes of defense, the Holston River constituted a formidable barrier on the south. The three small creeks running south through this tableland to the river were appropriately numbered and named, from east to west, First, Second, and Third Creeks by Knoxville's founders. If First and Second Creek were flooded by constructing simple dams to inundate their narrow flood plains, enemy entry into the town from the east would be virtually impossible. A flooded Third Creek would only slightly hinder an attack from the west. A perfect defensive position that would protect the town from an attack from this direction could be constructed on the high east–west ridge located between Third and Second Creeks. White's Hill was located at the highest elevation point on that ridge. Kingston Road (today's Cumberland Avenue/Kingston Pike) runs parallel to the ridge on the south side. The north side of this ridge overlooked the East Tennessee and Georgia Railroad (now the Norfolk Southern).

A smaller ridge northeast of the fort provided perfect sites for defensive entrenchments. Earthworks would be constructed on the crests of this ridge, including Summit, McGhee, and Asylum Hills; artillery fire from these points could be directed into the valley where the railroad was located, and beyond. College Hill, the site of East Tennessee University, was a high eminence above the mouth of Second Creek which anchored a defensive line to the river. The highest ground east of town included Temperance and Mabry Hills. If heavily fortified, this semicircle of high ground would protect the town of Knoxville, which nestled on the tableland below; on the other hand, if these ridges were captured by an invading enemy, the town would be subjected to direct artillery fire. The capture of the high bluffs on the south side of the Tennessee River opposite the town would pose a serious threat from enemy artillery fire.

On April 26, 1863, Major General Dabney H. Maury, commander of the Department of East Tennessee, wrote to James A. Seddon, Confederate secretary of war, that he was worried about a possible invasion into East Tennessee because he did not have the forces to defend the area (*OR* 1889:pt. 2, 795). Apparently his concern was not shared by the Confederate leadership, as no serious efforts were made to fortify Knoxville until the next commander of the department, General Simon Bolivar Buckner, arrived at his headquarters in Knoxville on May 12, 1863. One day before this, General Maury wrote to General Joseph E. Johnston before leaving Knoxville that he thought with his present number of forces that he would be able to fortify and defend Knoxville from cavalry attacks or insurrectionary forces if he completed construction of small redoubts on the heights surrounding the town (ibid.:831). He also advised Johnston that if enough redoubts could be constructed to safeguard trestles and bridges, then without doubt there would be enough tools obtainable to also fortify Knoxville, if enough men could be conscripted to do the work.

A week later, the new commander, General Buckner, informed Brigadier General A. E. Jackson, "You have been assigned to the command of the force charged with the defenses intended to protect the public works in East Tennessee. . . . You will assign the force under your orders to the various works. . . . The engineer's estimate is larger than the force I can now furnish you" (*OR* 1889:pt. 2, 841–42).

In spite of all the concern expressed in these communications and the ease with which the town and its surroundings could have been fortified, until May 1863 no substantial fortifications had been added, and no known comprehensive plan had been prepared for constructing them. Even if a plan had existed, there still remained a shortage of manpower and it was doubtful that a reliable work force of conscripted labor could be employed.

The plan and design of the defensive works were finally assigned to Colonel Danville Leadbetter, a native of Maine. After graduating from West Point in 1836, he served for many years in the Corps of Engineers, working on defensive fortifications for the Pacific and Gulf Coasts. He resigned from the army in 1857, joining the Alabama militia and serving as the chief engineer of the state of Alabama for a year before enlisting in the Confederate army. O. P. Temple would cynically point out that this Confederate colonel "had been educated at West Point at the expense of the United States, and had taken an oath to support the constitution" (Temple 1899:394).

In November 1861, the Richmond command sent Leadbetter to East Tennessee to arrest, try, and hang all Union traitors who had participated in the bridge-burning scheme; he was then to oversee the replacement of the burned bridges and devise a plan to protect against further sabotage (Foote 1958). It was during this time that Leadbetter would reveal an extremely cruel aspect of his personality, which O. P. Temple attributed to his treasonous decision.

In his 1899 book, *East Tennessee and the Civil War,* Temple attributed Leadbetter's defection to the fact that Leadbetter, while serving in Alabama, reportedly "fell in love with a refined lady of the south and married her" (Temple 1899:394). Temple believed that because he "was a Northern man" that it was "necessary for him, in order to escape suspicion, to manifest extra zeal in behalf of his newly-espoused cause." His "extra zeal" while in command in Knoxville was focused on quickly punishing any Union supporter who had been arrested, regardless of the crime committed and without any consideration of the guilt or innocence of the person involved, or whether or not there had really been any crime committed at all. The cause he espoused after assuming full command was to eliminate the existing regular court-martial because it could not "keep pace with the exigencies of the occasion," the "exigencies" being an increasing number of political prisoners. Had Leadbetter succeeded in his efforts, he would have been able to "do away with political offenders" as he had "done at Greenville [*sic*]" (Temple 1899:396).

He served in various other capacities before becoming General Braxton Bragg's chief engineering officer in 1863. It was probably because Leadbetter had served in Knoxville in 1861 and was familiar with the terrain that he was assigned by General Buckner in the spring of 1863 to return and fortify the town (Eicher and Eicher 2001).

Leadbetter sited, designed, and began building a large fort on the imposing east–west ridge locally called "White's Hill," after the founding family of Knoxville. This ridge was located about one mile west of town and was the perfect location for a large fortification to defend against an enemy attack from the west. Leadbetter planned to construct a "star fort" at this militarily strategic location overlooking Kingston Road (Pike) on the south and the East Tennessee and Georgia Railroad on the north. However, the earthwork was only partially completed before the Confederates were forced to evacuate Knoxville in August 1863.

As a West Point graduate, Leadbetter must have been familiar with Dennis Hart Mahan's 1848 *Treatise on Field Fortifications,* and the "star fort" he began to build was of a sort Mahan described in his *Treatise.* The plan, which Mahan attributed to the French, was based on a square or rectangular walled fortification with triangular bastions placed at the four corner angles; a ditch or moat usually surrounded the fortification. The addition of projecting bastions created the "star-like" appearance. The bastions provided covering and interlocking fields of cannon fire that protected the curtain walls of the fort between the bastions from infantry attack (Mahan 1848).

The Confederates named Leadbetter's earthwork Fort Loudon, but shortly after construction began, it was renamed Fort Buckner. The fort would be finally renamed Fort Sanders by Union General Ambrose Burnside in November 1863, in honor of General William P. Sanders, who was killed by the Confederates during Longstreet's November siege of Knoxville.

As Buckner, Leadbetter, and the troops worked through the summer of 1863 to strengthen Fort Loudon and other hilltop defenses surrounding Knoxville, General Rosecrans's Army of the Cumberland in Middle Tennessee was flanking General Braxton Bragg's troops, which were moving south to Chattanooga. While the Confederate army in Knoxville was not directly threatened by Rosecrans at this time, the fortunes of the Army of the Cumberland would be a deciding factor in whether the Confederates would complete the fortification and continue to hold East Tennessee.

Fig. 11. Gen. Ambrose Burnside. Library of Congress.

By July 4, 1863, Confederate General Braxton Bragg had been maneuvered out of Middle Tennessee by the Army of the Cumberland, and his entire Army of Tennessee was in Chattanooga. At the same time General Rosecrans had been pushing Bragg's army into Chattanooga, General Ambrose Burnside, commander of the Army of the Ohio, was busy finalizing his plans to invade East Tennessee.

The former commander of the Army of the Potomac, Burnside had never expected to serve again in such a high position as he had suffered a disastrous defeat at the hands of General James Longstreet and his 1st Corps at Fredericksburg in December 1862 (Marvel 1991). Burnside had traveled to Washington after the battle to submit his resignation to President Lincoln, but Lincoln would not accept it, saying, "he had other fish for him to fry" (Poore 1882:201).

Earlier in the war, in February 1862, Burnside had won a significant victory by capturing Roanoke Island from the Confederates. In spite of his less than sterling performance at Antietam in September 1862, he had been promoted to the command of the Union Army of the Potomac. Had Lincoln accepted his resignation after the disaster at Fredericksburg, he would likely have disappeared into military oblivion. But Lincoln decided to give him another chance by appointing him commander of the Army of the Ohio in March 1863 (Marvel 1991). Burnside would excel in this capacity. His inspirational leadership, organizational skills, and wise military choices made under great pressure, along with his defensive plan of action during November 1863, kept Knoxville and East Tennessee safely in Union hands. As he made preparations to take his army to Knoxville, he had no idea that he was destined once again to cross swords there with his nemesis, General James Longstreet, and his 1st Corps.

One description of Burnside came from Charles Dana, a former editor for the *New York Tribune,* who upon his retirement in 1862 was hired as an agent for the War Department by Secretary of War Edwin Stanton. Dana served as deputy director to Stanton from 1863 to 1865 and was called the "eyes of the administration" by Lincoln. Dana, a fervent abolitionist, traveled with the troops, reporting to Secretary Stanton on contractor waste and fraud; he also reported on

Fig. 12. Charles A. Dana.
Library of Congress.

the behavior, performance, and character of many Union generals, particularly Ulysses S. Grant, who was believed to be a heavy drinker (Dana 1996 [1902]).

Dana was sent by Grant from Chattanooga to Knoxville in mid-November 1863 to assess Burnside's situation there. He described Burnside, who was thirty-nine at the time, as a "large man physically, about six feet tall, with a large face and small head and heavy side whiskers," as well as "well-educated, straight forth and manly." Dana added that Burnside was trusted and greatly beloved by his men, who called him "Old Burnie" (ibid.:138).

By the summer of 1863, Burnside was on the march, leading his men to East Tennessee to free the loyal Lincolnites from the yoke of Southern oppression (Tumblin 2013c). President Lincoln was elated; he was also pleased with the military strategy developed by Burnside and Rosecrans at Burnside's base in Cincinnati. They planned to create a pincer movement on General Bragg's right flank and rear by squeezing Bragg's army between Rosecrans's advancing forces in the south and Burnside's army to the east.

Burnside moved south in June 1863 to the Lexington, Kentucky, area, where he continued to strengthen his army, adding many East Tennessee Unionists who had fled to the Bluegrass State. Burnside's plan was to cross the Cumberlands on roads that were not protected by the Confederates because they were considered too impassable for a large military force (Marvel 1991). By August 16, Burnside felt the Army of the Ohio was primed for action, and in two weeks he had successfully executed his plan to move 18,000 men in five columns 250 miles through Kentucky to Knoxville on some of the most miserable roads in the country (Poore 1882). From Lexington, Burnside led his center column down what is now U.S. 25 to Williamsburg. His right wing, commanded by General Lucas Hartsuff, took a route south similar to that of present-day U.S. 27. Two columns of troops marched from central Kentucky and rendezvoused at Jamestown, where they joined up with Hartsuff's wing. The cavalry joined with these four columns at Huntsville; then the infantry moved on to Kingston and from there east to Knoxville, 45 miles away. On September 1, the cavalry rode through Jacksboro on to Knoxville, with Colonel John W. Foster leading the way; General Burnside arrived with the infantry on September 3 (E. I. Miller 1957).

Benjamin Perley Poore emphasized in his biography of the general that without the strength and courage of Burnside and the heroic determination of his troops, the treacherous march over the mountains would not have succeeded (Poore 1882). Chaplain Augustus Woodbury remembered General Burnside as being "the inspiring spirit of the march," who kept "his men in good heart" during this treacherous journey over the Cumberlands. He described the harsh trek: "The soldiers climbed the rugged ways with indomitable persistence and courage. The horses and mules connected with the army were tasked to the utmost. . . . In several instances, the animals utterly failed to drag the artillery up the acclivities; and their places were filled by men, who, with hands upon the drag ropes and shoulders to the wheels, dragged or lifted guns, caissons and wagons from height to height. The road was in some places strewn with the fragments of broken vehicles and harness" (Woodbury 1867:305–6).

Ben Perley Poore boasted that the march over such an impenetrable barrier "was an undertaking which throws the celebrated passage of the Alps into the shade." This incredible march from Lexington to Kingston was made in only 14 days. Colonel William Goddard believed that the tortuous trek was the "first time during the war that a commander had been cut loose from a base of supplies." Goddard said it was so exceptional an accomplishment that Burnside's plan of the march and "his application to undertake the expedition are on the files on the War Department" (Poore 1882:214–215).

Burnside had specific rules of conduct for his men during the Kentucky march listed in his General Field Order No. 2. Before entering East Tennessee he also strictly forbade his troops to loot or commit fraud upon the loyal citizens who had been so oppressed. Soon afterward he received a report from Colonel Frank Wolford regarding a 1st Kentucky cavalryman who had paid a resident for a lot of tobacco with Confederate money and planned to resell it to his comrades. Burnside asked Wolford to investigate the case. The man was found guilty and Burnside ordered him drummed out of the service, but because there were no drums belonging to the cavalry, all buglers in the command were summoned and the delinquent horseman was loudly "bugled" out (Marvel 1991). Burnside commanded that the peaceful inhabitants encountered during the march were to be treated with kindness and every protection was to be given by the soldiers to them and their property. In number 5 of this order, Burnside instructed that "prisoners of war . . . will be treated with every consideration consistent with their safe keeping, and any ill-treatment or insults to them will be severely punished" (Poore 1882:214). These rules of behavior continued to be strictly enforced during Burnside's tenure in Knoxville and were greatly appreciated by the local inhabitants, both Confederate and Union supporters.

Meanwhile in Knoxville, reports of Burnside's march into East Tennessee were circulated in hopes of raising the spirits of local Union supporters who had been disappointed many times by false rumors of his imminent arrival. It was the Confederate military that revealed to Knoxville's citizens that the Northerners were truly on the way when, on August 24, the Confederates commenced "shipping Southward in great haste, all their supplies of every description" (Temple 1899:471). Four months later, Parson Brownlow advertised in the January 9 issue of his newspaper that he, acting as the assistant special agent of the Treasury Department, would have for sale in January not only used "rebel Wagons, carts . . . and parts of wagons," which the "rebel absconding army" had left behind in early September, but also a quantity of iron, which would be very desirable to farmers (*Knoxville Whig* 1864a).

Buckner had been ordered to evacuate Knoxville posthaste by General Bragg, who had assumed command of the Department of Tennessee. Bragg realized that Buckner would be overwhelmed by Burnside; for that reason and because he needed reinforcements to defend against the threat from Rosecrans, he ordered Buckner's troops to join him at Chickamauga Creek in northern Georgia. The Richmond command also sent General Lee's right-hand man, General James Longstreet, with his battle-hardened 1st Corps of the Army of Northern Virginia to reinforce Bragg. Tennessee senator G. A. Henry must have been pleased with this decision, as he had warned the Richmond command in May that Longstreet was needed in Tennessee as the future of Virginia would depend on the successful defense of East Tennessee (Johnson and Buell 1887).

In Knoxville, most of the citizens who had supported the Southern cause disappeared at the same time Confederate troops were leaving for Chattanooga to reinforce Bragg. Avid Unionist O. P. Temple recounted that the town was left for several days without any law enforcement, leaving the populace to face possible pillaging and depredations from marauding Southern soldiers left behind. For almost a week, residents were anxious, scarcely leaving their homes; they had no idea when Union soldiers might enter the town and restore order (Temple 1899).

On September 1, 1863, a beautiful sunny day, Temple, "restless, anxious and sick at heart," walked down to the depot of the East Tennessee and Virginia Railroad at about 3:00 p.m. to find out whether Superintendent J. B. Hoxie had heard any news of a Federal movement into Knoxville. Around 4:00 p.m., while visiting with Hoxie, a fellow Union supporter, Temple heard the "clatter of horses feet and rushed

Fig. 13. Col. John W. Foster. Library of Congress.

out" to see an advance column of Burnside's cavalry galloping up Gay Street. Elated when he was told by one of the horsemen that they were Federals, Temple began running after the troops toward the center of town. Arriving breathless at the Lamar House (the present-day Bijou Theater), where the cavalrymen had stopped, he was summoned to the hotel parlor by a messenger to meet with the commander of the forces, Colonel John W. Foster of Indiana, and James C. Luttrell, the mayor of the town (ibid.).

Temple recalled the jubilation of loyal Knoxvillians on that first day of September 1863 in his 1899 book about the Civil War in East Tennessee, writing that immediately after Colonel Foster's arrival, "the people commenced pouring in. On the next day, the crowd had swollen to thousands, and on the third day, the day after Burnside entered, it had grown to tens of thousands. The streets were literally packed with human beings." Temple further remarked, "The bliss of that day will never fade from memory of thousands of persons present" (ibid.:476).

American flags that had been hidden suddenly appeared like magic. The rebel flag on a 'Liberty Pole' at the corner of Gay Street and Clinch Avenue, was taken down by Union soldiers (Newman 1939:2). Colonel Foster recounted in a letter to his family that when he and his men had ridden into Knoxville, the ovation they received "was never before during this war given to any army" and added that "all that afternoon and into the night, the streets resounded with yells and cheers for the 'Union' and for 'Lincoln.'" He explained to his family that he had discovered why the town was becoming more and more crowded with people from the countryside: the news of the Union occupation was being relayed by locals with gunfire from one place to another and "by signal fires on the mountains." (Temple 1899:478–479)

By September 3, the day Burnside entered Knoxville, people were arriving in droves from adjacent counties. Colonel Foster [wrote] in his letter of September 3 saying "Men who had been in hiding among the rocks and caves of the mountains, and had not seen each other for years . . . grasping each other's hands . . . while tears streamed down their cheeks." He added, "I have read of 'tears of joy' but never saw so much of it as here." In closing, Foster said, "General Burnside and the rest of the army will be in town this morning, and I must get ready to receive them" (Temple 1899, [Foster 1863:478–480). President Lincoln had been determined to rescue the loyal Unionists of East Tennessee ever since he had first heard of their "faithfulness amid general desertion in the South," and his fervent desire to rescue the loyal people of East Tennessee was finally a reality.

Ellen Renshaw House, the rebel teenager who hated Lincoln and Yankees with a passion, probably did not leave her home during these days of celebration. Furious that the Yankees had taken the town, she was probably seated at a window with her diary, observing the enthusiastic crowd of misguided country people, when she wrote that they "cut down our secessionist flag and danced over it." She childishly added that she would "much rather have it cut down than have their old rag flying from it" (Sutherland 1996:7).

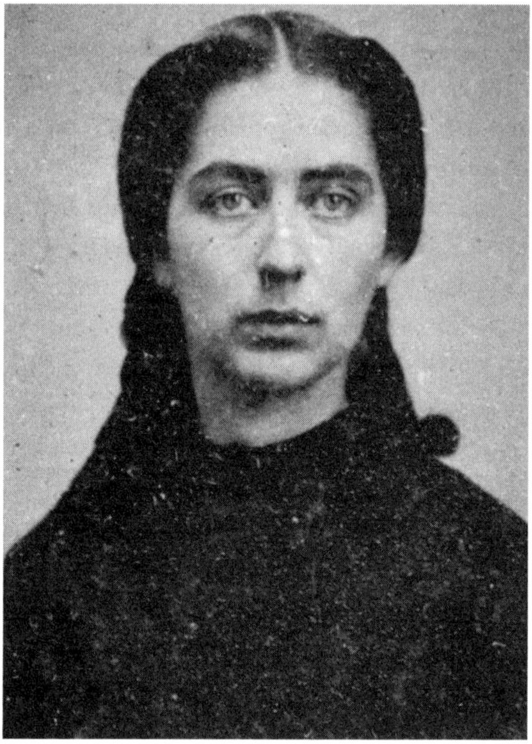

Fig. 14. Ellen Renshaw House. Courtesy of the Calvin M. McClung Historical Collection.

UNION TROOPS OCCUPY KNOXVILLE

On September 3, 1863, General Ambrose Burnside entered Knoxville, marching south on Gay Street, which was lined with thousands of cheering loyalists waving the stars and stripes they had hidden away during the Confederate occupation. The streets were decorated with Union flags "which had been concealed in houses or buried in the ground." Major Ben Perley Poore attempted to portray the raucous celebration in his 1882 biography of Ambrose Burnside, but he could only say that "it was a scene of grateful joy that baffles all description" (Poore 1882:216). When Burnside rode into town that morning, he was not only welcomed by Colonel John W. Foster but also "hailed as a deliverer" by thousands of people who came to greet him. Burnside dismounted at the Lamar House to greet the crowds of East Tennesseans who had come to Knoxville to welcome and thank him for freeing them from the "yoke of Confederate oppression." He responded to their enthusiasm by shaking hands for many hours with "plain old men and women from the country," who followed him from the Lamar House to his headquarters in the John Crozier House on Gay Street (Temple 1899:477).

So great was the desire of the people to see and welcome Burnside that, on September 4, arrangements were made for him to speak to the crowds of cheering people from the balcony of his headquarters. Temple recalled that "Burnside was an awkward, stammering speaker" that day, but he made up for his inadequacies by speaking from his heart with great sincerity. He praised the people gathered below for their undying loyalty to the federal government, and he reminded them that he had been sent by President Lincoln to liberate and protect East Tennessee from the cruel occupation of the Confederates. Temple described the profound outcome that Burnside's fumbling speech had on the crowds in eight simple words: "He won the undying love of our people" (ibid.:478).

Burnside would have little time to bask in their adoration, as President Lincoln wired him on September 10 with orders to "go about settling things in East Tennessee." Burnside had no more time to rest and regroup in Knoxville; he had been given a folksy but intimidating presidential command to take control of the entire East Tennessee region (ibid.).

Burnside's first step was the removal of the remaining Confederate army from upper East Tennessee. On September 7, Burnside left Knoxville with infantry and artillery for Cumberland Gap. After a forced march, he reached his destination two days later and personally demanded the unconditional surrender of the Southern garrison there. General Frazer, commander, accepted those terms, and Burnside's troops took "a large quantity of ammunition, two thousand stands of small arms, eleven pieces of artillery with their carriages and caissons, and twenty-five hundred prisoners" (Woodbury 1867:310).

The day after the surrender, Burnside asked Lincoln to relieve him from duty, as he was "suffering from a severe attack of the disease that had prostrated him during the summer." In a telegram, Lincoln refused his request, saying, "A thousand thank you's for the late success you have given us. We cannot allow you to resign until things shall be a little more settled." It now appeared that "things" would become comparatively quiet in the East and that the West would "become the scene of the contest of giants." The contest that was soon to take place would be "among the mountainous regions of northern Georgia and East Tennessee" (ibid.:327–328).

THE CONTEST IN NORTH GEORGIA AND TENNESSEE

General Rosecrans now occupied Chattanooga, and Burnside was being pressured to join him there. However, Burnside felt strongly that holding on to East Tennessee was more important than giving Rosecrans a hand; also, Lincoln's assignment would have been extremely difficult for him to achieve. Burnside found himself in an impossible situation: he was now supposed to hold the "line of the Holston, to occupy East Tennessee, to secure the gaps of the North Carolina Mountains" and at the same time concentrate his troops in Knoxville and prepare them to join Rosecrans in Chattanooga (ibid.). He was justifiably concerned as General Samuel Jones, with his 10,000 Confederate troops, were constantly harassing Burnside's outposts in upper East Tennessee. General Burnside believed that if he seriously reduced military strength at vital locations, his loyal East Tennesseans would once again fall into the hands of the Confederates (Humes 1888). Burnside made every effort to carry out his orders, but he refused to totally abandon Knoxville.

Leaving 600 men in Knoxville to strengthen the defenses of the town and prevent any enemy cavalry strikes, Burnside slowly moved his army south along the East Tennessee and Georgia Railroad, ostensibly with the intention of linking up with General Rosecrans's army in Chattanooga. His lead elements reached Cleveland, Tennessee, on September 18, only to find that an overconfident Rosecrans, believing he had Bragg on the run, had moved his army south to confront the Confederate forces spread out along Chickamauga Creek in Georgia. Washington expected Burnside to continue south to reinforce Rosecrans, and when Burnside did not respond, pressure from the Federal Command on Burnside began to increase.

Fig. 15. Gen. William S. Rosecrans. Library of Congress.

Charles A. Dana, assistant secretary of war, who was with Rosecrans's army, telegraphed Secretary of War Edwin Stanton on September 17 and again on the 18th saying that he had heard nothing positive from General Burnside (Dana 1996). A worried Lincoln sent Burnside several telegrams, urging him to continue south to Chattanooga, but a cautious and stubborn Burnside moved his Army of the Ohio southward only to Philadelphia, Tennessee, where he set up his headquarters (Seymour 1963).

On September 19–20, the Confederate Army of Tennessee soundly defeated Rosecrans at the Battle of Chickamauga. General Robert E. Lee had sent General James Longstreet and his vaunted 1st Corps of the Army of Northern Virginia to reinforce Bragg's army, and Longstreet's leadership had played a critical role in the Confederate victory. The Union army fled in panic back to Chattanooga, where they were quickly bottled up by Bragg's victorious army. Because Bragg's troops held the high ground on Missionary Ridge to the east and Lookout Mountain to the west, they were in control of the railroad, the river, and the best wagon roads as far west as Bridgeport, Alabama, which was the closest Union supply base to Chattanooga (Cozzens 1992).

Supplies could only be delivered to Federal troops in Chattanooga from Bridgeport by a circuitous route through the mountains north of the river, a distance of 60 miles (Grant 1886; Mosier 2006). The Federals, threatened with starvation, began eating their horses and mules as Bragg's lead elements began to probe northeast of Chattanooga along the Tennessee River in search of Burnside, who had been venturing downstream. After locating Burnside's forces, Colonel George G. Dibrell's Confederate cavalry brigade was sent to Philadelphia to attack any Federals they found. Colonel Frank Wolford's Union forces there were almost surrounded before they could pull back to their heavily fortified line at Loudon (Augustus 2000).

Events had obviously taken a sinister turn for the Federals in East Tennessee. President Lincoln was disgusted with Rosecrans and fearful that his plan to drive the Confederates out of East Tennessee was unraveling. He decided that a change was sorely needed in the high command in the western theater. On October 3, the President promoted General Ulysses S. Grant to Lieutenant General in command of the Union Military Division of the Mississippi, which included the Armies of the Cumberland, Tennessee, and Ohio. Grant replaced Rosecrans with General George Thomas as head of the Army of the Cumberland. His most trusted right-hand man, General William T. Sherman, was appointed head of the Army of the Tennessee, and he allowed Burnside to retain his position in the Army of the Ohio, because, as one Grant biographer wrote, "Lincoln had given him that command [and] there were very few first-rate Union generals around" (Mosier 2006:140).

When General Grant reached Chattanooga on October 23, his first priority was to lift the siege and get supplies to the starving Union soldiers there. Plans had already been made to open a shorter supply line from the west that would be safe from the besieging Confederates. On October 27, 1,800 Union soldiers quietly floated past Confederate pickets in 60 pontoon boats and repulsed the enemy sentries at Browns Ferry. Using the boats, they quickly built a pontoon bridge located out of range of the Confederate batteries on Lookout Mountain. Supplies could now reach the road north of the river and another pontoon bridge opposite Chattanooga, safe from the view and fire of the Confederates

Fig. 16. Gen. Ulysses S. Grant.
Library of Congress.

atop the mountain. A subsequent skirmish that cleared enemy troops out of Lookout Valley meant that the Union "cracker line" was now completely open, and Grant's army in Chattanooga began to receive food and supplies from Nashville via Bridgeport (Brearley 1871).

Grant initially believed that Burnside should evacuate Knoxville and concentrate his troops in Kingston, which was closer to Chattanooga, to enhance communication between the two. Burnside preferred to keep his forces in Knoxville for several reasons. He was extremely reluctant to abandon the people he had so recently delivered from Confederate occupation, and if his troops did join Grant's in Chattanooga, the need to supply them would be an additional burden for Grant. Another important consideration was the fact that there were no defensive fortifications in Kingston, whereas there were two earthworks in Knoxville that had been partially completed by the Confederates. Burnside believed that these earthworks could be strengthened enough to repel an attack and even withstand a siege (Poore 1882). He was proved correct a few weeks later. There were also rumors afoot that Bragg might send Longstreet to Knoxville. Grant sent Charles Dana to Knoxville from Chattanooga to consult with Burnside on the matter; after their discussion, Dana relayed Burnside's assessment by telegraph to Grant (Dana 1996 [1902]).

It was upsetting enough for the Confederate high command that Grant had broken General Bragg's siege, but now they were also forced to address the possibility of a mutiny by twelve of Bragg's senior officers, led by General James Longstreet. General Bragg particularly disliked Longstreet, who had earlier urged General Lee to appoint him to replace Bragg as commander of the Army of Tennessee. Longstreet loathed Bragg, and he deliberately chose to disobey Bragg's orders in Chattanooga, threatening his commander's success in the siege of the Union army there (Cozzens 1994). In addition to his troubled relationship with his officers, Bragg's troops also had no respect for him and thought he was an incompetent leader. He was seen as a cruel martinet who enjoyed chastising and demeaning his men (Johnson and Buell 1887).

In response to the petition requesting that Bragg be stripped of command and to the serious threat of a possible mutiny by his senior officers, President Davis traveled to Chattanooga in an attempt to resolve the problems there. One of President Davis's weaknesses as a leader was that he often stayed loyal to incompetent friends, and because Bragg was a favorite of the president, he was kept in command of the Army of Tennessee.

CONFEDERATES ATTEMPT TO EXPEL BURNSIDE

On October 29, President Davis wrote General Bragg and suggested that "you might advantageously assign General Longstreet with his two divisions to the task of expelling Burnside" (*OR* 1898:pt. 2, 554). Perhaps this questionable action was taken by Davis because he realized that Longstreet and Bragg could not effectively serve together in the same army. Or perhaps it was because Davis believed that the capture of Knoxville would put pressure on Bragg's immediate adversary, General Grant, who was well on his way to expelling General Bragg from the Chattanooga area.

Many Civil War historians have pointed out the shortcomings of Bragg as an army commander. The Southern historian Edward A. Pollard penned a harsh criticism of Davis in regard to his recommendations of Bragg. He said that Davis seemed "to have a singular fondness for erratic behavior. His visits to every battlefield in the Confederacy were ominous. He disturbed the plans of his generals; his military conceit led him into the wildest schemes." Because he feared that he would not receive the public credit he deserved for his "visionary projects," he often discussed in public the "general nature of his plans," thus forewarning the Union command (Pollard 1866:456).

Longstreet might have been disgruntled with this new assignment since his commander would still be Braxton Bragg; on the other hand, some historians believe that the general was glad to leave the Army of Tennessee as he had quietly coveted a higher rank and independent command in the western theater (Longstreet 1896). On November 5 Longstreet pulled his 1st Corps out of the entrenchments on Missionary Ridge and headed north to Knoxville via railroad to Sweetwater. Longstreet's battery commander, Colonel Porter Alexander, would later write in his memoirs that Bragg "never impressed me as a man of intellectual power—as a cool & clear thinker at all" (Alexander 1989:307). Although weakening his army by sending Longstreet to Knoxville as Grant was strengthening his forces in Chattanooga was a bad decision, General Bragg could not have chosen a tougher body of men for the assignment to capture Knoxville. Battle-tested veterans of 2nd Manassas, Fredericksburg, and Gettysburg, the 1st Corps of the Army of Northern Virginia included the nine crack infantry divisions of Generals Micah Jenkins and Lafayette McLaws, six outstanding batteries of artillery commanded by the capable Colonel E. Porter Alexander, and four brigades of cavalry led by the scrappy General Joe Wheeler (Seymour 1963).

General Longstreet had suffered devastating personal tragedies in 1862. He and his wife, Louise, had lost two children prior to that year, and they were to lose three more early in 1862 from the scarlet fever rampant in Richmond (Tumblin 2013b). In spite of these terrible personal losses, he returned to combat and for the most part had a

Fig. 17. Gen. James Longstreet. Library of Congress.

distinguished military career, serving second in command to General Robert E. Lee. Longstreet had loyally served General Lee as a corps commander, and Lee affectionately referred to him as his "Old War Horse."

He was loved by his men, and his leadership and bravery were outstanding, especially at the battles of 2nd Bull Run and Fredericksburg. His strong defensive position in the latter battle against his later nemesis, Ambrose Burnside, caused catastrophic casualties in the Union army and ultimately their total defeat. It was during that time that Longstreet was recognized as an innovative tactician and a master of defense, although he was blamed by critics for moving his troops too slowly into battle at Gettysburg and for criticizing the offensive tactics General Lee employed there (Wert 1993). The Knoxville Campaign would be his first independent command in an offensive role in the war, and responsibility for the outcome fell squarely on his shoulders.

Longstreet's success depended on rapid movement by rail to catch Burnside unprepared, but this choice of transportation was to present a huge challenge. As Longstreet left Tyner's Station on November 7, problems with the locomotives and poorly maintained track required the troops to detrain on the steep grades; because wood for the locomotives was scarce, the train had to periodically stop so that soldiers could chop down fence rails for the firebox. To top it off, the weather was unseasonably cold and rainy, and the dirt roads had turned into ribbons of mud. To make matters worse, from the outset of their campaign Longstreet's 1st Corps was suffering from a lack of supplies. General Bragg had promised supplies by the time they reached Sweetwater. As his troops left the train, Longstreet discovered the supplies were not there. According to Lieutenant Colonel Moxley Sorrel, Longstreet's chief of staff, the army was dependent on General Bragg for provisions, but he failed them miserably and the lack of adequate supplies impeded the troops for the rest of the campaign (Sorrel 1905). Troops had to go into the field to confiscate wheat and mill it into flour; there was a critical shortage of wagons and teams of animals, those provided were in inferior condition, and the draft animals were "feeble" (Wert 1993:341). Colonel Porter Alexander left the battalion in Sweetwater, waited for horses to arrive, and then left with an engineer to search the south bank of the Tennessee River around Loudon for a good place to build a pontoon bridge. The army continued the arduous journey north, struggling through ankle-deep mire for two more days. They finally stopped at the western outskirts of Loudon so they would not be discovered by the Federal troops on the north side of the river. Alexander, in the meantime, had found a site to build the pontoon bridge at Hough's Ferry ["Huff's" in soldiers' accounts], not too far from the burned railroad bridge near Loudon. The bridge had been deliberately destroyed by General Buckner during the retreat to Chattanooga earlier in August, and only the stone abutments and piers remained (Alexander 1989).

For this crucial assignment General Longstreet could not have chosen a more competent, innovative, or loyal soldier under his command than Colonel Edward Porter Alexander. Known to his friends as Porter, he was one of nine children born in Washington, Georgia, to a distinguished planter family (ibid.). Graduating third in his class at West Point, he taught engineering there before he was ordered to report for the Utah War between Mormon settlers and the United States Army in 1857–58. While there, he invented the code for the "wig wag" signal flags that was first used at the First Battle of Bull Run and helped turn the tide of battle in the Confederates' favor (Carruth 1884). As a lieutenant colonel in the Confederate army, he served as chief of ordinance under General Robert E. Lee at the battles of Second Bull Run and Antietam (Heidler and Heidler 2000a). Throughout the war, he was best known as a superb artillery commander and played a decisive role in the Confederate victories at Fredericksburg and Chancellorsville (Alexander 1989). In his comprehensive personal memoirs he wrote about his frustration in coping with the faulty artillery ammunition supplied to him in Gettysburg and later in Knoxville. One of his most stressful moments as a lieutenant commander occurred on the third day at Gettysburg, when he had the responsibility of deciding whether the defending Union artillery had been effectively silenced before what turned out to be an ill-fated charge on Cemetery Ridge (Gallagher and Noble 2000). After the Knoxville Campaign, when he was promoted to brigadier general, Alexander remained the chief artillerist for the Army of Northern Virginia until he surrendered with General Robert E. Lee at Appomattox Courthouse (Alexander 1989).

Just a month before Colonel Alexander identified an appropriate place to build a pontoon bridge for Confederate troops to cross the river, the retreating Union forces had salvaged their pontoon bridge in Loudon by dismantling and shipping the box boats used for their bridge back to Knoxville by train (ibid.).

From October 23 to 28, Union major Jacob Roemer's artillery farriers and blacksmiths had been busy making "thirty pounds of nails of various sizes for use in building a pontoon bridge over the Holston [Tennessee] River at Loudon. The nails were made from iron bars taken from a brick building near-by." Roemer noted in his *Reminiscences of the War of the Rebellion* that the bridge was soon completed, with "as many as two thousand men . . . employed upon it at the same time" (Roemer 1897:155).

In addition to dismantling the pontoon bridge for the trip back to Knoxville, Union troops earlier had to deal with a locomotive and cars that had been floated in pieces to the south bank of the river in Loudon and reassembled there to provide rail service for Union troops heading

Fig. 18. Edward Porter Alexander. From Francis Trevelyan Miller, *The Photographic History of the Civil War in Ten Volumes.*

toward Chattanooga to help Rosecrans. This matter had to be addressed in the quickest, most efficient way possible as they could not leave the locomotive and cars for the Confederates. The locomotive was fired up and driven at full speed toward the stone abutment, the "brink of the abyss" where the bridge once stood; the driver jumped from the train prior to reaching the chasm. In a dramatic description of the event, Colonel Sumner Carruth, who was standing on the river bank, said he heard the locomotive approach, "roaring like a wild bull . . . it leaped into the air with its cars and plunged head-long into the river; the agitated waters foamed and raged, then floated on as before. It seemed as if we had witnessed the drowning of a friend" (Carruth 1884:174).

Alexander may have known as he studied the river banks for a safe place to install a pontoon bridge that a Union locomotive and its accompanying cars rested peacefully beneath the surface of the water nearby. The location Alexander chose had to be close to the location where the tracks stopped in Loudon as the unwieldy pontoons were loaded on flatcars (Augustus 2000:69). Alexander discovered a suitable site about three quarters of a mile from Loudon. During the dark hours of the night of November 13, soldiers pushed the flatcars carrying the box boats quietly toward the river to avoid being discovered by Union pickets. The boats were then unloaded and dragged through the thick woods over rough ground down to the ferry site. Men from two companies of South Carolina Palmetto Sharpshooters manned the pontoon boats, which silently crossed the river (Alexander 1989). They were followed later that night by the entire regiment, which secured a "quite primitive" bridge by sunrise on Sunday, November 15. Because of the strong current and inadequate anchors, the completed bridge formed a huge, reverse letter "S" shape in the rapid current, but the bridge proved strong enough for all the troops to pass over, with Alexander's artillery following. One soldier who commented on the "queer bridge" over which he had cautiously trod advised that "no man should abuse the bridge by which he safely crosses" (Sorrel 1905:206).

General Ulysses Grant, now in command of the besieged Union army in Chattanooga, realized that General Bragg had weakened his force encircling Chattanooga but was apprehensive that Burnside could not prevent Longstreet from capturing Knoxville. At that time, Charles A. Dana, assistant secretary of war, was in Chattanooga for firsthand observation of how Grant was handling the siege. Secretary of War Stanton was also concerned about whether Knoxville and East Tennessee could be held by Federal forces. He ordered Dana to leave Chattanooga and head for Knoxville to evaluate Burnside's situation. Arriving on November 13, Dana had his first meeting with Burnside, whom he would later describe in his memoirs as "a very showy officer—not that he *made* any show; he was naturally that. When he first talked to you, you would think he possessed a great deal more intelligence than he really possessed." Dana reported to Stanton that "the town was fortified, though unable to resist attack by a large force. Up to this time Burnside had been very well off, for he had commanded a rich region behind Knoxville, and these had drawn food and forage. He even had about one hundred miles of railroad in active operation for foraging, and he had plenty of mills and workshops in the town which he could use" (Dana 1996:138–139 [1902]).

During consultations about the approach of Longstreet and his approximately 17,000 men, Burnside told Dana that he "would not long be able to resist such an attack and if Grant did not succeed in making a demonstration that would compel Longstreet to return that he must retreat." Burnside discussed various avenues of retreat, but by the next morning he had decided that he might not have to leave East Tennessee and "had even decided to send out a force to attack the enemy's advance" (ibid.:40). The next day, upon hearing that Longstreet's vanguard had crossed the river at Hough's [Huff's] Ferry, Burnside and Dana left Knoxville by train for Lenoir's Station, where Burnside had earlier ordered his men to build their winter quarters (Roemer 1897). The men were looking forward to a long respite and they thought the surrounding areas near the station were perfect for winter quarters. There was an open plain south of the railroad for a parade ground and winter houses; the Little Tennessee joined the Holston at this point and there were hundreds of second-growth pine trees growing on the hills surrounding the plain (Carruth 1884:175). About 5,500 men of the 9th Corps built their encampment in the midst of one of the forests (Cutcheon 1904:8) near a sizeable plantation owned by a member of the Lenoir family. Doctor Lenoir housed his slaves and overseers in over a hundred houses near his large fields which were full of corn and maize (Swift 1863). The troops commenced building an outsized oven to be used for a government bakery (Carruth 1884:175).

William Brearley noted that the pine forests provided all the wood needed for the "multitude of rows of six by ten one-half story log houses, arranged like a regiment 'marching in columns' by companies, with the 'distances' policed and graded into company streets." Brearley was excited about settling for the winter, and on November 15, after completing his hut which featured a brick fireplace and chimney, he set out to find some items for his abode and discovered a door in an old shanty which he acquired for his bunk. Brearley then added to his hut what he called "home luxuries;" a gun rack at the head of his new bed, a cracker box at the foot, and a shelf for his writing material. He would soon rue the fact that he had used a mildewed tent for roofing (Brearley 1871:8–10).

Forty-five year old artillerist Jacob Roemer, a German immigrant from Pennsylvania, created for himself a larger 8x10 foot log house, with a "wall tent fly roof." He proudly described in his memoirs the method he engineered to heat his log hut. "Just outside the house on the right of the front entrance, was a fire hole three feet deep; from the upper part of this a horizontal flue constructed of brick, extended through the house from front to rear, six inches below the ground and terminated in a chimney ten or twelve feet high" (Roemer 1897:156). Lieutenant Frederick William Swift of the 17th Michigan Infantry described the scene that a rain drenched Brearley, and a dry and warm Roemer, would witness shortly after midnight on November 16. Burnside had unexpectedly entered the camp with Dana to announce he would be taking personal command of his troops, and they were to prepare to abandon camp immediately. Swift described the scene as Burnside, their beloved commander, entered the camp on his favorite horse, "Old Bob." The men halted, opened to the left and right, and cheered him loudly as he passed. Burnside acknowledged their cheers by removing his hat, as was his custom, and greeting them with a broad smile which showed his "fine teeth" (Swift:1863).

The men immediately began to ready themselves, and prepared to carry out Burnside's orders. Their hopes for a long period of quiet rest over the winter months near Lenoir's Station vanished as they made preparations to leave.

Dana left Burnside at the Lenoir's Station encampment and quickly continued on horseback to Chattanooga, writing later that "so completely were the Confederates taking possession of the country between Knoxville and Chattanooga that had we delayed a single day we could have got out only through Cumberland Gap or that of Big Creek. We were four days in returning and Mr. Stanton became very uneasy" (Dana 1996:140–141). As Dana headed back to Chattanooga, Burnside, who was with his army in Lenoir City, advised his troops that he had made a decision to immediately attack the Confederate advance and slowly fall back to Knoxville. This strategy would, he hoped, draw Longstreet farther away from Chattanooga, making it more difficult for him to rejoin Bragg. If his plan worked, it would also allow additional time for the troops in Knoxville to complete the fortifications.

THE RACE TO CAMPBELL'S STATION

After failing to stop Longstreet's butternut and gray–clad columns from crossing the Tennessee River and turning the Union's right flank at Hough's Ferry General Burnside had realized the Confederates were heading east to cut him off from Knoxville. At 2:00 a.m. on November 16, he ordered his troops to abandon their main supply base and winter quarters at Lenoir's and make for the safety of fortified Knoxville, delaying Longstreet's advance as much as possible on the way (Augustus 2013). There was a need for great haste, and to prevent their supplies from falling into Confederate hands, Burnside ordered that the barrels of coffee, sugar, and flour be opened and "distributed among the men and what they could not take was thrown into heaps and burned." The men "watched as train after train was destroyed with their contents," as well as boxes of clothing, tents, ammunition, and about 100 wagons (Todd 1886:354). General Halleck was worried that Burnside would be overwhelmed by the pursuing enemy and defeated, but Burnside knew the area well and was aided by the sluggish and erratic movements of Longstreet's army. General Grant telegraphed Burnside on November 17: "You are doing exactly what appears to me to be right. I want the enemy's progress retarded at every point, all it can be, only giving up each place when it becomes evident that it can no longer be held without endangering your force to capture" (Burrage 1884:103). Burnside did exactly as his commander suggested, and the march to Knoxville began at 6:00 a.m. (Roemer 1897).

After crossing Hough's Ferry, McLaws's Division moved onto the Kingston Road and advanced towards Knoxville. Union forces retreated on Lenoir's Road (now Martel Road), which was located south of and parallel to Kingston Road before it turned north to join with that road just west of Campbell's Station. The Confederates hoped to reach the intersection of the road first, then block the junction of the two roads

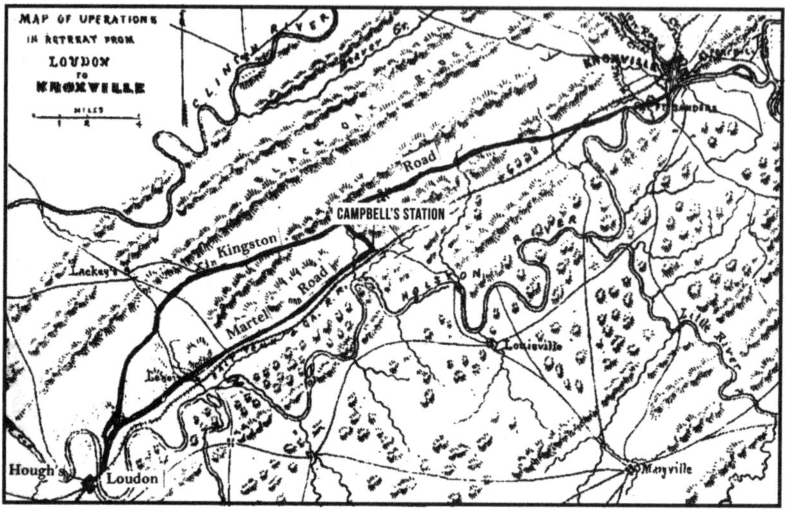

Fig. 19. Map showing routes taken by Confederate and Union troops from Loudon to Knoxville. Campbell's Station lies between Kingston Road and Black Oak Ridge. From Augustus Woodbury, *Major General Ambrose E. Burnside and the Ninth Army Corps*, 1867.

before the Union army could reach the crossroads, turn east, and retreat on the Kingston Road to the safety of Knoxville. Burnside had wisely dispatched a force to secure the junction before the mass of his troops retreated from Lenoir's. The 2nd Division under Colonel John F. Hartranft, who was "always prompt and always reliable, succeeded in the early part of the forenoon, in reaching Campbell Station." They had marched rapidly and reached the junction 15 minutes before the lead elements of McLaws's Division could cut them off. Augustus Woodbury would later minimize their accomplishment, writing that "it was an exciting race and our troops won" (Woodbury 1867:335).

THE BATTLE OF CAMPBELL'S STATION

The problem now facing General Burnside was how to delay Longstreet's advancing force so that his army could reach Knoxville and finish fortifying the town before the anticipated Confederate attack. In the early afternoon of November 16, Burnside deployed a battle line of infantry across the Kingston Road near the historic house belonging to Dr. William Nelson, which still stands behind the Taco Bell restaurant in Farragut. He placed his artillery on the high ground just east of the small village of Campbell's Station. The line of Federal infantry was anchored north of the Kingston Road by the 20th Michigan Infantry with Colonel Edwin Schall's 51st Pennsylvania. The flanks rested on wooded hills and anchored a narrow front of approximately a mile. These were battle-hardened men who had fought at 2nd Manassas, Antietam, and Fredericksburg, and they were definitely a match for Longstreet's vaunted 1st Corps (Augustus 2013; Davidson 1963).

General Longstreet's troops attempted to turn both flanks of the Union line, attacking across an open field under withering canister fire, but the Federals held. At about 3:00 p.m. Burnside ordered his troops to withdraw about 1,000 yards to the east and form a second line. Augustus Woodbury of the 9th Army Corps wrote that in a second attack when the Confederates came within short range, the Union artillery opened with grape, canister, and shell with fearful effect (Woodbury 1867:336–337). Brearley said that the "hills trembled under the reverberation" of the guns, adding that "seldom during the war had there been given so unobstructed a view of the whole field as spread itself out before our position." Firing cannons made great gaps in the Confederate ranks, which "would immediately close up and advance again." Brearley found himself fascinated by the guns as they fired, writing that "each gun seemed like a living, moving evil spirit surrounded with a halo of sulphorous [*sic*] smoke. Near one of the batteries when the wind would lift the smoke a little, we could distinguish a pair of boots which resembled Burnside's boots; and judging from an occasional glimpse of an old soft felt hat, which seemed to be nearly above them, we knew that somewhere between, our commander had his headquarters established" (Brearley 1871:24–25).

Augustus Woodbury proudly wrote, "The soldiers of the 9th Corps, with their comrades of the twenty-third, had met the flower of Lee's army, and had inflicted upon it a most damaging blow" (Woodbury 1867). When General Ferrero made his report of the action, he said,

"Never did troops maneouvre [*sic*] so beautifully and with such precision, changing positions several times while under severe fire, brigades moving forward to relieve each other, others returning, having exhausted their ammunition, changes of front, passing of defiles, were executed by men and officers so as to draw the highest praise from all" (Woodbury 1867:337–338). But Brigadier General Robert Potter reported that 249 Union troops had died while local residents stated that the "Confederates had only 91 killed "and over 300 wounded" (*OR* 1890:pt. 1, 380). Woodbury considered the Battle of Campbell's Station to be the most critical of the Knoxville campaign (Woodbury 1867:334).

BURNSIDE'S "MUD MARCH"

During the moonless night that followed the battle of Campbell's Station on November 16, General Burnside "having punished the enemy, mastered the field and saved his trains, drew off to Knoxville . . . in a forced march, joined by General Sanders's men who covered their retreat." Both Union and Confederate troops began slogging through the ever-present mud towards Knoxville" (Woodbury 1867). During the battle Burnside sent a wire to General Sanders telling him to take control of the Kingston Road so the Union army could safely retreat to Knoxville (Augustus 2013).

During the retreat from Lenoir's, the men labeled the thick mud created by frequent heavy rains "Tennessee Mud." William H. Brearley in his *Recollections of the East Tennessee Campaign* recalled that during the campaign, the mud was a great impediment. He described how the "liberal mixture of water and red clay soil" produced a thick sludge, which the troops laboriously "moved through" rather than marching. The consistency of the "Tennessee Mud" was almost "as slippery as soap, and sticky as wax . . . and it sucked in cannons, horses, mules and sometimes captured shoes of the men" (Brearley 1871). Brearley later described the march as "seventeen of the longest, weariest miles that it has ever been my misfortune to walk" (ibid.:25).

As he penned his history of the war, Major Cutcheon predicted that if the living members of the 20th Michigan were to vote on "which was the hardest day's march in their experience, it is probable that the majority would select the march from Lenoir's Station to Knoxville on November 16 and 17, 1863. The distance of more than twenty-four miles was made in a little less than twenty-four hours, during eight of which they were constantly under fire, and for two hours were engaged in a desperate struggle with a force more than ten times their own, supplied with artillery and accompanied by cavalry so superior to our own that we were in constant danger of being out-flanked [*sic*]and our line of retreat cut off" (Cutcheon 1904:77).

Burnside and his troops reached Knoxville hungry and exhausted from the march, most of it through red clay nearly three feet deep. Brearley recounted that he and many others slept while walking, and after being told they had two hours to rest upon their arrival in Knoxville, most men lay down on the mud and fell asleep (Brearley 1871:27). B.F. Thompson of the 112th Illinois was not one of the soldiers allowed to rest. His regiment was held in reserve and ordered to be ready immediately to respond if attacked by Longstreet. Thompson recorded that "a heavy detail from the regiment patrolled the streets all night to preserve order and prevent fast driving or a stampede in case of a night attack" (Thompson 1885:150–151). The men who had napped soon received an assignment to their battle stations and began working to prepare the defensive fortifications in Knoxville for the hammer blow to come. During the next 17 days, these two exhausted armies would slug it out for control of Knoxville and East Tennessee during one of the coldest winters on record.

4

FORTIFYING KNOXVILLE

POE'S ASSIGNMENT

William Brearley recorded that Captain Orlando Poe, chief engineer of the 23rd Corps, preceded the troops to Knoxville by two days, "having left us at Lenoir by order of General Burnside" to strengthen the defenses there for the upcoming Confederate assault. Poe, he continued, "by dint of uninterrupted labor had completed designs for defenses" by the time Burnside reached Knoxville with his men (Brearley 1871:25). An admiring Brearley wrote that "four original earthworks were 'pressed into service' without any very great remodeling, for although they had been constructed for an entirely different purpose and were necessarily illy [*sic*] adapted to the contingencies of a siege, the demand for *immediate* [italics in original] defenses was far too great, and the time allowed too limited to think of constructing others in their places which should conform in every respect to *rules* constructed for siege defenses" (ibid.:25–26).

Recounting his orders from Burnside in his official report, Poe said, "I was directed to select lines of defense around Knoxville, and to have everything prepared to put the troops in positions as fast as they should arrive. As I had been over the ground a great many times and had examined it in reference to this contingency, the examination directed was made very rapidly" (*OR* 1890:pt. 1, 305). Even though Poe was familiar with the ground and had graduated near the top of his class at West Point as a topographical engineer, he was facing a daunting task.

During the early years of the war, Poe had joined General George B. McClellan's staff and helped plan the defenses of Washington. Promoted

Fig. 20. Gen. Orlando Poe. National Archives.

to captain of volunteers, he later saw action in the Peninsular Campaign and at 2nd Bull Run and Chantilly. After an appointment as brigadier general of volunteers in November 1862 was denied by Congress, he was promoted to the rank of captain in the regular army, and in 1863 he became chief engineer of the 23rd Corps in the western theater (Taylor 2009).

Captain Poe had first entered Knoxville with the Army of the Ohio on September 3, and on September 7 was ordered by General Burnside to prepare Knoxville's fortifications for a garrison of 600 men. Poe described the fortifications designed by Leadbetter and abandoned by the Confederates when they hastily departed from Knoxville. Poe would base his plan on Leadbetter's aborted first phase of construction of two defensive works: "During the enemy's occupation of Knoxville, a very small beginning had been made toward the erection of earthworks. An insignificant line had been thrown up on the hill northwest of the college and a slight epaulment on the bluff overlooking the railway station . . . The plans for two works were submitted—one, afterwards known as Fort Sanders, on the site of the imperfect work first mentioned" (Poe 1888:731–32).

Adjutant General Henry Sweetser Burrage commented in his 1884 history of the 36th Regiment of the Massachusetts Volunteers that the fort was "not only unfinished, but was little more than begun" (Burrage 1866:102). On September 5, John Watkins, a gunner with the 14th Independent Battery, Light Artillery, 23rd Army Corps, who entered Knoxville from the west, noted in a letter written to his future wife, Sara Probert, on September 18 that the Confederates "had thrown up breastworks on two or three hills and that is about all they did do" (Watkins 1863b).

It was not long after Burnside arrived in Knoxville that he was ordered to seize Cumberland Gap from the Confederates. He took Poe with him, which delayed his progress on the defensive plans for Knoxville. During September, Poe submitted plans for forts on College and Summit Hills, but the work proceeded slowly because of the difficulty of transporting materials to Knoxville from the supply base in Kentucky. Poe was obviously thinking about what would be needed for the massive construction effort awaiting him, because he amassed 800 shovels, 500 axes, and 400 picks before leaving Kentucky for Knoxville. Progress was again delayed, this time for two weeks, when Poe was ordered by Burnside into combat at Bull's Gap. When Poe returned from the Gap on October 9, he immediately oversaw the building of an 800-foot-long pontoon bridge to connect fortifications south of the Holston (Tennessee) River to those in Knoxville (Booker 2015a). It was completed by the first of November using the same flatboats that had formed the bridge spanning the Tennessee River during the Union retreat from Loudon (Poe 1888:732; *OR* 1890:pt. 1, 273).

When Poe received orders from Burnside during the battle of Campbell's Station to return to Knoxville and strengthen the lines of defense there, he noted that only two forts "were in a defensible condition, *viz* that occupied by Benjamin's battery [Fort Loudon] and the one on Temperance Hill, the work upon them having been done by 600

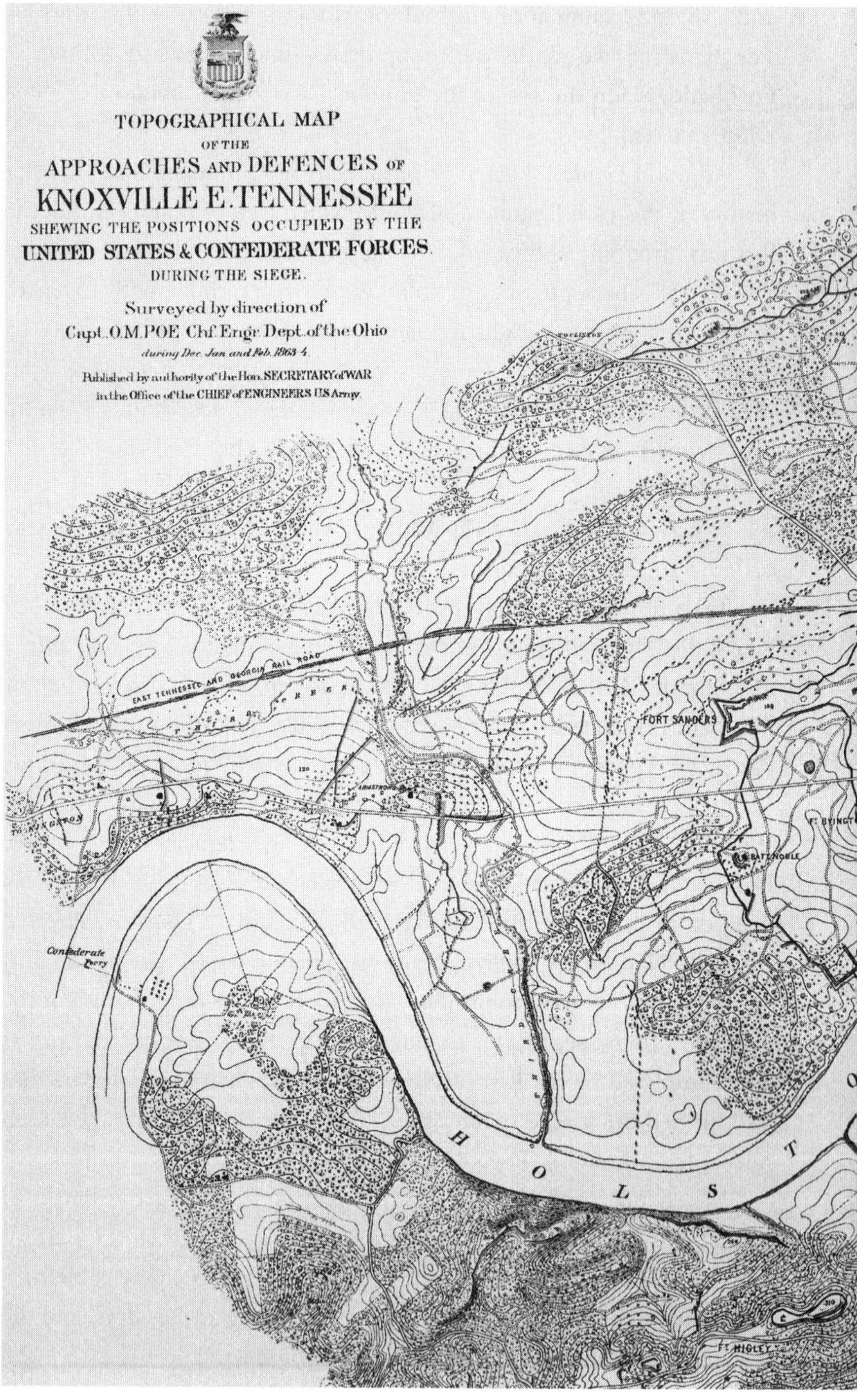
TOPOGRAPHICAL MAP
OF THE
APPROACHES AND DEFENCES OF
KNOXVILLE E. TENNESSEE
SHEWING THE POSITIONS OCCUPIED BY THE
UNITED STATES & CONFEDERATE FORCES.
DURING THE SIEGE.
Surveyed by direction of
Capt. O.M. POE Chf. Engr. Dept. of the Ohio
during Dec. Jan. and Feb. 1863-4.
Published by authority of the Hon. SECRETARY of WAR
in the Office of the CHIEF of ENGINEERS U.S. Army.
EAST TENNESSEE AND GEORGIA RAIL ROAD
FORT SANDERS
Confederate Ferry
H O L S T O
FT. HIGLEY

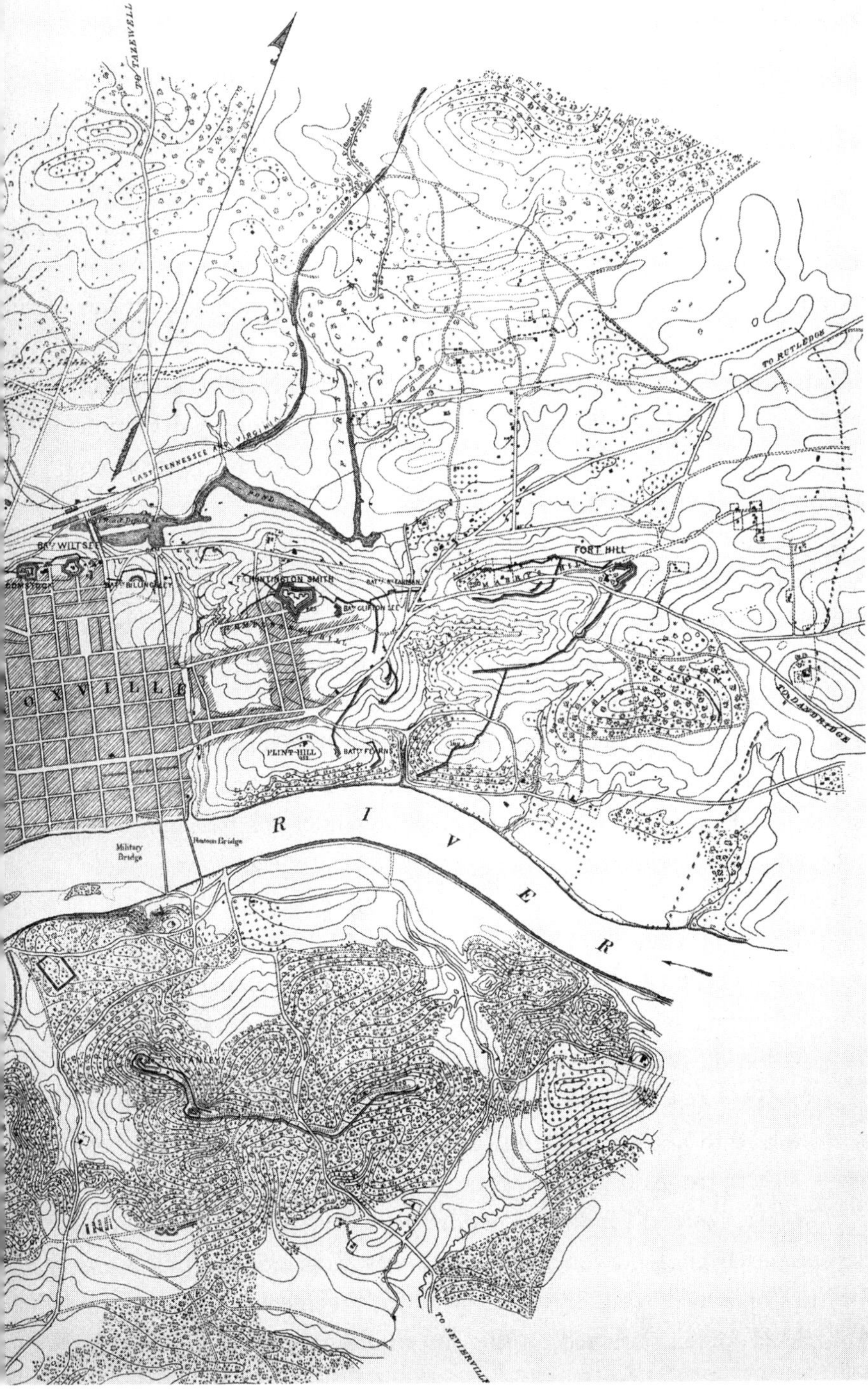

Fig. 21. The Approaches and Defenses of Knoxville, 1864. *OR Atlas*, Plate XLVIII-2.

troops belonging to the Engineer Battalion" of the 23rd Corps, who had been left to hold Knoxville during Burnside's retreat from Bull's Gap (ibid.:732).

When Poe was in Knoxville in early September, he described the earthwork on White's Hill, Fort Loudon, as an "insignificant line thrown up on a hill" (ibid.). In November, Poe had chosen to incorporate Fort Loudon and Fort Huntington Smith atop Summit Hill into a defensive design, noting that at that time Confederate Fort Loudon was "so far advanced toward completion that . . . [its] use without modification was compulsory" (ibid.). B. F. Thompson described the line from the Fort to Temperance Hill as "a parapet of three or four feet high" (Thompson 1885:162). In this study, *Webster's New World Dictionary* definition of a parapet is used: "a wall or embankment for protecting troops from enemy fire" (Agnes 2003).

Poe and his men were forced to build and build quickly on what was available to them at that time: Leadbetter's limited, initial construction of a strategic fort. Because of Poe's foresight, his troops had been supplied with adequate digging tools for the work to come. This fact is substantiated by the statement of Commander Burnside, who praised Poe by saying, "Captain Poe had before leaving Kentucky organized an engineer battalion from the Twenty-third Corps, and had by great efforts succeeded in bringing over the mountains a quantity of intrenching [*sic*] and other engineering tools. These proved to be of the greatest possible value to us during the siege" (*OR* 1890:pt. 1, 275).

While some Civil War historians attribute the design of Fort Sanders to Captain Poe, the Confederates had actually begun building the fortification they first named Fort Buckner (after their commander) under the supervision of General Leadbetter, the chief engineer of Bragg's army. The Confederates had changed the name to Fort Loudon before they were forced to flee Knoxville in August 1863. It is not known when the Southern troops began the work or how long they labored on it.

In fact, General Leadbetter had, in improving his preliminary defenses, wisely chosen a long, steep, east–west ridge about a mile west of town on which to site this strategically advantageous earthwork. A completed fort constructed on this site would have commanded two

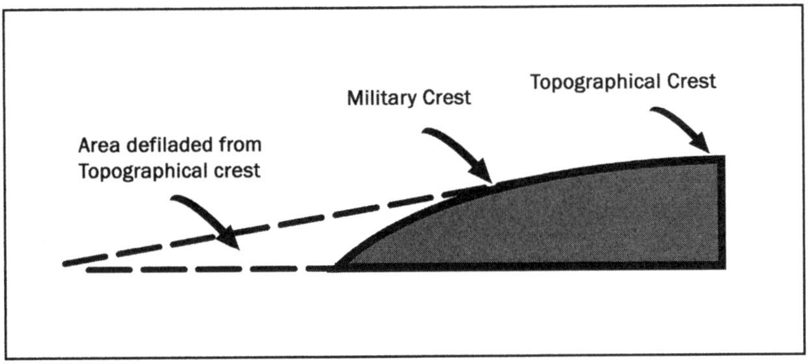

Fig. 22. Military Crest.

major routes into Knoxville from the west, the East Tennessee and Georgia Railroad located at the base of the northern slope of the ridge, and the Kingston Road at the base of the south slope. The location was militarily advantageous as Leadbetter had positioned Fort Loudon on the military crest of the western slope of the ridge, rather than on the topographical crest. Placing the earthwork fortification there allowed infantry behind the west wall of the fort, the most likely point of attack, maximum observation and direct fire, covering the slope of the hill to the west for 800 yards into the valley of Third Creek. Had General Leadbetter placed the west wall of the fort at the topographical crest of the ridge, there would have been a defiladed area, or "dead space," at the bottom of the ridge, where the attacking force could not be seen by the defenders. Another disadvantage to placing the fort on the topographical crest was that troops within the fort would become perfect targets for the enemy below as they stood silhouetted against the sky on the highest point of the ridge.

The problem created for defending infantry if fortifications are placed on a topographical crest becomes clear when one considers what happened to the Confederates defending Missionary Ridge during the Battle of Chattanooga on November 25, 1863. Engineers placed their trenches on the topographical crest of the ridge instead of the military crest (Bearss 2006). Because of the limited field of vision ("dead space") for the Southern defenders on the ridge top, the Federals were able to launch their attack out of sight at the base of the ridge and storm up

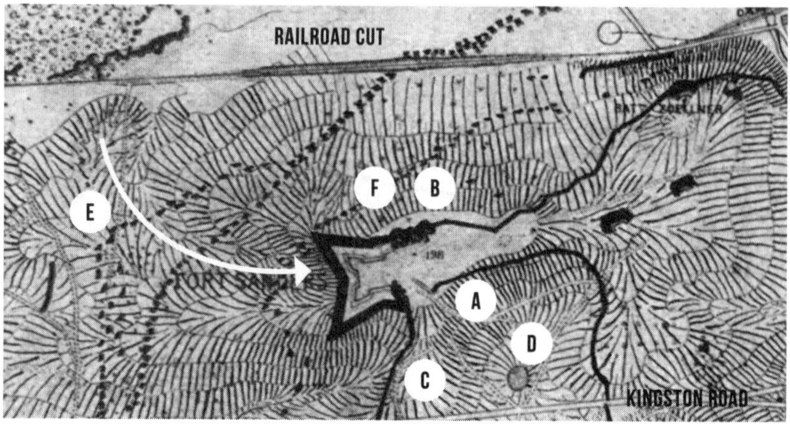

Fig. 23. Enlargement of Poe's topographic (hachure) map of the defenses of Knoxville. A) and B) Steep slopes along the north and south walls of the ridge; (C) incline, future site of 17th Street; (D) pond; (E) defilade, the sunken route of the Confederate attack; (F) sinkhole located north of the northwest bastion.

the dead space to take the ridge and win the battle. They routed Bragg's army in a key Union victory at Chattanooga—a victory that would help ensure that General Burnside and his troops would continue to hold Knoxville for the Union (Bearss 2006; Cozzens 1994).

It was obvious to Captain Poe as he began the work on Fort Loudon that any flaws in the fort's construction could not be corrected before the anticipated assault by Longstreet's 1st Corps. One very troublesome issue Poe immediately identified as a problem for Union troops was an adequate defense of the northwest bastion, which Confederate engineers had begun to build earlier under Leadbetter's direction. Military historian Earl Hess points out the problem in his book *The Knoxville Campaign:* "Even though the bastion was located as far down the slope from the natural crest as possible, it could not allow the Federals to cover all the ground along the line of approach" (Hess 2012:100).

Although the northwest bastion had been properly placed according to military engineering at the junction of the west and north curtain walls, these walls did not form a right angle because the fort had been laid out on the ridge top in the shape of an irregular quadrilateral whose east and west sides were not equal in length: the west side wall was 95 yards long and the east 85 yards long. This irregular shape caused the northwest angle (the angle vertex or highest angle of the shape) to project farther out than the southwest angle, causing the northwest bastion built at that angle to become a dangerously prominent "salient" and a critical defensive liability. ("Salient" is the military term for a defensive feature that projects beyond the main fortification.) In addition to this concern, the apex of the bastion was located about 800 yards from an abrupt slope, below which Confederate troops could not be seen. (Today, Metron Center Way runs north–south at the base of the slope, and the valley of Third Creek, where Tyson Park is located [see fig. 21], is west of Metron.) In addition to these grave concerns, because of its position it was possible for the enemy to surround the salient on three sides. These very visible liabilities must have stuck in the minds of the Union troops, and as they worried about defending the northwest bastion, many began to identify it simply as "the salient."

A greater concern for Union commanders was a long, wide gully (a swale) called "the defilade," which approached the northwest bastion of the fort from the base of the north side of the ridge on which the fort was located. As indicated above, a defilade is a hidden or covered way that allows an attacking force to approach its target relatively unseen. The dead space created by this particular defilade made it impossible for the Federals to fire directly down the capital of the northwest bastion straight into the defilade. The infantrymen defending the northwest bastion were located behind the curtain wall and had to turn their bodies at an oblique angle in order to provide covering fire into the dead space. This necessity created additional danger for these men since they had to expose themselves more in order to fire obliquely over the wall than if they stood shooting straight ahead.

Other Federal officers would comment on the condition of the Fort Loudon earthworks when they reached Knoxville on November 17. Captain Armour of the 79th Highlanders remarked that "little progress had been made toward its completion" (Armour 1898:7). Artillerist Lieutenant Samuel Benjamin said that the earthwork "offered no protection, as it was only one-fourth completed on the west, north, and south sides" (*OR* 1890:pt. 1, 43). If Benjamin was correct in his estimation, this means that about 24 yards of the west wall was complete along with

31 yards of the north and south walls. It is probable that most of the soil used to create the fortification that existed when the Union army entered Knoxville was excavated from trenches in front of the uncompleted west and south walls and from the interior of Confederate Fort Loudon. The "insignificant line on the hill" was probably first seen by Poe from the Kingston Road as he entered the outskirts of town. Only the partially finished south wall would have been visible. Both the north and south walls were created by adding earth on each side of the crest of the ridge.

Confederate commanders had also been acutely aware of the problems with the northwest bastion. Brigadier General E. Porter Alexander, chief of artillery of Longstreet's 1st Corps, criticized his fellow Confederate engineer General Leadbetter for his placement of that bastion in his own discussion of the northwest salient:

> "The Confederate engineer who laid out this work had injudiciously turned the salient angle of its northwest bastion directly toward the valley of Third Creek, just at the point where this valley allowed an approach, within 120 yards, completely covered from fire from the fort. The convex crest of the valley curved from this point to the east and south, and sheltered a large territory, affording space for many brigades to be held completely under cover, within distances from 150 to 400 yards of the enemy's entrenchments. These conditions made it the most favorable point for attack, and, indeed, the only one at all favorable north of the river." (Alexander 1962:483)

This "large territory" that Alexander described is now the location of Tyson Park (see figure 21). Alexander also commented in his memoirs that only "a few days after the 18th, the Union had completed an interior line which could have resisted an attack even if Fort Sanders was taken. By the time the battle took place, a second line had been constructed that could have possibly "survived the loss of the first" (ibid.).

The Poe 1864–1865 contour map (figure 21) illustrates the Knoxville area and Union and Confederate defenses. Figure 23 is an enlarged section of Poe's Knoxville hachure map which shows the northwest salient location at the top of the defilade. Hachure maps are a type of relief map that shows the physical geography of an area. Figure 24a is an enlargement of Poe's contour map showing the location of the Confederate muster ground, the path of the attack up the defilade, the rock outcropping seen in the Thompson 1922 aerial photograph, and the 80-foot Confederate trench.

What is commonly called "the Poe map" (figure 21) is labeled on the top left as the "Map of the Approaches and Defenses of Knoxville, Tennessee, Surveyed by the direction of Capt. O. M. Poe during Dec. Jan. Feb. 1863–4." At that time, triangulation was used to create contour lines; topographical features were sketched on paper marked with grid lines; and the direction was determined by compass bearings. Distances were determined by pacing or with the use of a surveyor's wheel (Nolan and Redmond 2012).

Whereas a hachure map creates an easily understood, three-dimensional relief of the area with more visually identifiable land forms, Poe's work was based on then-current scientific methods, which produced maps with more reliable distances and heights critical for military purposes. Before leaving Knoxville to join Sherman, Poe praised Major S. S. Lyons of the 4th Kentucky Cavalry, commending him for his mapping skills and abilities as a cartographer noting that Lyons possessed "a wonderful talent" for that "branch of science" (*OR* 1890:pt. 1, 43). Both of Poe's renderings of the topography of the fort area can be accurately compared to the present-day landforms. They clearly show the very steep, natural slopes located on the north and south sides of White's Hill, and these slopes can still be seen today.

Union soldiers entering the fort on November 17 immediately began carrying out the assignment that Burnside had given them. William Brearley recorded that they worked as hard as beavers and by nightfall they had completed a line of works (Brearley 1871). On the first day of the siege, Lieutenant Benjamin reported that "before the enemy had closed in, I dug two lines of pits for the pickets, about 80 and 30 yards from the fort—the second line to rally in if driven from the first." He also said by "dint of persuasion and demonstrating the impossibility of holding this position otherwise, I prevailed on General Ferrero to occupy the hill due south from the fort, on the other side of the road to

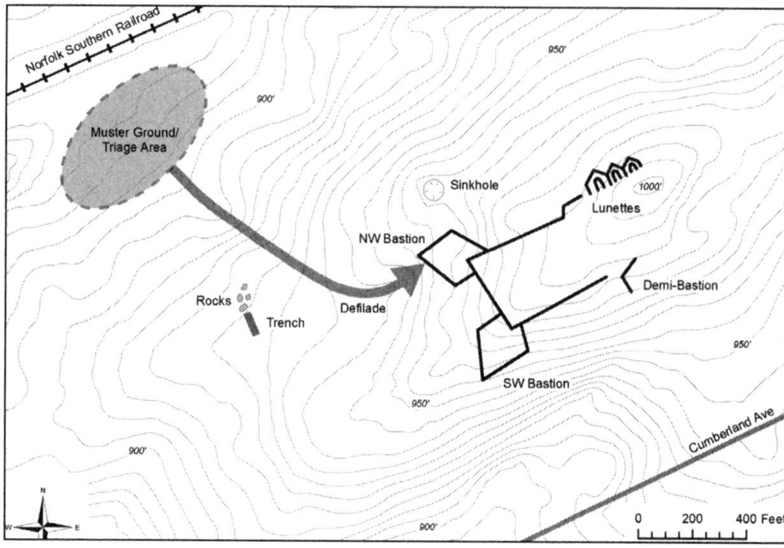

Fig. 24a. Contour map showing the location and shape of the earthwork of Fort Sanders on November 29, 1863. The arrow shows the route the Confederates took from the muster ground up the defilade to the fort. One can still see the defilade in Robin Thompson's 1922 aerial photograph of the battlefield.

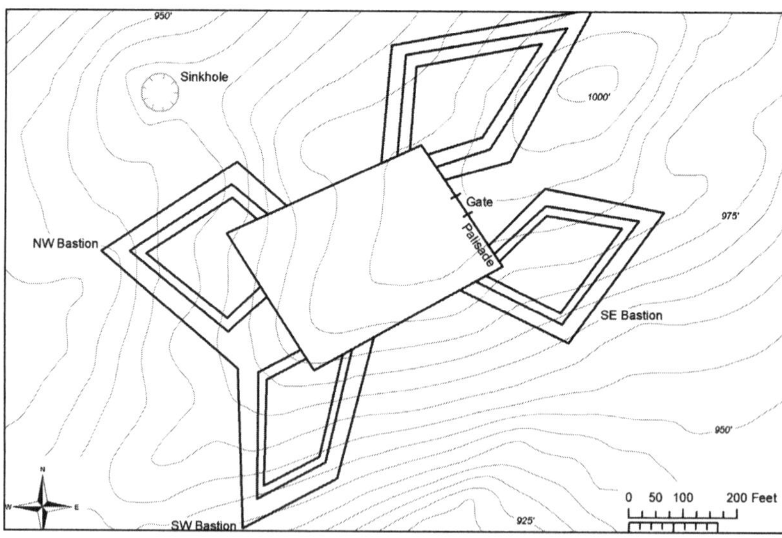

Fig. 24b. Contour map showing the location and configuration of the fort completed in 1865 under the supervision of General Davis Tillson.

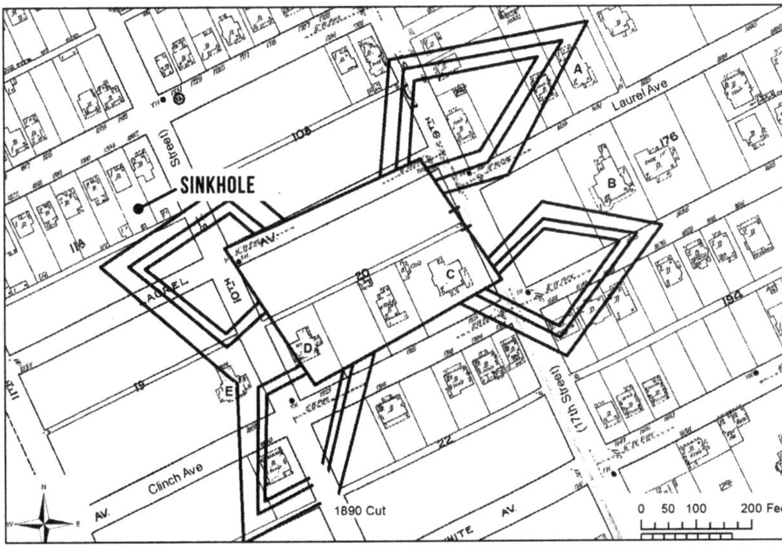

Fig. 24c. This map shows Fort Sanders as it was in 1890 overlain on a 1917 Sanborn map. The north/south cut made in the southwest bastion gave visitors access to the Blue-Gray Reunion into the interior of the fort. The jog in Laurel Avenue at 17th Street was created to extend the avenue westward into the fort for visitors. Engineers used soil from the north fort wall to fill the north trench, then Laurel was constructed on top of the packed fill. A) Location of former Harrison house; B) Location of former Pickle house; C) Carson/McDonald house; D) White Columns; E) Roddy house.

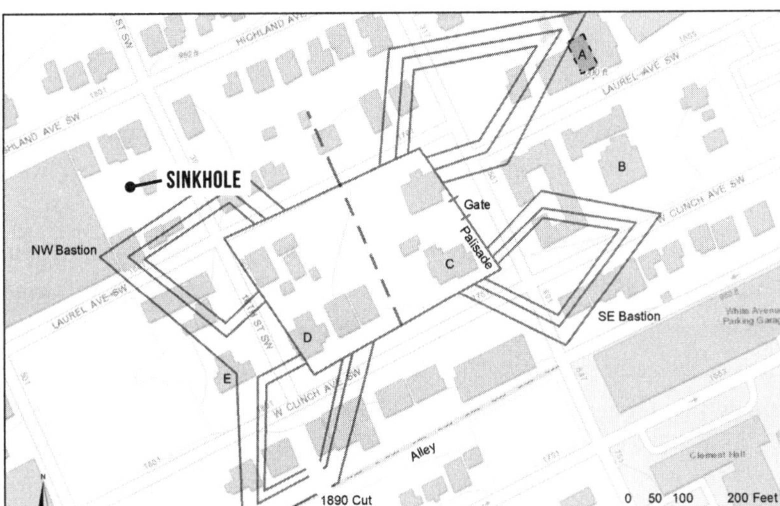

Fig. 24d. Map of Fort Sanders in 1890 overlain on a modern street map. Eighteenth Street has been dead-ended at Clinch Avenue. Laurel and Highland Avenues still jog to the north before turning west. The dashed line inside the fort interior indicates a change in the ground level for new housing. A) Location of former Harrison house; B) location of former Pickle house; C) Carson/McDonald house; D) White Columns; E) Roddy house.

Campbell's Station" (*OR* 1890:pt. 1, 342). Poe had also in advance of the arrival of the troops "located and marked on the ground a line of works" (Cutcheon 1993 [1902]:78). Brearley noted that rows of stakes were used to delineate where breastworks (breast-high defensive works/parapets) were to be constructed (Brearley 1871).

Work on Fort Loudon continued, with Poe directing the construction of infantry trenches, lines of earthworks around the artillery batteries, and dam building on First and Second Creeks (see figure 21). These trenches, small earthworks, and dams designed by Poe were swiftly constructed during the time between November 17 and the Confederate attack on November 29 in spite of the miserable weather and the constant, harassing enemy fire from the Confederate army that now almost encircled the town. "Four original earthworks were pressed into service," Brearley wrote. "Favorable intermediate positions were selected for 12 additional forts and batteries, and it was rightly conjectured that when our artillery should occupy them and the infantry had constructed connecting lines of breastworks, the position would be an unusually secure one" (ibid.:26).

Three main trenches or rifle pits connected the east end of Fort Sanders to two redoubts and a fort (see figure 21). A trench extended to the northeast from the fort to the eminence at the present intersection of Western Avenue and 11th Street, where Battery Zoellner was constructed overlooking the Second Creek Valley. Knoxville forts and batteries were named after Union soldiers who had been killed in action after Northern forces occupied East Tennessee in September. Battery Zoellner was named for Lieutenant Frank Zoellner of the 2nd Michigan. From Battery Zoellner the line of trenches and small earthworks followed this east–west ridge, ultimately reaching Fort Hill, which anchored the defensive positions in East Knoxville. The earthwork located on top of the hill at the university, Fort Byington, was connected to Fort Loudon by a trench, which curved from the base of the south slope of the hill northward to White Avenue. From there it curved northwest towards Fort Loudon. It was named Fort Byington in honor of Major Cornelius Byington, who fought with the 2nd Michigan and was mortally wounded on November 23. Another trench ran south from the southeast corner of Fort Loudon directly to the rear of the Cowan house, then curved west to present-day 17th Street just north of the Kingston Road. It crossed that road, then followed present-day Melrose south up to Battery Noble (Melrose Place). This small fortification was named for Lieutenant William Noble of the 2nd Michigan Infantry (Seymour 1963).

Poe described Fort Loudon in the *Official Records* as an irregular quadrilateral shape, 125 yards long, the west wall being 95 yards at the time of the battle. He added that the east side of the fort was open, the width between the walls there being 85 yards, and noted that a stockade was to be added in that space (*OR* 1890:pt. 1, 299).

The officers who directed the construction at Fort Loudon during the siege complimented the work completed by Union soldiers and citizens. Captain Poe was proud of the 9th Army Corps and the 23rd Regiment, calling them "chivalric rivals where duty was done," and expressed his satisfaction with "the manner in which his instructions and directions were carried out." Poe added that the loyal East Tennesseans who had fled to the safety of the Knoxville earthworks and were "pressed into service" had done an admirable job of construction, noting that their work had released "the almost exhausted soldiers who had no rest for more than a hundred hours" (*OR* 1890:pt. 1, 311, 317).

General Burnside was especially pleased with the African Americans who wielded the shovels, saying, "The negroes were particularly efficient in their labors during the siege" and "did good service." But he criticized the work of some of the local Confederate sympathizers, who "were not inclined, from disloyalty, to volunteer" (ibid.:275). Captain Poe agreed with his commander, observing that the rebels "worked with very poor grace, which blistered hands did not tend to improve" (ibid.:317). And like his superior, Poe praised the black laborers, whom he called "contrabands," saying, "And here I feel it is my duty to refer to the great value of the services of the contrabands. They were ever tractable and willing, and many of them came to me and volunteered to work. They did an amount of labor which was truly astonishing. Day and night they worked without a murmur. For the first week they labored regularly eighteen hours out of the twenty-four, and during the whole siege, out of nearly 200 we had at work, only 1 asked to be relieved, and he for only one afternoon" (ibid.:311).

Sergeant Tarrant of the Union 1st Kentucky Cavalry camped at a farm that belonged to the six daughters of Hugh A. M. White, the great-grandson of Knoxville's founder, James White. The farm and house where the White sisters lived was located east of Fort Sanders on the north side of Cumberland Avenue across from the present-day Ayres Hall. In the evenings Tarrant watched as black laborers made their way to the fort by lamplight to work all night strengthening the fortifications. He observed that "the labor of the male descendants of Africa's dusky race, the principal 'bone' of contention in the national conflict, was also freely 'confiscated' for the benefit of the service. A long double line of 'contrabands' might have been seen after nightfall marching in military order, if not with the exact military steps, in the direction of the forts and ditches, and just before daylight, they could be seen returning in the same order to the interior of the city" (Tarrant 1894:251).

Contrabands would continue to serve after the battle to come. Ellen House wrote on December 21 that it was essential for the Federals to rebuild the pontoon bridge to South Knoxville and that Union commanders were "pressing all the negro men to work on the pontoon bridge" (Sutherland 1996:69). The term "contraband" was used by the military to designate the status of "a slave who during the American Civil War escaped to or was brought within the Union lines" (*Merriam Webster Dictionary* 2017).

Perhaps Tarrant heard the contrabands singing during the night as they worked on the fortifications. Lieutenant Colonel Byron Cutcheon, 20th Michigan Volunteers, who fought at Fort Sanders, heard African Americans singing as they worked when he was stationed in Vicksburg in 1864. Cutcheon attributed the cheerful singing of plantation songs to the good nature of the members of the black troops attached to his corps; perhaps he was unaware that slaves called upon their cultural heritage to ease the pain of hard labor and sustain their spirit by singing. Newly composed freedom songs soon joined the vocal musical memories of African life.

The variety of African American spirituals is vast and constitutes one of the most important categories of American folk music. "And Many Thousands Go" was a freedom song that originated as slaves began to flee the plantations for Union camps. "Go Down Moses," first published in 1861, was sung by conductors of the Underground Railroad to identify themselves. Music during the Civil War was not only a source of solace and hope for African Americans but was of great importance to both Union and Confederate soldiers during this time of death, hunger, and upheaval (Werner 2006; *Army Mailbag* 1864).

INITIAL CONSTRUCTION OF CONFEDERATE FORT LOUDON

When Confederate engineer General Leadbetter began to build Fort Loudon, he wisely took advantage of the easily defended, steep slopes of White's Hill by adding walls along the northern and southern edges of the east–west ridge top, which increased the height the enemy would have to scale in staging an attack on the fortification (note A and B, figure 23). The widest part of this ridge top is located between Laurel and Clinch Avenues, and the highest part of the ridge extends between 17th and 16th Streets. The steep grade on the south side of the east–west ridge is broken midway by a more gradually sloping and wider, tongue-shaped incline, which begins today at Cumberland Avenue and narrows as it climbs northward up the hill crossing Clinch Avenue as it crests the ridge (C). This more gradual slope could be seen just west of a small pond where the University of Tennessee Law School now sits at the northeast corner of Cumberland and 16th Streets (D). Logically, in the early 20th century, engineers chose to construct 17th Street on this more gradual incline.

Two additional key topographic features can be identified on Poe's hachure map and also on an enlargement of Poe's contour map (figure 23). One is the "defilade" (E) or swale, at the west end of the fort, which played an important role in the November 29 attack by the Confederate army on Fort Sanders. This swale was a long, narrow,

E
D
C
A

Fig. 25. Barnard photographed Poe and O. E. Babcock in front of the northwest bastion (A) in March of 1864. Library of Congress. They are posing just east of the sinkhole (B) which Confederate artillerist Porter Alexander mentions in his memoirs. An enormous cut had been made (D) in the north wall (C) which was most likely created to bring equipment and supplies from the railroad into the fort. The three "humps" east of the cut are the lunettes (E).

shallow depression located between two gentle slopes that came together in front of the fort. The swale began at a point just south of the northwest bastion and ran west for about 120 yards before making a wide curve and then heading straight northwest, terminating near the tracks of the East Tennessee and Georgia Railroad. The swale provided a sheltered way safe from fire of the infantry manning the fort until attacking troops were almost within reach of the walls. An attack up either the steep north or south escarpments would slow an advancing enemy to a crawl and leave troops open to prolonged fire from the rampart above. The decision to attack from the west–northwest utilizing the cover the defilade offered was an obvious choice for Confederate officers planning the action.

Poe's hachure map and his amazingly detailed contour map both show the sinkhole and are key factors in the authors' placement of the northwest bastion at the intersection of 18th Street and Laurel Avenue. The sinkhole is easily identified on the hachure map by the circle which indicates a large depression north of the northwest bastion. On Poe's contour map the sinkhole is indicated as an interruption of a contour line that runs east–west on the north slope of the ridge. The contour line abruptly turns southwest, then northwest, and then north, forming a "dipper-like" anomaly. This is the large, limestone sinkhole, sometimes simply called a "sink" or a limestone sink, which Confederate artillery commander Porter Alexander described in his memoirs as being "a stone's throw" from the northwest bastion" (Alexander 1989:325).

This feature can also be seen in a March 1864 photograph of Colonel Orville Babcock and Captain Orlando Poe (figure 25), who stand posing a little to the northeast of the northwest bastion. The southern top edge (the "lip"), and the bottom of the large sinkhole can be seen behind and to the right of the men. One could easily observe the sinkhole before it was leveled in the fall of 2018 by standing on the sidewalk on 18th Street between Laurel and Highland Avenues and looking west. A hospital parking garage is now being constructed on the site.

Porter Alexander pointed out General Leadbetter's failure to see the sinkhole during his reconnaissance of the fort area immediately before

Fig. 26. Charles Faulkner standing at the base of the sinkhole described by Porter Alexander as being a "stone's throw" from the northwest bastion. The north side of an abandoned grocery store can be seen on the left, and the east wall of the Fort Sanders Hospital parking garage is in the background. Photograph was taken by Terry Faulkner standing on the sidewalk on 18th Street between Laurel and Highland avenues shooting west in June 2015.

the battle. He criticized Leadbetter's negligence with a tone of disgust, noting that the sinkhole was large enough to hold and provide cover for several hundred Confederate troops and intimating that if the sinkhole had been incorporated into the Confederate offensive plan, there might have been a different outcome to the battle (ibid.).

MANNING AND ARMING THE FORT

The battle-hardened 79th New York Highlanders, one of the first units arriving from Campbell's Station, were assigned to defend the critical and vulnerable northwest bastion. The Highlanders had accompanied the supply wagons on the exhausting trek east from Lenoir's to Knoxville. They numbered about 125 strong with the 17th Michigan as a reserve (Todd 1886). Captain Poe reported that by the time of the assault 12 days later on November 29, the number of soldiers located in the fort, connecting trenches, and additional small earthworks had increased to 500 men out of a total of 12,000 Union forces stationed in Knoxville. Union officer Byron M. Cutcheon later recalled, "The fort, known to us as Fort Sanders, was the key to the defensive positions, sweeping with its guns the space to the river on its left, the open slopes and hills in front, and enfilading to our line on our right nearly or quite to the point where Second Creek crossed the railroad, beyond the station, near which the right of our division rested" (Cutcheon 1904:78). Captain Poe described the garrison and the weaponry located within Fort Sanders during the siege as consisting "of Benjamin's and Buckley's batteries and one section of Roemer's (four 20-pounder parrots, six 12-pounder Napoleons, and two 3-inch rifled guns), and an infantry force made up of some 120 men of the 79th New York, 75 men of the 29th Massachusetts, 60 men of the 2nd Michigan, and 80 men of the 20th Michigan. About 40 men of the 2nd Michigan, under the command of Captain Charles H. Hodskin, occupied the banquette" (Poe 1888:742). A Civil War artillery battery would normally consist of six cannons. Counting the Parrots, Napoleons, and rifled guns, a total of 24 cannons were moved into the fort.

An earthen platform called a banquette was added to the counterscarp of the ditch in front of the northwest bastion of Fort Sanders. Infantry standing on the banquette could fire directly down the field in front of the apex of the bastion. Before any attacking forces could reach the ditch, the defenders would flee, running in the ditch to the south wall, where they could gain entrance to the interior of the fort.

Lieutenant Samuel Benjamin was in charge of moving the heavy artillery up the steep southern slope into the fort and positioning it along the walls. One writer described the ordnance collected by Benjamin as "motley" because each battery used a different caliber of ordnance (Nosworthy 2008). Benjamin's battery of 12-pounder Napoleon cannons were placed at the west curtain wall of the fort. One section of Captain Jacob Roemer's 34th New York battery was protected by the semicircular lunettes that composed the northeast angle of the fortification. These lunettes would later be incorporated into what became the northeast bastion of the completed fort. Poe described these enormous lunettes (see figure 24a as "the immediate eastward extension of the northern front" (Poe 1888:742).

As the ramparts of Fort Loudon were strengthened, additional artillery was brought into the fort. Lieutenant Benjamin commented on the difficulty of hauling the heavy guns up the steep slopes of White's Hill: "a gun [could not be] dragged into it until four hour's work, with two hundred negroes, had made ways, and cleared spaces for them" (*OR* 1890:pt.1, 742). When the New York Highlanders entered the fort, Captain Armour reported that the embrasures for the guns had not been cut in the critical west and north curtain walls (Armour 1878:9). That the African Americans not only hauled the cannons up the slope but also "cleared spaces" for them seems to indicate that they may have also prepared the platforms and embrasures.

During the time when Lieutenant Benjamin was overseeing the placement of artillery in Fort Loudon, he observed that the fort would be vulnerable to cannon fire from a location south of Kingston Road if the hilltop there remained undefended. He later wrote, "By dint of persuasion and demonstrating the impossibility of holding this position otherwise I prevailed on General Ferrero [the commander of the fort]

Fig. 27a. Samuel Nicoll Benjamin, Second US Artillery, was born in New York City in 1839. He entered West Point Military Academy in 1856, graduated in 1861, and served at West Point after the war in the Adjutant General Corps. He was twenty-four years old when the battle of Fort Sanders took place and thirty-eight when he received a Medal of Honor in 1877 for his notable service as an artillery officer. he died in 1886 and is buried on Governors Island. Brady photograph from National Archives.

to occupy the hill due south from the fort on the other side of the road to Campbell's Station. (Fire from that point would have taken much of our line in reverse)" (*OR* 1890:pt. 1, 342).

Benjamin was referring to the hilltop location of Melrose Place (the present location of Melrose Hall on the UT campus) where a redoubt, Battery Noble, was soon constructed. A battery of two of Buckley's Napoleons were placed there to prevent any possibility that the Confederates might seize the position and direct deadly flanking fire into Fort Loudoun. The troops manning Battery Noble would also be able to prevent enemy troops from approaching the town on Kingston Road or trying to attack the south wall of the fort. Lieutenant Benjamin was not only observant but also tactically skilled, thorough, and creative in his efforts to secure Fort Loudoun. In his official report on the battle, General Burnside singled him out for being "conspicuous for his efforts to strengthen his position" (ibid.:276).

Twenty-four-year-old Lieutenant Samuel Benjamin was an 1861 graduate of West Point. He chose a military career, serving throughout the Civil War in the 2nd United States Artillery Regiment, and was greatly respected for his military skills. In addition to the battle at Fort Sanders, Benjamin fought in numerous key battles including First Bull Run, the Peninsular Campaign, Antietam, and Vicksburg (McCullum 1899). In writing about the battle of Knoxville in his memoirs, Longstreet expressed his admiration for Benjamin whom he was acquainted with, both on and off the battlefield. He especially praised the artillery that Benjamin had available for the battle of Fort Sanders (Longstreet 1896). Longstreet's respect for Benjamin's expertise with his cannons would have significantly increased had he known that it was Benjamin who had achieved a direct hit on the tower of the Robert H. Armstrong house on the Kingston Road where Longstreet and McLaws had their headquarters (Seymour 1863). This house, first named " Bleak House," is now called Confederate Memorial Hall. It is owned by Knoxville Chapter 89 of the United Daughters of the Confederacy and is open to the public.

The science of gunnery was taught at West Point, and executing an exact hit such as the one Benjamin achieved on the tower of Bleak House necessitated familiarity by the gunner with four conditions: the explosive power of the gunpowder used "and its velocity; 2nd, the retarding agencies, air and friction; 3rd, the construction of the projectile tubes; 4th, the form of projectile calculated to attain a perfect result" (Greene 1858:261–280). Poe watched as Benjamin completed the preparations. Benjamin lined up the largest field rifle available, a twenty-pound Parrot. Estimating the distance to the Bleak House at 2,500 yards, he set the elevation accordingly and took careful aim. The gunner was signaled to take the shot which struck the tower, killing

G
I
H
F

Fig. 27b. Northwest bastion seen from the south, 1864 photograph. A) Ditch; B) northwest bastion; C) west wall; D) deepest point; E) revetment; F) glacis; G) 80-foot Confederate trench; H) woods; I) rock outcrop.

three Confederate sharpshooters and sending the rest running from the house. General Poe called it "the "prettiest shot of the war." Poe asked for a second, but Benjamin refused (Seymour 1963:141).

Benjamin was seriously wounded at the Battle of Spotsylvania during Grant's march on Richmond but lived to complete 25 years of military service; he was brevetted to the ranks of Major and Lieutenant Colonel during that time. In 1877, at the age of 38, he received the Medal of Honor and lived to cherish that honor for nine years, dying at the age of 47 (McCullum 1899).

DEATH OF THE GALLANT SANDERS

Another West Point graduate, 28-year-old General William Sanders, would come to the aid of Burnside as he sought to complete the defensive works. Sanders was born in Frankfort, Kentucky, grew up in Natchez, Mississippi, and graduated from West Point in 1856. He was a cousin of Jefferson Davis and in April 1861 was, according to his West Point classmate, Porter Alexander, as "intensely southern in his views of it (the war) . . . more so than any other Southern officer that I met . . . during the initiation of the hostilities." Alexander spent considerable time with Sanders in San Francisco while awaiting a steamship home from Washington state. He later wrote that Sanders, then a member of the Second Dragoons stationed in Utah, was "taking a brief rest" in San Francisco after a "remarkably long & swift march having pursued and caught" some deserters from his regiment. Sanders refused an invitation from Alexander to return with him via steamship and returned home overland after delivering the deserters to Utah. Alexander wrote later that Sanders at some point had changed "his mind completely" and finally chose to support the Federal cause "for reasons that Alexander never heard" (Alexander 1989:27–28). Captain Sanders first served in the defense of Washington, D.C., in the U.S. Cavalry between August 1861 and August 1862. He was an excellent horseman who fought in the Peninsular Campaign and at Antietam. General Burnside gave Sanders a command in the 23rd Corps of the Department of the Ohio before he and his men arrived in Knoxville, and he was brevetted in the field to the rank of Brigadier General in October 1863. On November 18 he was mortally wounded on the outskirts of Knoxville by Confederate sharpshooters located in the tower of Bleak House and armed with English Whitworth rifles (Seymour 1963).

Colonel Sanders was killed before his commission could be approved by Congress. He was unaware that his former friend, Edward Porter Alexander, with whom he had often dined, played billiards, and discussed the war in San Francisco in April 1861, was just outside Knoxville on November 18, directing cannon fire at Sander's dismounted cavalry as they kneeled behind a rail breastwork fence trying to hold back Confederate attackers (ibid.).

Sanders was a respected cavalry officer, and for the following two days, his dismounted troops with their breech-loading Spencer rifles showed their mettle as they held the Confederates back. Sanders knew the importance of armed soldiers on horses in war, and his men were equipped in much the same way that John Hunt Morgan's "Raiders" were outfitted earlier in the war. Sanders had served in the 2nd Regiment of the United States Dragoons, helping protect settlers in their travels west. In August 1861, the Dragoons (a European term for armed mounted soldiers) were called back east and redesignated the 2nd Cavalry Regiment by the War Department.

The advantages of well-trained horses and capable handlers became obvious early in the war. The flamboyant soldier of fortune, George St. Leger Grenfell, had helped train Morgan's rowdy troops using European methods. General George B. McClellan also traveled in Europe and became an exponent of many of the same methods that Grenfell taught. He wrote a manual on cavalry tactics published in 1861 and even designed a lightweight saddle based on saddles he had seen used in Europe (*New World Encyclopedia* 2017). The McClellan Saddle became standard issue for cavalry in 1859. McClellan would note after the war that during the final two years "no branch of the Army of the Potomac contributed so much to the overthrow of Lee's army as the cavalry" (F. T. Miller 1957:38).

Burnside had assigned Sanders and his men an extremely difficult task on November 17: to not only halt the Confederate momentum as they roared toward town on the Kingston Road, but also to hold them back as long as possible so that critical improvements to the defensive works within Knoxville could be completed prior to a major attack. Sanders willingly accepted the challenge (Kelly 2013). He established his 700 dismounted cavalry in a defensive line that stretched from the river, across Kingston Road, and over the imposing hill where the Second Presbyterian church stands today. The line of rails and rifle pits continued north to the East Tennessee and Georgia Railroad. From the morning of November 17, after Union troops arrived in Knoxville, until November 18, Sanders and his men heroically held this line in the face of withering fire, as Longstreet's forces sought to move forward into rifle and artillery range of the fort (Seymour 1863). Major Cutcheon noted in his book that the fighting on the hill was within clear view of the soldiers in Fort Sanders (Cutcheon 1904).

Entrenched behind the center of a barricade of fence rails located on the crest of the hill overlooking the Kingston Road were the men of the 8th Michigan, 45th Ohio, and 11th and 12th Kentucky cavalries. They had a single advantage; they were armed with seven-shot, breech-loading Spencer rifles. These repeating rifles could be fired 15 times a minute, whereas the Confederate infantry using their muzzle-loading weapons could fire only two rounds per minute (Marcot 1995).

At noon on November 17, a brigade of McLaws's Division hit the center and strongest part of the Union line, but the withering fire from the repeating rifles repulsed their charge. Unable to drive Sanders's men from the hill before nightfall, the Confederates waited until first dawn the next day to resume their attack. Confederate artillery chief Porter Alexander had discovered a way to bring the cannons forward under the cover of a deep ravine and set them up out of sight, close to the home of Robert Armstrong (Seymour 1963). The barrage of cannon fire aimed at the Union line from there splintered the fence rails, and sharp pieces of wood impaled the defenders. Southern infantry stormed up the hill, capturing the position on November 18. General Sanders, mounted on his snow white horse, had bravely ridden forward to the fence barricade during the attack, exposing himself to a galling enemy fire as he sought to rally his troops (Rule 1900). Porter Alexander later wrote "that poor Sanders was shot in the stomach while vainly endeavoring to rally his men and hold his breast works" (Alexander 1989:28). In another account, Sanders was wounded when he was walking back to cover with his aide (Seymour 1963).

Mortally wounded from the shot, Sanders fell from his horse near a lone cedar tree that stood atop the hill. Orlando Poe, while visiting Knoxville in September 1889, "pointed out the spot where General Sanders fell, near the tree on the farm of Mr. Jacob L. Thomas. Poe was certain that he fell within 20 feet of the cedar tree" (*Knoxville Daily Journal* 1889). Sergeant Eastham Tarrant was prevailed upon in 1891 by veterans of the First Kentucky Cavalry to compile their history, and he included a tribute written for Sanders by Chaplain W. H. Hornell. The chaplain had occupied the ground where Sanders fell and was lifting his fallen heroes "as they were shot down by the sharpshooters in the Armstrong House." Hornell wrote, "We were on our last struggle to save the day," adding that if Longstreet had assaulted Fort Sanders "at that first sunset . . . instead of the daybreak two weeks later, he would have been successful. But it seems as if Sanders's blood formed an impassable stream which no victorious Rebel could ever pass. Ten thousand men stood in arms repelling all advance into the city from that sunset hour which marked our slow retreat past the fort, forever to bear his name. Then night settled down over many a dying soldier to fall into the hands of others than ours." Hornell ended his account by saying that the "fatal little cupola, built for sights of peace, was made the high fort of death for many of us" (Tarrant 1894:240). Sanders had confided to his friend and classmate Captain Poe on the evening of November 17 that he had a premonition that death awaited him the next day, and he gave Poe some personal items to keep, including letters from 19-year-old Sue Boyd, a Knoxville girl he had hoped to marry (Foote 1958; Humes 1888).

Sanders was brought into town to the Lamar House, now the Bijou Theater. He was calm when the surgeon in attendance told him the wound was mortal, responding that "he had done his duty and served his country as best he could." The next day, when Sanders was told that death was near, he requested that a Christian minister baptize him.

Reverend Mr. J. S. Hyden, the chaplain of the post, honored his request. Burnside was holding Sanders's hand and crying as the sacrament of the Lord's Supper began. Then "suddenly the strength of the dying soldier failed, and like a child he fell asleep" (Humes 1888:75–76).

The procession to the burial site at the Second Presbyterian Church was led by Burnside and Reverend Thomas Humes, who conducted the service. Sanders was carried to the graveyard and buried by lantern light in an unsuccessful attempt to hide his death from the troops (Rule 1900). Humes, whose Irish father had begun building the Lamar House hotel in 1816, would later describe the event in his book *The Loyal Mountaineers of Tennessee,* published in 1888.

Sanders had sacrificed his life, leading his men in a heroic delaying tactic that provided time for the completion of the defenses and the arming and manning of the fort. Poe praised Sanders, saying, "the hours in which to work that the gallant conduct of our cavalry secured us were worth to us a thousand men each" (Rule 1900). Sanders had brought an abrupt halt to the tremendous momentum of the entire Confederate army as they charged towards Knoxville on the Kingston Road that morning of November 17.

On November 24, Assistant Adjutant-General Lewis Richmond issued General Field Order Number 31 and officially announced the death of Brigadier General William P. Sanders: "A life rendered illustrious by a long record of gallantry and devotion to his country has closed while in the heroic and unflinching performance of duty." The order then called for Fort Loudon to be renamed: "In memory of the honored dead, the fort in front of which he received his fatal wound will be known hereafter as Fort Sanders" (*OR* 1890:pt. 3, 241).

5

THE SIEGE OF KNOXVILLE

For many years there has been a controversy among military historians as to why Longstreet did not storm the town on November 18, when he had the Federals on the run. His ranking subordinate, General Lafayette McLaws, urged his commander to assault the fortifications immediately, before the Union soldiers could finish strengthening them. Known as "the master of tactical defense on the battlefield," Longstreet was seemingly hesitant to make an immediate and poorly prepared mass-offensive frontal attack on a strongly defended position. He had made this mistake when he reluctantly followed the orders of General Robert E. Lee and sent three divisions forward on that fateful charge later named for General George Pickett, one of the division commanders, at Gettysburg the previous July. In addition to his qualms over an immediate frontal attack, Longstreet felt the best course of action was to starve the Union army into surrendering Knoxville. He mistakenly believed he had successfully blocked their supply routes on the French Broad River east of town.

Union supporter Reverend Thomas Humes, who had been banished from his pulpit at St. John's Episcopal Church during the Confederate occupation and reappointed when Burnside took Knoxville, would later analyze Longstreet's failure to attack immediately. Humes, a smart and capable man who would become president of East Tennessee University in 1865, believed himself discerning enough to accurately analyze Longstreet's plan of action after the general's forces arrived on the outskirts of Knoxville. Humes attributed Longstreet's inaction to overconfidence in Bragg's ability to defeat the Union troops in Chattanooga. He wrote that Longstreet "sat down before Knoxville and with composure

Fig. 28. Thomas W. Humes. Library of Congress.

and wariness, and rather toyed with his supposed victim then contend with him as an equal adversary" (Humes 1888).

By the afternoon of November 18, the Confederates were able to move within cannon and rifled-musket range of the west battlements of Fort Sanders and had occupied the north side of the town beyond the railroad. While it was crucial for them to continue their investment in order to cut off the Union supply line from the east, Longstreet made a grave mistake: he stubbornly refused to move his troops far enough to the east to seal off the French Broad River. While a Union observer believed that Longstreet did not have a sufficient force to entirely invest the city, it appears that a major reason Longstreet chose the siege was his misplaced confidence in a faulty map of the Knoxville region provided to him by General Buckner in Chattanooga. The map showed the French Broad flowing into the Holston River below Knoxville (Seymour 1963). Longstreet was certain that the mouth of the French Broad was already controlled by Confederate forces and that supplies to the town had been choked off. Loyal Confederate sympathizers warned Longstreet that the French Broad River above Knoxville was open and that food provided by Unionists upstream was flowing into Knoxville. Sergeant Eastham Tarrant of the Union 1st Kentucky Cavalry, who was stationed in Knoxville during the siege, recalled, "The loyal citizens aided so much in sending down the French Broad River meat and grain in flats during the dense fog of the nights which prevailed at that period. An excellent officer by the name of Captain Doughty, maintained a small force up the river during the whole siege, and directed the efforts of the people in our behalf" (Tarrant 1894:254). What General Longstreet could not fathom was that the country people who lived along the French Broad River largely supported the Union cause. That river and those Unionists would play a very important part in the history of the war (Dykeman 1965 [1955]).

PREPARING FOR BATTLE

From November 16 to 18, while General Sanders and his men held the hill where the Second Presbyterian Church now stands, construction at the fort continued since the cannon and small-arms fire of McLaws's Division was not yet within accurate range. However, after Confederate forces took this strategic hill and moved closer to the fort, they began at once to dig rifle pits and cannon emplacements, and soon the Federals occupying the fort came under direct fire. An impressive Confederate trench with embrasured artillery positions suddenly appeared about 1,000 yards west of the fort. The trench was located on a hill south of Kingston Road just east of Drury Armstrong's home (present-day Crescent Bend), which had become the headquarters of General Joseph Kershaw (Angst 2012). A battery of Confederate cannon in this trench was under the command of Major Austin Leyden of the 9th Georgia Artillery Battalion, whose opening fire would signal the attack on Fort Sanders (Angst 2012).

Lieutenant Benjamin was irritated by the Confederate minié balls zipping through the air into the fort from these entrenchments and complained, "The rebel sharpshooters were very annoying" (*OR* 1890:pt.1, 343). "On the third day," Captain Armour reported, "the enemy advanced his picket line, and the bullets were singing over the fort in a very unpleasant frequency, which caused all hands, from the brigade commander to the drummer boy, to duck and dodge in a manner not perhaps creditable to our soldiers" (Armour 1898:9).

By November 20, sharpshooters were causing several casualties within the fort every day. In response, Lieutenant Benjamin "stuck brush in the parapet, along the interior crest, so as to screen us from sight, and enable us to look out without being seen. I also covered the embrasures with bags and barrels, so arranged as to see out without being seen" (*OR* 1890:pt. 1, 343).

Both Union and Confederate forces employed sharpshooters as an effective and deadly addition to infantry; often they were farm boys who were experienced hunters. Today the term "sniper" is used instead of sharpshooter for a rifleman who is a free agent and acts entirely on his own to hit his target from a concealed position. The Confederate infantry made good use of these talented marksmen, arming them with Whitworth .45 caliber rifles. These English rifles, which could cost as much as $1,000 each, were equipped with a 14.5-inch telescopic sight, which enabled the shooter to hit a target at 1,500 to 1,800 yards (Wicklund and Williams 2017). One important goal of every sniper was to take out officers during a battle, as this caused great confusion among the troops. Eliminating officers, such as the heroic commander General Sanders, in this manner was as much a psychological weapon as a tactical one (Sidlo 2008).

In spite of the harassing fire of sharpshooters, on the afternoon of November 18 the Federals raised the stars and stripes in the face of their enemy on a flag pole mounted on the west curtain wall midway between the southwest and northwest bastions (Armour 1898). This important event was met by a chorus of cheers from the besieged garrison. Captain Armour recalled, "The enemy also saluted it with a furious fire of artillery, but, although many of the shells burst in or near the fort, they did little or no damage. 'Our flag was still there'" (ibid.:9). First Lieutenant Ezra Parker of the First Rhode Island Light

Artillery wrote on Saturday, November 21, that in spite of the constant harassment, "the work upon the fortifications went steadily on" (Parker 1919).

By November 20, the Confederates had completed a line of rifle pits across Kingston Road 600 yards east of the hill that General Sanders had so stubbornly defended. Union artillerist John Watkins wrote that by the next day, "The rebels had got clear round us from the river on the west side of the town to the river on the east side of the town" (Watkins 1863b). In a report on November 25, Lieutenant Benjamin noted what he called an "enemy embrasure battery about the same elevation as the fort on a hill he estimated to be 700 yards to the west. This was the hill east of Kershaw's headquarters on Kingston Road, and it contained six 12-pounders" (Benjamin n.d.; OR 1890:pt.1, 343).

The site, which was named Morgan Hill after a former University of Tennessee president who lived there, is now the location of UT's Sorority Village. An archaeological survey and excavations were conducted there in 2010 by the UT Archaeological Research Laboratory prior to the construction of any buildings. The excavations uncovered dug-out gun emplacements connected by infantry trenches. Fireplaces had been dug into the west walls of these trenches (Angst 2012). The battery assigned to this position consisted of eight guns from Major Austen Leyden's 9th Georgia Artillery Battalion and the 2nd, 3rd, and 15th Regiments, South Carolina Infantry, on the advance line of Kershaw's brigade. Sniper fire from this location probably came from the 3rd Georgia Battalion Sharpshooters of Wofford's brigade (ibid.).

A Confederate battery was also established November 25 on Cherokee Bluff south of the Holston River. Six guns were floated across the river and hauled up the ridge and placed 150 feet above the elevation of Fort Sanders. Lieutenant Benjamin reported that Confederates manning this battery had a commanding view of the fort interior, and the elevation allowed the artillerists to direct reverse and enfilading fire on each front of the fort. To protect his men from this deadly bombardment, Lieutenant Benjamin added traverse trenches. Traverses placed in the interior of Fort Sanders would provide some safe passage as the troops moved about the fort (Benjamin n.d.).

It is believed that traverses were first created by General James Longstreet for use at the Battle of Fredericksburg in December 1862 (Davidson 1963). However, traverses are described in detail by Dennis Hart Mahan in his *Treatise on Field Fortifications* (Mahan 1862). The traverse was a barricade running perpendicular from the main trench along the walls at intervals, protecting the men on both flanks and allowing safe passage from one main trench to another. One author described traverses as follows: "Traverses were raised mounds of earth designed to defilade, or obscure from the view of the enemy, the interior spaces of field works. They also limited the area affected by explosions that might occur within gun positions" (Field 2005:17).

If earth was piled up to allow a passage from one place to another, it is likely that adjacent trenches were also involved, as well as other protective barriers. Commanding General Ferraro wrote in his official report of the battle that on the night of November 24 he had "erected traverses of cotton [bales] to protect the gunners" during the night (*OR* 1890:pt. 1, 352). General Burnside wrote in his final report on the Battle of Fort Sanders that during the Confederate bombardment from Morgan Hill preceding the attack on November 29, "the fort was so protected with traverses that only one man was injured during this heavy fire" (ibid.:277).

Captain Poe mentioned an additional traverse when describing the construction of the parade ground in the fort. He wrote that a 40-foot-wide parade ground was excavated into the slope of the hill forming a traverse (Poe 1888:742). An excavation into the slope of the hill indicates that the parade ground was created by digging a level area into the interior of the fort beginning at the west end. The location of the level surface of the parade ground at the west end of the fort was substantiated by Captain Tom Cumming, an adjutant in one of Wofford's regiments, who courageously entered the fort during the attack through a cannon embrasure and leapt down onto the parade ground (Nosworthy 2008).

CRUCIAL DEFENSIVE FEATURES OF FORT SANDERS

Two crucial defensive elements were incorporated into the irregular quadrilateral star fort design of the earthwork constructed on White's Hill: the bastions and the ditch. Angular bastions were built to project out from the corner of the west "curtain" wall of this fortification. Mahan did not recommend constructing a salient with an angle of "less than 60 degrees," as it would be "too weak to withstand the effects of weather; the interior space it encloses is too confined for the manoeuvres [*sic*] of the troops" and "it forms a large sector without fire" (Mahan 1862:7). A proper salient angle allowed defenders manning the bastions to protect the straight walls and adjacent bastions with direct gun fire. Embrasures cut into the bastions for cannons allowed these lethal weapons to cover the rampart walls and also adjacent bastions. A *pan coupe,* a cannon embrasure cut into the corner where the protruding bastion met the straight curtain wall, also provided additional cannon fire to cover the exterior sides of the rampart and southwest bastion.

Two bastions were constructed at the two corners of the west wall of the fort, the southwest bastion and the northwest bastion, which became known as "the salient" (see figure 24). The northwest bastion was the only one completed by November 17. Construction was begun on the southwest bastion by the Confederates, but this bastion was not finished at the time Burnside's army garrisoned the fort. Though smaller than the northwest bastion at the time of the siege, it commanded a large field of fire, which included the entire southwestern slope from the bastion to Third Creek and the Kingston Road (Cumberland Avenue) as well. While this bastion could be attacked from the west or southwest, such an offensive attack would not only place the assaulting troops under direct fire from cannon in the west curtain wall and the southwest wall of the northwest bastion but also from the artillery at Battery Noble. The southwest bastion covered an area of the present-day intersection of Clinch Avenue and 18th Street.

The Confederate engineers who began to build the large earthwork fortification had also realized that the placement of the northwest bastion presented a definite problem for defenders. The entrance to the defilade was located on the level area near the railroad tracks at the base of the ridge. Troops attacking from the northwest would be hidden as they mustered there, and also as they ascended the slope to the northwest bastion in the sunken area of the defilade; the men only became visible to those manning the fort as they reached the level area in front of that bastion and the west wall (see figure 23). It is amazing that Colonel E. Porter Alexander, chief of the Confederate 1st Corps Artillery, was able to see using his field glasses, into "the rear half" of the Second Creek valley because of the dead space of the defilade. Alexander believed the sunken pathway provided an additional advantage; he considered it impossible for Union troops manning the defensive trenches which extended east and south from Fort Sanders to successfully direct their fire into the defilade at an approaching enemy (Alexander 1989).

Lieutenant Benjamin, who had been appointed to oversee the work on the fort, realized there was a positive side to the location of this bastion. Once attacking forces had reached the leveled area at the west wall, they would be trapped and unable to maneuver as they were overwhelmed with cannon fire from both the northwest and southwest bastions.

Benjamin reported that he "made an embrasure in such manner that by taking out a few shovels full of earth I could train a gun on the northwest bastion sweeping its ditch and parapet. The parapet there was strengthened" (OR 1890:pt.1, 343). He added a 12 pounder in the northwest bastion at the point where the bastion joined the west wall, and also arranged for artillery fire to protect the capitals of both bastions. The addition of a hidden gun emplacement and one, possibly two, *pan coupes* helped to insure a successful defense, adding to his reputation as an exceptional artillery commander. In one area on the north side of the fort, a cheval-de-frise was added, composed of over 2,000 sharpened spikes captured by Union troops at Cumberland Gap. Set firmly into the ground at a 45-degree angle, they created a daunting barrier. If the spikes projected from the scarp or inner wall of the ditch, they inhibited attacking troops from reaching the parapet (Field 2005). As one moved east along the north parapet, the natural slope became steeper so it is likely the spikes were set in the scarp of the ditch.

The east end of Fort Sanders was left open at the time of the battle. However, semicircular earthworks had been added to the east end of the north curtain wall. These were lunettes, semicircular embankments with their cannons covering the north curtain wall (see figure 25) and the north side of the northwest bastion. Poe's early maps of the fort show three lunettes at the east end of the fort, but no mention is made of lunettes at the southeast corner of the fort in the Federal military reports. Poe's map shows a demi-bastion there. Concerning the northeast lunettes, Poe wrote that "three 12-pounders were so located in notches in the immediate eastward extension of the northern front as to admit of their firing into the left flank of the assaulting column" (Poe 1888:742).

The importance of these guns to the Union victory was emphasized by the Confederate general Lafayette McLaws, who defended himself at a court-martial brought against him by General Longstreet, who attempted to place the blame for the Confederate defeat on McLaws's shoulders. McLaws, in discussing the events that took place at the north curtain wall, said it was "the opinion of the distinguished officers who were engaged in the assault that if the skirmishers on the railroad side of the work [north] had silenced the enemy's fire from that side, as it was silenced by my line of sharpshooters [on the west] the work would have been carried in spite of all the other obstacles" (*OR* 1890:pt. 1, 491).

McLaws further commented that most of his men "were killed from a fire from the left of my line over which I had no control." The terrible cannon fire on his left came from the lunettes at the northeast corner of the fort (ibid.). Major Byron Cutcheon identified the battery responsible for the withering cannon fire as "a section of Roemer's New York battery" placed in semicircular redoubts immediately on the right of the fort. "It was his fervent opinion that Fort Sanders was saved by 'the steady, deadly, unremitting and unerring fire of the left flank of the Twentieth Michigan, and the devastating discharges of canister and shrapnel from Roemer's left section, just north of the fort . . ."(Cutcheon 1993 [1902]:86).

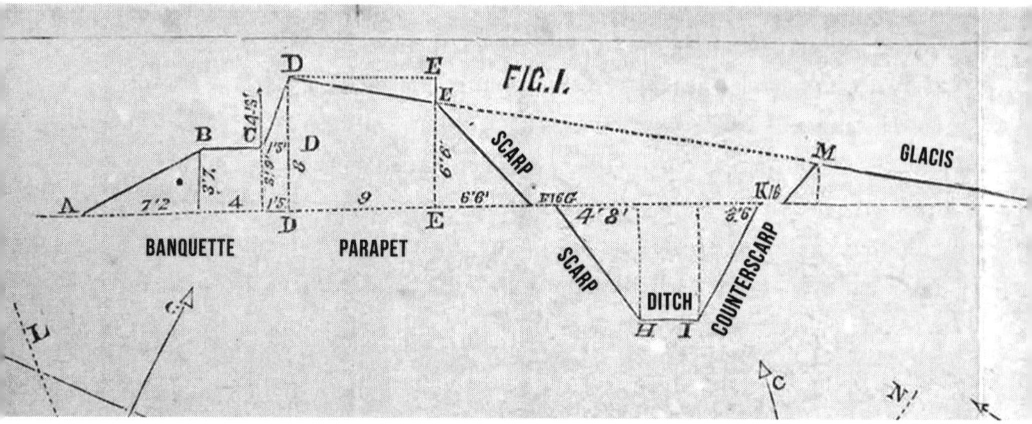

Fig. 29. Profile drawing of fort wall construction.
From Dennis Hart Mahan, *Treatise on Field Fortifications*, 1836.

The ditch was another critical defensive feature of Fort Sanders. Sometimes called moats, these ditches were never intended to hold water, although sometimes water collected in them after a hard rain. In military parlance a ditch is defined as a wide and deeply dug obstacle that hinders or prevents soldiers from reaching the walls of the fortification. If the ditch is deep enough and has vertical or acutely sloping sides (scarps), an assault would be seriously hindered or perhaps stopped before the infantry could reach the ramparts.

Captain Poe described the Fort Sanders ditch as follows: "The ditch was made twelve feet wide at the bastion faces and from six to eight feet in depth, depending upon the accidents of the ground, the average being about seven feet. The result of this location of the interior crest and depth of ditch, was an unusually high relief to the work, especially at the north-western bastion. The scarps were practically vertical, and the berme [*sic*] at the foot of the exterior slope was cut away. The counterscarps were continued until they intersected, and all the material between them and the curtain excavated to the general level of the bottom of the ditch, thus obviating all dead angles" (Poe 1888:742).

Additional information about the ditch came from Confederate officers who reconnoitered the fort early in the siege and from surviving infantry who encountered the ditch during their attack on November 29. As soon as they had established their siege line on November 21, the Southerners began reconnoitering their target. Many of their observations can be found in the records of the 1864 court-martial of Major General McLaws. Regarding the worrisome ditch, McLaws testified during his trial that before the battle he had suggested that if straw could be obtained, his men should be provided with bundles to be put in the ditch in case it was deeper than expected. As McLaws explained:

> And as the works of the enemy had not at that time been reconnoitered to an extent sufficient to give any positive knowledge of its strength, or of the depth of the ditch around it, I proposed to take bundles of straw, each man to carry a bundle, and fill up the ditch, *if there was any* [emphasis added]. (*OR* 1890:pt. 1, 484)
>
> There was a doubt about there being any ditch, because citizens had told us, and also some officers of artillery who had been in Knoxville when the works were constructed, so far as we constructed them, that the dirt to make the parapet had been taken principally from inside the work (Fort Loudon); that the fort was around the apex of a hill which had been smoothed off and the earth thrown to make a parapet, and if there was any digging on the outside it was in holes here and there with intervening high places, and that there was no regular ditch. (ibid.)

B. F. Thompson, a Union captain, quoted from a newspaper article he had clipped after the war and included in his book on the 112th Illinois. The article by an unknown author was entitled "Siege of Knoxville." The reporter emphatically stated that the "immediate vicinity of the fort had been jealously guarded from close observation and was a *terra incognito* to citizens as well as the Confederates. The deep and impassable ditch in front of Fort Saunders was as "much a surprise to Longstreet's assaulting columns as was the 'sunken road' to Napoleon's Imperial Guard as it made its last desperate charge at Waterloo" (Thompson 1885:160).

GENERAL LEADBETTER RETURNS TO KNOXVILLE

On November 25, Brigadier General Danville Leadbetter, the chief engineer of the Army of Tennessee, "the oldest Confederate engineer in service" and supposedly the most efficient, arrived from Chattanooga to help Longstreet assess the strength of the Federal defenses (Alexander 1989:383). Since Leadbetter supervised the initial planning and construction of the fort, Longstreet probably assumed that he would be able to quickly point out any weaknesses in its construction. After a "hasty reconnaissance of the enemy's entire position on the 26th," including observing the fort from the heights on the south side of the river, Leadbetter "pronounced the enemy's fort in front of [Major] General McLaws assailable" (*OR* 1890:pt. 1, 460). McLaws's men were situated to the front of the ditch of the west curtain wall (located at present-day 18th Street) and the northwest bastion at the corner of 18th and Laurel Avenue. Major Byron Cutcheon later said, "The storming column struck the fort at the point where the ditch was widest and deepest and the parapet highest and most difficult of access" (Cutcheon 1993 [1902]:82).

It is astonishing that General Danville Leadbetter, who oversaw the initial construction of the fort and should have been familiar with the topography around the works, neither remembered nor observed during his reconnoiter of the fort an extremely significant, natural offensive advantage. This topographical feature, which might have helped secure a victory for the Confederates, was the immense, flat-bottomed sinkhole described earlier. Alexander noticed it during the assault and later wrote, "within a stone's throw of the parapet there was a big limestone sink, making dead space in which several hundred men could stand—& the edge of it lined with sharpshooters" (Alexander 1989:325).

Alexander attributed the failure of the Confederate officers to use this natural feature to their advantage to General Leadbetter, who failed, for whatever reason, to point it out (ibid.). The south edge of this wide sinkhole can be seen in the March 1864 photograph just to the right of Poe and Babcock (see figure 25). It was extremely fortunate for the Federals that it was only during and after the battle that the Confederates became aware of its existence.

THE EXTERIOR DEFENSES OF FORT SANDERS

If the sinkhole had been filled with Confederate sharpshooters on that foggy morning of November 29, there may not have been the enormous number of Southern casualties to be removed from the ditch after a truce was called by Burnside. J. D. Cullen, the chief surgeon on Longstreet's staff, attended the wounded in the ditch and provided a detailed description of the obstacle the Southern infantry was expected to surmount, if they reached it alive: "the ditch on the west side of the work from shoulder to shoulder was from 12 to 13 feet deep and on the north front it was on average 10 feet deep, and that it was about 10 feet wide all around the work; but from shoulder to shoulder of the northwest bastion it was from 4 to 4½ feet deep, and here it was the assault was made. From the bottom of the ditch along the west front from shoulder to the top of the parapet must have been over 20 feet perpendicular, the same in the north front from the shoulder of the northwest bastion" (*OR* 1890:pt. 1, 491).

In addition to the ditch, other impediments to an infantry assault on the west side of the fort were constructed by the Federal defenders. To provide a clear field of fire, a grove of pine trees on the western and southern slopes of the hill was cut down. Colonel Cutcheon remarked on the removal of these trees: "The rounded hill upon which Fort Sanders stood had recently been covered with standing timber, mostly second-growth pine, which now and then a large oak tree interspersed. This timber had been chopped down, with the exception of a few trees, and the small trees used in making the platforms and revetments for the fort, and the tops and branches of the large oaks utilized in constructing an abattis in front" (Cutcheon 1993 [1902]:81).

The stumps of these trees were left one to two feet above the ground, and an ingenious entanglement was constructed using the stumps. When Poe visited the fort in September 1889, he discussed the use of the wire, saying that James B. Hoxie, who was "then in the employ of the military railroads . . . came to him and made the suggestion." Poe said that he had thought it was good idea and he "immediately acted upon it" (*Knoxville Daily Journal* 1889). Captain Armour related that Lieutenant Benjamin was responsible for laying the wire entanglement. Telegraph wire was stretched one night "from stump to stump in front of our most important positions, in order to form an obstacle to the advance of the enemy" (*OR* 1890:pt. 1, 318). Benjamin described the scene thus: "In front of the northwest bastion I made *abattis* concealed from the enemy by a small rise of ground and inside the *abattis* a little entanglement of telegraph wires" (*OR* 1890:pt. 1, 343).

The *abattis* (a French word meaning "felled trees") was a defensive measure described and recommended by Dennis Mahan in his *Treatise* (1861). Benjamin added an impediment of felled trees, stripped of leaves and smaller branches, and sharpened into points. These were placed side-by-side, then staked and wired down with branches pointing toward the enemy. Like other obstacles exterior to the ditch, an abattis would break the momentum of assaulting troops and hold them up under close musket fire from a defensive position (Benjamin n.d.).

In a letter to his father dated December 10, 1863, Edward Burruss (*mississippi confederates*.wordpress.com/2011/11/11/a-veterans-day-tribute) of the 21st Mississippi Infantry, Humphreys's Brigade, described the obstacles they faced as they assaulted the fort: "This fort is what is known as a Star Fort—the strongest of all forts—& it was the most immense work of any kind that I have ever seen. It was protected by an abattis of several hundred yards width" (Burruss 1863). In describing the attack by his division on the 29th, Major General McLaws was probably referring to the abatis when he said, "I ordered the assault in two columns, because there was *considerable felled timber* [emphasis added] and much broken ground between the positions of Humphreys's brigade and that of Wofford's" (*OR* 1890:pt. 1, 487).

Private William A. Osborne of the 29th Massachusetts described another clever obstacle that had been created by plowing. "The whole open space within our lines, directly in front of the fort . . . had been carefully plowed . . . with the furrows converging toward a point opposite the main battery. The furrows were wide and well defined" (Osborne 1877:270–271). The rationale here was that soldiers rushing over a piece of ground would instinctively move in the smooth hollows of the furrows, bringing them all together at the point where the furrows converged, creating chaos. Augustus Woodbury said that the fort was "strengthened by General Burnside's accomplished engineers Lieutenant Colonel Babcock and Captain Poe assisted by Lieutenant Benjamin, with everything known to their profession or available for their purpose" (Woodbury 1867:347).

In the still dark, foggy morning of November 29, the impediments of the sharpened stakes (which were wired together), toppled trees, stretched wire, and furrows would bring attacking forces together into a packed mass. Officers would not be able to recognize their troops, and the disorganized and confused mass of men would become victims of close-range charges of canister.

THE EARTHWORK OF FORT SANDERS READIED FOR BATTLE

After Union improvements had been made to Fort Sanders, Captain Orlando Poe in his official report written in January 1864 added a detailed description of the fort as it had been before the battle and mentioned that a stockade was to be added at the east end (*OR* 1890:pt. 1, 309). It appears that Poe closely followed the advice of West Point instructor Dennis Hart Mahan as he supervised the completion of Fort Sanders (Taylor 2009). As Mahan advised his students in his 1848 *Treatise,* "The Military Art, in all of its branches, is founded upon a comprehensive and thorough knowledge of the exact and physical sciences" (Mahan 1861:viii). It appears that Poe used Mahan's recommendations as much as possible in the time he had to complete the defensive fortification of Fort Sanders before the Confederate attack. Mahan wrote, "The exterior sides of the bastion fort should not exceed 250 yards, nor be less than 125 yards, otherwise the flanking arrangements will be imperfect . . . with a relief of 14 feet, the least that will present a tolerable obstacle to an assault, and an exterior side of 125 yards, the ditch of the curtain wall will be well-flanked." The ditch, he added, should be "12 feet wide and about six feet deep" (Mahan 1861, 1862:15–16).

Poe, in describing the defenses of Knoxville, wrote that Fort Sanders "is a bastioned earth-work, built on an irregular quadrilateral, the sides of which are, respectively, 125 yards southern front, 95 yards western front, 125 yards northern front, and 85 yards eastern front. The eastern front was entirely open, and is to be closed with a stockade; the southern front was about half done; the western front was finished, except cutting the embrasures, and the northern front was nearly finished. Each bastion was intended to have a '*pan coupe*'. The bastion attacked was the only one that was completely finished" (*OR* 1890:pt. 1, 309). Regarding Poe's description of the irregular quadrilateral, Henry Burrage of the 36th Regiment, Massachusetts Volunteers, recorded in his history of that unit that they held the west curtain wall of the fort, which "made almost a right angle at the fort, the northwest bastion being the salient" (Burrage 1884:109).

It is interesting that Poe does not mention the lunettes that were added to extend the north wall and the demi-bastions located at the southeast corner of the fort, which were added to provide fire along the south wall (Field 2005; figure 24). Mahan gave instructions in his *Treatise* on how to build a lunette, noting that it offered an artillerist an advantage because of the wider space in which to maneuver his weapon (Mahan 1861). At Fort Sanders this additional space would have provided the opportunity to place a cannon at an angle slightly parallel to the north wall; this could deliver the withering fire described by the Confederates who attacked up the slope to the north wall. The lunettes can be seen on Poe's map and also at the extreme left of the north wall in the photograph of Babcock and Poe taken in March 1864 (see figure 25).

THE BUCHTEL PRINT: PROBABLE APPEARANCE OF FORT SANDERS ON NOVEMBER 29, 1863

Various accounts of both Confederate and Union commanders and soldiers adequately describe aspects of Fort Sanders at the time of the battle, and there are many different engravings and drawings that also depict the fort on November 29, 1863. Some of these are more accurate than others, and several present a visual image of the battlefield and the fort "worth a thousand words" of descriptive text. The authors have chosen a reproduction of a drawing to illustrate the topography of the battlefield and the west end of the fort at the time of the Confederate attack. It was completed by a Union soldier, H. Buchtel of Company H, 104th Ohio, immediately after the battle (see figure 30a).

Buchtel's drawing was later reproduced and titled "Rebel Charge on Fort Sanders: Nov. 29, 1863." The original sketch was owned by T. W. Wallace, who lived at 1005 Chickamauga Avenue in Knoxville, when it was published in the *Knoxville News Sentinel* on November 25, 1934. It is a dramatic graphic illustration of Poe's written description of the fort and the landscape over which the attack took place.

The angle of the apex of the northwest bastion (A) points into the sunken area created by two sloping hills, which come together to form the defilade (B). The sunken area of the defilade slopes down from the apex of the bastion westward, providing a measure of cover for the Confederates as they approach the bastion. Some soldiers are climbing the steep scarp of the bastion from the trench (C) while others are about to enter the upper part of the defilade from different directions. A cannon is firing from the *pan coupe* (D) in the corner of the southwest bastion (E), sweeping the ditch along the west curtain wall and the northwest bastion. A gun in one of the lunettes at the northeast corner of the fort (F) can be seen firing parallel to the north curtain wall and the fire appears to reach the walls and trench of the northwest bastion. The

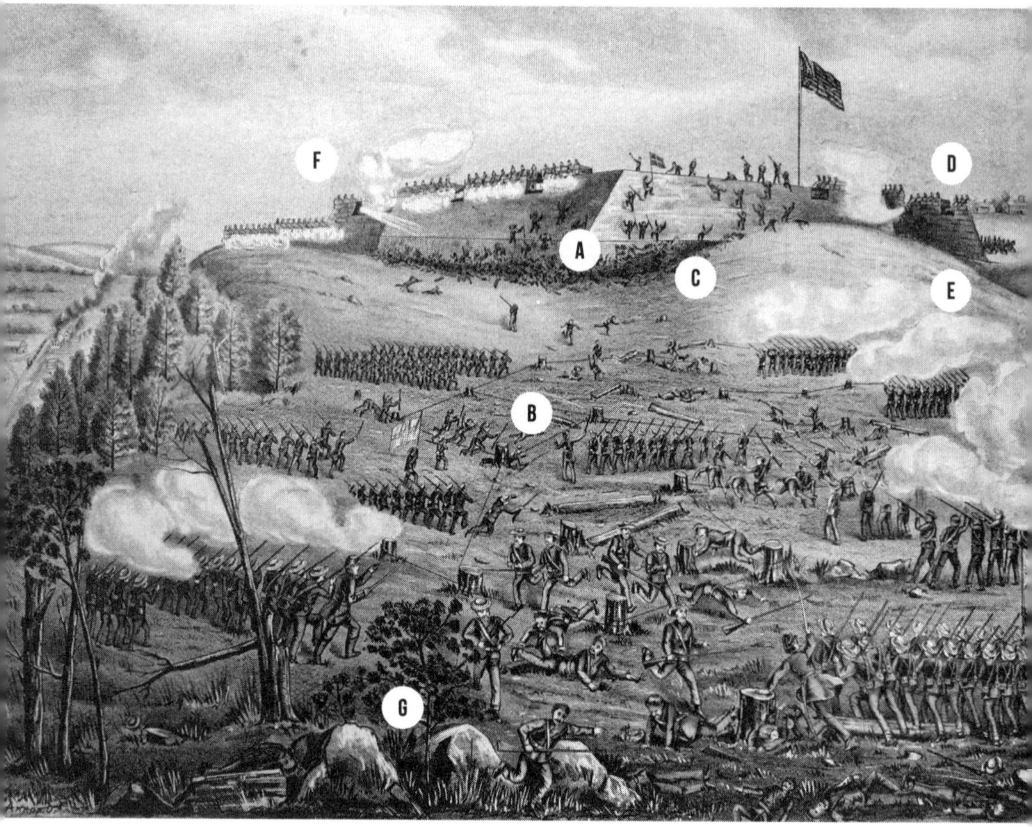

Fig. 30a. U. H. Buchtel's *Rebel Charge on Fort Sanders, Nov. 29, 1863*. Courtesy of Special Collections, University of Tennessee Libraries. (A) Apex of northwest bastion; (B) defilade; (C) soldiers climbing steep scarp from trench; (D) cannon firing from *pan coupe*; (E) southwest bastion; (F) gun in lunette firing on trench; (G) Buchtel's rocks, visible in figure 27b.

actual rocks Buchtel illustrated in the foreground of the engraving (G) can be seen at the north end of the 80-foot-long Confederate trench, visible near the woods in the enlargement of Barnard's photograph of the southern side of the northwest bastion (see figure 27b). The scattered remains of those rocks, the defilade, the vestigial outline of the trench on the southern side of the northwest bastion and the remains of Union rifle pits can be seen in the 1922 Robin Thompson aerial photograph of the battleground (see figure 48).

There are numerous engravings of the attack on the northwest bastion, but the authors believe for several reasons that Buchtel's is the most accurate. No engraving could have possibly been created that would illustrate the freezing temperatures and bitter weather during the siege and the weeks that followed. Only the words written by those who lived through those times can convey the terrible suffering and the scenes of death of men and animals during the winter of 1863 and 1864. Union and Confederate soldiers would continue the struggle to survive the hunger, cold, and physical hardships in those weeks to come after the battle. These men had no idea that they were fighting this war during the waning years of "The Little Ice Age." (see chapter 8)

Fig. 30b. Fort construction at Fort Butler, Virginia. *Pictorial History of the War of 1861.* A) Vertical supports for revetment; B) banquette; C) embrasure; D) wooden cannon platform in embrasure; E) soldiers constructing parapet; F) soldiers creating a berm.

6

LIFE, DEATH, AND BRAVERY DURING THE SIEGE

The lives of both Union and Confederate soldiers during the days of the siege included not only hard work, hunger, and bitter weather but also band music and singing. Drums, bugles, and the fife were common band instruments and were of great importance not only for entertainment, celebrations, and morale building, especially before battles, but bugles and drums were critical for conveying orders to the troops. Each regiment of artillery and infantry could have up to 24 band members, and the cavalry could have 16. General Phillip Sheridan's cavalry were key to Grant's success in the battle for Chattanooga, and his men helped contain Longstreet during his occupation of East Tennessee during the winter of 1864. He saw to it that his bands had special uniforms and the best horses because he firmly believed that music played a part in winning a war (Sheridan 1888).

When band members were not engaged in entertaining the troops, they were kept busy with numerous other activities, sometimes also serving as surgeons (Lanning 2007). Sergeant Eastham Tarrant wrote that the Wild Riders of the 1st Kentucky Cavalry "were enlivened every night by soul-stirring and patriotic airs of the band of the One Hundred and Twelfth Illinois. 'Yankee Doodle Dandy' was a favorite of Colonel Wolford and it was often played in their own peculiar style for his special benefit" (Tarrant 1894:252).

As the weary days of the siege passed slowly away, two memorable acts of bravery were carried out by Union soldiers during that time, and participants of each won Medals of Honor for their courage (Woodbury

1867). The first heroic deed occurred during a surprise sortie made at night into the Confederate lines on November 20 by the 17th Michigan. Led by 19-year-old Corporal John A. Falconer, this regiment set out to destroy a brick house and two log barns located west of the fort. Confederate sharpshooters were using the buildings as a picket reserve headquarters, and the sharpshooters there were making it difficult for troops to work within Fort Sanders. The property on which the buildings were located was on the east side of Third Creek, where Kingston Road (now Cumberland Avenue) crossed the creek. It belonged to a prominent Knoxvillian, Judge William Reese. The house, situated about 800 yards from the western front of Fort Sanders, had been vacated by Judge Reese's heirs and occupied by Southern sharpshooters, who on the evening of November 20 prepared supper before lying down to sleep on their blankets (Burrage 1884).

Major Frederick Swift was one of five men who volunteered for the dangerous assignment to burn the structures (Swift 1863). At 9:00 p.m. the "burners," carrying cotton, matches, turpentine, axes, and port fire, advanced with their regiment to the Confederate skirmish line. Only the burners continued to move forward towards the house; the rest of the regiment stayed put at the skirmish line, ready to help if needed. Upon discovering the presence of the burners, Confederate sharpshooters began shooting. Their gunfire was a prearranged signal for the waiting men, and their colonel "in a loud voice, as if commanding a brigade," ordered the entire Union line forward, the men shouting as they ran. Believing there was to be a full attack, the Confederate occupiers of the house quickly ran. One burner, when opening the door to the house, felt a skirmisher "dodge out under his arm." The men rescued "a kettle full of warm biscuits on the fireplace hearth," several gallons of blackberry brandy, some bacon, meal, and tobacco, and two boxes of cartridges before breaking up the furniture to set the house on fire. Seeing the house in flames, the regiment began to retreat. Firing the barns was more difficult as the logs were damp from frequent rains. Private William Brearley wrote that the burners quickly realized that "without support the barns could not be fired and sent word to the retreating regiment for help" (Brearley 1871:30–32).

The men turned about immediately and began firing. They had mistaken the order "to advance to the former position for one to begin firing . . . and a heavy fire was opened which for a time put the lives of the burners in the greatest danger." The position was quickly regained, but a retreat was soon ordered as all the buildings were aflame. The light from the blazing fires exposed only 200 retreating men to the Confederates. They suddenly realized that the "anticipated attack was instead a successful sortie," and their batteries began a furious cannonade. Brearley said of the sortie that it would "always remain a matter of surprise to [him] that but two of our men were killed" (ibid.:31).

As the regiment rested at the Union skirmish line watching the fire, some of the men commented on the "surprising warmth" emanating from Major Swift's pockets. Swift responded to the comments, saying: "I never felt so bad in my life as when I saw those biscuits in danger of burning" (Brearley 1871:32). Of the mission's success, William Brearley opined, "During the entire war there was not probably a more hazardous undertaking successfully executed than that evening's work" (Brearley 1871:32). Lieutenant J. Billingsly was one of the two men killed. In July 1896, Corporal John A. Falconer received the Congressional Medal of Honor for bravery in crossing the enemy picket lines and helping to destroy the buildings (*Military Times* 2014).

As Confederate forces continued to dig, encroaching eastward on Fort Sanders in preparation for an attack, the second great act of heroism occurred. This time, however, it cost the Union many of their best men and achieved nothing. As the day dawned on November 23, Union soldiers in the fort woke to discover that a rifle pit about 80 feet long had been thrown up in front of the Confederate skirmish line. Colonel Byron M. Cutcheon, who would also become a recipient of the Medal of Honor in 1891, described the scene: "On the 23d it was discovered that during the previous night the enemy had run a rifle pit from a piece of woods beyond the railroad on our left front, into the open field directly in front of the fort [see figure 32]. . . . Bushes from the woods had been set up in front of the parapet of the rifle pit, and from behind this screen the rebel sharpshooters commenced firing upon everyone seen moving within our works" (Cutcheon 1904:79).

A
E
F

Fig. 31. Southwest bastion. Library of Congress. In this photograph the camera was pointed towards the southeast, and it shows expansion of Fort Sanders' defenses after the battle. A) The "Hill"; B) westernmost defensive trench; C) Union camp; D) Cumberland Avenue; E) continuing excavation; F) apex of the southwest bastion; G) ditch.

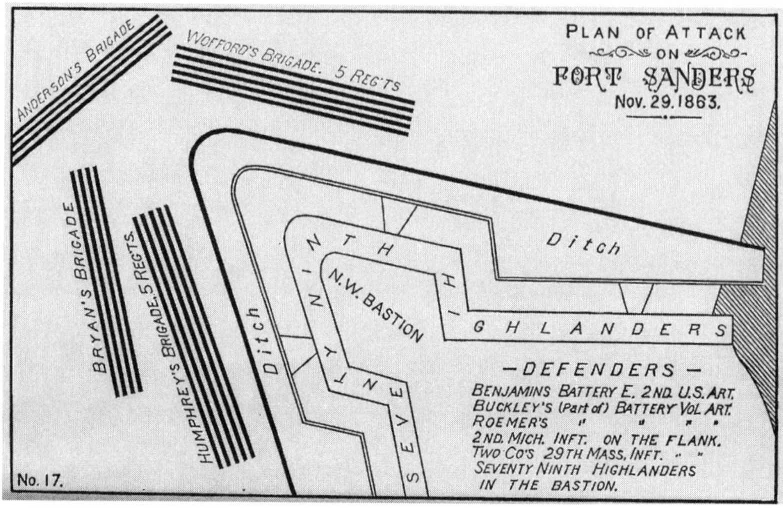

Fig. 32. Illustration of the Confederate plan of attack on Fort Sanders. From William Todd, *The Seventy-Ninth Highlanders, New York Volunteers*, 1886.

In an article first published in 1887, Major William M. Robbins, a member of the 4th Alabama Infantry, described the encroachment of the Southern pickets to the west wall of the fort: "During the night [of November 20] we were ordered to move our line up and dig rifle pits much in advance of our former position and within about 300 yards of the fort and its flanking works. By daylight we had a large number of rude, square holes dug waist deep in the ground (the best we could do with the time and the tools we had) in a line running parallel in the main to the face of the Federal works, but, nevertheless, curved considerably to the left and concealed in that part of the shrubbery" (Robbins 2004 [1887]:350).

The fort began taking fire from sharpshooters in the 80-foot-long rifle pit and adjacent woods. First Lieutenant Ezra Parker was ordered by General Ferrero to take out a sharpshooter hidden high up in a pine tree near that trench, a sniper who had already killed a number of men and almost put a bullet through Ferrero's head. Parker observed the woods through his field glass as a Union solider placed a cap atop a ramrod; a shot from the tree blasted through the cap in response. The tree and height of the shooter were determined by the smoke from the weapon. In another example of the accuracy of gunners in this war, artillerist Sergeant Frank Tucker, Battery D, was ordered by Parker to "load with solid shot [and] take his time about computing distance, elevation of piece and aiming it." Tucker then fired, and the next thing Parker saw was the "pine tree break off and topple over." The sharpshooter fell down with his gun in his hand, "jumped up and ran into a thicket in the rear of his tree." Parker continued: "Our men sent up a great shout. General Ferrero was delighted with such exhibition of marksmanship" (Parker 1913:47–48).

Determined to dislodge the sharpshooters from the woods nearby, General Ferrero on November 23 ordered an attack on the parallel by the 2nd Michigan, to be led by Major Cornelius Byington, who had lost thirty of his men at Campbell's Station. Captain Poe "strongly opposed" the attack, as did Lieutenant Benjamin (*OR* 1890:pt. 1, 343). General Ferrero reported that he acted "in accordance with instructions from the general commanding" (presumably General Burnside). Excluding those on picket duty, Ferrero ordered the 197 men of the 2nd Michigan "forward to carry the rifle pits at the edge of the woods on the left of my northwest front" (ibid.:349). Cutcheon said that the soldiers "were taken out of the rifle pits at 7 o'clock this morning [November 24] by Major Byington, and made a charge on the enemy's entrenched pickets" (Cutcheon 1993 [1902]:80).

From his position in one of the rifle pits, Major Robbins of the 4th Alabama witnessed the men of the 2nd Michigan "springing over their earthwork and dashing impetuously down the slope toward us." Robbins "hurried up in a moment the reserve battalion of the 4th Alabama to reinforce the men in the pits. And then ensued for a few minutes a fierce and deadly combat." Robbins admired the courage of the 2nd Michigan and compared their thinning ranks to those of the 4th Alabama. The "two veteran regiments," he said, had both been formed at the first call, and each had been reduced "by hard service with many battles to about 200 men each, but every man of them utterly fearless, splendidly daring, and knowing all about war" (Robbins 2004 [1887]:350).

Robbins was present when Byington "came on sword in hand, in front of his line exhorting them to follow him to victory to the very brink of our rifle pits, where he fell, desperately wounded within a few feet of me." Byington had been shot in his side and his leg broken. Robbins had him "carried back to the little piece of woods in our rear, made as comfortable as possible 'till he could be sent to the hospital" (ibid.). The 2nd Michigan had taken the works but only held it for half an hour. Before their reinforcements could come up, the Union soldiers "were repulsed by fresh troops the enemy had at hand" (ibid.). Robbins later wrote that the curve of the parallel to the northeast "proved to be of great service to us, for as our assailants charged in line parallel to and square against our right, they were enfiladed with terrible effect and the fire from our pits on the left, which hidden by bushes, had not been noticed" (Robbins 2004 [1887]:351).

While lying gravely wounded in the small woods with Robbins, Byington asked for the name of his regiment. Upon hearing the answer, Byington told him that his brother, who had been born in the North, had become a "Secesh" and was serving or had served in Robbins's brigade. Byington begged Robbins to send for him, only to learn that during the Chattanooga campaign, his brother had been killed (ibid.). Thirty-four-year old Major Byington was "left a prisoner in the hands of the enemy, and his leg was amputated by their surgeons." Exchanged on November 29, he died several days later (*OR* 1890:pt. 1, 354). The Union fortification on College Hill was named in his honor, and for his personal act of valor beyond the call of duty, Major Cornelius Byington would posthumously receive a Medal of Honor. The 2nd Michigan suffered a much greater loss that morning than the Union troops manning the fort would experience during the battle on November 29. In addition to the regiment's exceptional commander, Union combatants suffered 50 casualties according to General Ferrero's report (*OR* 1890:pt. 1, 349).

7

THE BATTLE OF FORT SANDERS

THE CONFEDERATES CLOSE IN

The Confederate decision regarding the point of attack became clear to the Union defenders of Fort Sanders as they began to observe the movements and deployment of the Confederate forces. They relentlessly began to close the gap between their lines and the entrenched Union pickets outside the west curtain wall of the fort. They could hear Longstreet's men at work on the ridge north of Fort Sanders connecting batteries with lines of rifle pits in preparation for a major assault. Captain Poe knew that the attack was imminent after the Confederates had captured most of the outer line of Union pickets "and driven the others . . . into the fort." Poe recounted, "we had not a picket 20 yards out from the fort and the enemy had secured the crest of the ridge which the work was on, beneath which they could mass troops night or day, within 80 yards of the works, without our knowledge." Poe had prepared his men well for the coming attack, noting, "Every man in the fort had his place assigned to him, and ate and slept in his place, so, on an alarm, they only rose and crouched by the parapet" (*OR* 1890:pt. 1, 343).

UNION PREPARATIONS FOR THE ANTICIPATED ATTACK

Union defenders had taken advantage of the lull that occurred as the Confederates established their battle lines after taking General Sanders's position on the Kingston Road. Lines of rifle pits were dug for their pickets at 80 yards and 30 yards parallel to the western wall and northwest bastion. The ground had been cleared of trees. The line of pits prepared by the infantry at 80 yards was used by sentinels who would give early warning of any threatening approach by the enemy. The pits located closer to the fort would serve the pickets as a second defensive position if they were forced to fall back from the first line.

The size and shape of rifle pits are now described and illustrated in infantry manuals and called "fox holes," and specially designed entrenching shovels are provided to soldiers. During the Civil War, the term "rifle pit" or "rat hole" was used to define a rough pit or a hole dug by infantrymen to protect them from enemy fire. The pits were excavated to a depth of about two and one-half feet with a parapet of about two and one-half feet high (OR 1890:pt. 1, 316). William Brearley called them "trenches," saying they "were of the most simple character, made by digging a ditch four feet wide and as many deep, throwing the earth excavated on the outside, making an embankment which was about shoulder high when we were standing in the trenches" (Brearley 1871:28). Some soldiers called a line of rifle pits a parallel. This term for rifle pits seems to be interchangeable in the diaries of soldiers.

The average soldier at this time was 5′8″ and weighed 143 pounds (Long 1971). Thus, a rife pit was cramped, but it provided a lot of protection from snipers and shrapnel. Sometimes soldiers on both sides who manned the trenches or connected rifle pits "made themselves a . . . fireplace by digging into the bank." Occasionally they would expand the pits so they could lie down. Captain Nason, 35th Massachusetts, wrote on November 30 that it was so cold the ice froze about a half-inch thick. The men addressed the freezing temperatures by making three fireplaces, adding room enough for ten members, and the company also "made the pit two feet wider to allow room to lie down" (White 2009).

Reverend Humes reported that before the siege many Union soldiers had cast off their overcoats, blankets, and tents during the escape from Campbell's Station and that the best way they could keep warm "when off duty was to crawl into . . . holes which they dug in the bank, back of the trenches" (Humes 1888:266). Will H. Brearley wrote of these earthen accommodations, "In lieu of tents, we dug holes in the banks, back of the trenches, and when off duty, two of us would crawl in, and the warmth of each other's bodies was the only covering" (Brearley 1871:34) (see figures 41a and b) Confederates dug fireplaces into the west banks of their trench on Morgan Hill just east of McLaws's headquarters at Bleak House in order to keep warm (Angst 2012).

During the early part of the siege, the rotation for Union picket duty during the day was quickly changed to night after two men were shot by Confederate sharpshooters as they made the switch. William Todd wrote that many men making their way to their pits at night through the wire entanglement, with which they were well acquainted, tripped and fell anyway and were able to measure "their length on the ground as they passed to and from the fort" (Todd 1886:374).

Pickets were assigned to an advanced outpost at a supporting distance to guard the fortification or to protect the main force during a battle. The guard was made up of between 40 and 50 enlisted infantry men and a lieutenant from each regiment. By regulation, picket duty was alternated regularly within the regiment. Henry Burrage noted that throughout "the siege both officers and men were on picket duty every third day. During this twenty-four hours of duty no one slept. The rest of the time we were on duty in the trenches, where one-third and sometimes one-fourth, of the men were kept awake" (Burrage 1884:105). Obviously this was the most dangerous work of infantrymen because if there were any major advance of the enemy they would be the first to be wounded, killed or captured. While likely unnecessary at Fort Sanders, a mounted sentry called a vedette would sometimes be employed in advance of such picket lines (Boatner 1959).

Longstreet's troops continued to encroach on the fort from the west and northwest. On the 28th they had captured most of the Federal rifle pits and forced Burnside's men into the ditch. Confederate sharpshooters now occupied the pits with the intention of keeping Federal riflemen below the parapet and preventing the artillery from using their guns during the assault. Lieutenant Benjamin, who had been carefully observing Confederate movements, noted that "the enemy had secured the crest of the ridge which the work was on beneath which they could mass troops night and day, within 80 yards of the work" without being seen (Benjamin n.d.). Captain Armour saw a large body of Confederate troops to his right (northwest) and believed that an assault was imminent (Armour 1898:12).

On November 28, Longstreet was also occupied with reassuring an officer about the attack ordered on Fort Sanders. In regard to the concerns about the depth of the ditch in front of the northwest bastion, Longstreet described the reconnaissance that he, General Leadbetter, and Porter Alexander had made on the west side of the fort on November 27: "The ditch at some points is probably not more than three feet deep, and five to six feet wide. At least, we so judged it yesterday in looking at a man who came down the parapet and walked over the ditch. In a letter to Major General McLaws on November 28, General Longstreet said "I have no apprehension about the result of the attack if we go with it with a determination to accomplish it" (Longstreet 1896:431) (see figure 31).

What Longstreet did not consider as he peered through his glass was that the soldier he saw walking over the six- to eight-foot ditch was crossing on a board (Seymour 1963). Sergeant Major J. A. Granberry of the 20th Georgia Regiment, Benning's Brigade, helped drive out Union soldiers in the rifle pits closest to the fort on the night of November 28, and they knew the ditch was deep. He recalled in an article published in 1910 that his brigade, on the night before the battle, "deployed as skirmishers in heavy line . . . advanced to the ditch around the fort, and knew that it could not be crossed without being bridged." He added, "If this had been done, the fort could have been taken easily" (Granberry 1910:24).

It may have been Granberry's skirmishers who at 9:00 p.m. on November 28 also staged a feigned attack using artillery and musketry on Fort Byington. Captain Jacob Roemer and his remaining troops were protected in a well-prepared fortification on College Hill. Most of his men had been placed in Fort Sanders. Roemer wrote that after dark, "Several hundred bullets and dozens of cannon-shots were exchanged and then suddenly everything became still." Roemer called all the members of the battery who remained and told them, "that which has just occurred was merely a feint: the real attack will be made before daylight in the morning." Roemer reported that soon after 6:00

a.m., Confederate troops fired all the guns positioned along the Union front "with the evident intention of smashing all the guns of the Union artillery" (Roemer 1897:170).

That evening, those in the fort were also on alert. In early morning, the Confederates began moving their brigades from their lines to their points of attack. General Joseph Kershaw described the movement of his brigade to "a long, shallow vale" that separated the armies (valley of Third Creek/Tyson Park area). It was "pierced by a small stream obstructed by dams at intervals, until the water in places was waist deep." His men "floundered through the water to the opposite side and stood shivering in their wet garments, while the cool air of the November morning chilled their whole frames." Most were thinly clad "and numbers of them barefoot." There was great suffering while they stood under arms "clasping with numbed hands the cold barrels of their muskets" (Dickert 1990:309).

Twenty-year-old South Carolinian Augustus Dickert, a member of Kershaw's Brigade, described in his 1899 history the solemn scene as he and fellow soldiers waited for the cannonade to begin. It had been almost 34 years after the war when he began to write his account of Kershaw's Brigade, but Dickert even then was able to graphically recall those gut-wrenching moments as they waited for the signal to attack. He wrote that the troops stood

> "silent, grim, and determined, as they awaited the coming crash! The crash with the thunder of the signal gun of Alexander's battery. Longstreet then saluted his enemy with the roar of twenty guns, the shells shrieking and crashing in and around Fort Sanders. Burnside answered the salutation with the welcome of fifty guns from the fort. . . . Salvos after salvos sounded deep and loud from the cannon's mouth and echoed and re-echoed up and down the valleys of the Holston. After the early morning compliments had continued ten or fifteen minutes, the infantry began to make ready for the bloody fray. The dread fortress was to be taken by cold steel alone. Not a gun was loaded in the three brigades. As the mist of the morning and the smoke of the enemy's guns lifted for a moment the slow and steady steps of the

> "forlorn hope" could be seen marching towards the death trap—over fallen trees and spreading branches . . . the brave men marched in the face of the belching cannon raking the field right and left." (Dickert 2004 [1899]:310)

William R. Carter was a Knoxville resident when he wrote his 1902 book, *Tennessee Volunteer Cavalry in the Great War of the Rebellion.* He describes the scene at 4 o'clock that freezing Sunday morning as the Confederate "assaulting column was formed of about 4,000 men . . . near where the Knoxville Woolen Mills now stand" (Carter 1902:117). This location was north of the railroad tracks near present 17th Street in the area where the round house and other railroad buildings were burned. Other regiments of infantry formed in the railroad cut below the fort and at the opening of the defilade. They waited silently for the signal to attack. "At about daybreak on the 29th, the enemy suddenly opened a terrific artillery fire on Fort Sanders, which was immediately responded to by Union guns all along the lines." As the Union artillery barrage slackened Confederate troops began to move forward with a yell (ibid.). As his men prepared for the attack in the freezing darkness, General McLaws wrote that it was obvious to him that Union troops knew the assault was coming and that it was "probable they knew where it was going to be made, for while I was talking to Colonel Ruff on the railroad the enemy threw a shell, which burst over the woods just to the rear of us through which Colonel Ruff's command (Wofford's brigade) was passing, assembling by regiments for the assault" (*OR* 1890:pt. 1, 489–90).

Private Edward M. Burruss of the 21st Mississippi, Company D, waited in reserve for the signal to attack; he described the scene in a letter written after the battle: "About half an hour before day break we were drawn up in line of battle as near the fort as possible without being seen & awaited the signal which was to be the opening of a battery in quick succession on our right as soon as the gunners could see to shoot. My eyes were watery from cold but this became more so from deeper cause as I looked down the line of half clothed, less than half shod heroes & saw their knees actually smiting together & their teeth russling [*sic*] like dry bones—but not from fright; watched their look of calm confidence & then thought of the terrible struggle that awaited them" (Burruss 1863 letter: mississippiconfederates.wordpress.com/2011/11/11/a-veterans-day-tribute).

At 5:30, a horseman galloped up to Fort Byington in the dark with an order for Roemer from Lieutenant Benjamin. It read: "Capt. Roemer, send to Fort Sanders fifty rounds of 10 pound shrapnel, fifty 20-second fuses, and all available canister, without delay, by your own teams, under escort." Roemer watched later through his glass as the team "plunged and tore along . . . at a dead gallop" towards the east end of the fort (Roemer 1897:172).

"HERE THEY COME BOYS, LOOK SHARP"

At daylight, a signal cannon was fired by Leyden's battery just east of the Armstrong House. This opened the 20-minute Confederate artillery bombardment on the fort. Second Lieutenant John Watkins, 48th Pennsylvania Regiment, was in the fort and described the shelling in a letter dated December 15, 1863, to Sara Probert in Ohio: "shortly after day light the rebels opened on us with all their Artillery, and I tell you the shell came around and above us pretty thick. Almost the first shell that came over killed a horse within three rods from where our gun stood [in the northeast redoubt (see chapter 10)]. They kept up there [*sic*] shelling for ¾ of an hour maybe and by that time they had a force in position to charge the fort . . . and on they came with a yell eight columns deep and one in reserve . . . about 5000 of them [so the prisoners said] . . . and with a yell they came on about 5,000 of them" (Watkins 1863a).

When the Confederate cannonade slacked off, signaling the infantry to advance, the men soon came into view under heavy covering musket fire, which was directed at the northwest bastion from the Southern sharpshooters in the rifle pits. A Federal officer shouted, "Here they come, boys, look sharp," as columns of gray-clad infantrymen with fixed bayonets emerged from what Major Cutcheon described as a heavy white fog that had "settled over the lowlands and in the hollows between the hills" and looked like a "a vast sea of milk." The dense fog reached "nearly up to the fort" (Cutcheon 1993 [1902]:81).

As the Confederates moved up the slope from the tracks, "the guns of Benjamin, Buckley and Roemer poured out 'thunder and lightning.' As they approached the fort, the well-known rebel yell was heard above the roar of the battle, then the black-throated monsters of the fort, double and triple shotted, pierced the advancing column through and through, making wide gaps which were quickly filled" (Carter 1901:117). Private William Rule described the attackers as they continued to move forward: "Yet proudly and defiantly the gray, grim and grizzled moved into the 'jaws of death'" (Rule 1900:173). Confederate Private Burruss watched as "his fellow Mississippians made the assault on Sanders . . . a nearly impregnable Yankee bastion." He saw the "colors of the two regiments as they struggled forward through bushes & briars & over rocks & logs" (Burruss 1863, letter). Byron Cutcheon described the scene from his viewpoint in the fort:

> "we presently saw a column of rebel troops burst out of the mist, coming on at the double-quick, directly toward the completed bastion of the fort. On they came, by columns of battalions, line on line, brigade on brigade, with arms at trail, heads down, with little or no yelling, but with a steady tramp, tramp, tramp and a low "hep, hep, hep", they rushed forward in an apparently irresistible surge toward the west front of Fort Sanders. The moment they showed out of the fog the fort opened with canister and shrapnel, cutting gaps in the advancing column. But still they came on without hesitation or wavering, until the leading line struck the wire entanglement, which they had failed to notice in the dim light and the fog, and many of them went down in confusion and disorder. The impetus of the charge was broken, and it was well-nigh impossible to regain formation." (Cutcheon 1993 [1902]:82)

The men of the 79th Highlanders on picket duty had watched the fireworks from Longstreet's cannonade as chips flew from stumps around their heads. Upon seeing the Confederates charge from out of the mist they rushed as fast as they could to the southwest bastion. Only a single plank spanned the ditch and as they scrambled to cross it "two or three men were thrown over" (Todd 1886:386).

William Todd continued the story of their retreat into the fort, saying, "Just as we were plowing over the plank, the roar of the artillery, volleys of musketry and yells of the Rebels broke upon our ears from the direction of the northwest bastion. Not a shot had been fired from the fort until the enemy was within fifty yards of the muzzles of our pieces." After removing the plank and arriving at their post, they found their "comrades actively engaged in repelling the assault. The attacking party had reached the ditch before we gained our position, and such a scene was being enacted that was difficult for pen to describe. The artillery depressed to the lowest point was hurling double and triple charges of canister into the masses of the enemy. Some of our men were firing over the cotton bales and others through the embrasures" (ibid.:389).

The men of McLaws's Division led the assaulting column on the northwest bastion; Wofford's Georgia Brigade was on the right and Humphrey's Mississippi Brigade on the left. These two brigades were followed in close order by Bryan's Brigade as a reserve. General G. T. Anderson's Brigade of John B. Hood's Division, commanded by General Micah Jenkins, was stationed to the left of Wofford's and Humphreys's brigades with orders to attack the fort on the north side; if the leading brigades were successful in entering the fort, Jenkins's Division was to then sweep around to the open east end of the fort and prevent the Federals from escaping (Seymour 1963).

Lieutenant Benjamin observed that "in less than two minutes from their appearance Wofford's and Humphrey's brigades were in the ditch" (*OR* 1890:pt. 1, 344). In the semidarkness, members of the Wofford and Humphreys units who had made it through the abatis and the wire entanglement had intermingled in the converging furrows. The men had shifted to the right and stumbled into the 10-foot-deep section of the ditch along the west curtain wall. Adding to the increasing confusion, Bryan's reserve brigade now slammed into the melee, pushing their comrades into the ditch, where the closely packed soldiers could neither advance up the slippery slope nor safely retreat from what had become a killing field. Once in the ditch, the attackers now confronted the 20-foot-high exterior scarp with no berm on which to secure a firm foothold that would allow them to climb up the slope. Adding to this disadvantage, the defenders had poured water down the steep slope during the freezing night, and according to Major General McLaws, "the parapet was hard frozen and a heavy ice crop was formed by the moisture from the bank, which prevented the men from obtaining a foothold, and the absence of a berm upon which the men could mount and start from" (*OR* 1890:pt. 1, 491). Captain B. F. Thompson of the 112th Illinois would vividly recall that ice had formed "on the water in the ditch and the almost perpendicular walls of the ditch and parapet were as smooth and slippery as a wall of marble" (Thompson 1885:161). Much less of an impediment to the Confederates was the wire that had been stretched in front of the fort. General Poe would later respond to a question about whether the wire was effective in demoralizing the Confederates. "No," he replied. "They were veterans and were made of material which is hard to demoralize" (*Knoxville Daily Journal* 1889).

Joseph Stockwell Manning was an eighteen-year-old sergeant in the 29th Massachusetts Volunteer Infantry who described the fierce assault: "The rebel infantry pored [*sic*] into upon us, scaling the parapet and climbing through the embrasures, but as fast as they did so, we shot them down, and they rolled back into the ditch which surrounded the fort." Describing his feelings as he repeatedly loaded and shot, he said, "Never in my life did I experience such a savage feeling. It seemed to me that I could not load and fire fast enough, and although my fingers were numb with cold. I was in a fever of excitement" (Harris 2014:2).

According to General McLaws's personal account of the assault, he was at Major Leyden's battery on Morgan Hill when the bombardment commenced, and he saw his troops advancing "in grand style" toward the fort. By the time he reached Wofford's Brigade, however, the Confederates were falling back to the cover of the defilade, the officers telling McLaws that it was "impossible to mount the parapet" and that several officers had been killed or wounded in the attempt. McLaws rallied and re-formed the regiments again under partial cover about

500–600 yards from the fort, but the brigade commander told him it was useless to resume the attack. General Longstreet gave McLaws permission to withdraw. In the meantime, Anderson's Brigade "came rushing to the assault in the same place where [McLaws's command] had attempted it, but was repulsed at once and retired" (*OR* 1890:pt. 1, 490).

When the lead column of Longstreet's troops charged the fort on the "double quick" (slow run), Lieutenant Benjamin reported heavy musketry fire directed at the northwest bastion from the enemy rifle pits (*OR* 1890:pt. 1, 344). No fire came from the onrushing columns, for they had been ordered to storm the fort with fixed bayonets and without firing a gun. According to Captain Armour and Lieutenant Benjamin, not a shot was fired from the fort until the enemy was only 10 yards away. The Federals then opened fire with double- and triple-shot canister from two cannons in the northwest bastion. They also started firing what they called a "flank gun" in the *pan coupe* and began sweeping the ditch along the northwest bastion with canister. The infantry poured what Amour and Benjamin called a "destructive fire" over the cotton bales and through the artillery embrasures into the seething mass of humanity below them. From the north front of the fort, the New York Highlanders, 2nd Michigan, and 29th Massachusetts directed a murderous flanking fire into the ditch. The Highlanders were stationed in the northwest bastion and the 2nd Michigan and 29th Massachusetts defended the north wall (Armour 1898:14).

As the sun rose at 6:30, Roemer watched from Fort Byington. He described the scene: "There stood brave Benjamin with his fifty rounds of shrapnel, each fitted with a twenty second fuse. Lighting the fuses with his cigar, he hurled them one after another, over the parapet into the ditch below, to intensify the terror already prevailing there and on the ground in front" (Roemer 1897:172).

Lieutenant Benjamin had cut the 20-second fuses to five seconds on the Parrott artillery shells sent to him by Roemer and placed them in rows along the banquette tread of the west and north walls of the fort. Scraping the fuses, he said to a nearby officer, "Captain where do they seem the thickest?" The captain pointed to an embrasure with one of Benjamin's guns and said, "Through that embrasure." Swift wrote,

"As quick as thought Benjamin coolly lights the fuse from his cigar and tosses the shells over into the ditch among the crowd, exploding them with terrible effect." Benjamin said, "I guess they will find that warm medicine as he tossed in the shells." As the shells burst, "yells, screams, and groans attested to their bloody work" (Armour 1898:14).

As the Confederate fire slackened and the first wave of attackers retreated to the rear, a cheer went up from Benjamin, Armour, Cutcheon, Watkins, and the other men in the fort: "Huzzah, Huzzah, Huzzah!" This was answered by a chorus of the rebel yell from Anderson's Brigade, who broke out of the woods and stormed the northwest bastion and north wall. Private Joseph Manning, who had been separated from his regiment, described the desperate fight that ensued: "Three of the enemy's colors were planted upon the parapet, but were quickly shot away, and a hand-to-hand fight followed, the officers using their swords, the men their bayonets and the butts of their guns. Even the artillery men took part, using their axes and the rammers of their guns as weapons, the enemy being finally obliged to withdraw, after losing heavily. General Ferrero who commanded the fort called out: 'There are lots of them in the ditch. Go out and get them.' A detail of our regiment was sent to the left and one from the 2nd Michigan to the right to sweep the ditch." Manning waited until he thought they had entered the ditch and then he "jumped upon the parapet, slid down the outside of the fort and landed among the rebels" (Harris 2014:1–3).

In spite of the fact that he was the only Union soldier present, he confronted the 16th Georgia infantry color bearer and other Confederates, demanded their surrender, and held them until the Michigan boys arrived. Two hundred in the ditch were taken prisoner, and Manning's bravery earned him a Medal of Honor (Dodge 2001). Before leaving the ditch, Manning helped to recover a rebel flag from underneath the body of the color bearer. After arriving at headquarters he presented it to Burnside, who took him "by the hand and complimented . . . him in the most flattering language" (Harris 2014:3). In the midst of this brutal struggle, the flag of Humphrey's 17th Mississippi was also captured by Sgt. Jeremiah Mahoney, Co. A, 29th Massachusetts earning him a Medal of Honor (*Military Times* 2014).

Captain B. F. Thompson with the 112th Regiment of Illinois Volunteers watched the battle from his position on a hill south of the Holston River; he described the Confederate assault in his book published in 1885 thus: "we could see the solid gray mass, line after line as they pressed forward to the assault. As they strained to see through the veil of smoke and listened to the noise of artillery, bursting shells, and the "sharp quick rattle of musketry," the suspense was terrible, as they knew that "upon the successful defense of the fort depended the fate of the whole army." When they heard the cheers of soldiers in the Union lines, they knew the attacking forces had been repulsed. Then, "the cloud of smoke lifted and revealed to our straining eyes a scene of carnage seldom witnessed even amid the horrors of war" (Thompson 1885:163).

Estimates for the length of time during which the carnage at Fort Sanders took place have ranged from 20 to 45 minutes, according to observers on both sides of the battle. Sergeant J. H. Granberry wrote "that not a gun was fired from the fort until our forces broke in retreat from the explosion of the hand grenades thrown into their ranks; . . . just one volley was fired into our retreating ranks" (Granberry 1910:24).

A truce of five hours was declared at noon to tend to the wounded and bury the dead. John Watkins was among the Union defenders who immediately climbed on the parapet to look down at the dead and wounded Confederates in the trenches. He described the scene in a letter to his future wife, Sara Probert: "Most all of the wounded were calling for water," which, Watkins wrote, "was about the only thing they ask for when first wounded." He continued: "The ditch in places was almost full of them piled one on top of the other, and such groaning I never heard. The dead were lying in all imaginable shapes the wounded on top of them and dead on top of them again, and the ground was strewn with them all along their route" (Watkins 1863a). Captain B. F. Thompson of the 112th Illinois was even more graphic in his description of the slaughter in front of the fort: "Men literally torn to pieces lay all around, some in the last throes of death, others groaning and their faces distorted under the extreme pains from their severe wounds. Arms and limbs, torn from their bodies, lay scattered about, while at every footstep we trod in pools of blood. . . . Over a hundred dead bodies were taken from the ditch alone, while the vast number of the wounded were being carefully carried within our lines, to receive the best care in our hospitals" (Thompson 1885:164).

In Augustus Woodbury's history of the battle, he noted that "96 bodies were found in the ditch and within three or four yards of it" (Woodbury 1867:347). One estimate of the Federal loss in the fort was eight killed and five wounded (*OR* 1890:pt. 1, 345). Captain Armour of the 79th New York Highlanders wrote that "the loss sustained on that November morning by the defenders of Fort Sanders was only about 20, of whom 4 killed and 5 wounded belonged to my regiment" (Armour 1898:17). Compared to the Federal casualties, the numbers of Confederate dead and wounded were staggering. According to the *Official Records,* 129 were killed, 458 wounded, and 226 missing (*OR* 1890:pt. 1:475). Augustus Dickert criticized Longstreet for ordering the assaulting columns to fall back, saying that "the most glorious victory of the war was lost by the ill judgment of one man" (Dickert 1990:311). Historian Maury Klein labeled the Confederate effort to retake Knoxville as the "most bungled, inept and ill- fated campaign in Confederate annals" (Klein 1997:40–42).

The number of soldiers in the Confederate army killed in 20 minutes of action is astonishing, and the descriptions above of the carnage suggest that there was an even greater number of deaths. Twenty-four-year-old William Rule, a captain in the 6th Tennessee, would write in his 1900 *Standard History of Knoxville* that the sexton of Bethel cemetery at that time, W. D. Winstead, an old Confederate soldier, said that of the more than 1,600 Confederates buried in Bethel Cemetery "there were buried . . . in the southeast corner 300 bodies of soldiers killed in the battle of Fort Sanders." Rule added that the sexton told him the 300 were buried immediately after the battle, and that 92 were exhumed later from the battle ground and interred there (Rule 1900:584). In addition, it is known that at least one Confederate officer was buried at the field hospital and possibly others were interred there as well.

While the weather certainly played a significant role in the Confederate failure to capture Fort Sanders, the shocking disparity in casualties between the two armies indicates that the construction of the fort offered its defenders extraordinary protection from an infantry that was numbered among the best in action during the war. Captain Armour praised the earthworks that shielded his New York Highlanders, saying, "protected by earthworks, we had great advantage and were enabled to inflict upon the enemy losses out of all proportion to that suffered by ourselves" (Armour 1898:16). Captain Poe probably best summarized the opinion of the troops about entrenching: "A feeling of intense satisfaction pervaded the whole command, and many persons assured me of their conversion to a belief in 'dirt digging'" (*OR* 1890:pt. 1, 317).

Confederate sharpshooters in the rifle pits realized the assault had failed when they saw their comrades being carried back down the defilade on litters. From his rifle pit, Lewellyn Shaver witnessed the removal of the Southern wounded and would later write, "No words were required to convey the sad tidings." He described the scene: "a solitary litter was seen advancing toward us over the field in our front; then, another and another, and on, a sad procession was silently threading its way to the rear." He saw "blood dripping from the litters" . . . and heard the "groans of the mangled occupants who had led the charge, as they passed through our line on the way to the rear" (Shaver n.d. 1867:26).

Sergeant Granberry of the 20th Georgia, who occupied one of the rifle pits dug by the Confederate sharpshooters on the night of November 28, saw the Union white flag of truce go up on the west wall after the battle. He watched as "the Federals swarmed out of fort," and he and the men "mingled with them between the fort and our picket line where the dead and wounded lay." Granberry thought the Federals, because it was their Sunday-morning inspection time, "presented quite a contrast to the appearance to the Confederates . . . with their clean linen and polished shoes." He said that the dead and wounded were removed during the first thirty minutes of the truce (Granberry 1910:24). The speed with which the wounded were moved back to their lines was due to Burnside's generosity in allowing the Confederates to use Federal ambulances (Seymour 1963:207).

There are several accounts of Union and Confederate troops mingling during the truce in the area between the fort and the Confederate picket line, where the wounded and dead lay. Charles Walcott reported that the "21st Massachusetts's boys met some of the 'Palmetto Sharpshooters' when they caught a pig together, and killed and divided equally" (Walcott 1882:289). Several of the opposing officers also met together and talked. Porter Alexander wrote that "he was in front of the lines during this respite from battle and was in conversation with Ferrero, Poe, Babcock, and Benjamin, with whom he had previously been acquainted" (Alexander 1989:144–145). Benjamin noted that while conversing with Alexander, the Confederate artillerist praised Burnside's maneuvering at Campbell's Station (*OR* 1890:pt. 1, 342).

Union Army Captain B. F. Thompson wrote in his *History of the 112 Regiment of the Illinois Volunteer Infantry* that for two hours after the truce was called by Burnside, both Northern and Southern troops "mingled together upon friendly terms, between the lines; the former assisting in burying those who had a few hours before, in obedience to the firm demands of duty, they had deliberately slain" (Thompson 1885:165). At the firing of a cannon at 7:00 p.m., the hostilities began again (Seymour 1963). Rifle pits were reoccupied, and the relentless watching and shooting continued.

Ellen House was kept awake most of the night. She described what she saw and heard: "I could see the flash of cannons where I was in bed, since during the night there was very heavy firing of musketry, and I could hear our boys cheering" (Sutherland 1996:52).

DEALING WITH DEATH

The Southerners had little time to deal with their dead with dignity, so they seem to have chosen the most practical and expedient way to bury their comrades as the subfreezing temperatures had made the ground solid. They had two options: to bury the bodies in open rifle pits or trenches or to chop individual grave pits in the frozen ground. It would have been almost impossible just to bury the 98 bodies recovered in the ditch alone in the time allowed by the truce (Seymour 1963). Sergeant Granberry wrote that "our dead were collected and we buried them, ninety-seven in number, in one grave" (Granberry 1910:24). This corresponds with the account of Charles Chapman, who said that the

Fig. 33. William Rule. Courtesy of the Calvin M. McClung Historical Collection.

Confederates transported the bodies well behind their own lines for burial in a long ditch (Chapman 1863). This "ditch" was most likely the 80-foot-long "trench/parallel" that Major Byington and the men of the 2nd Michigan had taken from the Confederates on November 23 but failed to hold. It is also possible that some of the dead were left exposed until the weather permitted suitable graves to be dug.

An eyewitness to the immediate aftermath was a young boy, W. P. Martin, who ventured out to Fort Sanders shortly after the battle. In a 1922 newspaper article, Martin described the burial of the Confederate dead on the battlefield to a reporter: "The confederates had been granted a respite to bury their dead, and Mr. Martin declared that only enough earth to cover the victims had been used. On one grave, near a small pine, a Confederate officer was buried and a small head-board put up to mark the site. No markers were used on the other graves according to Mr. Martin. Many of the victims were later taken up and given burial elsewhere" (*Knoxville News Sentinel* 1922).

In his *Standard History of Knoxville,* Captain William Rule of the 1st Tennessee Infantry wrote about his trip to the battlefield several days after the battle with a friend, a fellow Union supporter, Samuel T.

Atkin. Rule vividly described the macabre scene they witnessed; they saw the "ground where the soldiers had been hurriedly buried . . . their bodies protruding from the ground, being rooted out by hogs." Rule's companion was a compassionate man, and after returning from the battleground, Atkin advocated for the proper burial of the Confederate dead. A wealthy friend agreed to "pay the expense incurred," provided Atkin would have the work done (Rule 1900:175).

Atkin was a former coffin manufacturer who had prospered in the iron business during both the Confederate and Union occupations. He contacted 37-year-old James H. Renshaw, a local carpenter and undertaker, who agreed to make neat pine boxes for every corpse. The bodies, most of them unidentified, were buried for four dollars each and were reinterred in the Bethel (Confederate) Cemetery on Bethel Avenue, where other Confederate soldiers were earlier laid to rest when their army had occupied Knoxville. According to Rule, 92 men were buried there (ibid.).

It is unclear, however, with the ground frozen solid, how the Confederates were able to bury their dead comrades immediately after the battle. Assistant surgeon Robert P. Myers said the Federals allowed them to bury the dead during the truce, but he was "not permitted to go near the fort guarded by a strong picket line" (Myers n.d.). Perhaps the Confederates were not allowed to immediately bring in their fallen comrades from the ditch and burial was delayed. Charles Chapman wrote in a letter that they had to carry the wounded and dead from where many of them lay to the Southern lines (Chapman 1863). In a diary entry on December 5, Ellen House said that some Confederate dead were not buried on the day of the battle, and on January 1, 1864, she wrote in her diary that she hoped that while Grant was in Knoxville on his inspection tour, he would "send out to the Battle field & have the men they pretended to bury covered over. I am told there are any amount of arms and legs sticking out, and there was one whose face was uncovered" (Sutherland 1996:79).

Grant may have addressed Ellen's concerns before leaving Knoxville, but there were more buried Confederate dead to be dealt with as late as the first days of March, 1864. Sergeant Major Alvin M. Woolson, a member of the Ohio Volunteer Artillery, entered Knoxville with his regiment on March 7. The next day, the first order given the men was to "rebury the dead confederates on the slope west of the fort." Woolson described the scene they encountered there: "bodies had been tumbled into rifle pits and slightly covered. They had been exposed to the weather for several months and the rain had washed the earth away, leaving arms and legs exposed, and, in some instances, the entire body of a Confederate soldier, was entirely exposed, and by the actions of the sun and rains, and the decaying remains of these unfortunates, the odor arising was unbearable. We were obliged in many instances, to dig new graves or trenches and dig them deeper in order to decently inter them" (Miller 1914:25).

Before a battle, the regimental surgeon would establish a field hospital beyond the range of enemy artillery or a forward aid station outside the range of small-arms fire (Robertson 1984). The Confederate field hospital near Fort Sanders was probably located at the entrance to the defilade situated at the west end of what is presently Forest Avenue where the Campus Point Apartments now stand, as this was the safest area most accessible to the battlefield.

On December 1 the body of Lieutenant Colonel Henry Thomas of Wofford's Brigade was disinterred from the area of the field infirmary and buried in the private Lonas cemetery on Middlebrook Pike (Brown 2011). That other Confederates were buried near the field infirmary where they died is suggested by reports that, as the Crown Point Apartments were being built in 2005–07 on Forest Avenue, human bones were uncovered by the workmen.

CARING FOR THE SICK AND WOUNDED: HOSPITALS IN KNOX COUNTY

Parson Brownlow, in the January 9, 1864, issue of the *Knoxville Whig*, informed his readers that the "military authorities have taken all the Churches but one, and all of the Hotels of Knoxville and converted those into hospitals" (*Knoxville Whig* 1864a). The number of wounded on both sides who were treated in Knoxville hospitals after the November battle was overwhelming. William Todd of the 79th Highlanders wrote that the "Confederates left their sick and wounded in Knoxville and Union doctors immediately took over their hospitals" (Todd 1886:404). By January 1864, two thousand patients, Union and Confederate, were being treated in five Union military hospitals. The main military hospitals included the Tennessee School for the Deaf built in 1848. This beautifully restored building was later used as Knoxville's City Hall and presently houses Lincoln Memorial University's Duncan School of Law (McRary 2012a).

Information about feeding those soldiers hospitalized in the School for the Deaf was recovered on May 29, 1992, when the profile of a large, barrel-vaulted, Civil War brick oven was exposed by street construction at the intersection of Western Avenue, and Broadway and Henley Streets. The oven had been built into the slope of the hill below the hospital and then covered over with earth to help retain heat in the bricks as the bread was baking. Charles Faulkner and a University of Tennessee colleague, Chuck Bentz, were called to investigate and record the historic feature that had been revealed in a construction trench. The oven walls were three bricks thick, and the heavily fired clay floor was covered with ash and charred wood. Mid-nineteenth-century cut nails were found; some were embedded in pieces of charred wood, indicating that wooden boxes and construction material had been used to fire the oven. Unfortunately, construction immediately continued after examination of the site, and the oven was reburied before further study could be conducted (Faulkner n.d.; National Archives 1864).

In addition to the Tennessee School for the Deaf, the Lamar and Bell House Hotels, four downtown churches, the Knox County Courthouse, and a block of stores were put to use for the wounded (McRary 2012a). Ellen House went to one of these stores immediately after the battle to help wounded Confederate soldiers. She wrote afterwards in her diary that two or three of the severely injured men were lying on the floor without "a spark of fire" in the room. Each "had lost a leg or an arm," and there were no blankets to cover them on the coldest day they had suffered thus far during that winter (Sutherland 1996:53).

Fig. 34. Melrose Place. Former Confederate Major Thomas O'Conner married Fannie House, Ellen Renshaw House's sister, in 1870. O'Conner, a wealthy businessman, was killed in a gunfight on Market Square in 1882. The property was sold to the university, and the house was replaced by a dormitory. The circular driveway, however, survives as a city street today. Courtesy of the Calvin M. McClung Historical Collection.

A hospital located in an elegant Italianate home built in the 1850s by Colonel John J. Craig, stood on the crest of a hill south of Kingston Road just west of the town. This house, which was located almost directly opposite Fort Sanders, and the vast estate that surrounded it were called "Lucklow" by Colonel Craig. An important Union defensive position was added here in November 1863. The estate would later become known as "Melrose Place" (Tumblin 2012).

When Henry Burrage entered Knoxville on September 17 with the 36th Massachusetts, the property was owned by an avid Union supporter, William Powell, who warmly greeted him and "invited Colonel Morrison and Major Draper to make it their headquarters" and "also designated a chamber for the sick of our regiment." Burrage described the earthwork with two cannons that was built atop this hill close to the house: "A few feet from the southwestern front of the house, a small earthwork called Battery Noble was thrown up by our men, in which was placed a section of Buckley's battery" (Burrage 1866:101–102).

The grounds of this estate remained an unknown burial site for soldiers and horses until after 1875, when workmen began to dig a pond on the property (Tumblin 2012).

Mary Boyce Temple, the only child of O. P. Temple and his wife Scotia Hume Temple, was about nine years old when her father purchased the property from William Powell. Temple named the 20-acre estate "Melrose Place," in honor of his mother-in-law's home in Scotland. He became a gentleman farmer and filled the estate with orchards, ornamental trees and shrubs, and vegetable and flower gardens. He added to his lawyer's income by selling strawberries grown at Melrose Place. Temple sold his estate in 1875 to Thomas O'Conner, a onetime Confederate major who had married Ellen House's sister, Fannie. They soon continued to embellish the grounds by adding a large artificial lake between his house and Kingston Road. It is said that as the lake was being dug, gruesome evidence emerged of the terrible battle that had raged on the ridge almost directly north of their home.

"When workmen were excavating for the artificial lake, bones of men and horses, bullets and minie balls, pieces of uniform, both blue and the gray, rifles and other mementoes of the battlefield were found in great quantities" (ibid.). If one accepts the story about the macabre discoveries that emerged from the soil at Melrose, then one could surmise that the irreverent depositing of human remains of both Union and Confederate soldiers, together with those of horses, was necessitated by a critical need for burial sites close to the fort during the afternoon of November 29, 1863.

The Scottish place names used by O. P. Temple have lingered on that ridge south of the battleground into the present century. The old lane leading from Kingston Pike that includes the circular drive is called Melrose Place. It terminates at Melrose Avenue, where Melrose Hall is located. It was the addition of a lake to the grandiose estate of Thomas and Fannie House O'Conner that gave Knoxville the street name, Lake Avenue (Rothrock 1946; McNabb 1991).

In the summer following the battle, issues of the *Army Mail Bag* solemnly described a ritual journey of wounded soldiers who were carried from the train station to South Knoxville for treatment in a Federal hospital: "Almost every night the train arrives from Chattanooga. A long and mournful procession of ambulances file down Gay Street, and continue their march to and over the bridge, until the weary sufferers are safely welcomed at the hospital tents on the banks of the beautiful swift running Holston. A large number of tents have been erected two or three hundred yards above the bridge. We learn that 'Holston Hospital' was organized on the 4th of July and there are beds for 1000 men" (*Army Mail Bag* 1864; Booker 2015b).

The hospital, General Hospital No.1, was later enlarged. Four hundred tents were added, each to be occupied by six men, enough for "2,400 wounded Union soldiers who were being sent from Sherman's army." Sergeant Major Alvin M. Woolson, who while crossing the treacherous Cumberland Mountains had been crippled so badly with inflammatory rheumatism that he could no longer walk, adds a most interesting account of how these wounded men were kept warm in their tents during the winter of 1864, thanks to the ingenuity of army engineers (Miller 1914).

The hospital sat above the bridge on a "gentle declivity" of "about 15 to 20 degrees." Engineers excavated twenty ditches "four feet wide by three feet deep" and extended them to the bottom of the declivity, a ravine, about 500 feet below the hospital area, where each ditch connected to a fireplace in the ravine. At the top of each trench, a chimney 20 feet high was constructed. The ditches "were covered with a double thickness of boards" except for the last 20 feet at the bottom of the ravine, which was "covered with flagstone." Twenty flues "covered with two inches of sand" were created; each was "500 feet long from the ravine at the bottom to the top." Over each flue "twenty tents were placed so there was plenty of space." When the fire in the ravine connected to the flue, "the heat and smoke would pass up the hill through the flue to the chimney at the top, and after the fire got well started, the draught would be complete between the tents." When fires in the ravine "got well started it made the temperature in the tents comfortable even in the coldest weather" (Miller 1914:90–91). Woolson personally enjoyed the benefits of that heat as he occupied one of the tents. He wrote that "when we wanted to warm our feet we simply set up on the edge of our cots and placed our feet upon the ground." He added that it was believed "that no like arrangement for heating tents was made during the Civil War" (ibid.:91).

Another Union hospital is described in the *Army Mailbag* as a convalescent camp, "situated on a beautiful place of cleared ground about a mile west of College Hill. There are about 400 men at the camp representing a large number of regiments, but the majority from Kentucky and Tennessee. These convalesces are put on guard duty, and those able to work are put in a government garden which is quite extensive, near the camp" (*Army Mailbag* 1864).

Today, stories abound that most antebellum houses in West Knoxville sheltered injured soldiers from both armies and that blood stains can still be seen on wooden floors in some of these houses. Several are said to be haunted. At least two antebellum historic houses still standing on the north side of Middlebrook Pike in West Knoxville were used as Confederate hospitals. "Middlebrook Hospital," as it was referred to in Confederate records (McRary 2012a), was the residence of mill owner Gideon M. Hazen and his wife, who were still grieving the loss of their son Gideon Jr. (known as "Gid") that November of 1863. Gid had left "Brook," as the house was called, and joined Colonel John Hunt Morgan on his first raid into Kentucky in 1862. He was captured by Union forces and died a prisoner in the Dry Tortugas. Mrs. Hazen entered a state of denial about her son's death and began placing a candle in a window to welcome Gid home every night until her death.

The hospital at "Brook" was under the supervision of Dr. William M. Piggott, Wofford's Brigade, McLaws's Division. Ellen House, who constantly ministered to wounded Confederate soldiers—securing medicine, food, clothing, and even cutting up the carpet from the family living room to make blankets—wrote in her diary on December 18 that Dr. Piggott was now in serious need at Middlebrook. His hospital was located outside the Hazen house "in tents, and is very much in need of blankets, clothes, &c." House called it "Wofford's Hospital" for his brigade, which had taken terrible casualties as they led the charge against Fort Sanders (Sutherland 1996:67–68). The commander of the brigade was Lieutenant Colonel Solon Z. Ruff, who was killed in the attack (Seymour 1963:193–196). This well-preserved antebellum house still stands on Middlebrook Pike.

Confederate artillery commander Porter Alexander recorded that while camping near the Hazen house, he visited an Englishman, Captain Steven Winthrop. A former captain of "Her Britannic Majesties 24th Infantry," Winthrop was recovering from surgery in an upstairs bedroom of "Brook" for a wound he received while rallying his troops in an attack on General Sander's breastworks on November 18. Winthrop was hit in the "base of his neck tearing up his collar bone so that some inches of it had to be amputated." Alexander climbed the stairs with his camp dog, Buster, who had never set paws in a house before. The dog ran up and down the hall "a time or two and & then, a window at one end being opened, he took a flying leap through it." Buster was not seriously injured and, of course, was unaware that he was a source of great humor for Porter and "even Winthrop in all his bandages." The men laughed together until they were "sore over the idea of Buster's astonishment when he found himself falling through the air outside of the window." Alexander recalled later that this was one of the days during the war that stood out vividly in his memories: "the success of the little private fight for the rail breastworks put us all in fine spirits, and we never doubted that but that within a very few days we would have Burnside & all his people prisoners" (Alexander 1989:321).

The second home on Middlebrook used as a hospital was a fine two-story brick house built by Jacob Lonas in 1850; it has recently been restored. Jacob's great-granddaughter, Mary Dowell, who was born in 1897, lived there all her life (Anderson et al. 2009). Mary, the family historian, genealogist and a good friend of the authors, often recounted two family stories about their home place and the Civil War. She told us about a crooked maple tree that stood in the front yard when she was a child: During the Civil War the house served for a time as a hospital and soldiers used to tie their horses to "a maple tree in the front yard of the house." As a young child, Mary was familiar with that tree, where hungry horses had "chewed the bark off . . . creating a permanent bend in it." She also recounted a family story about a wounded Confederate officer who was being tended in an upstairs bedroom of their house. He observed from a window there that some of his troops were trying to break into the smokehouse below. The officer drew his gun and called out the window that he would shoot any man who tried to enter the structure (Dowell 1986; Norris 1982).

On December 5, Colonel B. C. Christ, 9th U.S. Army Corps, and three of his regiments were searching for a retreating Georgia regiment when he stopped at Gideon M. Hazen's paper mill near Middlebrook Pike. There they discovered 130 sick and wounded Confederate soldiers. In another house, as he passed near the mill, he found more of the same and was appalled to see "many of them destitute of medicines, rations or medical attention" (*OR* 1890:pt. 1, 360). Papermill Road was named after Hazen's mill on Third Creek, which was located near the current-day western junction of Interstate 40/75 and 75/640 (bypass) (Rothrock 1946).

The suffering of the Confederate wounded is graphically described in the diary of Lieutenant Robert P. Myers, a 16th Georgia Infantry Regiment surgeon, who said he was the only medical officer in Wofford's Brigade on the Fort Sanders battlefield. Myers wrote that on the morning of November 29, the temperature was brutal and the ground frozen solid: "as I would wash the water would freeze on my hair & beard before I could wipe it off although I was before a large fire. . . . the wounded sufferd [*sic*] much—I had large fires on the field to keep them warm—my hands became so cold while dressing the wounded I had to warm them" (Myers diary, n.d.).

DAYS FOLLOWING THE BATTLE

Weary Union soldiers had no respite after the battle as Longstreet's troops remained in their trenches and continued to harass them, keeping the penned-up Federals on alert for the next five days. Major Fredrick Swift wrote in his diary that Union pickets suffered enormously during this time. He described the weather, noting that it rained "hard for a couple of days then turned very cold and some of the poor fellows in the rifle pits almost perished. When relieved after dark they had to be helped out of the pits and back to the trenches. Their pits were small and deep and clayey soil had not absorbed the water and they could not drain the pits, for fear of the sharpshooter" (Swift 1863, diary).

Longstreet was well aware during those cold and rainy days following the battle that he did not have sufficient ammunition, nor were his troops physically capable of launching another attack on the fort. Even though General Bragg had been defeated by Grant's army at Chattanooga on November 25 and the Confederates were repulsed by Burnside four days later, Longstreet did not prepare to end the siege until December 1. The Confederate commander waited to leave Knoxville until he was sure that General Sherman, who was moving with 25,000 of his men from Chattanooga to Knoxville, would continue northward, rather than return south to pursue Bragg's troops into Georgia,

Around midnight on December 4, the last of Longstreet's hungry and largely barefoot army silently departed in good order from their battlements and slowly moved east to Bean's Station and Rogersville. In an effort to deceive the troops in Fort Sanders into believing the siege was still on, the troops occupying the trench on Morgan Hill were ordered, before departing, to stoke the fireplaces they had dug in the west wall of the trench (Angst 2012).

On December 6, Sergeant Henry White left his place on the Union picket line to enjoy his new freedom; he wrote about a small excursion he took to a nearby Confederate entrenchment: "I took a stroll over the rebel works; they had got up some strong entrenchments; broken and burned guns were strewed around the ground. I noticed hides of cattle cut up to make shoes and saw one pair of shoes made up" (Walcott 1882:294). William Todd, 21st Regiment, Massachusetts Volunteers, was happy that they could now stand up inside the fort without being shot at. He wrote that the men "began at once to clean inside the grounds and pitch tents in more convenient places" (Todd 1886:404).

It was an exciting day in 2010 when archaeologists with UT's Archaeological Research Laboratory, directed by Michael Angst, discovered the long north–south infantry trench on Morgan Hill that Confederates had abandoned the night of December 4. As the trench was excavated, the row of fireplaces that had been dug into the west wall of the trench and two cannon emplacements were found, along with a broken, alkaline-glazed pottery jug made in South Carolina. The hearths contained evidence of the final activities of the occupants before their departure the night of December 4. Historic accounts were proven true, as remains in the fireplaces were carefully excavated; the Confederate occupants of the trench had thrown every nonessential flammable item available into the small fireplaces to keep the fires burning as they escaped. Nails from burned boards and metal parts of wooden wagons were found in the fireplaces, which had been filled in, along with the trench, probably over a hundred years ago (Angst 2012).

SHERMAN ARRIVES IN KNOXVILLE

Two days after the Confederates vacated their positions, General Sherman, accompanied by Assistant Secretary of War Charles Dana, reached Knoxville with three army corps: the 4th Corps, including Major General Gordon Granger and General Philip Sheridan, and the 11th and 15th Corps, with Major General William Sherman (Sherman 1875). The troops left Chattanooga on November 29 but were delayed in reaching Knoxville until December 6 because of the additional time it took to build a trestle bridge near Loudon to cross the Tennessee River. Charles Dana, who had accompanied Sherman to assess the condition of the troops of the Army of the Ohio and evaluate their performance during the siege, soon reported, "The utmost constancy and unanimity had prevailed during the whole siege, from Burnside down to the last private; no man thought of retreat or surrender" (Dana 1996 [1902]:155).

One of the soldiers in Sheridan's 4th Corps, Lieutenant Marcus Woodcock of the 9th Kentucky Infantry, who had marched into what he called "the famous city of Knoxville," spoke scornfully of Longstreet's siege and "boldly [*sic*] repulse" in his *Memoirs:*

Fig. 35. Gen. William Tecumseh Sherman. Library of Congress.

> But where were the rebels? "the nest was there and warm, but the bird had flown;" yet he had left abundant evidence of his rashness. All around the parapets and in the ditches of one little fort could be seen the marks of a recent desperate conflict—desperate in every sense of the word for there a chosen body of heroes had attempted in one single charge to decide the fate of an army, and they had acted in every way worthy of the occasion. But it is already known to the world how Longstreet attempted to reduce Burnside's army to such a state of destitution that it would have to surrender, and how when he heard the fourth Army Corps was coming he attempted to take the city by assault, and how he met with an awfully bloody repulse, and how he decided to leave Burnside alone, and how he pulled up stakes and went further east. (Noe 1996:246)

General Burnside had earlier informed Grant that he was running out of provisions, but Sherman was never convinced that starvation stalked the Army of the Ohio in Knoxville. Dana noted that Burnside had 20 days of provisions, much more than he had at the beginning of the siege (Dana 1996). General Sherman's suspicions were confirmed when he was honored upon his arrival in town with a celebratory turkey dinner and all the trimmings, which had been put together with a variety of contributions by the local populace. It had taken a great effort to assemble the ingredients to create such a meal, and those attending were shocked when Sherman expressed his surprise at the extravagance of the dinner he was served when the rank and file in the trenches were on short rations. The general became more agreeable upon inspecting Fort Sanders and the other Knoxville fortifications the men had constructed. He complimented the garrison, telling the troops that the works seemed nearly impregnable and pronounced them a "wonderful production for the short time allowed for their selection of ground and construction of work" (Sherman 1875:381–382).

General Burnside at the time of Sherman's visit naively believed that Longstreet would voluntarily vacate East Tennessee (ibid.). He made a critical mistake during that time when he convinced Sherman that he had sufficient troops to guard Knoxville and, if the need arose, drive the pesky Longstreet back to Virginia. Sherman, who had little desire to use Burnside's East Tennessee army in any offensive operations and who had described East Tennessee as "my horror" (*OR* 1890:pt. 3, 297), left for Chattanooga on December 12, leaving General Granger with only 10,000 men of the 4th Corps to help dislodge a potentially threatening Confederate army just up the river.

W. R. Carter agreed with Sherman's assessment regarding Knoxville's fortifications. Arriving in Knoxville from Sparta on December 15 with the men of the 1st Tennessee Volunteer Cavalry, he described their approach to the fort after passing "through Longstreet's main line of works." He wrote: "Shortly after passing this point we caught sight of Fort Sanders and Benjamin's 'Dogs of War' which were still peeping through the embrasures looking bold and defiant. The huge fort and long lines of new-looking earthworks which crowned the hills and ridges which almost encircle the town bore the marks of battle." When they reached the point where Reservoir Street crossed Gay, they "passed through Burnside's main line, the yellow clay towering high above" their heads (Carter 1901:113).

Poe, who had supervised early construction of the fort, was more pessimistic about the quality of the works, believing that the victory was due to the mettle of the soldiers defending Fort Sanders rather than the state of the fortifications. He stated in his official report that "the work was . . . very weak, and should have fallen by the ordinary chances of warfare; but the garrison were picked men" (*OR* 1890:pt. 3, 343). The *Nashville Daily Union* printed a description of the fort two weeks after the battle on December 13, 1863: "No part of the fort is complete. . . . One bastion in the northwest angle, and the parapet on the west side are only up. . . . Temporary traverses were made by cotton bales, and also two salients from which guns could sweep the ditches on the north and west" (*Nashville Daily Union* 1864).

COLLATERAL DAMAGE TO KNOXVILLE'S CIVILIAN POPULATION

As for the collateral damage, innocent townspeople caught up in the traumatic siege and battle were fortunate that the focus of the confrontation was a mile from the center of town. On November 19, the Confederate artillery had lobbed a few shells from a battery on Tazewell Pike; after that they apparently decided that indiscriminate cannon fire was a waste of ammunition, especially since half the Knoxville citizens under bombardment were Confederate supporters. It is a remarkable fact that only one innocent person was reported killed by the sporadic gunfire during the siege, a little girl killed by a stray bullet (Gordon 1904; Seymour 1963).

The damage to the civilian population would understandably begin to increase in late November and early December of 1863. Two descriptions of Knoxville by Union soldiers prior to that disruptive time differ substantially. Artillerist John Watkins arrived in Knoxville in September with the 48th Pennsylvania regiment and his portrayal of the town was grim. He wrote to Sara Probert that: "Knoxville must have been quite a place before the war began but it looks now as if it were the oldest place in the world and been allowed to run down ever since it was built" (Watkins 1836b). Colonel Sumner Carruth who entered Knoxville in October with the 25th Massachusetts Volunteers, described the town in a more appealing way, perhaps because he found a cookie shop "open for trade in gingerbread and apples." His memory of the town in 1884 was that his "men found it much better built and more city-like than they anticipated. There were large railroad stations and freight houses, hotels, markets, a university, asylum for the deaf and dumb, numerous churches and schools, and street lamps for gas" (Carruth 1884:172).

The worse damage to the civilian population was the destruction of their homes, many of which were deliberately burned by Federal troops in retribution or to clear an area of houses that might be used as Confederate sniper positions. Ellen House wrote on Tuesday, December 1, that the city was "completely ruined, scarcely a fence standing. The sidewalks are like a stable yard, and the stench is horrible, particularly from the hospitals and there are one hundred and fifty of them" (Sutherland 1996:57). William A. Huddart of the 1st Ohio Infantry Regiment, who traveled up from Chattanooga to Knoxville was impressed with the defensive works but not with the "run-down" town he had been sent to protect. Writing home to his father in Ohio on December 13, 1863, he said, "Knoxville is one of the strongest positions I have ever seen. The town, too, has been at one time a splendid place but is now pretty well run down. Many of the houses have been burned down and the Breast Works have been thrown up along every one of the principal streets" (Huddart 1863, letter).

Ellen House recorded another planned demolition of homes in her journal on January 2, 1864. She had heard that Union troops intended to "pull down three more houses on Summit Hill to make room for more guns" (Sutherland 1996:79). A northern reporter visiting Knoxville shortly after the battle described the devastation: "Burnt houses and solitary chimneys over one whole quarter of the city, showed that the heart of East Tennessee loyalty had not been without its sufferings"

(*Knoxville Whig* 1864a). Another observer described widespread homelessness and reported that one quarter to one half of the houses had been burned down (McKenzie 2006).

The worse conflagration had occurred on November 23 as the Confederates began to tighten their positions on the besieged Federals. To prevent their capture by Confederates, Union troops set fire to the East Tennessee and Georgia Railroad roundhouse, shops, and dwellings on the north side of the tracks near present-day 17th Street. As the buildings burned, condemned ammunition stored in the roundhouse by the Confederates exploded "making an extensive conflagration lighting up the city and the surrounding country as bright as day" (Osborne 1877:152).

Later, on March 5, 1864, Brownlow's *Knoxville Whig* reported that there was "shocking dilapidation of this town in the last six months. One third of it has been destroyed and the balance greatly marred and injured. . . . all our public buildings, the University, the Deaf and Dumb Asylum, the cemetery, and their fences and grounds are more or less injured and defaced" (*Knoxville Whig* 1864d).

Even what later became the University of Tennessee did not escape the devastation of the battle and military occupation of 1863–65. In 1866, a student enrolled in what was then called East Tennessee University described the campus: "There was a bare hill, and on its summit, three dilapidated, unattractive old buildings, with nothing whatever to embellish the surroundings—hardly even a blade of grass. The footprints of carnage were everywhere visible; buildings without windows or doors; the remains of earthworks, ramparts with cannon embrasures and gun platforms; rifle pits and a group of abandoned soldier graves in garish unloveliness scarred the hillside, making what had been a comely college lawn, green and refreshing, a desert waste" (O'Steen 1994:14). Drury Dryden, Ohio Light Artillery, was billeted in a university building and related that "we are now in the college, on College Hill, the highest in town. There is one thing nice about it—there is one of the largest libraries in the state in this building, mostly old books. A great many are carried away by the soldiers. I should like some myself" (Dryden 1989:7).

BURNSIDE LEAVES KNOXVILLE A HERO

Burnside had suffered from a lingering intestinal illness for months and had first tendered his resignation because of this problem on September 10, shortly after taking Cumberland Gap from the Confederates. He was refused by Lincoln, who sent a telegram thanking him for his success at the Gap but adding that he could not allow him "to resign until things have settled down in East Tennessee." Although Longstreet still remained in upper East Tennessee, Lincoln accepted Burnside's second request to be relieved from duty in order to recover from his illness. At this time, Burnside had for "transportation up and down the valley . . . five locomotives, 22 cars and about a hundred miles of track—from Loudon to the vicinity of Bulls' Gap" (Fink 1957:87). Perhaps because of his long illness and fatigue, Burnside thought this was sufficient, and as he awaited his furlough, he became uninterested in trying to remove Longstreet from upper East Tennessee. General Sheridan described Burnside as "inactive and apathetic, confining his operations to an aimless expedition whose advance extended only so far as Blaine's crossroads, whence it was soon withdrawn." Sheridan describes the operations in East Tennessee in his memoirs as constituting a "series of blunders, lasting through the entire winter." He attributed this state of affairs largely "to the fact that the command of the troops was so frequently changed" (Sheridan, *Personal Memoirs* Vol. I, XVII, 1888:335–336).

Burnside had regained his vigor when he and Sheridan met in Versailles, France, in September of 1870. Both traveled often through the countryside accompanied by Count Bismarck during the German invasion of France visiting active battlefields and studying German military tactics. (Sheridan, *Personal Memoirs* Vol. II, XIX, 1888)

Burnside left Knoxville on December 12 for Cincinnati. Mrs. Burnside joined him in Cleveland, and they traveled home to Providence, Rhode Island. After a well-deserved rest, the general was ordered to begin recruiting for the 9th Army Corps; and on April 11, he left Providence for Annapolis, where he took command of the 25,000-strong

9th Corps, which would join Grant on his Overland Campaign to capture Richmond (Poore 1886).

Benjamin Perley Poore in his 1882 biography of Burnside described Burnside's military prowess during his time in East Tennessee saying that, "the defense of Knoxville, against the superior forces of Longstreet, was an admirable exhibition of military skill and science. In fertility of resources, in sagacity, in the comprehensiveness and thoroughness of his plans and the vigor of their execution his merits were remarkable" (ibid.).

Burnside not only received the admiration of military leaders and the men who served under him in East Tennessee, but he was also greatly respected by both Union and Confederate residents and local dignitaries for his fair treatment of everyone and his determination to keep them safe by enforcing the laws. Captain B. F. Thompson wrote in his 1882 history of the 112th Regiment, Illinois Volunteer Infantry, that Burnside was "kind, generous and humane, to citizens and soldiers alike; he won the profound respect of all and imparted confidence and courage to all" (Thompson 1885:155). Augustus H. Pettibone, the congressman from Tennessee's First District and himself a former Union officer, spoke at Burnside's graveside service in September 1881. He described with emotion the deep affection East Tennesseans felt for Burnside, and as he placed a sprig of laurel on the old soldier's grave in Providence, Rhode Island, Pettibone said, "Among our mountains hundreds of children have been named for him for he won the heart-love of our people" (Poore 1882:223).

Pettibone and others who loved Burnside probably did not know that the general's name would remain in our vocabulary today for a different reason, although the two syllables forming his name are reversed. Burnside was known for his impressive, thick crop of bushy hair, which grew down in front of his ears, then curved inward along the top of his jaw. An immaculately groomed mustache joined the terminus of each sideburn to create an impression of strength and determination. He kept this style of "sideburns" into his old age after his hair had become snowy white.

GENERAL JOHN G. FOSTER ASSUMES COMMAND

Major General John G. Foster replaced Burnside on December 11. Unfortunately, he was not well liked by either the Union troops or the local populace (Seymour 1963). Foster, who was also unwell, began on December 15 to address the problem of Longstreet's continued presence in the area. He sent Major General John Parke and Brigadier General James Shackelford's cavalry division northeast on the Morristown Road to Rutledge and Bean's Station under the command of Parke. The 9th and 23rd Corps Artillery was moved out of Fort Sanders that same day by mule team along with Roemer's and Buckley's batteries, but the heavy guns in the fort could not be transported over the almost impassable muddy roads (*OR 1890*: pt. 1, 241). The remaining section of Buckley's battery and a guard of convalescents were left to defend Fort Sanders and Lieutenant Benjamin reported for duty as chief of artillery. General Phillip H. Sheridan and his men were called from headquarters in Sevierville to Knoxville after a detachment of Longstreet's rear guard made feints from Blaine's Crossroads against Knoxville. Sheridan was eager to leave Knoxville, but was ultimately left in charge of dealing with Longstreet. Foster had been forced to pass command to Parke as "the hardships of winter had reopened an old wound received in the Mexican War. . . ." Granger assumed authority after Parke, and finally the command was "unloaded" onto a resentful Sheridan (Sheridan 1875:1, 153).

After General Longstreet was informed that Sherman had returned to Chattanooga, he received a wire from Richmond placing him in sole command of his army. It was then that he decided to turn on the Federals who were now nipping at his heels. He ordered General Bushrod Johnson's 2,400-man division to attack the Union infantry and cavalry, who had paused for two days at Bean's Station. The surprised Federals took cover in the town's commercial buildings, including the well-known three-story brick tavern and hotel, which would become an armed fortress. They came under heavy artillery fire from Porter Alexander's batteries, and finally the Union defenders retreated from the town and set up a defensive line three miles west of Bean's Station. Holding back the advancing rebels the next day, the Federals abandoned Rutledge during the night and pulled back to Blaine's Crossroads and Knoxville (Smith 1999:17–19).

Longstreet chose not to send his hungry and ill-clad infantry in pursuit, and on December 19 he moved his army south to establish winter quarters around Russellville and Morristown. This portion of the upper Tennessee Valley had been scarcely touched by the war, and the general found the surrounding countryside a bountiful commissary for his starving troops, much to the discomfort of both Unionist and Confederate residents of the area. Like locusts, the Southern foragers and later the Northerners swept through their fields, ate their stock, and emptied their barns and smokehouses. Men in both armies were encouraged and even compelled to live off the land since they carried little or no "hard cash" to buy food (Robertson 1984). In his memoirs, Longstreet recalled:

> Before Christmas [we] were in our camps along the railroad, near Morristown. Blankets and clothes were very scarce, shoes more so, but all knew how to enjoy the beautiful country in which we found ourselves. . . . Stock and grain were on all farms. . . . The country about the French Broad had hardly been touched by the hands of foragers. Our wagons immediately on entering the fields were loaded to overflowing. Pumpkins were on the ground in places like apples under a tree. Cattle, sheep, and swine, poultry, vegetables, maple sugar, honey, were all abundant for immediate wants of the troops. . . . The enemy were almost as much in want of the beautiful foraging lands as we, but we were in advance of them, and left little for them. . . . For shoes we were obliged to resort to the raw hides of beef cattle as temporary protection from the frozen ground. (Longstreet 1896:445–446)

Augustus Dickert, a member of General Kershaw's brigade, wrote about the success they had in obtaining a little "bite" to eat from the locals: "We foragers had the instinct (or acquired it) and the gifts of a 'knight of the road' of worming out of the good house-wife little dainties, cold meats, and stale bread and if there was one drop of the 'oh be joyful' in the house, these men of peculiar intellect would be sure to get it" (Dickert 1990:329–330). The bounty of this garden of Eden on the French Broad quickly disappeared for the vulnerable farmers who had planted and nurtured it, as well as for the Union and Confederate armies who picked it clean during that winter of 1864–65.

In February 1864, the East Tennessee Relief Association was organized to raise money to feed and clothe the several thousand white and black refugees "who had trudged into Knoxville from East Tennessee farms starving and almost naked." The association raised more than $200,000 to assist the refugees and Knoxville began to administer relief to these victims of the war (Newman 1939:2).

8

THE WINTER OF 1864

Unforeseen events took place in upper East Tennessee in 1864 that had a sobering effect on both armies. First and foremost, the weather was horrendous; it was the coldest winter on record. No one could have known at that time that the cause of their great suffering was the result of what is now known as the Little Ice Age. It was not until 1939 that François E. Matthes named and defined this phase of planetary cooling, which took place mainly in the Northern Hemisphere (Matthes 1939). The generally accepted time period for the Little Ice Age is between 1500 and 1900, but the dates vary according to geographical locations. This change in the climate is believed to have been caused by a reduction in the number of sun spots that warm the earth, volcanic explosions, and changes in ocean circulation and in the orbital cycles of the earth. References to the frigid weather during this period in East Tennessee are ubiquitous in the accounts of the ill-prepared soldiers who suffered through it in the winter of 1863 and early 1864. A special correspondent from Longstreet's army wrote on December 11, 1863:

> To one subject I would call your attention. Thirty-five hundred men are to-day barefooted, without other means to protect them from the inclemency of the season than the rags they may strip from their backs. When you remember that the weather is so cold that water freezes in ten minutes after nightfall—that the icicles which fringe the mill-races are as thick as a man's body, and that the poor soldiers are driven to the extremity of cutting up the reeking, bloody hides of slaughtered beef to form a temporary pair of moccasins, which may

> last only ten or twelve hours of marching at best, you can imagine somewhat of the sufferings to which our brave troops are exposed. They are useless to the service in their present condition, and unless Government or people can afford relief promptly, few among them will ever again be in condition to take their places in the ranks of our country's defenders. (*Richmond Whig* 1864)

On December 23, soldiers in upper East Tennessee found that recent rains had washed bridges away and cut deep gullies into the roads. From the last of December to January 1, 1864, constant rain was accompanied by high blustery winds, and on New Year's Day the temperature dropped to 29 degrees below zero. Water sources were frozen solid. Federal soldiers wrote that railroad ties and huge logs were burned to provide warmth, and notes exist in a diary that a house was even set afire so the men could keep warm. A Federal cavalry picket post on Bays Mountain froze to death. It was reported that four of the dead were lying on the ground and two were standing with their loaded muskets still at their sides (Smith 1999:83–85).

The Southerners fared even worse. Surgeon Robert Myers of the 16th Georgia Volunteer Infantry said that while in camp at Bean's Station, "This morning as I put water on my tooth brush, it froze before I put it to my mouth" (Myers n.d.). Many of their soldiers were barefoot or wore only makeshift shoes of cowhide. Lieutenant Colonel Moxley Sorrel recalled, "It was bitter winter weather, the ground was hard and sharp, and not less than 2,000 of our little army were without shoes" (Sorrel 1905:215). Confederate Brigadier Commander Basil W. Duke described the severity of that winter of 1864 in East Tennessee in his *History of Morgan's Cavalry*, first published in 1867: "There is no word in the English language which adequately expresses how cold it was. Our horses, already tired down and half starved, could scarcely hobble. Those of the enemy where [*sic*] in worse condition, and it is scarcely an exaggeration to say that for ten miles a man could have walked on dead ones. They lay . . . frozen in every conceivable and revolting attitude, as death had overtaken them in their agony" (Duke 1960:564–565). Byron Cutcheon would designate the East Tennessee campaign as the "most trying period of our entire service." In his 1904 book he identified it as "the 'Valley Forge' of the Tennessee campaign" (Cutcheon 1904:91).

The solidly frozen French Broad River prevented any shipment of critical subsistence supplies that might be available from upper East Tennessee to the Union army in their Knoxville base. Porter Alexander's understated description of that time of despair was this: "It was a campaign of much hardship" (Alexander 1989). Both sides were running low on food. Living off the land, roving Confederate foraging parties had already laid bare large areas of the countryside, and in his excellent book *Campaign to Nowhere,* David C. Smith wrote, "Even the most loyal Union families, many with men serving under the same flag, were not spared, for the urgency of the moment left no room to give loyalty its proper consideration. So serious was the plundering and robbing of these helpless people that on January 4, [Union] General Sturgis issued special orders to his field commanders that any soldier found one mile from camp without a pass in writing, would be arrested" (Smith 1999:87).

Confederate troops "marched out of one valley and into another. They left behind an area almost destitute, where more than 50,000 men and their animals had ravaged field and storehouses in their constant search for food . . ." (Dykeman 1955:116).

But Longstreet refused to vacate upper East Tennessee in spite of the terrible weather, diminishing food supply, and his embarrassing defeat at Knoxville. Oliver Temple wrote that the Union failure to drive Longstreet out of the area was the "cause of the greatest calamity that ever befell the people of East Tennessee. It brought upon them actual famine." Tens of thousands of people fled to Knoxville "to be fed and clothed by the Union army, the charity of the locals and the generous people in the north" (Temple 1889:514).

GENERAL GRANT VISITS KNOXVILLE

Union commanders in Knoxville had multiple concerns. Grant wanted the Confederates out of Tennessee, then Grant could choose when and where to begin his spring campaign rather than the enemy choosing for him (Catton 1968). Grant decided to pay a visit to Knoxville and steamed up the river from Chattanooga for an inspection tour and to assess the feasibility of transporting supplies to Knoxville over existing roads from Lexington. He set out in the midst of some of the coldest days of the winter, arriving in Knoxville on January 1, 1864. He visited attorney Oliver P. Temple and his wife, Scotia, at their home while in Knoxville. Temple would later note that Grant, who was widely known for his love of cigars and drink, neither smoked nor drank that evening (Temple 1899:517).

Reverend Humes would later write that "Grant's reputation for unaffected sincerity of manners was confirmed to those who formed his acquaintance" (Humes 1888). Temple met again with the general the next day at the Federal headquarters located in the Park House on Crooked Street to discuss the condition of the roads though the Gap. Temple recorded that at this meeting Grant's aides confided to him that a plan was being considered for a possible spring campaign up the French Broad Valley into North Carolina to divide the lower from the upper Confederacy (Temple 1899:518). In his *Memoirs,* however, Grant barely mentioned his Knoxville visit and said nothing about considering a possible spring campaign into the Carolinas (Grant 1886). He had probably at that time already made up his mind to capture Atlanta, the industrial center of the deep South.

After arranging to have railroad connections between Chattanooga and Knoxville secured and maintained, General Grant left Knoxville on January 5 in freezing weather for Kentucky via Cumberland Gap. He had not specifically ordered General Foster to immediately confront Longstreet's army and force him out of the state. Grant continued to evaluate the condition of the roads as he returned to his headquarters in Nashville via Cumberland Gap and Lexington. One of Grant's biographers described the arduous trip: "The journey made in mid-winter was full of hardship and danger. The mountains were covered with ice and snow and the thermometer was ten degrees below zero. In many places it was impossible to ride, and Grant and his party were compelled to dismount and lead their horses. The general in advance had many falls" (Boyd 1885:207).

Because of the lack of supplies and the dangerous weather, it is likely that Foster was greatly relieved that Grant left Knoxville without ordering him to move aggressively on Longstreet. Foster had been wary of forcing his troops to fight a defensive battle on Longstreet's choice of ground, as he knew his adversary was at his best as a field tactician in those situations. He favored the adage "let sleeping dogs lie," choosing to believe the Confederates in upper East Tennessee did not present a serious threat to Knoxville.

While General Longstreet had been soundly whipped in his attempt to capture Knoxville on November 29, the Army of the Ohio continued to have great respect for his abilities and the élan of his vaunted 1st Corps. General Grant did not share Foster's lackadaisical attitude about the future plans of Robert E. Lee's "Old War Horse" for East Tennessee. On January 8, he telegraphed his commander, Major General Henry Halleck, in Washington: "Owing to the want of clothing, particularly shoes, in Foster's command, it is impossible to move more than 60 per cent of his men until they are supplied. Clothing is now on the way, and it is hoped will be in Knoxville within one week from this time. I have directed Foster then to attack and drive Longstreet at least beyond Bull's Gap and Red Bridge. In the mean time I have directed the Ninth and Twenty-third Corps to be pushed on to Mossy Creek, the Fourth Corps to Strawberry Plains, and the cavalry to Dandridge, to scout and forage south of the French Broad and threaten Longstreet's flank" (*OR* 1891:pt. 2, 43).

THE SUFFERING IN KNOXVILLE

It was bitterly cold and miserable in Knoxville that January of 1864. There were frequent deep snows, and streets were often covered with mud five inches thick. Smallpox was spreading. Ellen House wrote that several "of the wealthiest people in Knoxville were trying to sell their parlor furniture" (Sutherland 1996:80). An order had come out on January 6 "forbidding any one from buying anything except those that take the oath as Loyal [*sic*] citizens, not even a dose of medicine or a spool of thread" (ibid:82). Jails were crowded with Confederate prisoners, and Dr. Piggott said those who were sick recovered "from force of nature" as he was "unable to get . . . medicine or liquor for them" (Sutherland 1996:81–91).

Friday, January 15, found General Foster recovering in Knoxville from a wound he received in the Mexican War, which had reopened after his horse fell on him. Foster had been relieved of his field command, which was placed in the hands of General John Parke, Burnside's chief of staff during the Knoxville siege and General Samuel Sturgis, chief of cavalry of the Army of the Ohio.

Ellen House remained steadfastly undeterred in her efforts to do everything she could to help Confederate prisoners. She washed and mended their clothes, baked biscuits and bread, cut up carpets for blankets, and went begging down the main streets for food and clothes. On January 15, she was livid when she recorded on that day that her "Father went and took the oath" of loyalty to the United States. She added that the worst of it was that he had taken with him Reverend Humes, who had forced them to move a few days earlier from their rental home, to speak in his behalf (Sutherland 1996:89).

Ellen continued to endanger herself and her family by publicly and privately declaring her hatred of the Union occupiers. Her journal is filled with comments about the despicable troops that occupied Knoxville. She honestly believed that "she could kill a Yankee and not a muscle quiver." She did not stop hoping that Longstreet would "whip" Grant and take Knoxville (ibid.:). Her hopes were not totally unfounded, as things were still not "settled" in East Tennessee.

LONGSTREET CONTINUES TO THREATEN KNOXVILLE

In December, Longstreet still posed a threat to Knoxville, and the Union cavalry under the command of General Samuel Sturgis moved to the east and met scattered contingents of Southern horse soldiers. A sharp engagement was fought at Mossy Creek (now Jefferson City) on December 29; when the temperature plunged below zero on January 1, 1864, the dead and wounded from this battle froze solidly to the ground (Smith 1999:83).

Reverend W. H. Hornell, although a noncombatant in the 1st Kentucky Volunteers, could usually be found at the front "attending to the wounded and seeing the fighting well done." Long after the battle of Mossy Creek, Hornell recalled that "during the ever-memorable cold new year of 1864 he had once slept on the front pew of a Mossy Creek church as that building "resounded to the groans of dying heroes." He wrote that his men had "froze to the ground in their blood ere I could reach them from the farther end of the line; and after we had driven them back in defeat, the dead of both sides were gathered for burial, and they were as stiff as blocks of ice" (ibid.).

The eastward push by the Union army after the first of the year was based as much on the need to secure forage along the French Broad River as it was to threaten Longstreet's left flank and capture his base at Russellville. After weather conditions improved, Sturgis's cavalry, with infantry following close behind, moved out of Mossy Creek; after encountering little resistance, they occupied Dandridge on January 14. Realizing his left flank was now vulnerable, Longstreet sent his army to recapture Dandridge, and two days later his troops pounced on the Federals encamped there. Considering the force of the Confederate attack, Parke believed that the 1st Corps had been reinforced by elements of General George Pickett's Division from Virginia. While this was simply an idle camp rumor, Parke decided it was unwise to face Longstreet head-on and pulled his army all the way back to their supply depot at Strawberry Plains. On January 19, Parke's troops abandoned their depot at the "Plains" and sought safety in heavily fortified Knoxville (Smith 1999).

By this time, General Grant had become totally disgusted with General Foster's performance as commander of the Army of the Ohio and replaced him on February 9 with a 33-year-old West Point graduate, Major General John M. Schofield. Three days earlier, Grant had telegraphed General Thomas that two divisions were with Longstreet and that he was reinforced by troops from the east, indicating that the enemy intended to secure East Tennessee if possible. While rumors of

Longstreet's reinforcement were unfounded, General Grant was now seriously considering his antagonist to be a very real threat. Longstreet continued to make preparations for another strike at Knoxville, moving his army headquarters to New Market the next day. Three days later, a division of Confederate infantry crossed the river at New Market on a pontoon bridge, and some of these troops traveled within six miles of Knoxville (ibid.). Reports were received that details of Union troops were at work on forts within the city in preparation for an attack, and the troops were justifiably concerned that Longstreet planned to strike soon. However, Longstreet was quite aware that another attack on Knoxville would be futile without reinforcements. Receiving no support from Richmond, Longstreet abandoned his base at Strawberry Plains and moved back up the valley to Mossy Creek on February 22 (ibid.).

On March 1, General Schofield had taken his army as far as Morristown; and two days later, Ellen House noted that he was said to be on the Knoxville side of Morristown. On March 11, she wrote that Union pickets had been driven in the night before. Ever hopeful that her "saints" were still contemplating an attack on Knoxville, Ellen continued her reckless and dangerous condemnation of the Yankees and was forewarned by a Union officer that her conversations and actions had led officials to believe that she was "a very violent rebel, one who would sell her soul and body for the benefit of the Confederates." The officer advised Ellen that she might be sent south if she did not become more "prudent" (Sutherland 1996:113).

Ellen would have been elated had she known about the plan Longstreet expected to present to President Davis and General Lee in Richmond. Longstreet wanted to lure Union troops away from the Federal offensive planned for northern Georgia by General Sherman. He traveled from East Tennessee to the Confederate capital, where he presented an ambitious proposal to march back through East Tennessee, retake Knoxville, and invade Middle Tennessee, thereby forcing the armies of Grant and Sherman to Kentucky, where Confederate sympathies were still strong. His strategy was scrapped due to a lack of supplies and manpower, shortages that were now seriously affecting the Southern armies. On April 7, 1864, Longstreet's command was ordered back to join Lee's Army of Northern Virginia in anticipation of Grant's drive south to move on Richmond with the Army of the Potomac (Longstreet 1896:469).

On Friday, April 8, Ellen House, too, was commanded to leave Tennessee as she had accumulated "a great many charges." Ellen was certain that Parson Brownlow, who had labeled her a "she devil," was responsible for this final decision of Union officers. His articles in the *Whig* probably had some effect on Ellen's departure as he often called for the removal of "hateful and disgusting rebel women—traitors to the government . . . brazen as the Devil, with little sense and less prudence." Brownlow was firmly convinced that these she-devils "should be sent south and made to stay there throughout the war . . . without any regard to their positions or associations" (*Knoxville Whig* 1864d). She was ordered South and was to leave Knoxville on Monday with Dr. Piggott and Dr. A. C. North from the Papermill Hospital. She was gravely concerned that she might forget to take all the things she would need for a lengthy stay in Georgia with friends but was certain that she would *not* forget her derringer. After leaving on April 11, she finally arrived in Eatonton, Georgia, on September 1. Ellen would return to Knoxville on June 1, 1865 (Sutherland 1996:127–28, 169).

On April 12, Major General Schofield issued Special Order No. 103: the 3rd Brigade was to hold the railroad bridge at Loudon and to "protect the railroad between that point and the Hiwassee as far as practicable, and hold the railroad bridge and supply depot at the Hiwassee as long as may be necessary." Schofield was aided by Brigadier General Jacob Ammen, commander of the 4th Division, who was ordered to spend as much time as possible training the troops and to provide additional protection for four critical points in East Tennessee: Knoxville, Cumberland, Loudon, and Hiwassee. He ordered Brigadier General Davis Tillson, who had been placed in charge of completing the fortifications in Knoxville in December 1863, to hold Knoxville "at all hazards and against any force, however large," while instructing the regiment in Kingston to remain in place "for protection of quartermaster's property and for other such duty as may be required" (*OR* 1891:pt. 3, 339). On May 2, 1864, a Federal scout reported that "all of

Longstreet's forces have gone to Richmond except Buckner's division, four brigades of infantry and one of cavalry, the infantry at Saltville, Virginia, and the cavalry at Pound Gap. All transportation, forage, etc. has been sent out of Tennessee. Rebels claim Buckner has 6,000 men" (*OR* 1892:pt. 2, 7).

Many loyal East Tennesseans felt that the exit of General Longstreet and his 1st Corps from their region marked the end of the Confederate threat to the embattled Army of the Ohio and their Unionist supporters, but Richmond was not about to give up East Tennessee completely. While the ranks of Confederate soldiers in upper East Tennessee were depleted and commanded by less competent leaders, parts of the region still remained under Southern control, and throughout the summer of 1864, both blue- and gray-clad cavalry patrols continued to cross sabers in the valley.

JOHN HUNT MORGAN RETURNS

On June 24, 1864, one of the largest squads of Confederate cavalry under commander General John Hunt Morgan moved through Big Creek Gap from Kentucky into Anderson County and ventured as far south as Knox County. General Morgan wired General Lee in Petersburg, Virginia, on July 11 to report that there was only "a small force at Knoxville"; and the next day General J. L. Sandford sent a message to Colonel J. B. Palmer, District of Western North Carolina, Ashville, instructing him to move on to Knoxville and "make a demonstration toward the position of the enemy in order to attract his attention from other movements that will be on foot at the same time" (ibid.:701, 708). The Confederates continued to let the Federals know that they were still close at hand, and the Federals continued to strengthen their fortifications in anticipation of a sudden strike.

Finally, in August 1864, Governor Andrew Johnson heeded the cries of loyal East Tennessee citizens for aid and ordered Union cavalry commander General Alvan C. Gillem at the Strawberry Plains base to push his troops up the valley and clear the Southerners out of that part of the state once and for all. The Confederate army, now under the command of General John Vaughn, pulled back from Mossy Creek, and General Gillem moved forward to a base at Bull's Gap (Smith 1999).

The Confederates stubbornly continued the fight in upper East Tennessee, and the appearance of the unpredictable and destructive John Hunt Morgan at Jonesboro was especially unwelcome news to nervous Union commanders and soldiers occupying Knoxville. Morgan, who had escaped from an Ohio prison earlier, was given command of the Trans-Allegheny Department on August 22, which included East Tennessee and southwest Virginia. At the time he was being quietly investigated for criminal activities in Kentucky. Morgan immediately began to plan a raid, and his arrival in Jonesboro from Abington, Virginia, on August 31 with additional troops greatly cheered Vaughn's weary men. They readied themselves to fight with what was left of "Morgan's Raiders" and their infamous leader, the "Thunderbolt of the Confederacy." Morgan's plan was to quickly attack Gillem's army and drive the enemy from Bull's Gap, move on to Rogersville, force Union troops there to surrender, and perhaps move as far down the valley as Knoxville. Morgan's men, anxious for battle, started for Greeneville with about 1,600 poorly equipped troops, which included portions of General John C. Vaughn's Brigade (Ramage 1986).

Morgan was not destined to carry out his plan. Reaching Greeneville on September 3 at 4:00 p.m., he decided to encamp there and attack Bull's Gap the next day. Morgan established his headquarters at the home of his friend Katharine Williams, the mother of Captain William Williams, a staff member. (This impressive house still stands in Greeneville and is open to the public.) Morgan stationed pickets on all roads leading into Greeneville. It is believed that Mrs. Williams's daughter left for Bulls Gap to alert Gillem after hearing rumors of Morgan's approach. Basil W. Duke, Morgan's brother-in-law and second in command, recounted in *A History of Morgan's Cavalry* that at daylight on September 4, 400 Union cavalry "dashed into Greeneville and were followed in a short time by Gillem's whole force." Morgan left the Williams house with a staff member, Major C. W. Gassett, who later told Duke that they had found every street guarded and "took refuge in the open cellar of a house." Discovered by a Union patriot, Gassett escaped, and Morgan returned to the Williams house, where he was "killed in the garden." Duke admitted that it was "not known whether he surrendered or was offering his resistance" (Duke 1960:539). The much-admired "Thunderbolt of the Confederacy" was dead at age 39.

Confederate sympathizers in Knoxville began to accuse the Federals of brutally murdering Morgan in cold blood after he had surrendered, and Parson Brownlow was eager to prove the accusations were not true. He made inquiries to the U.S. Headquarters at Bull's Gap, and Lieutenant O. C. French, a member of Gillem's staff, responded on September 9 by sending Brownlow the September 5 testimony of Captain J. T. Rogers, who was with Morgan at the time he was shot. Rogers testified that he was with Morgan in the Williams garden, hidden in some bushes. He said that a soldier in a brown jacket rode up to the garden, and as he and Morgan thought he was a Confederate soldier, they left the bushes and started towards the garden fence.

They stepped through the fence, and as the unknown soldier demanded their surrender, Captain Wilcox and other Federal soldiers rode up. Duke said he hastened toward Wilcox "looking back in the direction of Gen. MORGAN. I saw him throwing up his hands, exclaiming, 'O God!' I saw nothing more of him until he was brought to the street dead. I am satisfied that JOHNSON and myself were fired on after we surrendered, but by men so far from us that it must have been impossible to know that we were prisoners. I asked Capt. WILCOX to leave a soldier with me after I had surrendered for from such a distance that I am satisfied the men did it innocently. I, however, do not condemn them for firing on me after I surrendered under the circumstances. If General MORGAN surrendered before being shot I do not know" (*Knoxville Whig* 1864e).

A grief-stricken Basil Duke recounted that Union soldiers "broke down the paling around the garden, dragged him [Morgan] through, and while he was tossing his arms in his dying agonies, threw him across a mule, and paraded his body about the town." Rogers was given permission from Gillem to help wash and dress Morgan's body. Duke said that Morgan had been "taken from the hands that defiled it, by General Gillem . . . and had been sent to our lines under flag of truce" (Duke 1960: 539–540).

Brownlow was vindicated; Union troops had not deliberately shot General Morgan in violation of the rules of war. He informed his readers about what he had found, publishing in the October 2, 1864, edition of the *Whig and Rebel Ventilator* all the correspondence he had received from the U.S. Headquarters at Bull's Gap. Then he attempted to destroy the heroic Southern image of Morgan by ending with these caustic remarks: "A more infamous coward never made a noise in this rebellion. All the clothes MORHAN [*sic*] had on—vest, pants and boots—were uniform, and had either been stolen in Kentucky, or taken from a Federal prisoner after he was captured and murdered. Our Federal boys did a good job when they killed MORHAN, and they are entitled to the lasting gratitude of every remaining horse and mule in Kentucky and Tennessee" (*Knoxville Whig* 1864e). Confederate sympathizers continued to hail him long after the war as a "Lost Cause" hero, along with other southern cavalry officers such as Nathan Bedford Forrest, John S. Mosby, and Jeb Stuart (Thomas 2014).

Had Brownlow lived to be 107 and was still of good mind, he surely would have become apoplectic upon hearing that the Kentucky United Daughters of the Confederacy erected a bronze statue of General Morgan on horseback on the lawn of the Lexington courthouse in October 1911 and that public funds helped pay for it. One hundred and seven years later, in October 2017, Lexington government leaders had the statue of the mounted Morgan, the Southern "American Robin Hood," removed from its granite base. His statue left the courthouse lawn in the back of a truck accompanied by a bronze, treasonous Confederate companion, his successor in East Tennessee, General John C. Breckinridge (Costello and Sayers 2017). Only time will tell whether they see the light of day again.

LONGSTREET LEAVES FOR VIRGINIA

Despite Gillem's victory at Greeneville and the death of General Morgan, the macabre military dance of advance and retreat continued to play out in the valley. Gillem remained at his forward position at Bull's

Gap and repaired the railroad to his supply base at Strawberry Plains. The next move of Morgan's remaining brigade of "two hundred and seventy-three effective men" in this cat-and-mouse game was to send a raiding party behind Union lines to cut Gillem's supply line by destroying the railroad bridge at Mossy Creek on October 20. General Gillem then moved down to New Market to be closer to his supply base. After resupplying his army there, the general moved his troops back up to Morristown, where a sharp battle ensued. It ended with a Confederate retreat to Russellville (Smith 1999:195–196).

On September 27 General John C. Breckinridge assumed command of the Department of East Tennessee and Southwest Virginia after Morgan's death, and by the first week in November, 2,000 reinforcements were sent from North Carolina to strengthen General Vaughn's army in order to take Bull's Gap (Heck 1976). Breckinridge led the raid that drove General Gillem from the Gap under the cover of darkness in an attempt to reach Strawberry Plains. The pursuing Confederates were hot on his heels, caught up with the Federals on November 14, and gave them a good thrashing (ibid.). Although Vaughn's army never got by the Union base at the "Plains," Knoxville got a final scare when it was reported that squads of Rebel cavalry were passing around this place. Gillem's army quickly recovered, and in a few weeks it became part of a 6,000-man force that now moved up the Holston Valley via Bean's Station and finally pushed Vaughn's force back into Virginia (Smith 1999). The Union high command could finally report that "East Tennessee was now comparatively free from danger of Confederate invasion or raids" (Thompson 1885:198).

9

AT WORK ALL THE TIME ON THE FORT

SECURING KNOXVILLE FOR THE UNION

Although by the end of 1864 virtually all of East Tennessee was under the control of the Federal army, the region continued to be plagued by Confederate cavalry raids in 1865. Guerrillas, with their hit-and-run tactics, were a particular nuisance, as these marauders kept attacking the supply line of the East Tennessee and Virginia Railroad through the region. It became a major problem to keep the Federal garrisons throughout upper East Tennessee supplied. Only 20 miles of this railroad had been repaired east of Knoxville by late March, and on the 24th of that month it was reported that 300 Confederates in a scouting party were going to attack Morristown (*OR* 1897:pt. 1, 23).

On March 11, 1865, about one month before the war would end, Major General George Thomas directed Major General David Stanley, commander of the 4th Army Corps of the Army of the Cumberland, to move three divisions (about 45,000 soldiers) through Huntsville, Alabama, to Knoxville by rail to protect the crews working to restore the East Tennessee and Virginia track and trestles. Stanley was also ordered to block the mountain passes in order to prevent a possible retreat of Lee's army in Virginia south into the mountains.

Union army contingents stationed in Knoxville in early 1865 included the 1st Colored Artillery Regiment, the 10th Michigan Cavalry, and the 1st and 2nd Tennessee Infantry regiments. Companies A and B of the 2nd Ohio Heavy Artillery were listed on duty at Fort Sanders until August 1865. To emphasize the importance of Knoxville as a critical base that would ensure continued Union occupation of the region, on March 11, 1865, General Thomas gave this order: "A depot will be established at Knoxville for accommodation of the whole of East Tennessee" (ibid.:21). Uncertainty about the future stability of the region during 1864 would directly affect military decisions made in regard to the town until the war ended. Work immediately began to secure Knoxville, the headquarters of the Army of the Ohio and a central supply depot. Determined efforts to transform a vulnerable Fort Sanders into a larger and more formidable defensive deterrent had begun soon after the November 1863 battle and continued for another year and a half.

Since Knoxville was a strategic point for military forays into Confederate-held upper East Tennessee during much of 1864, the town was teeming with Union soldiers arriving by rail from Chattanooga. But it was the local garrison, not the transient soldiers, that furnished the manpower for the initial repair after the battle and the continuing defensive additions to Fort Sanders. The garrison appears to have largely consisted of units from Sherman's 4th Corps and the 9th and 23rd Corps of the Army of the Ohio (ibid.). Joseph L. Rogers of Company D, 11th New Hampshire Infantry of the Army of the Ohio, was obviously referring to the continuing work on Fort Sanders when he wrote his wife from Knoxville on January 27, 1864, that "we are having a very good time here although we have no time of our own being at work all the time at the Fort" (Rogers, letter 1864). Private Drury F. Dryden of the 19th Independent Battery, Ohio Light Artillery, wrote to his sweetheart and future wife, Gettie Goss, that he had been "in a fort by itself . . . and had been "building quarters, building forts, etc." (Dryden, letter 1989).

The best description of the work on the fortifications by Union soldiers stationed in Knoxville in the months following the battle can be found in the diary of Private Michael Houck of the 19th Ohio Battery, 23rd Army Corps. Houck's diary was written between January 1 and December 31, 1864, and although his daily observations are brief, from the beginning of the year to the middle of March, while he was permanently stationed in Knoxville, he often focused on his work on the fortifications in town. While not identifying Fort Sanders by name (only Fort Negley and College Hill were identified), Houck's description of his daily military routine clearly reflects how the troops were used to repair and expand Fort Sanders. There seems to be a set pattern for his work schedule: three to four days of fort construction, followed by one to two days of guard duty (Houck, diary 1864).

The number of days recorded when the earthworks were repaired and expanded by Houck were as follows: 7 in January and 12 in February, but only 6 in March, as on the 15th of that month he was sent to what was called "the front" in upper East Tennessee. His diary does not indicate the frantic work pace that occurred before the battle took place. Private Houck wrote that he had considerable free time. On January 8, he recounted that "our Boys went rabit [*sic*] hunting," and the next day he wrote, "Had a good dinner of rabits [*sic*]. No mention of starvation rations" (ibid.). Sergeant Major Alvin Woolson noted that "there were 2000 men working on the fort and stockade, so it did not require much time to erect it" (Miller 1914:86–87).

An unusual and creative defensive measure was implemented at this time to enhance the fort walls, a process Reverend Thomas Humes described in his book *The Loyal Mountaineers of Tennessee*. Humes said the soldiers fastened "locomotives and driving wheels . . . to the defenses with rope, by cutting which could be sent rapidly downhill to repel an assault" (Humes 1888:280). The locomotives and wheels would have been found in the ruins of the roundhouse, which was burned before the battle on November 29. While it is unlikely that these heavy objects could have been launched down the slope of the parapet, they could have been launched from the edge of the steep north and south slopes of the hill.

On February 9, 1864, General John Schofield assumed command of the Army of the Ohio, replacing General Foster. Will Brearley recalled that during this time there were numerous rumors circulating among the inhabitants. Frightened residents continually reported their concerns to Union occupiers. On one day citizens would hear that Longstreet was on his way to Virginia to join Lee. Another day might be met with reports that Ewell's Corps had joined with Longstreet and the siege would soon be renewed (Brearley 1871).

A report on the defenses of Knoxville in March 1864 listed 123 officers, 3,507 enlisted men, and 10 field artillery (*OR* 1891:pt. 3, 209). However, the roster of the Knoxville garrison was to be diminished in April and May as General William T. Sherman, in preparation for his Atlanta Campaign on May 4, 1864, combined three armies: the Army of the Tennessee, commanded by General James McPherson; the Army of the Cumberland, with General George H. Thomas as commander; and the Army of the Ohio, under the command of General John M. Schofield. On April 10, General Sherman wired Grant that at the appropriate signal, Schofield should leave a "select garrison" of the 23rd Corps in Knoxville and rendezvous with the rest of the army, which was assembling in northern Georgia to prepare for the march on Atlanta (ibid:331). In the same month, the 9th Army Corps, once again under the leadership of Burnside, was in Annapolis, Maryland, to join Grant who was now in overall command of the Army of the Potomac and planning his epic drive on Richmond (ibid:749).

While battle-ready troops were leaving Knoxville, their place was being taken by convalescing soldiers brought north by train from Chattanooga, where the hospitals were overcrowded with wounded soldiers from Sherman's Atlanta Campaign (Billings 1870). The *Mailbag* reported that these soldiers were transferred to the Holston Hospital on the south side of the river (*Army Mailbag* 1864). It appears that the veteran ranks of the Army of the Ohio had thinned considerably in Knoxville by the beginning of the summer of 1864.

POE, BABCOCK, AND THE CONTINUING WORK ON THE FORT

While the enlisted men who labored at Fort Sanders from late 1863 to early 1864 remain anonymous for the most part, two engineering officers often cited for their excellent work, Captain Orlando Poe and Colonel Orville Babcock, were in charge of the work on Fort Sanders during this period. Captain Poe was introduced earlier in this study as General Burnside's chief engineer in Knoxville, and is often credited with the design and construction of Fort Sanders. However, Poe neither sited, began the construction of, nor oversaw the completion of Fort Sanders. But he did design the overall plan of defense for the town and chose the western fortification as the major defensive earthwork.

Confederate General Danville Leadbetter chose the site on White's Hill, determined the layout of the fortification there, and oversaw initial construction of the work before abandoning Knoxville as Burnside approached the town in August 1863. Before the chief Confederate engineer fled, the partially built fort apparently resembled the structure defended by the Federals on November 29 of that year. In his 1889 visit to Knoxville, Poe said that "his original instructions . . . were to erect three forts that could be occupied by 600 men and used as a defense against cavalry attacks" (*Knoxville Daily Journal* 1889). In his narrative published the year before this visit, he wrote that when he entered Knoxville in early September 1863, Fort Sanders was "so far advanced toward completion that . . . [its] use without modification was compulsory" (Poe 1888:735). His military companions, however, did not share his opinion about the defensive preparedness of the fort. While there is no doubt that Poe was in overall command of strengthening the Knoxville fortifications in preparation for a Confederate attack, Lieutenant Samuel Benjamin was in charge of the needed improvements. Benjamin wrote in his official report: "Work went on night and day under my sole direction. The Engineer officers of the Corps being occupied with other points of the line, no assistance or advice was asked or received except I altered a portion of the rifle pits so as to contract the line and not be forced to fire over our own men." General Burnside verified Benjamin's involvement in the battle when he reported that "Lt. S. N. Benjamin, who *commanded* Fort Sanders [italics added], situated on the northwest angle of the line, was particularly conspicuous for his efforts to strengthen his position" (*OR* 1890:pt. 1, 276).

It is surprising but understandable that Captain Poe left Knoxville soon after the battle, arriving home before Christmas for a "well-deserved leave and the warmth of family and friends back in [Navarre] Ohio." In January 1864, it was there, while enjoying time with his first-born son, that Poe wrote his official report on the Battle for Knoxville for his superiors (Taylor 2009).

The report Poe wrote for War Department officials before leaving home again in early 1864 would be incorporated into the multivolume set eventually titled *The War of the Rebellion: A Compilation of the Official Records of the Union and Confederate Armies*. Primary source information such as Poe's began to be collected in the War Department in 1864. In 1866, a joint session of Congress passed a resolution ordering that such letters, military orders, maps, diagrams, correspondence, and so on, both Union and Confederate, be compiled and published under the auspices of the War Department, and between 1881 and 1901, the *Official Records* (*OR*) were published, containing 128 books in 70 volumes (Heidler and Heidler 2000b).

Poe soon returned to the South, but this time to Nashville, as he had been assigned to the headquarters of the Military Division of the Mississippi. He traveled to Knoxville during an inspection tour of East Tennessee fortifications in March and posed with Orville Babcock for a photograph taken by his friend George N. Barnard, who had been appointed the official photographer for the head of engineering of the Division of the Mississippi. Babcock and Poe posed in front of the northwest bastion (see figure 25). Barnard's official photographs while in Knoxville were transmitted to the War Department in Washington, along with Poe's report on April 11, 1864 (*OR* 1890:pt. 1, 315).

Later writing about that Knoxville visit, Poe noted that the works were strengthened and fortified but was troubled that more care than necessary was expended in the west end while the eastern front had been neglected (Poe 1888). His comments reinforce the probability that continued construction on the open east end of the fort had become a priority of the new commander, who considered the present threat from the Confederate army to be coming from the east instead of the west. This was Poe's last visit during the war to the place where his reputation as the hero of the Battle of Fort Sanders originated. In late April, he was appointed Sherman's chief engineer and joined his campaign to capture Atlanta.

When Poe left his command in Knoxville in early December, he was replaced by his assistant chief engineer, Lieutenant Colonel Orville Babcock, who continued to work on the repair and enlargement of Fort

Sanders. Poe had praised Babcock in his official report, writing, "Always ready with the most practical advice, he cheerfully gave it and it never passed unheeded" (*OR* 1890:pt. 1, 321). By March, when a photograph of the northwest bastion was taken (see figure 27b), this battlement had been repaired, suggesting that in spite of the last three months of daunting weather, work on the fort had proceeded with great speed.

Colonel Babcock had also received his engineering training at West Point, and after graduation he was stationed with the Army of the Potomac until February 6, 1863, when he was named the assistant inspector general and chief engineer of the 9th Corps (McCullum 1899). During the Knoxville Campaign, he directed the construction of the crucial bridge across the (Little) Tennessee River that allowed Union troops to move quickly during Longstreet's advance up the Tennessee Valley. With Captain Poe, he constructed the vital pontoon bridge across the Holston (Tennessee) River at Knoxville, linking the town with the south side of the river where the Federals were constructing defensive earthen fortifications. During the siege , he and Poe had a 1,000-foot, handmade iron cable stretched across the river to prevent Confederates from floating a large raft downstream to destroy the pontoon bridge. A 1,500-foot log-and-chain boom was later constructed and placed farther up the river (Seymour 1963). On January 23, 1864, Major General John Foster, commandant of the Army of the Ohio in Knoxville, issued General Orders No. 12, stating that "Lt. Col. O. E. Babcock is hereby announced as acting chief engineer [of the Department of the Ohio]. He will have entire charge of all matters relating to positions, defenses, bridges, &c." However, no records have been discovered to indicate that Babcock was still directly involved with the continuing construction of Fort Sanders between January and March 1864 (*OR* 1891:, pt. 2, 191).

TILLSON TAKES COMMAND

Babcock would leave Knoxville on March 29, 1864, after being named an aide-de-camp to General Ulysses Grant. He joined Grant and the Army of the Potomac in the Overland Campaign which began during the first week of May and culminated in the capture of Richmond the

Fig. 36. Gen. Davis Tillson. From Francis Trevelyan Miller, *The Photographic History of the Civil War in Ten Volumes.*

following year (McCullum 1899). However, from the study of construction at Fort Sanders, by early 1864 Colonel Babcock apparently was under the command of Brigadier General Davis Tillson, appointed by Foster on December 31, 1863, to oversee the defenses of Knoxville. Foster announced that General Tillson was "assigned to the command of the defenses of Knoxville, Loudon, and Kingston, Tenn., and will supervise the erection of the fortifications at those places. His headquarters will be at Knoxville" (*OR* 1898:pt. 1, 509).

Thirty-three-year-old Tillson, a native of Maine (1830–1895), was well-qualified for this assignment, as not only had he been in charge of the defenses of Cincinnati and the works protecting the Louisville and Nashville Railroad, but he had also raised two regiments of artillery while there and had been appointed the chief of artillery for fortifications for the Army of the Ohio (Eicher and Eicher 2001). He recruited, trained, and became captain of the Volunteer Light Artillery, 2nd Maine Battery. Tillson and his men acquitted themselves well at the battles of Cedar Mountain and 2nd Bull Run; and in March 1863, he was commissioned as a brigadier general (Dodge 2000).

General Tillson suffered an injury to his leg shortly after entering West Point in 1849. In the spring of 1850 doctors decided the infected leg needed to be amputated. Tillson returned to West Pont in April on crutches, but found it difficult to perform the necessary duties, and by September of 1851 he had resigned and returned home to Rockland, Maine. He worked as a civil engineer, was elected to the state legislature, and shortly thereafter became Maine's Attorney General. Tillson was appointed by President Lincoln as a customs inspector, but he resigned from this post to organize the 2nd Maine Battery. He had been fitted with a cork prosthesis in 1852 and was concerned about being rejected from service. He was immediately accepted at the muster station as the officer in charge was a West Point classmate. It is reported that the officer said to Tillson; "I know you, and I would have passed you if you had lost both arms and legs." Tillson became captain of the 2nd Maine Artillery. He swiftly rose through the ranks and by the war's end, he was a brevet major general (Jastrztembski 2018; accessed online 7/17/2018, https://emergingcivilwar.com/2018/06/12/general-davis-tillson).

Tillson arrived in Knoxville in January 1864 and quickly undertook the tasks that had been assigned to him by his commandant General John Foster. These included working to restore the damage to the fort that had occurred during the battle and also the enormous responsibility of overseeing the construction of two additional bastions, and a stockade to the east end of the fort, and a defensive stockade that extended along the western-most trench from the southeast bastion to the river. General Foster added to Tillson's duties on January 6, 1864, when he issued General Order No. 6 which read: "All able-bodied colored men between the ages of eighteen and forty-five within our lines, except those employed in the several staff departments, officer's servants, and those servants of loyal citizens who prefer remaining with their masters, will be sent forthwith to Knoxville, Loudon, or Kingston, Tenn., to be enrolled, under the direction of Brig. Gen. Davis Tillson, chief of artillery, to be composed of troops of African descent. The commanding officers of divisions and posts are charged with the execution of this order" (*OR*, 1900:series 3, vol. 4, 11).

After arriving in Knoxville, General Tillson would soon meet Reverend Humes and Ellen House's father. Humes rented Tillson the House family residence but failed to inform the family that they had to vacate immediately. When Ellen heard about this affront she was furious and her anger is evident in her diary entry on January 12, in which she questions the morality of Reverend Humes. Although Ellen's father, Samuel, a former plantation owner in Georgia, visited Tillson and requested that they be allowed to stay in their home, it was for naught. The family was forced to move out on January 13 into a cold, empty schoolroom that had been rented to them by their friend, Rachel Currey. There was no kitchen, and the single room was in such a state that Rachel's husband, Richard Currey, who scrubbed the floors, said "He never saw as dirty a place except a stable" (Sutherland 1996:88).

Tillson, while in Cincinnati, had helped form the full regiment of the Ohio Volunteer Heavy Artillery to which Sergeant Major Alvin M. Woolson belonged. Woolson's regiment entered Knoxville on March 7, 1864, and remained there until July 25, 1865, when most of the members were mustered out. During his time in Knoxville, Woolson completed a rough drawing of the area including the fort and the town. Using his map, the authors have solved a longstanding mystery as to where Reverend Humes' rental house was located in the town. Woolson placed Tillson's headquarters, the former home of the House family, on the southeast corner of Crooked Street (now Union Avenue) and State Street (present 200 State Street) (Miller 1914:86).

General Tillson might have been overwhelmed with the work that needed to be done to complete Fort Sanders had it not been for his time at West Point, his familiarity with Mahan's *Treatise,* and his experience in building fortifications. One would assume as the chief of artillery for fortifications for the Army of the Ohio, Tillson would not be without a copy of the *Treatise*. He had been commended for his defensive works in Cincinnati and the works that protected over 160 miles of L&N track between Louisville and Nashville. It would have been immediately obvious to Tillson that adjustments would need to be made to Mahan's detailed recommendations for bastioned forts built on flat terrain; but where possible on the ridge top location of Fort Sanders, he probably attempted to follow Mahan's guidelines that recommend when the ground for an entrenchment is level, the profile for the entrenchment should be constructed perpendicular to the ground surface (Mahan

1862). It is believed that Tillson most likely had the base of all the ridge-top entrenchments leveled, and the authors used the measurements seen in this profile to determine the approximate width of the walls (ca. 59 feet), which would have included all the elements (banquette, revetment, scarp, ditch, and so on) seen in Mahan's drawing (see figure 29). The limited area of ridge top may have caused the width of the walls to vary, as the slopes of the existing ridge may have influenced the shape of the bastions. We also studied Mahan's text on how to build the entrenchments, palisades, and bombproofs so that we could better understand how these elements of the fort were probably constructed.

THE 1ST REGIMENT, U.S. COLORED HEAVY ARTILLERY

There were 423 free blacks and 2,370 slaves in Knox County at the beginning of the war (Rothrock 1946). Many enslaved people, in addition to their work in the fields, caring for animals, training horses, and performing household tasks, had learned such useful trades as carpentry, blacksmithing, brickmaking, and masonry, and were sometimes hired out by their owners to perform special tasks for others (Faulkner 2017). They had made the bricks and built many of the brick homes in Knox County. Freed slaves had become teachers, teamsters, saddle makers, and shoe makers. Many of these skills were needed by the Federals, who by the summer of 1862 were facing a shortage of troops.

Congress passed the Confiscation Act on August 6, 1861, which "empowered the president to receive into service of the United States as many persons of African descent as he deemed proper for the repression of the Rebellion" (Williams 1888:86). Congress soon passed additional legislation allowing Negroes to be drafted for naval or military service. By late 1862 vigorous recruitment of black soldiers had begun. The Emancipation Proclamation issued by President Lincoln on January 1, 1863, freed all enslaved persons in the states of rebellion and allowed them to serve in the Federal army. Williams reverently proclaimed the good news again in his book, published fifteen years after Lincoln's proclamation, that: "The grand policy of emancipation and the military employment of the American slave have been officially proclaimed . . . swept forward with the force and majesty of its importance" (ibid.:112).

Many Northerners objected vehemently and sometimes violently to blacks serving in the military. Lincoln initially justified his decision for issuing the proclamation to a Wisconsin resident, a judge, in a practical rather than an ethical way. He explained: "The slightest knowledge of arithmetic will prove to any man, that the rebel armies cannot be destroyed with Democratic strategy. It would sacrifice all the white men in the north to win the war." He informed the judge that "freeing the slaves has given us two hundred thousand men raised on Southern soil. It will give us more yet. If all the posts now garrisoned by black men are abandoned and put in the battlefield or cornfields against us, we would be compelled to abandon the war in three weeks." Lincoln then shared some information that had offended his morality: "there have been some men base enough to propose to me that if I returned to slavery the black warriors of Port Hudson and Olustee," I would regain the respect of "the masters they fought. Should I do so, I would deserve to be damned in time and eternity. Come what will, I will keep my faith with friend and foe" (Wilson 1888:108–109). Parson Brownlow berated horrified Southerners in an article entitled "The Enlistment of Negroes" in the *Knoxville Whig,* writing, "A fearful howl has been raised by the Southern chivalry, because a portion of the Federal army are receiving the services [of] Negro soldiers. Such enlistments they regard as an insult and a wrong to the south, and to civilization" (*Knoxville Whig* 1864b).

The War Department had instituted the Bureau of Colored Troops in May 1863 to help create a division of "conscripts," as African American soldiers were often called. These black troops helped enormously to relieve white soldiers of many backbreaking duties such as building roads and fortifications. Tennessee was third in the number of African Americans aiding the Federal cause; 20,133 served in the Union army. Of the 178,000 black soldiers who served in nearly every military department of the United States Army, 36,847 were killed, wounded, or missing in 449 battles, and at least 21 men received the Medal of Honor (Williams 1888; Wilson 1888). Author Joseph T. Wilson's experience serving with the black troops during the war and his research afterwards

Fig. 37. Joseph T. Wilson. From *The Black Phalanx: African American Soldiers in the War of Independence, the War of 1812, and the Civil War*, 1890.

led him to conclude that more than 278,000 African Americans served in the Union forces (Wilson 1888).

Joseph Wilson and George Washington Williams, both freeborn U.S. veterans, each undertook an effort to obtain statistics, document historic events, collect anecdotes and describe the mindsets of black soldiers who served in the Civil War . . . in spite of the difficulties of compiling this information shortly after the war ended. We, as authors and writers, found ourselves very grateful to these determined and extraordinary men who succeeded in recording and publishing this priceless material for the ages.

Joseph T. Wilson (1837–1890) was born free in Norfolk, Virginia, and received some education in Massachusetts before sailing off to the South Pacific on a whaling vessel. He was in Chile working on a railroad when he heard about the war in the States. He returned immediately and enlisted in New Orleans to fight for the Union. He was seriously wounded in the Battle of Olustee in Florida and received an honorable discharge. Wilson settled in Norfolk and became a journalist, poet, an activist, and politician who was a lifelong advocate of civil rights for African Americans.

After receiving the title of Colonel in the Grand Army of the Republic (G.A.R.) he was commissioned by this veterans' organization to write a book on the history of black participation in U.S. wars, a very difficult task in the early 1880s. He entitled the book *The Black Phalanx: A History of the Negro Soldier in the Wars of the United States 1777–1812, 1861–65* (Wilson 1888). He chose the term "black phalanx" to emphasize the need for black communities to remain united in order to survive the post-Civil War Reconstruction years with their civil rights intact: The "phalanx was an ancient Greek infantry formation that depended for success on total cohesion" (Varon 2018). Wilson's book was publicly acclaimed as a landmark history of African American soldiers in the U.S.

George Washington Williams (1849–1891), who was born free in Pennsylvania, was also an American veteran who fought in Mexico to overthrow Emperor Maximilian. After returning to the States he became a minister, lawyer, politician, and a historian who published two important books on African Americans in the U.S. in the 1880s, *The History of the Negro Race in America 1619–1880* (1882), and *A History of Negro Troops in the War of Rebellion* (1887). The former was the first book published on the history of African Americans in the U.S. The latter provides critical information regarding the experience of black troops in the Civil War.

As hopes for winning the war faded, the Confederate leadership, well aware of the effectiveness of Federal "colored troops," considered and rejected the possibility of recruiting African Americans into their army. Having vehemently espoused the belief that "inferior blacks" were not worthy of being Confederate soldiers, most believed "that centuries of servitude had made the Negro slave incapable of any civil or military service" (Williams 1888:67). Howell Cobb, a Georgia politician, described the Southern dilemma when he said that when the time comes that you can create a soldier out of a slave, we will know our rebellion is doomed (Williams 1888).

On April 12, 1864, the Federal army announced that General Davis Tillson would continue the organization of African American troops in the District of East Tennessee and care for the contrabands in Knoxville (*OR* 1892:pt. 1, 339). Contrabands were escaped slaves who came under the protection of the Union army. When General Grant was in Knoxville in January 1864, General Tillson applied for permission to raise a regiment of "colored" heavy artillery for the defense of Knoxville. General Grant referred Tillson to the Colored Bureau for the requisite authority and designation (Mussey 1864). The 1st Regiment, United States Colored Heavy Artillery, was mustered on February 20, 1864, and served with Tillson's 2nd Brigade. A year later the heavy artillery regiment had reached a full complement of 1,800 men. Since a heavy artillery unit would have their battle stations in Knoxville's fortifications and were charged to maintain these structures, it is reasonable to conclude that they also continued to construct and improve them. During the Civil War, the term "heavy artillery" referred to large-caliber cannons that were primarily used for defensive purposes in fortifications, although they could also be used for offensive operations on the battlefield. These included the 3-inch ordnance rifle and 10- and 20-pound Parrott rifles (Woodhead 1996). It is not known how much specific training the African American 1st Regiment soldiers received in actually firing these weapons.

Tillson's efforts to recruit soldiers for training in heavy artillery was successful, as in late January 1864, "Lieutenant-Colonel Thomas J. Morgan of the 14th U.S. Colored troops, stationed in Gallatin, Tennessee, was ordered to Knoxville to consult with General Davis Tillson as to raising a regiment of heavy artillery." He reported regarding this assignment that: "There is an excellent state of feeling in the Department of Ohio touching colored troops, General Tillson and staff, and others high in rank . . . are warm friends of the move" (Williams 1888:129).

In addition to serving as the major military workforce that continued to build and maintain Fort Sanders in 1864–65, the black regiment undoubtedly built and perhaps even manned other small defensive outposts in the Knoxville vicinity. Many federal earthworks called redoubts, or redans, were built during the war to protect wooden railroad trestles, which were critical for Union transportation and thus an inviting target for Confederate partisans and cavalry. Redans were semicircular or V-shaped earthen defensive structures that housed at least one cannon (Smith and Nance 2003).

In 2007, a well-preserved redan was discovered by the authors while walking on the Third Creek Greenway in Knoxville. The redan had been built on an eminence that overlooks the present concrete bridge of the Norfolk Southern, the former East Tennessee and Georgia Railroad, over Third Creek. While no documentation about this particular redan has yet been found, it is likely that the First Regiment African-American Heavy Artillery soldiers built this earthwork since they were a significant military work force building and maintaining fortifications in 1864. The redan was acquired by Knox County, added to the county park system, and dedicated as a Civil War historic site on March 2, 2017 (Norrell 2017; Steely 2017).

It has been recorded that the U.S. government's original plan was to use African American soldiers as garrison troops in order to release white troops for combat. They were often assigned a disproportionate amount of heavy labor and fatigue duty, such as erecting batteries and hauling cannon. Largely because of the prejudice of Union army officers, this injustice continued even after black soldiers consistently proved their bravery in battle (McPherson 1991). Finally, on June 14, 1864, the United States War Department issued a directive, reading in part: "Accordingly the practice which has hitherto prevailed, no doubt from necessity of requiring [African American troops] to perform most of the labor of fortifications, and the labor of fatigue duties of permanent stations and camps, will cease, and they will only be required to take their fair share of fatigue duty with white troops" (*OR* 1900:431).

In mid-May, the United States military began to publish a weekly Knoxville newspaper—the aforementioned *Army Mailbag*—which was distributed to Union soldiers every Saturday. The paper remained in print until October 8, 1864. It mentions the presence in Knoxville of the

79th and 104th Ohio Infantry Regiments, the 2nd Ohio Heavy Artillery and its "fine" brass band, the Illinois Elgin Battery, and several Federal cavalry companies, including the 10th Michigan, which had engaged in most of the combat in upper East Tennessee. The African American 1st Regiment, which was based in Knoxville through September 1865, also received mention. While filled with stories about the trials and tribulations of bored soldiers, the *Mailbag* frequently described the activities of the black artillery regiment; and in September, it reported that the unit had excellent soldiers (*Army Mailbag* 1864).

On October 28, 1864, Confederate General John C. Vaughn reported to his superior officer, Major General John C. Breckinridge, that "they have at Knoxville two negro regiments and one Ohio, say 350 muskets in the Ohio regiment. The negroes are variously estimated from 800–1,800" (*OR* 1892:pt. 3, 858).

A general order was issued on April 12, 1864, from the headquarters of the Department of the Ohio by Major General Schofield. General Order No.103 commanded Brigadier General Tillson to complete the defenses of Knoxville under his personal direction and make them "as formidable as practicable." The order strongly stated that the town "must be held at all hazards and against any force, however large." In addition to these responsibilities the general and his 2nd Brigade were instructed to, "if practicable, protect the railroad bridge at Strawberry Plains" and the tracks from Knoxville to Loudon (*OR* 1891:pt. 3, 338–39).

Brigadier General Z. B. Tower, inspector general of fortifications, Military Division of the Mississippi, reported to his commander, Major General George H. Thomas, after an inspection of the defenses of Knoxville that "the defensive line of Knoxville, commenced by Captain Poe, Engineer Corps, immediately after its occupation by our army, owes much of its progress to General Davis Tillson, commanding at this post during the past year. He has evinced much skill in laying out the connecting lines, and an uncommon energy in their execution, and it is a pleasure to bring his services in the defense of the post to the notice of the commanding general" (*OR* 1897:pt. 2, 251).

GENERAL TILLSON AND THE FREEDMAN'S BUREAU

General Tillson would continue his work with African Americans in the postwar South. The general had earned a stellar reputation during the war for his competence in the field and his organizational abilities. Thus, when he offered his resignation after the war ended, it was rejected, and he was put in charge the Bureau of Refugees, Freedmen, and Abandoned Lands commonly called the "Freedmen's Bureau." President Lincoln appointed Major General Oliver Otis Howard to serve as commissioner of the bureau during its short lifetime. Tillson was appointed an assistant commissioner, serving first in Memphis and later in Georgia. He was mustered out of the service on December 1, 1867 (Wilson and Fiske 1889).

Congress had foreseen the need to create the Freedmen's Bureau in March 1865 to assist freed slaves in the devastated communities of the South during Reconstruction; impoverished whites also benefited. An office was opened in Knoxville in 1866 (Newman 1939). The bureau provided food, clothing, and housing, built hospitals and schools, and offered legal assistance for the freed slaves. Teachers sent to Knoxville by the bureau conducted classes in reading and writing and provided training in useful skills that would help ensure freed slaves were able to obtain work. While serving in Georgia, Tillson managed to convince qualified whites to fill needed positions at the bureau and required that standard contracts be drawn up to ensure that freed slaves would receive fair pay for their work. Because of the Southern Homestead Act, Tillson had some success in settling former slaves on abandoned or confiscated lands (Cimbala 2005). In one instance he helped provide travel from Greensboro, Georgia, to Little Rock, Arkansas, for three men who were reported to be agents for 150 families of freed men who wanted to "settle in Arkansas under the Homestead Act" (Hayden et al. 2013:937–939). On the occasion of Tillson's departure from his headquarters in Augusta, the mayor hosted a public ceremony to honor him for the outstanding work he had done during a critical time in Georgia's history (Hatfield 2015).

After the war ended, the residents of Speedwell, a small town in Claiborne County, Tennessee, also sought to assist freed slaves in adjusting to a new life. There had been few slaves in their county and most had been house servants. It is believed that most slave owners in this Union area of East Tennessee had freed their slaves before the war ended, and the freedmen had been allowed to live on farmland in the Hoop Creek Community. In 1981, some African Americans still lived in this area (Holt 1981).

An archival example of the concern shown for the freed slaves by citizens of the Claiborne County area can be found in a 1976 book by Lawrence Edwards entitled *Bits of Memory*. In this memoir, Edwards recounted his memories of growing up in Speedwell. He told a story about how the local residents who, after the war ended, recognized that "there was a problem: what to do with the freed slaves." Without any assistance from the Freedmen's Bureau, the residents there "set aside a little area . . . near a large spring located on the VanBebber property in Greasy Hollow." Every family was given enough land for "a garden and a cabin, with arrangements for a little cow pasture and a corn patch . . . and a little church." Edwards thought that perhaps there had been a schoolhouse also. A cemetery was located for their families near the small community. Edwards wrote that by the time he was born in 1907, everything there had completely disappeared. He added that the freed slaves "kept their names given them by their former owners, their native names having been long since forgotten" (Edwards 1976:33–34).

10

UNDERSTANDING POST-BATTLE CONSTRUCTION AND ITS EFFECT ON THE LANDSCAPE

PHOTOGRAPHS AND DRAWINGS

Unfortunately, no photographs have been discovered that were taken of Fort Sanders before the battle took place in November 1863. The official 1863 contour maps of Poe and Tillson provide a line drawing of the fort and its placement on the landscape; however the shape of the enclosed fortification is drawn as a rectangle rather than as an irregular quadrilateral described by Poe (Poe 1888:742). The authors are aware of no extant drawings, engravings, or photographs of this fortification before the battle took place. Had there been cameras available to anyone during the siege, there would have been neither time nor motivation to use them.

Several drawings and prints published after the battle illustrate the bastions, west curtain wall, and the landscape in front of the wall in perspective. These may help to visualize how this part of the fortification might have looked at the time of the attack. Some appear to be more accurate than others, such as the Buchtel print (see figure 30a).

The issue of how the fort looked after completion is confused by General Tillson's drawing of Fort Sanders as a perfect-square star fort. Between late December 1863 and April 1864, Private John G. Orth, also represented Fort Sanders as a square star fort, as do the artists in 1886 and 1888 drawings of the bird's-eye views of Knoxville (see figure 45).

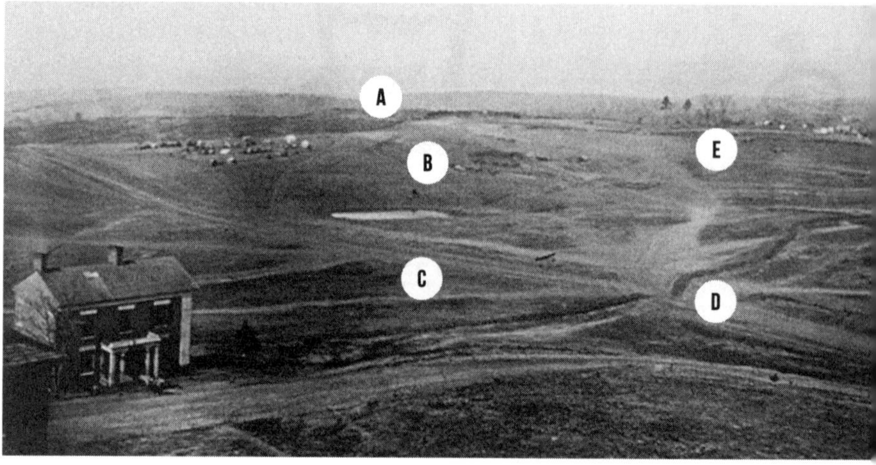

Repairs and further construction of the fort became the responsibility of General Tillson in December 1863. There are few references in the *Official Records* that relay much information about the construction occurring during Tillson's command, but aspects of the stages of construction can be seen in several photographs taken during this time. These photographs bear witness not only to the changes that transformed a small fortification into a goliath "Keep of East Tennessee" but also to the landscape surrounding it.

THE PHOTOGRAPHS OF GEORGE N. BARNARD

George N. Barnard (1819–1902), a New York photographer and personal friend of Orlando Poe, took official photographs in Knoxville in March 1864, almost four months after the battle at Fort Sanders. Before the war began, Barnard had worked as a portrait photographer in Matthew B. Brady's Broadway studio in New York City. Brady's talent with a camera had won him a gold medal in the international competition for photography at the 1851 London World's Fair. In the years following Barnard's addition to his staff, Brady became renowned

Fig. 38a. First two sections of George Barnard's 1864 panorama of Knoxville at White's Ridge. Library of Congress. A) Fort Sanders; B) westernmost borrow pit; C) Kingston Pike; D) Poe's defensive trench; E) easternmost borrow pit; F) White sisters' barn; G) orchard; H) White sisters' house.

as a Civil War photographer and acknowledged as the "father of photojournalism." His photographs of Civil War battlefield scenes strewn with the dead still speak to the carnage of that war more graphically than words ever will (Hoobler and Hoobler 1977).

Brady became interested in documenting the Civil War when extensive photographic coverage on such a grand scale was unprecedented. After receiving permission from President Lincoln in 1861 to undertake this task, Brady, at his own expense, outfitted a group of twenty photographers, called "Brady's Photographic Corps," who used traveling studios on horse-drawn wagons that could be driven into a combat area. The added wooden enclosure was filled with an assortment of cameras, chemical tanks, tripods, glass plates, and a small darkroom. Barnard became proficient in the collodion, a wet-plate process of photography, and was sent by Brady to photograph the 1861 inauguration of Lincoln; he was later chosen to be a member of the Photographic Corps (ibid.).

In 1864 Barnard was appointed the official photographer for the chief engineering official of the Military Division of the Mississippi, first commanded by Grant, and then by William Tecumseh Sherman in the spring of 1864. The subsequent official photographs Barnard took in Knoxville in March 1864 were transmitted to the Department of War in Washington, along with the reports of Captain Orlando Poe, chief engineer of General Burnside's army, on April 11, 1864 (*OR* 1890:pt. 1, 315). Barnard and Poe traveled with Sherman to Atlanta, where Barnard continued serving as Sherman's official photographer in Georgia, and during General Sherman's March to the Sea. In 1866 he published photographs of the devastation that occurred in the wake of Sherman's scorched-earth policy during that campaign, entitled *Photographic Views of Sherman's Campaign* (Davis 1990; Schmid 2017).

Barnard was facing northwest on March 19, 1864, when he took these two photographs from the cupola of the main college building (Purcell, 2007). The building was surrounded at that time by the fortification known as Fort Byington. It was located on what was then called "Barbara Hill" after William Blount's daughter who was one of the first women to attend the college (Creekmore 1976). These two photographs of Fort Sanders and the surrounding area show a desolate scene familiar to General Tillson as he supervised work on the fortifications. It is a photograph which has been extremely valuable to the research of the authors as it reveals significant features of the landscape and can be used to pinpoint modern locations.

A bleak, ravaged, and treeless landscape is seen in this panoramic view (figure 38a). The topography of the area can be clearly observed because very few trees remain between the south slope of the ridge and Kingston Pike other than the magnolias which surround the White sisters' house. The location of Fort Sanders can be identified to the left (A). Just southeast of the fort above the pond one can distinguish the westernmost borrow pit (B). Kingston Pike is south of the pond (C) and crosses Poe's easternmost defensive trench (D). To the north one can see the easternmost borrow pit (E), and south of that enormous excavation is the White sisters' barn (F), orchard (G), and their two-story house (H).

A closer view of the landscape (figure 38b), shows Fort Sanders (A) looming above the tent camp. Poe's westernmost defensive trench (B) begins at a point below the rectangular area (C) where the southeast bastion will be added and continues southward on the west side of the slope where the tent/hut camp (D) is located. Seventeenth Street will be built northward up this slope beginning at approximately point (E) on the Kingston Road (F) just west of where the Cowan house (G) will later be built. Sophronia Strong Hall was built in the area of the Cowan house in 1926. One can see the westernmost borrow pit (H) and pond (I) where the future UT Law School will be built. A tent camp, probably for cavalry soldiers, is located on top of the easternmost borrow pit (J). The easternmost defensive trench (K) crosses Kingston Road and continues up the hill to Fort Byington. According to the Ogden map of West Knoxville the easternmost excavation had been filled with earth, leveled for development and platted by 1895.

An exciting discovery was made because of the detail which could be obtained when this digital photograph was greatly enlarged. Revealed to us was the westernmost borrow pit (G) which is being excavated for fill dirt that was hauled up the slope in wagons (probably Studebaker wagons) for use in the construction of the fort. One can see a steep cut on the northern edge of the pit, two lines of wagons, and a dark outline which looks like a "check mark" (H) etched into the earth south of the wagons which probably indicated the boundaries of the area to be excavated.

The scene was probably staged for Barnard's photograph. Earth-hauling wagons are neatly lined up in front of the borrow pit. A canvas-covered wagon at the west end of the line was possibly used to carry digging tools. These are probably Studebaker wagons, manufactured by the Studebaker Corporation in South Bend, Indiana (Erskine 1918). During the war, the US government contracted with the company to supply these wagons which released their contents mechanically. The company survived, changed with the times, and in the mid-twentieth century began to manufacture the famous Studebaker automobiles (Longstreet 1952). One can distinguish a path created by the wagons as they traveled slightly southwest, then turned up the slope onto the path heading northwest to the palisade area. Army engineers in early 1864 had to go farther afield to find suitable soil because the supply of softer topsoil in the immediate vicinity of the fort had been exhausted. The authors' field research revealed that the ridge on which the fort is located is underlain by a hard cherty subsoil observed in soil profiles

A
C
B
E
G
D
F
I

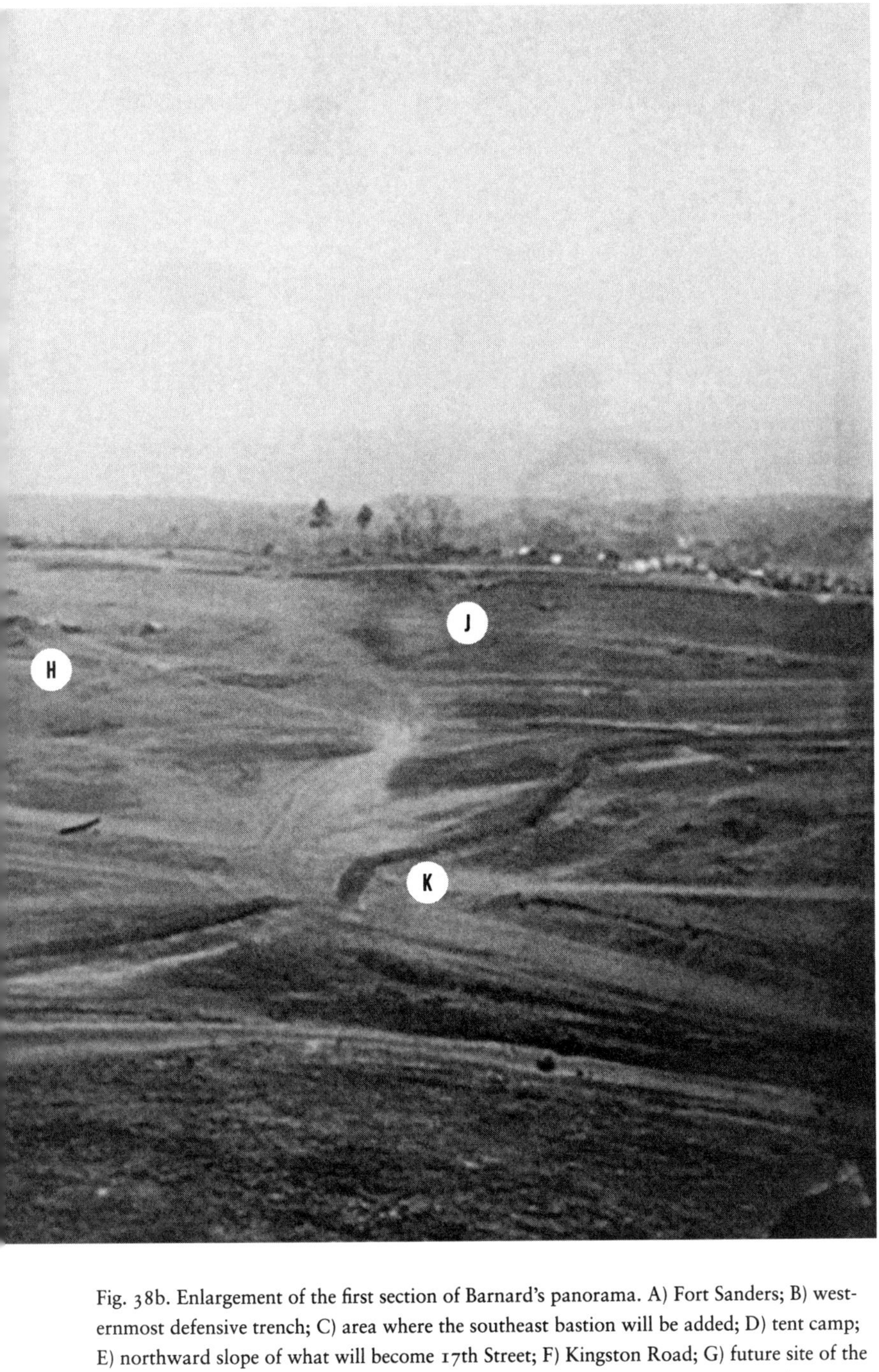

Fig. 38b. Enlargement of the first section of Barnard's panorama. A) Fort Sanders; B) westernmost defensive trench; C) area where the southeast bastion will be added; D) tent camp; E) northward slope of what will become 17th Street; F) Kingston Road; G) future site of the Cowan house; H) westernmost borrow pit; I) pond; J) tent camp and easternmost borrow pit; K) easternmost defensive trench.

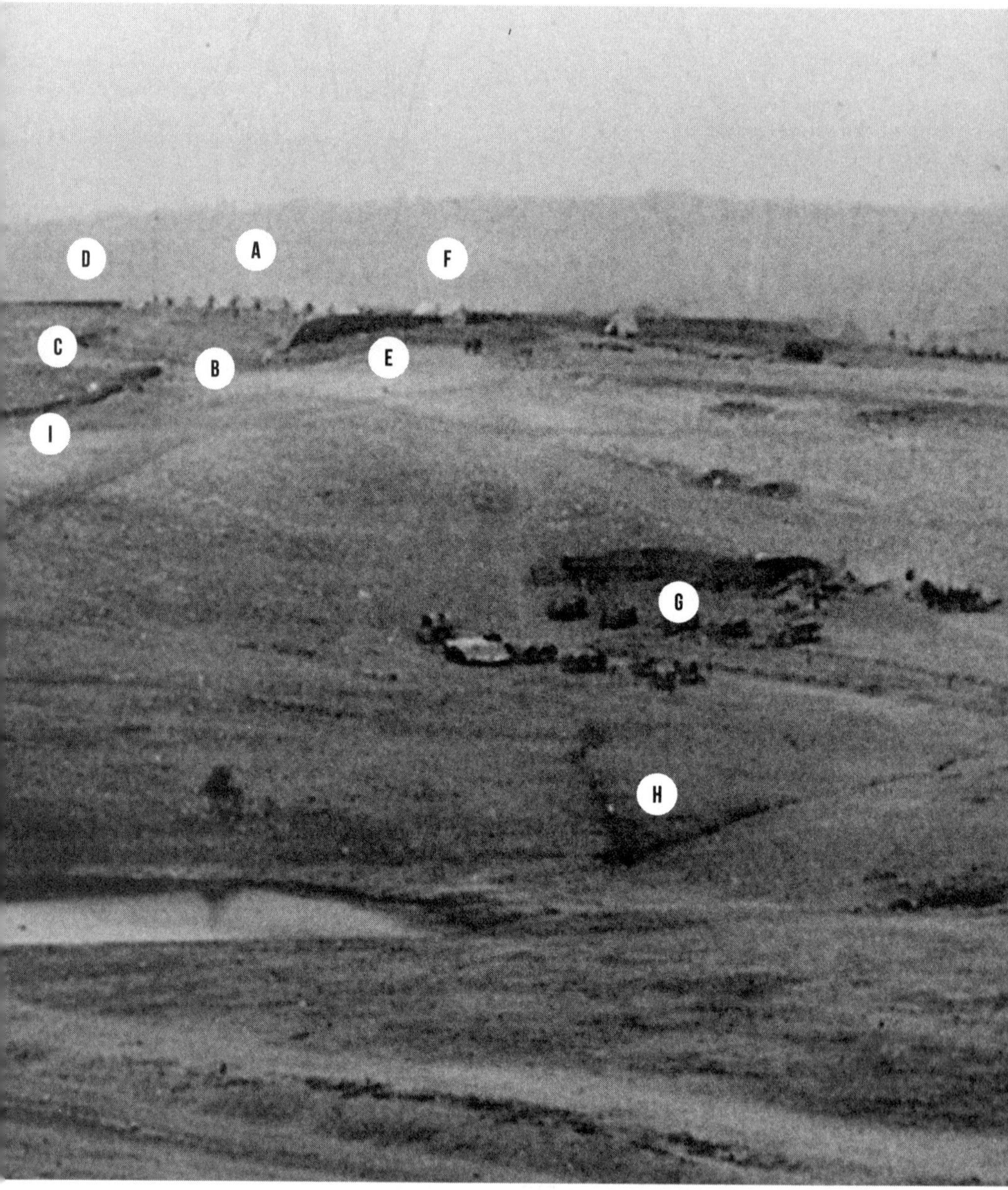

Fig. 38c. Enlargement of the second section of Barnard's panorama, shoing the westernmost excavation pit which was made into an amphitheater for the 1890 reunion. It later became a Knoxville park. Above the excavation one can see the stockade which stretches across the ridge. A space has been left where a gate will be added. The stockade terminates at the east side of the "rectangle" where the southeast bastion will be added.

Fig. 38d. Enlargement of photograph showing the enormous easternmost excavation pit above the White sisters' barn. The orchard south of the barn most likely contained apple trees and may have been the campsite from which cavalryman Sergeant Tarrant observed black laborers march eastward to the fort in the evenings. The Kingston Road is in the foreground.

created by foundational excavations for Fort Sanders Manor, which was completed in 1922. This stratum would have been much more difficult to dig with hand tools than the soil on the south slope of the ridge, where the borrow pit was located. Natural deposition on this slope created a deeper layer of softer colluvial clay soil, a looser sediment deposited on slopes from rain and sheet wash, which could be much more easily removed with picks and shovels. This same type of soil might have been identified by engineers in the easternmost excavated area seen in figure 38b (J).

The borrow pit was transformed into the amphitheater for the 1890 Blue-Gray Reunion and later became a park. Remnants of this sunken area can still be seen today at the southeast corner of Clinch Avenue and 16th Street. The Masonic Lodge stands close to the western edge of the visible sunken remnants of the amphitheater/park and the recently built Knoxville Place Apartments now fill the remainder of that area located behind the Masonic Lodge.

A multitude of details of the landscape are revealed in this enlargement of the fort area. A new tent camp within the fortification (A) was probably added for soldiers working on the fort. It is located above the rectangular area where the southeast bastion will be constructed (B). The original configuration of Poe's trench, which connected to the demi-bastion, forms the west perpendicular line of this rectangle (C). The narrow black, east/west line above the south wall (D) is a wooden revetment built under Tillson's supervision which will retain earth for construction of a standard parapet (see figure 29). The stockade extends from the southwest to the northeast (E) and is designated not only to provide for the construction of an entrance gate (F) but also to retain and support packed earth which will be used to construct the southeast and northeast bastions. One can see that earth has already been packed at the interior and exterior base of the stockade to help support the palisade. Beneath the westernmost excavation pit (G) is a dark "check mark" (H) dug into the earth, which is the outline for the extension of the borrow pit. There is a better view of the defensive trench (I) which can be seen behind the Cowan house (see figure 42b). In this figure a row of post holes dug for the construction of a sturdy defensive stockade can be seen on the east side of the trench. This stockade was added along the entire length and is described later in the text in detail by Jacob Roemer, a member of the 34th New York Independent Battery.

Barnard's photograph dominated by the figures of Captain Orlando Poe and Colonel Orville Babcock in front of the northwest bastion (see figure 25), in context with the entire north face of the fort, provided a wealth of information about the location of the fort and was vital to locating the current site of the northwest bastion. Paths crisscross the sloping landscape behind and to the right side of the men. One path borders the east edge of the large limestone sinkhole (B) that Confederate artillerist Porter Alexander described in his memoirs. This sinkhole, along with the 1922 Thompson aerial photograph (see figure 48), places the northwest bastion at the corner of Laurel Avenue and 18th street. Before it was destroyed, the sinkhole could be seen west of 18th Street between Laurel and Highland Avenues (see Figure 26).

One can see the apex of the northwest bastion behind Poe and Babcock and the solitary soldier (A), who was probably placed there for scale, as well as the sinkhole (B). The north wall of the fort stretches eastward on the top of the ridge from the northwest bastion towards 17th Street (C). It is interrupted midway by an enormous cut through the earthen fort wall, which also extends into the ridge top itself (D). After much deliberation about the purpose of this huge gap, which would have made the fortification vulnerable if present at the time of the battle, we decided that the gap was obviously created after the battle and are now convinced it was made to bring heavy equipment, cannons, ammunition, and other supplies into the fort from the adjacent railroad.

This is the only photograph showing the three lunettes seen in Poe's and Tillson's maps. They appear on the far left (E) and look like enormous piles of soil that were placed on the crest of the ridge and extend down the north side of the slope a bit. One can see the outline of the ridge top in the spaces between the earthen mounds and also to the east of those earthworks.

The Barnard photograph of the south side of the northwest bastion (figure 27b) is an excellent image taken from the south in March 1864. One can see that the berm has not yet been added back to the scarp

B
A
C
D
J
K
L
M

Fig. 39. Western section of Barnard's 1864 panoramic view of Knoxville taken from south of the Holston River. A) Tent/hut camp; B) Fort Sanders; C) Fort Byington; D) shebangs/ground dwellings for soldiers; E) tent camp for cavalry; F) mounted cavalry; G) White sisters' barn; H) Kingston Road; I) easternmost excavation; J) soliders' path from ground dwellings to spring; K) William Blount's temporary home; L) spring; M) Holston River; N) East Tennessee and Virginia Railroad stone piers for bridge; O) Second Creek.

of the bastion. With the camera pointed to the northwest, the photo includes the trench (A) in front of the west curtain wall (C), the south side of the northwest bastion (B), the deepest part of the trench (D), and the desolate stump-ridden landscape over which the Confederates launched their attack (F). The woods where Confederate sharpshooters were located can also be seen.

When enlarged, this photograph reveals the 80-foot Confederate trench adjacent to the woods, and also the rocks seen in Buchtel's engraving of the attack (see figure 30a) and the 1922 Thompson aerial of the battlefield and defilade (see figure 48).

Barnard's photo of the northwest bastion (figure 53) is an excellent view of the feature taken in March 1864. Because Barnard was standing a little north of the bastion and shooting southward, he also captured the ridge tops south of the river. This photograph confirms the fact that the fort builders not only removed the softer topsoil of the ridge, but they also had penetrated the deeper and harder clay subsoil in order to deepen the ditches and procure additional soil for the fort walls (A). In the foreground of the photograph one can see the cherty clay subsoil (B) in the ditch that overlies the bedrock of the ridge. There are three cannon embrasures in the northwest bastion and two cuts in the wooden revetment on the south side of the bastion where cannons would have been placed. A berm (C) is seen in this photograph, which was taken the same day and time as the photograph of Poe and Babcock in March 1864. The berm of the northwest bastion had been cut away before the battle, but it was added again soon afterwards, probably so that soldiers could use it to repair and maintain the bastion. Bare soil on the bastion slopes and walls of the fort would have suffered erosional damage during the rainy years following the war. It is safe to assume that because of the smooth, pristine appearance of the bastion wall, any damage to the fort walls was carefully repaired before Poe returned to Knoxville on his March inspection tour. However, not all debris had been removed for the photograph; one can see empty sandbags (D) that have tumbled down the slope and rest on the side of the ditch in front of an embrasure.

A soldier (E) stands at attention on the west curtain wall between the northwest and southwest bastions. To the left of the lone sentry, one can see a part of an interior timber structure called a revetment (F). This wooden "wall" kept the packed earth that formed the earth parapet behind it from slumping into the fort. Large, square vertical posts support the retaining walls made of horizontal planks, which were probably constructed according to Mahan's instructions in his *Treatise.*

Elements described by Mahan in his *Treatise* can be distinguished in an engraving of Camp Butler in Newport News, Virginia, from *Pictorial History of the War of 1861,* which shows Union soldiers constructing an entrenchment similar to Mahan's drawing in figure 30b (Leslie 1862). Instructions in Mahan's *Treatise* offer valuable time-saving information to those in command of overseeing construction of fortifications. For the aspect of construction shown in that particular figure, Mahan would have advised reading his chapter titled "Manner of Throwing up a Work." The soldiers at Fort Sanders also may have been situated as they worked according to Mahan's guidelines: "Experience has shown that, in ordinary soil, a man with a pick can furnish employment to two men with shovels; that, not to be in each other's way, the men be from four-and-a-half to six feet apart; and finally, that a shovel full of earth can be pitched by a man twelve feet in a horizontal direction, or six feet in a vertical direction" (Mahan 1861:33).

Dennis Hart Mahan (1807–1871) was the son of Irish immigrants who graduated first in his class at West Point. He spent several years in Europe studying at and evaluating military schools. His singular purpose after resuming his academic position at West Point was to teach and publish all he had learned in school and abroad so that his students would be well-prepared if they were ever engaged in warfare. Devasted after being forced to retire in 1871, he committed suicide.

THE JOHN ORTH MAP

Between late December 1863 and April 1864, Private John G. Orth, a member of the 23rd Corps, 118th Regiment, Ohio Volunteer Infantry, Company G, from Arcadia, Ohio, was apparently stationed for a time around or within Fort Sanders. He drew the only known existing map of the interior and area immediately surrounding the fort (figure 40).

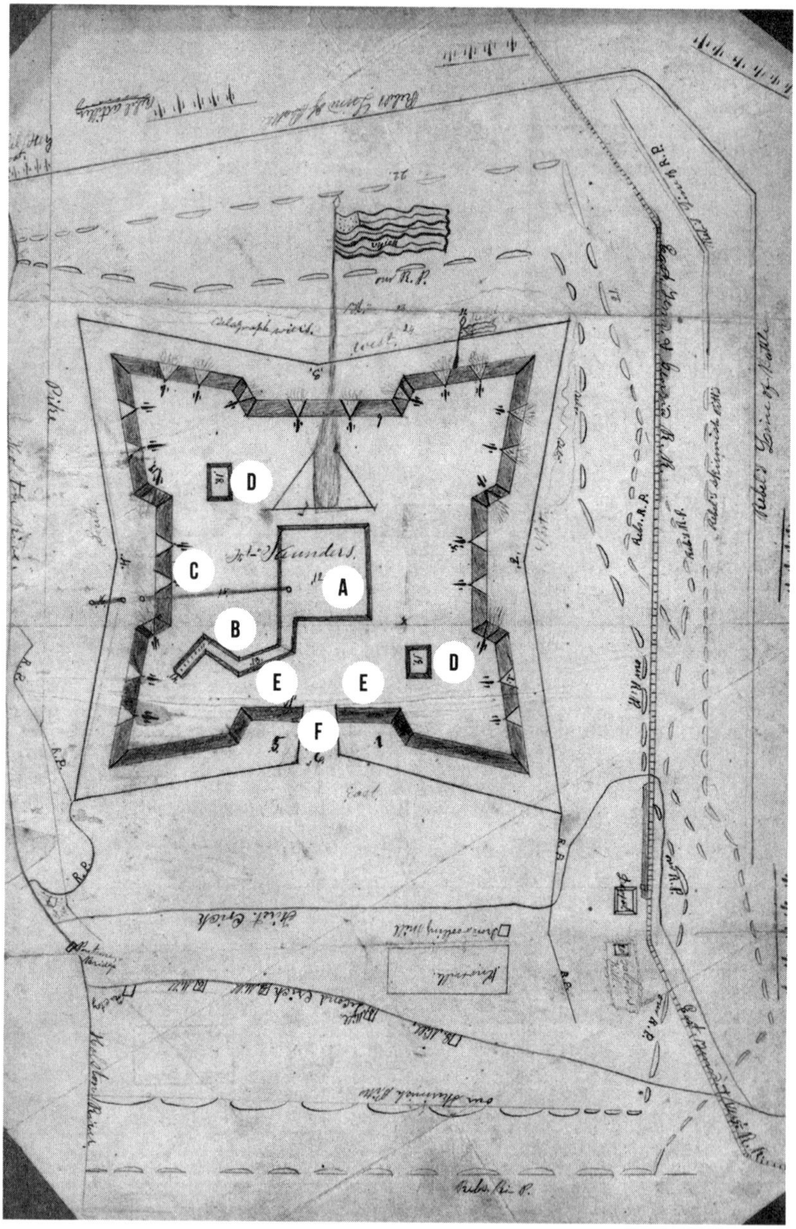

Fig. 40. Orth map of the interior of Fort Sanders. A) magazine B) entrance to magazine C) underground drain for magazine which connects to the south wall trench D) cistern E) stockade F) entrance gate.

It is possible that Orth came to Knoxville with Sherman's relief force in early December, as the 118th Regiment is not listed as a participant in the siege and battle of Knoxville. Because that regiment appears to have only seen action at Mossy Creek on December 29, it may be that they were serving as a reserve unit in Knoxville. Orth would have then moved south with the 118th as part of Sherman's army in the Atlanta campaign in April 1864.

We know that he was in Knoxville on January 8 because on that date a Confederate soldier, a member of the 8th Texas Cavalry named Ephraim E. Dodd, was hanged on "gallows hill." Authorities executed the spy, "who had passed our pickets in a Federal uniform," wrote Parson Brownlow in the next day's *Whig*, "on the very spot where, two years ago, the rebels hung our Union men" (*Knoxville Whig* 1864c). Orth places the "gallows hill" on his drawing; the authors believe the location was between Grand and Forest Avenues and 12th and 13th Streets, near Battery Zoellner. The incident is mentioned not only by Brownlow but by Orth and Ellen House as well. Dodd had been imprisoned since December 17, and Ellen House had visited him several times in jail, even supplying him with shirts (Sutherland 1996:80–84).

Although Orth represented the fort as a "square star fort," his drawing is significant not only because he documented in detail the fort's interior and exterior features but because he also added details of the landscape around the fort. He numbered and identified all the features in an accompanying key. Only those features directly associated with the fort provided on his key are included here. The descriptions are in his own words and spelling:

> (1– 5) is the ditch outside the fort; (6) is the dovar [door?]; (7) is the poart [port] holes [cannon embrasures]; (8) the guns; (9) is the parapitt; (10) the side which is stockaded with timber and is occupied by the infantry; (11) is the rebel flag on the corner the enemy maid the assult Sun morning Nov. 29 1863, and had it planted once and the barer of it was completely riddled with balls and the flag captured by the 9th corps; (12) is the ammenizion [ammunition] magazere [magazine]; (13) is the Gball [entrance hall to magazine?]; (14) is the stairs entering

> the hall and col [?] [this work is all underground]; (15) is an undergd ditch or drain to mag; (16) is a drain to the ditch on the outside of the fort; (18 and 19) is the cisterns containing water.

Orth's drawing of the fort and his notations detail many interesting features that were constructed in the fort, but unfortunately this drawing has no scale so it is difficult to determine exactly where these would be located on the present landscape. However, since the location of the interior has been identified, the approximate location of these features can be determined.

The ammunition magazine (often called a powder magazine or bombproof) dominates the drawing of the fort interior. The garrison was aware that they were subject to enfilading fire and resulting shrapnel. Thus, the bombproof they built was entered by an elaborate "Ghall" [*sic*], which zigzagged downward to the interior chamber and prevented shrapnel from entering that room, which contained ammunition and powder. This passage, as well as the interior space it accessed, was probably constructed of heavy timbers or logs and covered with sandbags. A similar timber-lined, underground bombproof was excavated at another Civil War site, Fort Pocahontas in Jamestown, Virginia (Maynard 2012). The Fort Sanders bombproof was finished just two days before the Confederate attack. In his book on the 79th Highlanders, William Todd wrote that on November 26 the pickets who had come in from duty ate their meager breakfast and were ordered to "join with those already working on the bombproof . . . which was completed by noon that day providing safety for telegraph operators and their equipment and also served as a powder magazine" (Todd 1886:380).

Orth's drawing indicates that the magazine was located at the center of the fort. Based on extensive research, including examination of the present ground surface of the interior area of the fort, we believe that the approximate center is located at the rear of the present-day Ronald McDonald House in a paved, east–west alley. A depression in the pavement was evidently created by a subsidence of the asphalt surface. While this depression could be the result of recent construction such as a sewer line, it is also possible that it was caused by the partial collapse of less compact or organically enriched soil fill in the magazine. Similar pavement slumping over late 19th century privy sites in downtown Knoxville has been observed in archeological excavations. (Garrow 1984).

In his drawing, Orth shows 24 guns (18 without counting the *pan coupes*), which would have required considerable shells and powder. Such magazines were sometimes called bombproofs, indicating that they were also used as shelter during heavy bombardments. Lieutenant Benjamin said that General Ferrero used it as his command post and that it also served as the telegraph center (Benjamin n.d.). On October 24, 1864, a Union army communiqué from Knoxville to the headquarters of the United States Military Telegraph, Division of the Mississippi, relayed information that "during the siege . . . we built a line to all the forts, and operated them day and night" (*OR* 1900:854).

A detailed description of the telegraph communication within the Union lines was provided by Henry J. Broadwell (or Bardwell), who served in the Signal Corps (Brown 1974 [1896]) which connected General Burnside's command post to other fortifications during the battle. While visiting the 1913 National Conservation Exposition held in Knoxville, he was interviewed by a local reporter and described the problems members of the Corps had with laying and maintaining these critical lines of communication:

> "In that day, the old signal telegraph train was used, as well as the flags, and the work of this service was most dangerous.
>
> The signal telegraph train . . . was a detachment of wagons, each carry [*sic*] a complete outfit, consisting of a mile of wire, telegraph instruments, and slender ashen [*sic*] poles to hold up the wires.
>
> Knoxville was the central station, and at different times we had the lines at Fort Sanders, Fort Cameron and at Temperance hill. When we wanted to establish communication between and [*sic*] two places, the wagon would be driven over the ground and the wire unwound; the poles would then be put up, and the instruments attached, after which all was in readiness for work. We did not use the Morse code of telegraphy then, but had a magnetic dial and spelled the words out, so that no knowledge of telegraph as it is known now was required.

> I remember that we were greatly bothered by people in the community who sympathized with the other side, cutting our wires and for a good many days this was kept up. General Burnsides [*sic*], however, finally got exasperated and placed guards along the lines, with orders to shoot the first man, not a soldier, caught tampering with the wires. You can bet we had no more trouble then." (Broadwell 1913)

Other features on the Orth map include two rectangular cisterns located at the east and west sides of the fort. These must have been brick-lined like most mid-19th-century cisterns found in Knoxville. All of the 19th-century cisterns studied in Knoxville were circular and appear to have been filled by a roof rainwater catchment system, with a down-pipe emptying into the cistern (Carnes 1982). There is no indication on Orth's map of inlets into the fort cisterns and there are no roofs from which rain water could be caught. It is likely that these cisterns were filled with barrels of water from Third Creek to supply the horses and mules with water and also the troops during emergencies.

The American flag is at the west end of the fort (see figure 40), probably in the exact location it was placed during the siege and battle. Orth's drawing shows the stockade (with the sallyport, or entrance), at the east end, which encloses the interior of the fort by connecting the northeast and southeast bastions (see figure 40). A later photograph of the fort taken from the south bluff of the river shows earth piled on the west side of the stockade, which has been extended down the south slope of the ridge. This extension provided support for the earth, which was piled against it to create the southeast bastion. In only a few months, the open east side of the fort was enclosed, substantially strengthening this fortification.

THEODORE SCHLEIER'S PHOTOGRAPH

The latest known photograph of Fort Sanders was taken by Schleier in early 1865 from the top of the bluffs south of the Tennessee (Holston) River. The fort and surrounding area are shown in the westernmost frame of a four-section panorama. Schleier was a Prussian immigrant who had opened a successful photography studio in Nashville, married into the Knoxville family of Joseph Knaffl in 1862, and finally moved to Knoxville in 1866 (Hoobler 1986; Karnes and Coddington n.d.). Several changes in Barnard's 1864 landscape (figure 39) surrounding the fort are evident in Schleier's 1865 photograph.

This photo seems to indicate that Union occupiers realize the war is going to end soon. Fort Byington (A) looks as though it is beginning to deteriorate. The earthen holes that soldiers had been occupying in the Barnard photograph have been filled and the soil in that area (B) has been smoothed over. The path to the spring (C) has almost disappeared and part of the eastern defensive trench behind the white building which connected to Second Creek from Kingston Road appears to also have been filled in (D), but the section extending up the hill still remains (E). The East Tennessee and Virginia Railroad stone piers still stand ready to support a new railroad bridge (F).

Behind College Hill and north of Kingston Road several long rectangular buildings for stabling horses/mules have been added to the landscape (G) and a tent camp for the cavalry (H). The stalls probably opened onto the road running between the two buildings, helping to achieve maximum warmth for the animals. Equines were indispensable to the Union war effort and it was critically important that they be cared for as best as the war conditions allowed.

The buildings seen in this photograph are almost identical to those seen in a Union remount depot at Giesboro, Maryland, near Washington, D.C. Between one and three million horses and mules are estimated to have died during the war, and constant resupply was required. Giesboro was one of two depots created by the government where personnel purchased new stock and fed, sheltered and trained these reliable, hard-working animals (Miller, ed., 1957). The depots also provided a place for ill and exhausted veteran war horses to convalesce so that they could be returned to battle (Cederwald, 1928). At Giesboro, the Union army handled 170,622 horses in 1864, exclusive of 12,000–13,000 artillery horses (Miller, ed., 1957). No information could be found on the number of equines which would be housed in a building of this size.

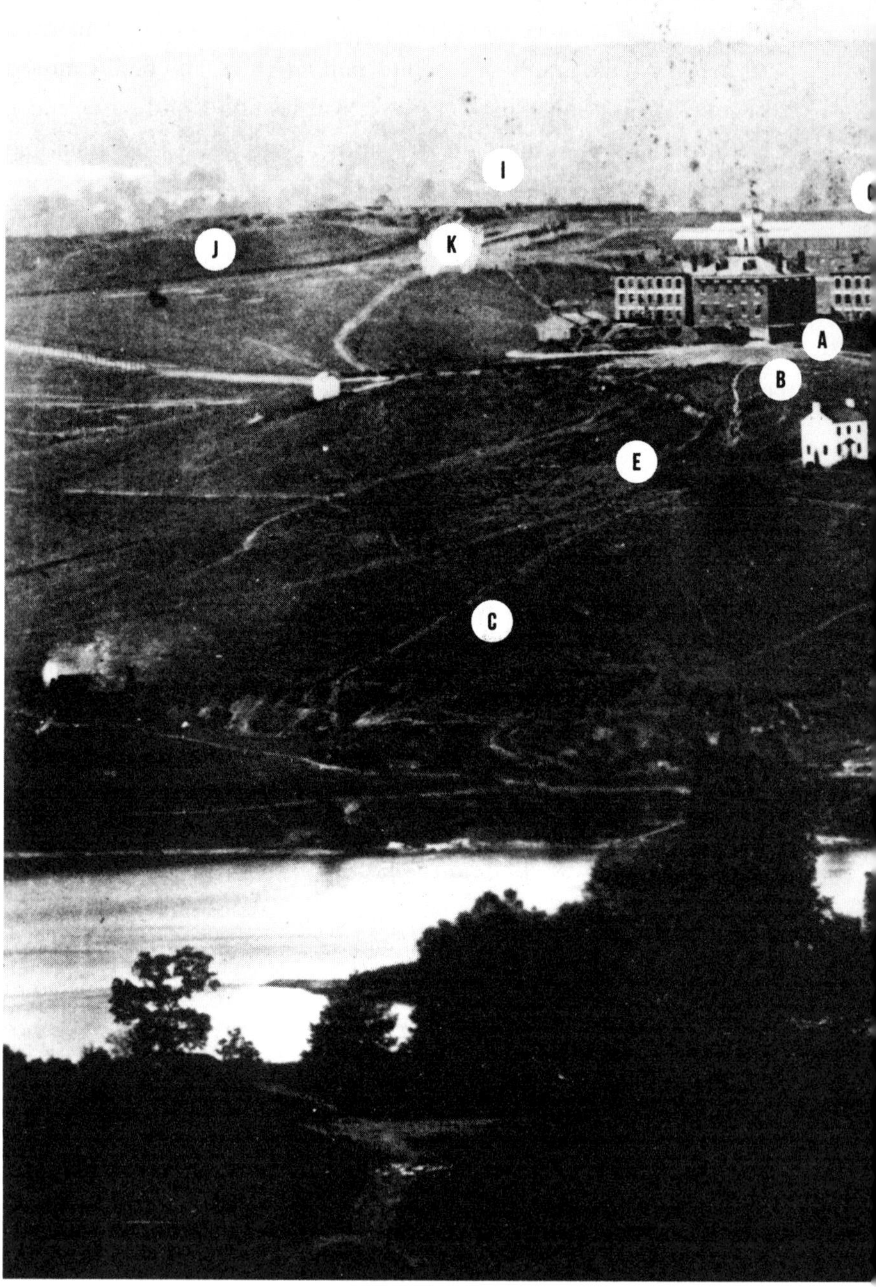
I
J
K
A
B
E
C

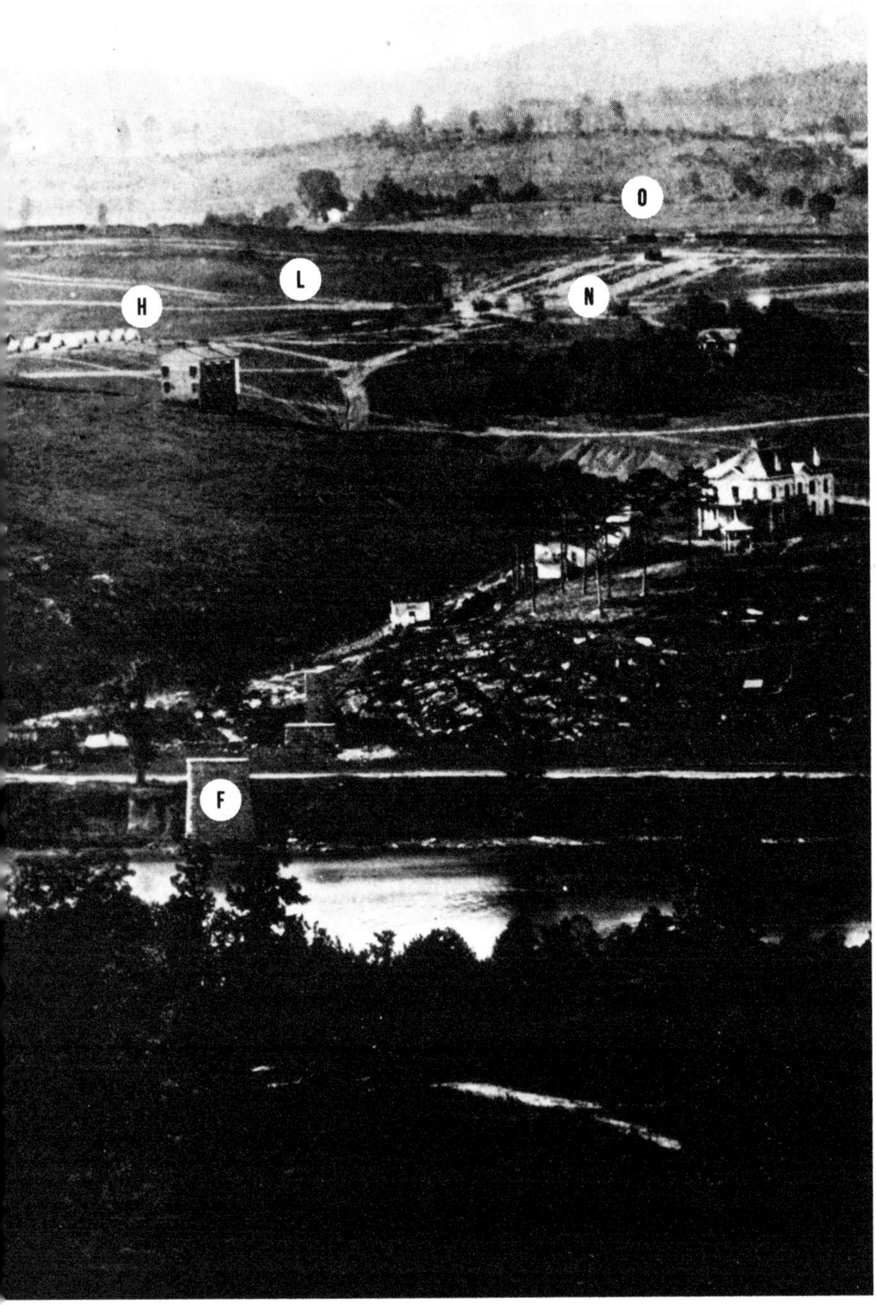

Fig. 41a. Theodore M. Schleier's 1865 panorama of Knoxville. A) Fort Byington; B) site of earthen holes, now filled, from Barnard photograph; C) former path to the spring; D) now filled eastern defensive trench; E) remaining trench; F) railroad piers; G) stables; H) cavalry tent camp; I) Fort Sanders; J) westernmost defensive trench; K) construction activity around the southeast bastion; L) excavation pit; M) excavation roads; N) exposed strata; O) Battery Zoellner structure.

Fig. 41b. Detail of Schleier's 1865 panorama showing Battery Zoellner. O) Battery Zoellner's structure; N) exposed strata.

Left of the stables one can see Fort Sanders (I) and the westernmost defensive trench (J). Details are lacking but there appears to be construction activity at the southeast bastion (K). A new road had been created by wagons carrying earth up to the southeast bastion from the westernmost borrow pit located behind the small pond (see figures 38a–c). The camp which was located north of Kingston Road at the site of Sophronia Strong Hall has disappeared.

To the east of White's ridge the huge excavation pit (L) dominates the landscape. The north side of the pit has been cut back farther and the tent camp which was on top of that cut has been moved, probably relocated to the east of the new horse barns. Well-used east/west roads are seen in the excavation (M), indicating that tons of earth have been removed from the pit since Barnard took his 1864 photograph. There are parallel strips of light-colored earth (N) which might have been exposed as topsoil was removed for additional earth.

At the highest point of the top of the parallel strips the authors made an exciting discovery about Battery Zoellner which has had very little written about it. Zoellner was a substantial structure (O) with sharply defined angled scarps and one gun embrasure facing southeast; another gun emplacement might have faced the railroad but the north side of the structure is not visible. Soldiers who manned Zoellner were probably responsible for managing the "gallows" which Orth showed on his map as being located in this same area, now at the intersection of Western Avenue at 11th Street.

When looking at this photograph one realizes that the White sisters unfortunately no longer have a barn behind their house. It has been removed! If one accepts Roemer's statement that the wood used to build revetments for Fort Byington came from "boards and shutters taken from the College, and of similar materials obtained in the neighborhood," then one must surmise that the sisters' barn boards may have been reused for the Fort Byington parapets (Roemer 1897:166).

THE WAR ENDS AND FORT SANDERS IS ABANDONED

Lee surrendered the Army of Northern Virginia on April 9, 1865, to Grant in the little village of Appomattox Court House. Just five days before, an inspection report was submitted to Major General George H. Thomas, commander of the Military Division of the Mississippi West of the Allegheny Mountains, by Brigadier General Z. B. Tower, the inspector-general of fortifications, Military Division of the Mississippi, Nashville. He reviewed the state of preparedness of all major earthworks in Knoxville, writing, "This city, the keep of East Tennessee, is well-fortified, and though the works are not finished they are sufficiently advanced to admit of good defense against *coup de main* or siege" (*OR* 1897:pt. 2, 213).

He then described the overall plan of defenses: "Seven enclosed works, eight batteries, and about two miles of infantry entrenchment constitute the defenses of Knoxville." An evaluation of Fort Sanders followed: "This large fort of bastion form is intended for twenty-one guns, the embrasures of which are nearly all finished. The work needs a good magazine and 21 platforms. The interior is not excavated deep enough to give good cover to the defenders. The ditch should be deepened and the scarp trimmed" (ibid.:214).

Tower ended his evaluation of Knoxville's defenses with compliments for the work of General Davis Tillson: "The defensive line of Knoxville commenced by Captain Poe, Engineer Corps, immediately after its occupation by our army, owes much to General Davis Tillson, commanding at this post during the past year. He has evinced much skill in laying out the connecting lines, and an uncommon energy in their execution, and it is a pleasure to bring his services in the defense of his post to the notice of the commanding general" (ibid.:215). Tower and Major General Thomas would soon hear that the battle at Appomattox Court House would be the last battle of the Civil War in the state of Virginia.

The war there ended in the home of Wilmer McLean on the afternoon of April 9, 1865. General Robert E. Lee surrendered his Army of Northern Virginia to General Ulysses S. Grant. A formal parade and the stacking of Confederate arms was arranged for April 12, and after that solemn ceremony ended, over 26,000 officers and soldiers, having agreed to the terms of their parole, were allowed to return home with their horses, side arms, and luggage (Winik 2001).

Ellen House, who was still living in Eatonton, Georgia, was devastated. She wrote that now "the people of the South are slaves—to the vilest race that ever disgraced humanity" (Sutherland 1996:165). Ellen would begin her journey home to Knoxville in an open wagon, sitting on her trunks. Other Confederate surrenders would follow in Alabama, North Carolina, Louisiana, Mississippi, Oklahoma, and elsewhere. Jefferson Davis was captured by Federal troops on May 10, 1865, in Georgia (Ballard 1997), and on August 20, 1866, President Andrew Johnson issued a proclamation stating that the insurrection had ended (Long 1971).

In the 1880s, two Union veterans, William F. Fox and Thomas L. Livermore, began the very difficult task of compiling statistics gleaned from state and federal records to determine how many deaths had resulted from the Civil War. Their totals included deaths from combat, wounds, starvation, disease, or accidents. For over ten decades, their numbers have stood as reliable estimates: 618,222 men died in the Civil War, 360,222 from the North and 258,000 from the south" (Hacker 2011; *Civil War Trust* 2018). However, research conducted by J. David Hacker, a Binghamton University demographic historian, based on newly digitized data collected from 19th-century census records, increases the death toll to a minimum of 750,000. Hacker's research was published in *Civil War History* (Hacker 2011) and has been said to be one of the most significant pieces ever to appear in the journal (Gugliotta 2012).

Several Union regiments would remain in Knoxville after Lee's surrender on April 9. Among these units were the 1st Colored Heavy Artillery, the 2nd Ohio Heavy Artillery, and the 10th Michigan Cavalry which was listed as on duty until August 1865. Organized in June 1864, the 1st Heavy Artillery were mustered out of service on March 31, 1866. In 1872, a Chattanooga reporter described Knoxville in the spring of 1865 as "the strongest fortified city in the South" (*Knoxville Press and Herald* 1872).

While the Union troops serving here were occasionally called out to deal with lingering guerrilla activity, they primarily guarded the restoration of the East Tennessee and Virginia Railroad and the telegraph lines. Another duty of the troops was to keep order among soldiers garrisoned in Knoxville and manage problems caused by Confederate sympathizers and by rowdy discharged soldiers who flooded the town after the war ended (McKenzie 2006). In May and June 1865, Union troops from Knoxville were sent to western North Carolina to block mountain passes and assist in the capture of Confederate president Jefferson Davis as he fled south, trying to reach a haven in Texas (Winik 2001).

That Fort Sanders was still a military installation in March 1866 is suggested by the mustering out of the 1st Colored Heavy Artillery during that month. Because President Johnson issued the proclamation ending the war in August 1866, it is reasonable to assume that Knoxville's Fort Sanders was abandoned in that month and its name given to an existing fort in Wyoming so that General William P. Sanders's name would continue to be remembered and honored. The Wyoming Fort Sanders protected travelers on the nearby Overland Trail and workers on the Union Pacific Railroad. The War Department maintained the fort until 1882. In July 1868, a meeting to consider the route of the Union Pacific Railroad was held at the Wyoming Fort Sanders, and a photograph exists of the notable people who attended the conference, including Generals Grant, Sherman, Sheridan, and Gibbon (Revere 1960).

The authors have not found any documents indicating that Tennessee's Fort Sanders was officially decommissioned or abandoned. In a list of 46 Civil War forts, Fort Sanders was one of only five that were neither documented as decommissioned or abandoned. Two were in Virginia, and three were in Tennessee. In addition to Fort Sanders, the Tennessee forts were Fort Pillow and Fortress Rosecrans (*Civil War Journeys* n.d.). All three were earthen fortifications, and there was probably little of value for the federal government to salvage. The journey to oblivion had begun for this historic structure that had served Union troops so well on November 29, 1863.

11

FORT SANDERS FROM 1866 TO 1900

After Fort Sanders was abandoned in 1866, the area surrounding it reverted to farmland where wandering cattle grazed. Photographs taken during the 34 years before the turn of the century show that the barren landscape around the earthen fort remained open and largely undisturbed until around 1880, when houses began to be built near the eastern boundary of the fort. The site of the fortification itself continued to be a place of great interest for curious residents, relic hunters, and the men who had fought there. Children "played about the crumbling structure," and the flat interior of the fort was used by a former teacher and resident of the area who "would take groups evenings to the old Fort for astronomical observations" (Yoe 1949).

Descriptions of the fort became sparse as it began to deteriorate and its historic significance faded in the minds of the populace. One article mentioning the old fort was published in an 1872 issue of the *Knoxville Press and Herald.* This newspaper reprinted an article entitled "Chattanoogan Taking Notes" originally published by the *Chattanooga Times* on June 4. The reporter wrote, "The old landmarks of the war have been pretty well obliterated and the immense wall that surrounded the city in 1864–65 has been leveled down except for a few outlying forts. Old Fort Sanders for the possession of which one of the severest battles of the war was fought on the morning of November 21st [*sic*] 1863, would hardly be recognized by its defenders or assailants" (*Chattanooga Times* 1872).

Based on other descriptions and photographs of the fort published near the end of the 19th century, the condition of the fort as described by this writer appears to be exaggerated. An assessment of the town, however, was favorable in 1872. Another reporter wrote, "The town had a clean wholesome look, is healthy and pleasantly situated and is rapidly acquiring a look of solidity seen only in our older and wealthier communities" (*Knoxville Press and Herald* 1872).

During the first decade after the war, the citizens of Knoxville seemed anxious to forget the "recent unpleasantness," as Southerners were apt to call the conflict, and began to pay little attention to Fort Sanders and its bloody legacy. It is noteworthy, for example, to consider the July 4, 1874, visit by General Burnside to Knoxville. Arriving by train that summer morning, his itinerary included a parade around town but did not include a visit to Fort Sanders, the site of his greatest Civil War victory. After a speech, he boarded a train and left Knoxville, a place where he was revered by hundreds of Union and Confederate supporters after the war's end (*Knoxville Weekly Chronicle* 1874). Burnside never returned and might not have ever known that his primary defensive fortification on White's Hill would be carved away by road building, earth removal, and residential development. The virtually treeless, war-torn property located on White's Hill, with the consent of the five granddaughters of James White who still owned the historic property, was soon to become a victim of 19th-century urban expansion.

THE FATE OF THE FORT IS SEALED

The first major impact on the area surrounding the fort was the incorporation of the City of West Knoxville (West Knoxville Charter 1889). This was closely followed by the construction of streets extending westward from Knoxville to the east end of the fort. The first of these early major thoroughfares was Clinch Avenue. The *Knoxville Daily Chronicle* reported on June 15, 1873, that "Col. C. M. McGhee is carrying out a valuable improvement over in the West end. He is cutting down Clinch Street from the railroad, westward and making fills near the bridge over Second Creek and near Fort Sanders. This grading extends Clinch Street as far out as Fort Sanders, and makes it an easy and pleasant drive" (*Knoxville Daily Chronicle* 1873). A bill from Charles Waring & Company dated September 1, 1873, lists a number of street gradings in 1872 and 1873 in what was then called the West End, including the excavation of 3,629 cubic yards of earth on Clinch. The bill also states that "Clinch Avenue can now be used as a road-way from 2nd Creek to the top of the fort." Clinch can be seen in the 1886 Bird's Eye view extending behind part of the southeast bastion up into the fort. This extension would later become the driveway for the Pickle house (see figure 44a). The fort with its projecting eastern bastions extended almost to 16th Street. However, the steep hillside on which the fort was located, along with the formidable walls and trenches of the fort itself, delayed further street building and improvements until the late 1880s (Charles Waring & Company 1873). It was not until November 1889 that the City Council of the new town of West Knoxville chose to continue improvements to Clinch Avenue to 8th Street (now 16th Street) (West Knoxville Council Minutes 1888–97).

The land boom in West Knoxville in the 1880s and 1890s sealed the fate of Fort Sanders. Before the war began, the six White granddaughters had inherited a large tract of land that included the fort site from their father, Hugh Andrew May White. A reporter for the *Knoxville News Sentinel* researched and related the interesting history of the land where the battle of Fort Sanders took place in a 1922 article, 57 years after the Civil War ended. "In the year 1820," the reporter wrote, "a tract of about 70 acres which included the site where the Battle of Fort Sanders was fought . . . was given to Joseph Greer by the State of Tennessee in the form of a land grant. Two years later an exchange . . . was made between Greer and Charles McClung for the tract" (*Knoxville News-Sentinel* 1922).

Charles McClung was the son-in-law of Knoxville's founder, James White, and the surveyor hired by his father-in-law to lay out the town of Knoxville in 1791. In 1832, Charles gave this land to his son Matthew McClung, who later sold the tract to Soloman D. Jacobs for the sum of $2,000. The land came back into the White family when Hugh A. M. White, grandson of James and Mary White, paid $7,000 for it. Hugh was a successful banker and merchant; he and his business partner, Marcus D. Bearden, owned several steamboats that operated on the Tennessee River between Chattanooga and Knoxville. Hugh's six daughters inherited his property along with his fortune after his death in 1860. The sisters would greatly benefit from the eventual sale of this land, which extended from Cumberland Avenue north over White's Hill to Highland Avenue. In the 1920s, house lots were selling in some sections for as much as $11,000 ($154,000 in 2016 dollars) to $15,000 each (ibid.). The White homestead with its gray, two-story frame house and orchard was located between White Avenue, Cumberland, and present-day 12th and 13th Streets (see photograph in Seymour 1963:161; note that the caption is erroneous). In the Fort Sanders neighborhood, White Avenue is the only remaining vestige of the presence of these descendants of Knoxville's founder.

The six White sisters were socially prominent and graciously entertained both Confederate and Union officers during their respective occupations of Knoxville. In 1934, Charles Rodgers, the son of Lucy White Rodgers, recalled that as a boy he overheard his mother and her sisters reminiscing about their friendships with the Confederate soldiers prior to the arrival of the Federals in the fall of 1863. He recalled that the ladies talked about how apprehensive they were when Union forces occupied the town. Their fears soon completely subsided as they found many of the young officers to be "wholly courteous and likeable" (Davis 1934). Soon the White sisters were again hosting lively parties at the old home place, which many years later would be replaced by the University of Tennessee Home Economics building and Hoskins Library.

On the morning of November 29, 1863, the sisters were surely silent and fearful, wondering what the future would hold for them as they listened to cannon fire coming from Fort Sanders. Things were to turn out well for the White sisters, as after the war they married into prominent Knoxville families and the land they had inherited continued to grow in value. In the 1870s, a tract of land appropriately named White's Addition was divided into parcels, and the lots were sold to individuals eager to move away from the smells, smoke, and soot of town. Charles Rodgers, Lucy White's son, became a "real estate man" who would profit from selling the land belonging to the sisters. Charles disposed of much of the sisters' big West Knoxville tract which included the fort's location. Sounding nostalgic about his childhood, he told stories to Lee Davis, a *News Sentinel* reporter, about how he and other neighborhood youngsters had collected relics in the fort and had played about the crumbling structure. Charles Rodgers, however, was a practical, politically savvy man of his times and ended his reminiscing by making it clear to Davis that "there was no anti-Yankee feeling involved in the razing of the fort." He explained further "that the fort covered two blocks of choice sites." Rodgers added that the fort was simply "removed to make way for residential development"(Davis 1934).

The onslaught of development in the area of the fortification and the battlefield itself began when James D. Cowan, a wealthy merchant who married one of the White sisters, purchased an entire block in White's Addition fronting on West Cumberland Avenue in 1879. The property was located between present-day 16th and 17th Streets (the latter was originally Fort Sanders Avenue) and extended northward to the bottom of the slope of the old fort (see figures 42a and b). James and his wife, Ann, built a palatial estate located where Sophronia Strong and Clement Hall dormitories stood on the University of Tennessee campus. The centerpiece of the estate was an elegant and very expensive three-story brick house in the Second Empire style, which featured a kitchen with running water, large dining room, parlor, music room, library, six bedrooms, two baths, a huge basement with a bowling alley, a four-story central tower, and a standing water tower (Avery 2000).

POSTWAR PHOTOGRAPHS OF THE FORT

Photographs taken in the 1870s show the Cowan house, outbuildings, and extensive grounds, including the view (see figure 42a) taken from a point looking northwest. The mansion faces the present Phil Fulmer Way (A), West Cumberland Avenue (B), and the east boundary of the estate is defined by future 16th Street (C) and a wall of stacked hand-hewn limestone blocks (F). A graveled road, the beginning of future 16th Street, extends from Cumberland Avenue north past the greenhouses (D) and ends at what is believed to be a guest house or the home of the Cowan's gardener (G). The University of Tennessee purchased part of this property in 1920.

E
D
F
C
B
A

Fig. 42a. 1870s photograph of the front of the Cowan house and grounds, looking northwest, with Fort Sanders in the background. Courtesy of the Calvin M. McClung Historical Museum. For key, see page 233.

E
F
B
A

Fig. 42b. 1880s photograph showing a part of the westernmost defensive trench which extends from the southeast bastion south to Melrose Place. Courtesy of the Special Collections, Virginia Tech University Libraries. A) Infantry trench; B) filled in postholes for the old stockade which followed the line of the western trench to the river; C) rear of Cowan house; D) cistern; E) greenhouses; F) gardener's house; G) Kingston Road; H) Melrose house.

Only the two-story house, which historians usually call the "gardener's house," remains of the estate and is still owned by the university (ibid.). Because it was located near the three large greenhouses and has been called the gardener's house for years, it is reasonable to assume that it was home to Michael Hoey, an Irish immigrant who worked for James Cowan as a gardener, floral designer, and "lawn maker" for twenty-two years until his death in the fall of 1894. Hoey was said to be one of the finest lawn makers in the country (*Knoxville Journal* 1894). The University of Tennessee completed the restoration of this earliest dwelling (130-plus years) remaining in the Fort Sanders area in 2018 for use as a classroom. It is located at the corner of White Avenue and 16th Street. To the right of this building, a track or path begins where the road ends at the gardener's house (close to future White Avenue) and continues up the hill to the east side of the fort. This track would later become the northern extension of 16th Street. Just east of this track one can see the edge of the borrow pit (H) (also see figures 38a–c). The entire length of the south curtain wall (J) of Fort Sanders with its two bastions (I, K) is captured against the skyline. The southwest bastion completed in 1865 (K) is visible at the west end of the fort, and pine trees (L) grow near the slope of the bastion. In 1890, a south–north cut at the location of a cannon embrasure in that bastion (K) would be made to allow reunion visitors into the fort.

The top of the enormous southeast bastion with its embrasures looms against the sky at the east end of the fort (I). This stunning photograph of the fort graphically shows the awesome size of Fort Sanders in 1865 and testifies to the truth of Charles Rodgers's statement in 1922 that the fort "covered two blocks of choice building sites" (Davis 1934). Other photographs of the fort and the area surrounding it were taken around 1888 by members of the New England Press Association, who toured the southeastern states of North Carolina, Tennessee, Virginia, and Maryland, taking pictures of the countryside and places of interest. These photographs can be found in the New England Press Association Album, which is preserved in the Virginia Tech University Library (New England Press Association n.d.) On their visit to Knoxville, members of the group took several photographs, of which two have been used to identify the true location of the fort.

Figure 43 shows the eastern end of the north wall and part of the northeast bastion. The houses located east of the bastion remnants are on a street initially named Grove and later renamed Laurel Avenue. The photographer stood on the northwest bastion facing east and photographed part of the north wall (A), northeast bastion (B), and the trench (C). Two houses are visible farther east; the occupant of the house closer to the photographer was listed in the 1888 Knoxville City Directory as G. A. Rumsey (Knoxville City Directory 1888–1922). The Rumsey house (D) can also be seen on the 1917 Sanborn map (Sanborn Insurance Company 1917). The tower of the W. H. Simmonds frame house can be seen above the roof of the Rumsey house. The Simmonds (E) house stood on the crest of the hill at Laurel and 15th Street as early as 1882. A plank fence painted white surrounded the yard and kept large animals off the lawn (*Knoxville News-Sentinel* 1922).

The photographer was standing on the northwest bastion when he shot the southwest bastion seen in figure 42a. To the left in the photo is the tower of the Cowan house (E) set behind the location of Melrose (F). A straight line of underbrush extends south from the road. This line (G) marks the unfinished route of the Knoxville Southern Railroad chartered in 1887. The Knoxville Southern Railroad was purchased by the Louisville and Nashville in 1902 and is now part of the CSX system.

As seen in figure 42b, the third view of the westernmost defensive trench (A) of Fort Sanders taken by the New England Press photographers is especially important in determining the exact location of Fort Sanders. It was taken at the east end of the fort with the camera facing south towards the back (north side) of the Cowan house (C). A large standing brick cistern is located immediately to the rear of the mansion, supplying water for the bathrooms and kitchen facilities (D). The greenhouses (E) are located in the eastern side yard, and at the far left the gardener's house is partially visible (F). The two-story brick house still stands at the corner of 16th Street and White Avenue, situated adjacent

C

Fig. 43. 1880s photograph of the Rumsey house facing east and showing the northeast bastion and the trench along the north wall. Courtesy of the Special Collections, Virginia Tech University Libraries. A) North wall; B) northeast bastion; C) trench; D) Rumsey house; E) Simmonds house tower.

to the top of a limestone wall that faces 16th Street. Portions of this wall still remain, along with the gardener's/guest house. In the foreground is the Union infantry trench (A), which was still in fair condition at the time the photo was taken. This trench ran from the southeast corner of the fort toward the Cowan house, crossed the Kingston Road (G) (now Cumberland Avenue), and continued southward up the hill, roughly following the direction of present-day Melrose Avenue. The trench connected to a Federal earthwork called Battery Noble at the top of a ridge, on which was located the Thomas Powell house (later Melrose house) (H). This house sat directly opposite Fort Sanders.

In this photo, a line of postholes (B) east of and running parallel to the trench was for the first time identified by the authors as the remnant of a stockade installed by Tillson. We rechecked this photograph for postholes after reading an account of a Union soldier stationed in Knoxville emailed to us by Steve Cotham in January 2018 and were stunned that we had not recognized these earlier. Alvin Woolson and Steve Cotham get the credit for this major discovery. Woolson wrote: "From the Holsten [*sic*] River to the Fort a stockade was made of poles from 8 inches to 12 inches in diameter, placed in the ground and sharpened to a point at the end. These poles were in the ground about eight to ten feet and extended out at least twenty feet" (Miller 1914:86). If the posts had not been pulled by scavengers after the war, they were certainly pulled by Cowan employees before the house was completed. The holes were refilled with lighter-colored soil than the earth surrounding them.

BIRD'S EYE VIEWS OF KNOXVILLE

Two important drawings of the town and areas surrounding it were published in 1871 and 1886. These images were drawn in perspective from an imagined point high above the landscape and illustrate a panoramic view of Knoxville and portions of the surrounding areas. The former only shows the city as far west as the university, but the 1886 view, published by Norris Wellge and Company of Milwaukee, Wisconsin, shows Fort Sanders at the far left of the image (Beck and

Fig. 44a. 1927 Thompson photograph of the Pickle mansion with Fort Sanders Manor in the background. Note the driveway rising from Clinch is similar to the road leading up to the fort interior behind the southeast bastion as seen in the 1886 Bird's Eye View of Knoxville. Courtesy of the Calvin M. McClung Historical Collection.

Fig. 44b. 1927 Thompson photograph of Pickle mansion looking north. The limestone and brick walls retain remains of the southeast bastion. Courtesy of the Calvin M. McClung Historical Collection.

Paul 1886). The drawings are fairly accurate, but there are errors in the image. Fort Sanders is misrepresented as a square star fort (A). Grove Street (later Laurel Avenue) (C) and Clinch Avenue (D) are both mislabeled (see D and E), and the extra "street" (E), mislabeled Clinch, was mistakenly added by the artist. Clinch Avenue terminates at the top of a slope behind a modified southeast bastion and provides entry into the east end of the fort.

The Pickle house (B) would be built in 1899 behind this same modified bastion, and the old path up into the fort from Clinch would serve as the driveway for the house. The Rumsey house seen in figure 43 was built in 1888 a block east of future 17th Street on the north side of what

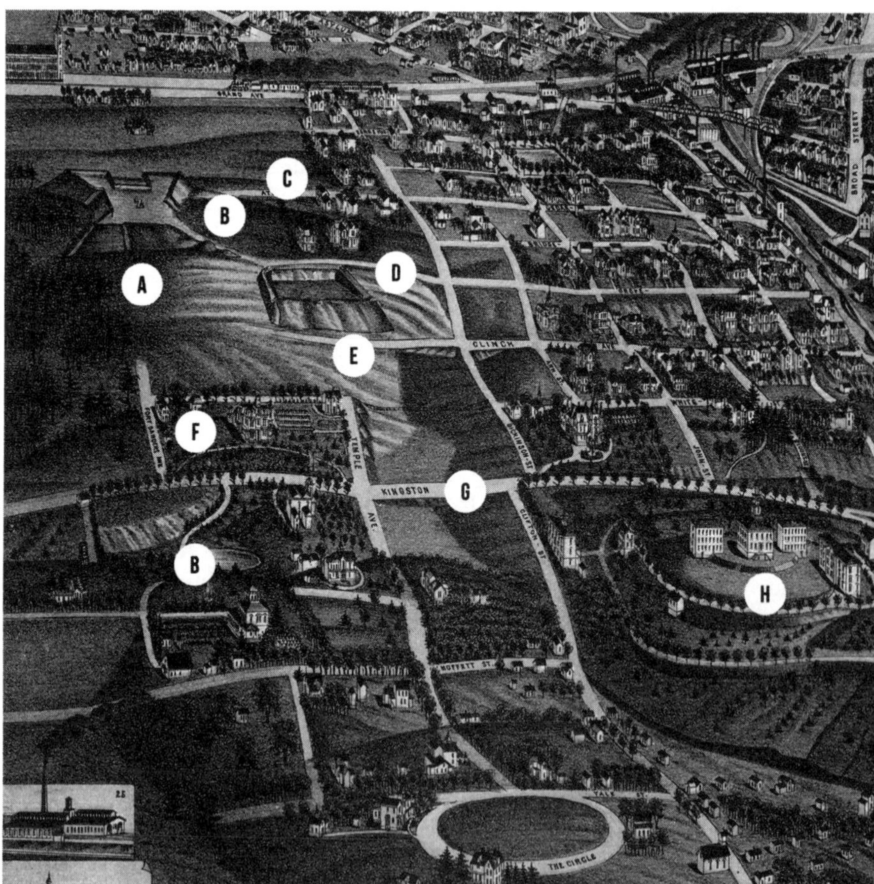

is now Laurel Avenue. The Cowan house (F) faces Kingston Pike (G), and to the northeast of the Cowan estate is the borrow pit excavated for fort construction (E). This rectangular pit was excavated on the south side, rather than the north side, of future Clinch Avenue to future White Avenue and between 15th and 16th Streets. The way in which the borrow pit is rendered creates an optical illusion that makes this excavated area appear as a reservoir of some kind with above-ground walls. The borrow pit became an amphitheater in 1890 for the Blue-Gray Reunion, a picnic area called the "Commons" in the 1940s, and later a rose garden (Ferguson 2011).

Fig. 45. 1886 Bird's Eye View of Knoxville. Courtesy of the Calvin M. McClung Historical Collection. For key, see above.

12

PRESERVING MEMORIES AMID CHANGING TIMES

KNOXVILLE ENTERS A PERIOD OF GROWTH AND RECONCILIATION

Like many of her fellow Knoxvillians, Ellen House carried her wartime grudges into the postwar period. After her return to Knoxville, Ellen's life in a boarding house next door to Parson Brownlow, the murder of her favorite brother in 1865, and the death of her father in 1866 did not help to soften her attitude towards Unionists, for whom she continued to express bitter hatred.

Ellen wrote on September 8, 1865: "We certainly live in horrible times. Scarcely a day passes some one is not killed" (Sutherland 1996:186). She avowed that the "the Devil seems to be walking at large in East Tenn" (ibid.:195). Feelings continued to run hot between the winners and losers of this war, and Ellen wrote of drunken fights, beatings, hangings, shootings, and drownings of both Union and Confederate supporters and blacks and whites. Added to Ellen's resentment of the continuing Union occupation in Knoxville was the fact that she wanted the family to leave their boarding house for a home of their own. She bitterly wrote that she was one of many who were "almost crazy to get to housekeeping . . . but houses are very difficult things to get. There are so many Yankees here, that every place is filled with them" (ibid.:177).

By October 1865, the House family had a new home and began taking in boarders. One of their first boarders was a young clerk from Nashville, a nondrinker, a rebel, and a chess player named James Fletcher.

Ellen and James fell in love, were married in 1867, and settled in Knoxville (ibid.:202–3).

Knoxvillians of both leanings began to mellow as time passed, and their rigid stances softened. By 1880, old animosities began to fade away among the local war generation as memories of the terrible conflict's horrors grew dim. The majority of citizens, including those who had supported the Confederacy, realized that Union occupation actually had been good for Knoxville in terms of money flowing into the city. By 1870, the population had tripled from an estimated population of 5,300 in 1860 (Deadrick 1976), and the Knoxville Board of Trade had been established to advertise Knoxville to the outside world. In the ten years that followed, in addition to free public schools, a second newspaper, a theater, a town doctor, a city board of health, a library, street cars, a telephone company and a number of businesses had opened. Most residents believed that "their modest town stood on the brink of profound changes and that they would need one another to make those changes as beneficial to themselves and the city as possible" (Wheeler 2005:5).

A souvenir packet created by McCrary and Branson in 1889 featured illustrations of important buildings in Knoxville, street views, and the scenic terrain that surrounded the town. This beautifully designed packet was likely sold everywhere in town during the 1890 Blue-Gray Reunion. The flowery text touted the town as the literary, commercial and political metropolis of East Tennessee and one of the best distributing centers in the entire South. How could one not pack up and move to Knoxville after reading that its location compared to "the blizzard stricken north and the torrid south" offered a climate "equal to that of the most favored country in the world" (McCrary and Branson 1889:15).

The population of the city when this souvenir packet was published was about 22,535 (Deadrick 1976) and was growing. Large numbers of Northerners, many of whom had fought in the area, were settling in Knoxville, creating businesses, or seeking employment in numerous commercial and industrial businesses. Historian Todd Groce wrote that former East Tennessee Confederates during this time were ambivalent about lauding "The Lost Cause," as they now found it necessary to "live peacefully for their economic and social benefits." They were practical people and realized that "little could be gained by keeping alive old memories which might antagonize former enemies who were now business partners, neighbors and even friends" (Groce 1999:159).

HONORING WAR VETERANS

Many of the younger generation in Knoxville had not fought in the war, nor suffered the loss of their property, nor gone hungry as had older natives of the city. They were not haunted by animosity toward either "Yankees" or "rebels" and began to honor the dead of both sides of the conflict. Even before the war ended, Knoxvillians were decorating the graves of those who had worn both the blue and the gray in the Knoxville National Cemetery, where the Union army soldiers are buried, and the Bethel Confederate Cemetery. In the decade before the 20th century, a national reconciliation spread through the country, spurred by "memory creation"—that is, the memorialization of heroes and battles through monuments. Between 1867 and the late 1890s, the majority of Confederate and Union memorials were added in cemeteries and were funereal in design, expressing admiration of deceased soldiers and grief over their loss. National Military Parks were established at this time; the earliest sites preserved as parks were the battlefields of Chattanooga and Chickamauga in 1890, and both Union and Confederate soldiers were honored there (Paige and Greene 1983).

Bethel Cemetery was the burial ground for the Confederate soldiers in Knoxville. The cemetery was given this name after the Knoxville Ladies Memorial Association acquired the cemetery in 1873. Usually buried in trenches, about 1,600 soldiers were interred from 1861 to 1863, including the unknown dead from the battle of Fort Sanders. Four metal and stone tablets record the names of those Confederates known to have been "killed in the Battle of Knoxville 1861–1865." About fifty Union prisoners of war were buried in a separate area (McRary 2012c).

On Memorial Day, May 19, 1892, a monument was dedicated by Confederate veterans to the soldiers buried in the cemetery. Lloyd Branson, one of Knoxville's most distinguished artists had designed and a Union veteran, George Whitaker, had carved an "eight foot, six inch soldier . . . judiciously scaled to appear life size taking account of the 48 foot elevation and the distance from which it would be viewed" (Tumblin 2013a; Smith 2015).

The National Cemetery located on Tyson Street in Knoxville was established in 1863 by General Ambrose Burnside. It was reported in 1867 that there were 2,600 Union soldiers buried here. Calvin "Cal" Johnson (Caldonia), a former slave, had been hired to oversee other freed slaves in burying Union soldiers during the occupation. Johnson received a government contract after the war ended "to gather dead bodies throughout the region and convey them here for burial." The cemetery was expanded to add room for 600 more graves so that soldiers first buried in the Cumberland Gap area could be reinterred in the National Cemetery. Cal Johnson was 21 years old in 1865; and over the next 60 years, he became one of the wealthiest African Americans in Knoxville (Booker 2017). A Knoxville park was named in honor of his contributions to the city as an alderman and philanthropist (McRary 2012b).

African American soldiers were also buried in the National Cemetery early in the Federal occupation of Knoxville. In December 1863, Steven Ray, although not a Union soldier, was interred in the cemetery. Ray was a "teamster" who apparently was highly regarded for his service to the Federal army. Four members of the 1st Regiment, U.S. Colored Heavy Artillery, were buried that same year; and after African Americans began to be recruited into the Union army in early 1864, the number of internments increased dramatically. In 1865, 14 soldiers of the United States Colored Heavy Artillery, 40th United States Colored Infantry, and one soldier in the 14th USCI were interred (Welsh 2013).

Union veterans wanted a taller memorial built in the National Cemetery than the Branson monument and had designed in 1900 what was then the largest Union monument in the South. Dedicated in 1901, it was destroyed three years later by a "a powerful bolt of lightning . . . that was heard for miles." The bronze eagle that topped the shattered base "was flung into the street with its wings 'closely cropped at its body as if the work had been done by an instrument.' With the help of Captain William Rule, sufficient funds were raised to repair the monument base and hire Baumann Brothers Architects to complete the project. The new monument featured an eight-foot-tall Union soldier, and its height topped the Confederate memorial in Bethel Cemetery by four feet" (Neely 1999; Tumblin 2013a).

Women of the South, left alone to survive the personal and family hardships brought about by the war years, became empowered during the war; and they came together after it ended for a purpose: to glorify the "Lost Cause" by depicting it as a courageous struggle by Southerners to retain their way of life against impossible odds (Gallagher and Noble 2000). The United Daughters of the Confederacy was established in Nashville, Tennessee in 1894, and the organization was formally named in 1895. The women fought for pensions for Confederate soldiers, became fundraisers, documented battlefields, and installed monuments in cemeteries to the men who had fought for the honorable "Lost Cause." They defended the secession and the right to self-government, espoused the virtues of the antebellum South, and developed pro-South lesson plans for their children (Cox 2003). In the late 19th and early 20th centuries, as they gained political power and funds, they began placing heroic statues of Confederate leaders on the lawns of county courthouses and town squares (Foster 1987). The Ellen Renshaw House Chapter of the Tennessee Division of the United Daughters of the Confederacy 2624 was formed in Knoxville in 2000.

Digby Seymour described the meetings that he attended as a child with his mother, who belonged to a Knoxville chapter of the United Daughters of the Confederacy. He said that he enjoyed singing the old "rebel" songs with the women each time they met (Seymour 2008). In an effort to keep the "the Lost Cause" alive in the early 1950s, the Daughters created divisions of the "Children of the Confederacy" for youth under 18 who were blood descendants of honorable Confederate soldiers. They sought to maintain the prewar racial and social order for the next generations (Gallaher and Noble 2000).

Local veterans' organizations were formed so that those who had fought together could stay connected. Larger organizations such as the United Confederate Veterans, formed in 1865, helped to care for indigent veterans, orphans, and widows of veterans. A year later, the Grand Army of the Republic (G.A.R.), was founded in Decatur, Illinois in 1866 by Benjamin F. Stevenson. Members of this organization became advocates, lobbying for voting rights for black veterans, promoting pensions for vets, and supporting Republican candidates. They also helped to establish Memorial Day as a National holiday. Peak membership was over 490,000 in 1890 (Knight n.d.). Numerous reunions, including Knoxville's Blue-Gray Reunion, would finally bring the veterans of both armies to meet face to face in remembrance and brotherhood (Hathaway 1971).

13

DISAPPOINTMENT AND CELEBRATION

FEDERAL GOVERNMENT REFUSES TO PURCHASE FORT LAND

In addition to honoring the war dead in Knoxville's military cemeteries, there was a movement among Knoxville citizens who had participated in the war to acquire Fort Sanders and develop it into a military park in early 1890. On January 25, Robert N. Hood, a Knoxville attorney, sent a letter of introduction and a memorandum of a contract to Leonidas C. Houk for the sale of Fort Sanders to the federal government for a military park. Houk was a member of the U.S. House of Representatives from Tennessee's Second District, a leading Republican in East Tennessee, and a former colonel in the Union army (Langston 2000).

In the letter, Hood related: "General Alger was in Knoxville, in company with congressman Bliss of Michigan, and by the way the late lamented Col. Goodlee, was with the party and also Gen. Poe, the engineer who constructed Fort Sanders; in company with the gentlemen of Knoxville. I visited Fort Saunders with the party, and it was unanimously agreed that the Government should purchase the property" (Robert N. Hood, Letter 1890). General Russell Alger had served in the Civil War in the 5th Michigan Cavalry, where he was brevetted to the rank of general in the Union army. He also served as the 40th secretary of war and was the 20th governor of Michigan (Bourasaw 2004); Michigan Historical Commission 1924). Attorney Hood ended his letter by saying, "I hope that Congress would include the appropriation asked for, enough money and provide for the erection of a statue to the late Gen. A. E. Burnside. The loyal people of East Tennessee remember Gen. Burnside, as their savior and redeemer, from a yoke of bondage that was equal to, if not worse, than Egyptian bondage" (Robert N. Hood, Letter 1890).

General Alger and his party arrived by train in Knoxville on September 17, 1889. With the group were Colonel A. P. Bliss, a Michigan congressman; Colonel George H. Hopkins, assistant adjutant general of the G.A.R.; and General Orlando Poe, who was still greatly admired and respected by the people of Knoxville. General Poe led the men on a tour of the fort the next morning, and the gentlemen were impressed, regarding it as a prominent and historically important feature of the landscape.

Poe gave a detailed account of the battle, and his remarks were published by the *Knoxville Daily Journal.* As to the location of Fort Sanders, he said that the fort was built "on the *western* slope of the hill," the military crest (italics added). Poe told again the story of the miraculous cannon shot by Lieutenant Benjamin and the mortal wounding of General Sanders. He also praised the bravery of the Confederates who stormed the fort and responded to the frequent criticisms of General Longstreet's decision to attack what was thought to be the strongest point of the fort. General Poe said that had he been on the Confederate side, he would have "advised him to attack just where he did attack" (*Knoxville Daily Journal* 1889).

After bidding farewell to their hosts, General Alger and his party left Knoxville for Crawfish Springs, Georgia, where 12,000 Union and Confederate veterans were attending a reunion and plans were being made for the nation's first military park at Chickamauga (*Hallowed Ground* 2013; Veal 2013). Alger was a member of a committee of the Society of the Army of the Cumberland, formed in 1888; this group had taken the first step in purchasing ground at Chickamauga for a park. Seven years later, the Chickamauga National Battlefield Park was dedicated (Paige and Greene 1983). Veterans of the battle were able to identify and describe the events that took place at important areas of the battlefield, and these sites were documented with large cast-iron markers that still stand.

The memorandum of the sales contract for the Fort Sanders site contained the detailed description of eight acres that can be exactly located on modern maps of the Fort Sanders neighborhood. The contract to sell Fort Sanders to the federal government was between the owner, James D. Cowan, husband of one of the White sisters, for $5,000 per acre for all of the land included within the eight acres. It is noteworthy that no further documentation has been discovered to indicate that the federal government was interested in purchasing the land. Because the government was already deeply involved with the acquisition of the enormous Chickamauga battlefield, there may have been no desire to invest in more battlefield property. By early 1890, the Chattanooga battlefield had been added to that preservation project. And in May 1890 a bill was introduced to the U.S. House of Representatives to purchase 7,600 acres of these battlefields for $125,000 (ibid.).

THE BLUE-GRAY REUNION OF 1890

Having failed in their attempt to get federal funding to purchase and preserve a part of Fort Sanders, it appears that prominent Knoxvillians were still not ready to give up on saving the fort. An improved economy and the convenience of railroads provided the means for those interested in touring Civil War battlefields to travel long distances in order to satisfy their curiosity.

In January 1890, a reunion in Grand Rapids, Michigan, of the 17th Michigan infantry, which had fought at Fort Sanders, caught the attention of several Knoxvillians who were interested in hosting those same veterans at a future reunion in Knoxville (*Knoxville Daily Journal* 1890a). Included among those interested were members of the local Ed Maynard Post of the G.A.R. and the Zollicoffer Camp. While separate Union and Confederate reunions had already been held in various parts of the country, this was the first event of its kind that would bring former adversaries together in a more fraternal spirit. Knoxvillians had a significant fort and battlefield for visitors to see, in addition to stories to share about the siege and descriptions of an extremely bloody battle. They also had a desire to make money from tourism, and were optimistic that a successful reunion would create new interest in preserving the old fort.

In March 1890, city leaders decided to host a reunion and invite both Union and Confederate veterans who had fought in the battle of Fort Sanders, their families, and others interested in visiting Knoxville. With seven months to prepare, they quickly began to advertise the event, which they had named the "Veterans Reunion at Knoxville" in national newspapers. The Ed Maynard Post sent special invitations to the 8,000 G.A.R. posts in the country, as well as to organizations of Confederate veterans, and emphasized that anyone who had fought at Fort Sanders would "be a specially invited party" (Conklin 2005:93). Not only was there advertising to be done, but there were also old roads and streets to be improved and others to be built; an outdoor amphitheater to be constructed; housing for visitors to be identified; mattresses, linens, and cots to be stocked, rented, and sold; mementos to be manufactured; food and drink to be supplied; a fireworks display to plan; and an enormous enclosed venue to be erected.

A large number of committees were formed, and one of the first orders of business up for discussion was where to stage the indoor activities for the 22,500 residents of Knoxville and the thousands of anticipated visitors. While constructing some kind of permanent structure for the festivities was contemplated, it was deemed more practical and cheaper to find a temporary structure such as a tent. The problem was solved when a huge tent used by the Barnum and Bailey Circus was found. Priced at $600, it could hold 15,000 people. While finding the tent proved relatively simple, transporting it to Knoxville from its storage place in Milwaukee proved more problematic and costly. The tent measured 212 × 262 feet, weighed eight tons, and required two railroad flat cars to transport it. It arrived in Knoxville on August 4 and was set up on the west side of the fort near the southwest bastion east of what is now 19th Street (ibid.).

Because most of the activities planned for the reunion would take place in West Knoxville, the details for the events that would occur there became largely the responsibility of the West Knoxville Town Council. The site of the fort itself was quickly chosen for the festivities since it was still largely an open field devoid of houses. A critical element for a successful event was safe access for visitors to the fort and tent site. The fort at that time could be reached from town only via Clinch Avenue to 8th Street (now 16th St.), then by taking a right turn there and making a short trip up the hill to Laurel. A left turn onto Laurel would take a visitor into the fort (ibid.). Several street improvements were proposed on the West Knoxville Council agendas in 1890, Laurel Avenue and 8th Street were macadamized in April and May, respectively, and sidewalks were added on Laurel. Ninth Street (future 17th Street) had not been built (West Knoxville Council Minutes 1888–97). As early as 1887, a streetcar line had been planned from the center of Knoxville to Fort Sanders. On November 10, 1887, the *Knoxville Tribune* reported, "The West End street railway company will commence laying the track out Clinch Street, west from the custom house, within a few days. The ordinance giving the right of way over the street will pass final reading Friday night. The company promises to begin work and complete the line to Fort Saunders [*sic*] at once so that the public may have the benefit of the road by the first of the year, if not sooner" (*Knoxville Tribune* 1887).

On October 6, preparations were still underway for the influx of visitors. "There was a plea on that day by the reunion decoration committee that everyone on the main streets should finish decorating their homes and businesses with flags and bunting "not later than Monday evening, October 6" (Conklin 2003:100).

Vendors in the Market House competed with each other to put up the most festive decorations. All the businesses around the square decorated their storefronts as well, and many added lights. Large pictures of Grant and Lee with the words "Our Country" hung from the second stories of store fronts. One store window featured cuttings from the cedar tree that was still growing near the spot where General Sanders was shot. Other evergreen cuttings used for decoration were taken from pine trees that had "grown up in the field where blood ran like water." According to the *Journal* reporter, the new pine growth now covering the ground there had obliterated "all signs of blood" showing that the carnage of the war was now gone and forgotten; and the green boughs cut from those pines used in decorations also affirmed that "those brave men who lost their lives shall ever be kept green in the hearts of those who come after them." Every aspect of the reunion was meant to celebrate the reuniting of the country (*Knoxville Daily Journal* 1890b).

On October 6, a headline article announced that on the day before, between 2:00 and 5:00 p.m., "the streets leading to Fort Sanders where the big reunion tent is stretched . . . were lined with approximately 5,000 people." The reporter added a flowery description of the tent: "The big tent is a sight in itself. A perfect mountain of canvas rearing aloft its head to the skies" (*Knoxville Daily Journal* 1890c). Descriptions of that day's activities continued: "the most active work today will go on in building the monster amphitheater for people to witness the gorgeous fireworks display on Thursday night." At that time, the amphitheater that the *Knoxville Tribune* reported would hold 7,000 people, was only half completed. This huge outdoor venue had been shaped from the earlier massive borrow pit created by the labor of Union soldiers from 1863 to 1865 (*Knoxville Tribune* 1890). Portions of this sunken amphitheater are still visible at 1612 16th Street near the Masonic Lodge.

From October 7 to 9, 1890, more people streamed into Knoxville by train, carriage, wagon and horseback, and sought out their accommodations. The New York Highlanders stayed at Camp Vendome, one of only 10 hotels in Knoxville at that time (Conklin 2005). The Reunion Organizing Committee had wisely begun in August to place cots in empty public buildings and arranged transportation for visitors to campsites at Lake Ottossee (now Chilhowee Park). A large number of the thousands of visitors found rooms in private homes, while many veterans and other attendees chose to camp in Fort Sanders itself. The Knoxville Rifles went in to camp on Monday night and remained there until the reunion was over. A detail of that organization also guarded the tents each night. The *Knoxville Tribune* reported that "young soldiers at Fort Sanders say they enjoy camp life hugely" (*Knoxville Tribune* 1890).

The following descriptions of reunion activities were reported in the *Knoxville Journal* and the *Knoxville Tribune,* and were taken from an excellent article by Forest Conklin in the East Tennessee Historical Society's *Tennessee Ancestors*. The reunion was extensively covered locally and written about in regional and national newspapers.

The first day of the reunion, October 7, was filled with receptions for visitors hosted throughout the town by prominent citizens and by veterans' organizations at their headquarters (*Knoxville Daily Journal* 1890d). Celebrations began on the second day late in the morning with a parade of veterans, escorted by members of military and civic organizations. The line of the march wound through the main streets of the Knoxville business district and then headed out Clinch Avenue to the fort. The *Knoxville Daily Journal* reported that thousands of spectators followed mainly on foot but also in "conveyances." Prior to their arrival, workmen had set up seats "over the very best ground on which the main charge of Longstreet's force was made." They saw "numerous small tents used by military companies as quarters between the large tent and . . . the old ditch running along outside the old fort." Also, "Sentries paced up and down protecting their property and the workers from annoyances" (*Knoxville Daily Journal* 1890e).

After arriving, the attendees assembled in the "Big Tent" and listened to speeches by notable guests. The key address was written by the guest of honor, General James Longstreet, who because of a wound received in the Battle of the Wilderness, had his prepared remarks read by the Honorable E. A. Angier of Atlanta. The *Knoxville Daily Journal* humorously reported that no effort had been made to keep the general out of Knoxville this time and that he was "one of our honored guests and [met] with a cordial welcome." Colonel Henderson said in his speech regarding the battle that the "brave Highlanders were one of the chief obstacles to getting inside the fort." His remark was said to have "brought down the house" *(Knoxville Daily Journal* 1890e). The fort presented a picturesque scene. "Places where the cannons had been stationed" were occupied with "stands" of every kind, and plenty of souvenirs were to be had.

On Thursday, October 9, people trooped back to the fort for a "peace jubilee," where veterans "who thirty years ago were engaged in shooting each other, met as brothers who now lived together in peace in a united country." They shared personal stories of the war and talked about the "valor of the American soldiers, their brave deeds in battle and their heroic marches to sure death" (*Knoxville Daily Journal* 1890f).

That evening was labeled the "climax" of the reunion, and a huge crowd entered the "amphitheater" ready to be entertained by a highly touted fireworks display. The crowd was not disappointed as the display seems to have rivaled present-day 4th of July spectacles. The introduction to the program included geysers, two hundred pyric sparrows, grand borealis illuminations, a huge silver fire wheel, a ruby cluster, and two dancing skeletons. There were several set pieces 75 to 100 feet wide. The final piece, the battle of Fort Sanders, was set off to the accompaniment of a band. It was a representation of the fort illuminated with "lance works of cinnamon tints." There were thunderous roars as cannonading began, bombs flew towards the fort, and houses burned. The fiery scene concluded "with the explosion of large rockets" and battery fire. This fabulous fireworks display was a fitting ending to an enormously successful reunion, and the organizers felt that they "had met their objective to create a better and more fraternal spirit among the veterans in arms" (ibid.).

The enthusiastic, energetic, and efficient organizers had no inkling that a single surviving panoramic photograph of the fort taken during that special gathering would provide the key that 120 years later would unlock a 21st century mystery: the discovery of the lost location of Civil War Fort Sanders within the neighborhood that eventually inherited its name. The photograph itself was lost to Civil War historians as it had been erroneously identified as a circus event when it was first found because of the presence of the huge Barnum and Bailey tent. It had been properly identified by 2008 as an 1890 reunion gathering at Fort Sanders when McClung Collection archivists were sorting through a collection of Thompson photographs and was available during the planning for the Civil War Sesquicentennial (Cotham 2017).

The exact day the photograph was taken during the reunion is unknown, but the likely date is October 8, when a series of speeches were given in the tent. The photographer stood on the roof of the cupola of the Cowan house, pointed his camera with its panoramic lens towards the northwest, and captured the entire south wall of the fort. After hours and hours of study of this digitized photograph, which fortunately could be enlarged at the click of a mouse, the authors were finally able to identify features of the fort that, upon first glance, now seem quite obvious.

Beginning in the foreground, one can see the base of the former location of the Cowan house cistern (A). The early track of Fort Sanders Avenue, which can also be seen in the Bird's Eye View of Knoxville (see figure 45), begins at the lower left (B) and then loops westward towards the entrance to the tent (C). The Barnum and Bailey tent with two flags awaits reunion visitors (D). Several trees can be seen just west of the southwest bastion (E). These same trees are also seen in the background of the Cowan house photograph immediately west of the southwest bastion (see figure 42a). A rectangular tent connects on its west end to the larger tent and to the bastion on the east end (F). The capitol (or apex) of the southwest bastion appears to have a well-worn path leading up into the fort (G). A cut into the southwest bastion allows horse-drawn carriages to bring visitors into the west end of the fort interior (H). Visitors are standing along the level track, which would later become the alley between White and Clinch Avenues, and 16th and 18th Streets (I). A steep vertical cut looms behind the track, and one can see deep eroded gullies at the top of the cut (J). The year 1875 was the rainiest year on record in Tennessee, and the rains seem to have taken a toll on this intimidating defensive feature, which was obviously added after the battle under Tillson's direction, as this vertical cut is not indicated on Poe's 1864 map (see figures 21 and 24a). The track was put to good use by the reunion planners and this steep cut and leveled alley, which still can be seen, is another definitive piece of evidence as to the exact location of Fort Sanders.

The cut (H) in the south wall of the southwest bastion was a main entrance into the west side of the fort. There was another route at the crest of the ridge, which could also access carriages to this area where the 1863 attack took place at the northwest bastion. An extended Grove Street (future Laurel) ran in front of the Harrison house, which is located on the right side of the photo (M) east of future 17th Street (K). The ditch of the south wall at this point has been filled with some type of material, probably gravel, which appears as a white area.

Panoramic photographs taken at this time often distorted distances, and in this case the distortion caused the Harrison house to "jut"

SOUTHWEST BASTION
D
G
F
E
H
C
B

Fig. 46. 1890 photograph of the Blue-Gray Reunion taken from the top of the Cowan house. Courtesy of the Calvin M. McClung Historical Collection. A) Former location of the Cowans's 1870s brick cistern; B) Fort Sanders Avenue; C) Fort Sanders Road extension to tent entrance; D) Barnum and Bailey tent; E) pine trees west of southwest bastion seen in Patrick's 1901 photo [figure 47a]; F) rectangular tent connecting large tent to southwest bastion; G) path to apex of southwest bastion; H) visitor access road to fort interior; I) east/west track and future alley between Clinch and White Avenues and 17th and 16th Streets; J) vertical defensive cut above east/west track; K) future 17th Street; L) southeast bastion with eroded cannon embrasures; M) Harrison house.

forward and appear as if it were located on Clinch Avenue instead of Grove. Many have mistakenly called this the Pickle house, which was not completed until 1899. The Pickle house was built on top of the truncated northern portion of the southeast bastion (L) on Clinch slightly to the west of the Harrison house located on Grove. Although the two houses are similar in appearance, the footprints of the houses seen on the Sanborn map are distinctive. The 1900 *Knoxville City Directory* also verifies the street addresses for these homeowners (Knoxville City Directories 1888–1922). In 1886 Clinch ended at the southeast bastion; a trail picked up from there and continued northwest along the top of the truncated remains of the bastion and then into the fort. The trail became the driveway into the Pickle property from Clinch (see figure 44a).

THE BATTLEFIELD ENCAMPMENT: REUNION OF 1895

Five years after the highly successful reunion of Union and Confederate veterans in 1890, the Blue and Gray met again in the city to celebrate the new era of reconciliation. This was the 14th Annual Encampment of the Sons of Veterans, founded in 1881, and the event took place from September 15 to 18, 1895. Beginning on September 11, reunion news made the front page of the *Knoxville Journal* every day until the gathering ended on September 19, when newspaper space began to be filled with stories of the upcoming dedication of the Chickamauga Battlefield National Park in Chattanooga (*Knoxville Journal* 1895).

Visitors began arriving on Sunday and Monday, September 15 and 16, and were greeted by citizens lining each side of Gay Street. Storefronts and light poles were bedecked in red, white, and blue decorations. The guest of honor at the Encampment Reunion was Governor William McKinley of Ohio, who arrived on September 17. The next day McKinley led the official parade through the downtown area, but the route of the marchers did not lead west to the fort as it had in 1890. An evening fireworks display authorized by the West Knoxville City Council ended the day. On Thursday, the encampment drew to a close and many traveled south to Chattanooga for the national dedication of the Chickamauga-Chattanooga battlefields. During the encampment, visitors were heard to complain about the small attendance, especially by "people from the North" (ibid.).

There is little doubt the Knoxville promoters were disappointed that the event had not measured up to their expectations. It may be that 30 years after the war, veterans had settled into their midlives, and the memories that had bound them to the site and to each other were rapidly fading. Certainly the battle site was not a primary focus of this event as it had been in 1890, since the three-day schedule did not include even a single official visit to the nearby fortification; however, visitors and veterans went anyway. The *Knoxville Journal* on September 16 reported, "Hundreds went out yesterday to what is left of Fort Sanders and looked over the ground where Longstreet's and Burnside's veterans wrestled with each other on that cheerless November morning in 1863" (ibid.). To the authors' knowledge, no formal photograph was taken of visitors to the fort site.

Veterans expressed their dismay at the condition of the fort. Many of those present remarked that it was a pity the fort had not been preserved and agreed that "it should have stood throughout the years to come as a monument to American valor." John Watkins, the previously mentioned Union artillerist, was shocked to find a large house standing less than 100 feet from an embrasure at the northeast corner of the fort, where he had helped man a cannon during the battle. Watkins, a gunner with the 14th Independent Battery, Light Artillery, 23rd Army Corps, was stationed in one of the enormous lunettes that formed the northeastern defense of the fort. He immediately wrote to his wife, Sara, who had remained at home in Ohio, noting, "Went to Fort Sanders, looked the place over and talked with old soldiers and some other people about it, but it will soon be of the past—the boys are helping to tear down the parapets to find bullets and they get lots of them—We can locate the place where our gun stood alright, but now there is a big house built within 100 feet of it and a road has been graded right through the works where we were" (Watkins, Letter 1895).

Watkins's letter, sent from Knoxville in 1895, provides another key piece of evidence as to the location of Fort Sanders. In addition to locating the site of the lunettes at the east end of the fort near 17th Street instead of 16th, the comments Watkins made regarding the newly built house 100 feet from his battery provide more proof of the location of the fort on the military crest. By the time Watkins saw the J. B. Harrison house at the 1895 encampment, it had stood on the north side of Laurel, just east of present-day 17th Street, for five years. Watkins probably did not meet Harrison during the 1895 reunion, but surely he must have admired the beautiful three-story, brick, Queen Anne mansion that Harrison, a successful Knoxville clothier, had built on the street that now gave curious visitors access to the old fort. Harrison was only one of a large number of well-to do Knoxvillians who wanted to live in the new town of West Knoxville.

14

DEVELOPMENT OF WEST KNOXVILLE

THE FINAL BLOW

The boundaries of the new town chartered in 1888 included the land between Second Creek on the east to Third Creek on the west, and the tracks of the East Tennessee and Georgia Railroad (now Norfolk/Southern) and the Tennessee River. The West Knoxville City Council soon passed ordinances changing the names of streets in this area: Kingston Pike was renamed Cumberland Avenue, 9th Street was changed to 17th Street and Grove Street to Laurel Avenue. In spite of the hilly topography, new streets were laid out on the north side of Cumberland in a grid system. Sidewalks, waterworks including fire hydrants, sanitation systems, schools and churches were built. As new roads were added, the Civil War fort located within the new town, instead of being honored, became an impediment to progress, an engineer's nightmare, and a supply depot of earth for fill dirt. As new streets were being cut through the fort, development accelerated from increased sales of lots in what was named White's Addition. Construction of new houses along Clinch and Laurel rapidly proceeded westward. The earliest house to be built on the eastern end of the 1600 block of Laurel Avenue near the fort was the J. B. Harrison home at 1631 Laurel Avenue, completed by 1890.

Distinguished residents who had helped plan the successful Blue-Gray Reunion were certainly aware of the historic importance of the old fort. Many serving on the council must have continued to think of it as a possible money maker for the city, as in March 1891 the West Knoxville City Council recorded that Fort Sanders was still a "plus for the city" (West Knoxville City Council 1888–97).

Those Knoxvillians who wanted to preserve the fort may have enjoyed a slight reprieve in the 1890s, but land sales in the area of West Knoxville were quickly increasing. The tract of land owned by Hugh A. M. White, inherited before the war by his daughters, began to be sold in piecemeal lots until the turn of the century. West Knoxville with all its amenities was annexed by Knoxville in 1897. Knoxvillians who wanted to live in the new suburb were probably uninterested in whether the old fort was preserved or not. The fort area, which covered almost two blocks, was destined to become prime real estate.

In spite of the rapid sales of land located on and near the fort site, portions of it were still visible at the turn of the century. An 1897 street map of Knoxville shows no streets in the three blocks from Laurel to Cumberland between 17th and 21st Streets (Crozier 1897). Captain William Rule built his family a house on the southwest corner of Clinch and 16th Street close to the east end of the fort. Rule was twenty-four years old when Confederates began building the fort and he lived in Knoxville his entire life, so his description of the earthworks in 1898 can be trusted: "Its condition at the present time (December, 1898) is as follows: A street runs through the center of the fort with three or four residences upon it, which would be available as quarters for officers. The long slope to the west and north, up which the Confederates made such a gallant charge, is still open country and the line of the fort is well preserved" (Rule 1900: 177). The street mentioned by Rule is probably Laurel, which is present on 1897 maps of the area. Three of Brownlow Patrick's photographs taken in 1901 tell us that Rule was describing the south and west walls and a part of the southwest bastion. A fourth photograph taken by Patrick also reveals that there were remnants of the northeast bastion (see figure 47d).

The next major disturbances to the fortification were the construction of 17th and 18th Streets; the former would cut through the south wall and the northeast bastion, and the latter through the northwest and southwest bastions. The most formidable construction elements of the fort were located on 17th and 18th Streets; and because heavy equipment such as mechanized, steam-powered bulldozers, and graders were not invented until the 1920s, earthmoving had to be done by hand or with draft animals. The completion of these two streets was delayed not only by the presence of the fort walls and bastions but also by the steep grades required because of the sloping sides of the ridge.

A copy of a report from a contractor for his work in these areas was added into the record, along with the November 1894 minutes of the West Knoxville City Council. He wrote that "boulders and detached masses of rock made street construction at the intersection of 9th Street (17th street) and Laurel very difficult because . . . the ground was hard and dry, and would be harder to excavate than ordinary earth, although, a portion of the work was the filling from the old fort" (West Knoxville City Council 1888–97). An 1892 article in the *Knoxville Daily Tribune* reported on the December 23 meeting of the Town Council of West Knoxville. E. H. Flenniken, a local contractor and member of the council from 1888 to 1891, had recently died, and he was honored during the meeting. He had served as the Street Committee chairman for his entire term of service as an alderman and was fully in charge of work on streets and other incorporation improvements when more than $100,000 was expended (*Knoxville Daily Tribune* 1892).

The authors believe that the jog in Laurel at 17th was the point where the first direct impact was made in 1890 on the fortification. To create access for visitors during the reunion into the interior of Fort Sanders, it was necessary to extend the street in front of the Harrison house (future Laurel Avenue) through the northeast bastion into the fort. To avoid having to cut through the highest parts of the bastion with picks and shovels, the road was turned northward (on future 17th) with a 90 degree angle where the south side of the bastion attached to the east wall stockade, and then the road again angled 90 degrees to the west onto Laurel Avenue through the bastion wall, which connected to the north curtain wall (see figures 24c and 24d).

There is a substantial difference in the north–south lengths of the two blocks affected by the northeast bastion in this area. The distance of the east end of the block at 17th from Highland to Laurel is about 88 yards; and the distance of the east end of the block at 17th from Laurel to Clinch is about 101 yards, a difference of 13 yards. The west end of the block between Laurel Avenue and Highland is about 95 yards at 18th Street. The width of the east end of that block at 17th Street is 88 yards. This difference of 7 yards results because Laurel angles toward the northeast, and it creates a block at 17th that is 7 yards less wide than the west end of the block. The angle created by Laurel may be the same angle of the north wall of the irregular quadrilateral fort. The jog on Laurel is about 20 yards, and the reverse jog on Highland, also necessitated by this difference in the widths of the blocks, is about 26 yards wide.

It was not until August 1892 that the West Knoxville Council decided that "if finances are good the grades on 9th Street will be done the coming year," and in August 1894 it was reported that "the estimated work on 9th Street from Highland to Clinch would cost more than appropriated for it" (West Knoxville City Council Minutes 1888–97). Despite these difficulties, John Watkins's letter of September 19, 1895, indicates that 17th Street was graded at that time. By 1900, a drivable Laurel must have extended to 17th past the Harrison house and also to Clinch past the new Pickle house. One sees these completed mansions in the 1901 Patrick photograph of the northeast bastion (see figure 47d). City of Knoxville engineers had begun to deal with grading a route for 17th Street down the hill from its crest at Laurel to connect with Highland, which would necessitate another jog in that road.

Although 17th Street was open to traffic in 1900, apparently it was still treacherous, indicated from a fatal surrey accident caused by the street's steep grade. Mr. and Mrs. Michael J. Condon and their out-of-town guests, Mr. and Mrs. Mortimer F. Shea, left the Condon home on Asylum Avenue for a surrey ride to Fort Sanders. The carriage turned left at the intersection of Laurel with 17th and started down the steep hill towards Cumberland Avenue where the lane up to Melrose Place began. A slight offset at the intersection of 17th and Melrose matches that of Poe's westernmost defensive trench as it crossed Cumberland and ascended up the entrance lane to Melrose Place. When crowded by another vehicle on the narrow, unpaved street, the horses became frightened and ran down the steep hill. The horses were out of control when they reached Cumberland, and the surrey was hurled into the gate at the entrance to Melrose Place (see figure 34). Both men were killed, and the women were badly injured (Tumblin 2012).

It took even longer to complete 10th Street (later 18th Street) from Highland south to Clinch. In this case, a steep grade was not the problem, but the northwest and southwest bastions were. The northwest bastion lay at the intersection of 10th and Laurel, and the southwest bastion was located at the intersection of 10th and Clinch. Although the northwest bastion presented surmountable problems to continuing the construction of 10th, such as earth removal, dealing with the deep north–south cut into the southwest bastion was a more serious issue. This was the exact location where 10th Street should have continued down the south slope of the ridge to connect with White Avenue. The extension of 10th Street from Clinch to White Avenue was never built. Engineers probably considered it too dangerous or too difficult to continue construction of this street down the steep slope. This cut into the bastion, created to allow reunion visitors into the fort, and which is visible in the 1890 reunion photograph, can be easily identified again in a Thompson panoramic photograph of White's Ridge made in 1922. This later photograph shows large rocks placed in the cut to help stabilize the soil and probably to prevent its use as a treacherous shortcut from Clinch to White Avenue. The appearance again in a 1922 photograph of this 1890 manmade cut into the bastion is further proof of the location of the southwest bastion at 10th (18th) Street and Clinch. Eighteenth Street begins again on White Avenue at the base of the slope in direct line with the cut and connects south to Cumberland Avenue. City engineers and others who study KGIS maps must sometimes wonder why 18th Street between Clinch and White Avenues was never constructed. It was not until August 1897 that the City Council voted to establish the grade on 10th Street north to Forest Avenue. The grading and construction of that section would not be completed until after West Knoxville was annexed by the city.

15

FORT SANDERS AFTER THE DAWN OF THE 20TH CENTURY

DEVELOPMENT ON THE FORT SITE BEGINS

In March 1892, optimistic members of the West Knoxville City Council declared, "We feel proud of West Knoxville, and look forward next year to having the finest residences erected that have ever been built in Knoxville" (West Knoxville City Council Minutes 1888–97). Beautiful houses began to line the streets of the new town, but it was almost a decade before homes began to be built in the area within the walls of Fort Sanders. The fort's south wall along Clinch Avenue between 9th (later 17th Street) and present-day 18th Street was the first to be modified by UT engineering professor William Carson, who built his two-story brick house on the northwest corner of 17th and Clinch.

The presence of the fortification created some serious problems for road building and home construction. In addition to the earthen walls of the fort, there were the four enormous bastions to be dealt with. Trenches needed to be filled, bastions leveled, and streets built before lots could be sold. The steep slopes along the south and north sides of the fort were also a challenge. Minutes of the West Knoxville City Council taken in December 1892, describe the problems the situation presented to development of the town: "Owing to the topography of the town being in the main high and rolling and . . . streets were located along sides of hills. . . ." Residents had constructed homes before some very steep street grades were cut and other areas filled; and it was only with the cooperation of property owners who largely funded "thousands of feet" of rock walls that the roads were constructed. (ibid.). Built between 1900 and 1930, these expensive hand-hewn limestone, marble and brick retaining walls are prevalent on the north side of Clinch Avenue between 16th and 18th Streets and they still effectively retain the earth.

By the 40th anniversary of the battle, much of the fortification had disappeared. A newspaper article described the condition of the fort: "only a few traces of the old defenses remain which have not been re-excavated for the foundations of elegant homes" (*Knoxville Daily Journal and Tribune* 1903). A study of Fort Sanders using maps and city directories reveals that access to the interior of the fort that had been surrounded by the fort walls had impeded construction of street houses on the two blocks between 16th and 18th on Clinch and Laurel (Knoxville City Directories 1888–1922).

The Harrison house, built in 1890, was located east of the fort on Grove Street, which would become Laurel Avenue. This street had originally been a soldiers' path on the top of the ridge leading to their campsite and into the fort. Two photographs of this house (see figure 47d) show that a portion of the northeast bastion located behind the rear of the house was still intact. The Pickle mansion, also built east of the fort immediately north of the partially destroyed southeast bastion, was not completed until 1899 (see figures 44a and b). This house was built on the second lot east of future 17th Street, which remained at that time a dirt track crossing the crest of the ridge.

The only sidewalk east of the fort location on Clinch Avenue in 1890 was made of planks and extended several blocks on the south side of the street (*Knoxville News-Sentinel* 1948). According to city directories, it was not until 1913 that Clinch Avenue crossed 17th Street. The 1700 block on Clinch between 17th Street and 18th Street does not appear to have been paved until after that date. This was probably due to the fact that the north side of Clinch in this area abutted the steep embankment of the south wall of the fort and the defensive ditch that was located at the base of that wall. Street building meant filling in the ditch and removing the earthen wall. The most expedient way to fill in the ditch and widen the street was to push the fort wall into the ditch.

There is physiographical and archaeological evidence that, as Clinch was built, some of the mixed cherty clay/loam fill earth from the south wall was also deposited on the south side of the street to level the slope between Clinch and the almost vertical cut to the alley so that houses could be built on the south side of Clinch. This cherty clay fill of the southwest bastion was also evident in a construction trench in the backyard of the James Monday apartments at 1738 Clinch. A steep driveway into the Saratoga apartment complex at 1800 West Clinch separates the two apartment buildings and the 1700 and 1800 blocks of the avenue. This driveway was built where the 1890 cut in the southwest bastion was located.

The same mixed cherty clay/loam fill from the southeast bastion was also identified in the profile of an excavation for a house basement at the southeast corner of Clinch Avenue and 17th Street (1644 Clinch). The east–west profile studied by the authors extended almost across the entire front of that lot. Fill had obviously been pushed from the southeast bastion of the fort to build Clinch and was again used to level the area south of Clinch for homes in the 1600 block. The sequence of house construction westward along the avenue from 1900 to 1920 would indicate that the construction of Clinch advanced slowly.

The William W. Carson house was built in 1903 at what was to become the northwest corner (1705) of Clinch and 17th Street, and it remained the only house on the north side of the street until 1909, when a house was built on the adjacent lot. The Carson house sits at a slight southwest-to-northeast angle to Clinch and this may indicate that the house was aligned with the south fort wall (see figure 47c). It was two years later, in 1911, that the Briscoe house, now called White Columns, was built on the northeast corner of the intersection with future 18th Street. It took two more years before 18th Street was completed to Clinch, and the point where the 1890 cut into the southwest bastion halted construction. In 1914, a year after 17th Street crossed Clinch, four houses had been built in the 1700 block west of this intersection on the north side of Clinch (Knoxville City Directories 1888–1922). The Pat Roddy Jr. family home had been completed on the northwest corner of 18th and Clinch by 1917, according to the Sanborn map of that year (Sanborn Insurance Company 1917).

Development of the western end of the 1700 block of Clinch was undoubtedly delayed by the large southwest bastion located there. Completion of the cut and roadway up into the fort for the 1890 reunion had resulted in some destruction of the southwest bastion and the photograph of the reunion shows that earth was also being robbed from the bastion at that time (see figure 46). However, there was considerable earth left that would need to be removed before development could continue westward.

There was no development west on Laurel in the 1700 block during that time period, probably due to the remaining earthworks of the fort. The north wall, the ditch, and the northwest bastion had to be dealt with in that area, and developers did the obvious. They used the fort walls and bastion to fill the ditch and level the area north of Laurel for houses. The 1922 aerial photograph (see figure 48) shows that the earliest homes were built between 1911 and the early 1920s.

THE FINEST RESIDENCES EVER BUILT IN KNOXVILLE

An article written by Lucy Curtis Templeton in 1949 for the *Knoxville News-Sentinel* reveals that this west Knoxville neighborhood was truly unique (Templeton 1949). The neighborhood became an enclave of interesting and gifted residents; entrepreneurs, artists, musicians, lawyers, authors, historians, politicians, engineers, philanthropists, professors, and civic leaders strolled on the ubiquitous sidewalks and drove their motorcars on the streets of Fort Sanders. Many residents traveled abroad frequently. Some worked in factories and stores and lived more ordinary lives in more modest homes. All could either walk, drive, or ride a trolley to town, church, or school. They had their own band and croquet club. Some children who lived close to the mill pond near Forest and 13th Street caught bullfrogs there and fried up the legs (Conroy 1954). Children played together, and when it snowed, if they didn't have a sled, they made one from a chair turned upside down; sometimes they even sledded down the most forbidding street of all: 17th Street. A future Pulitzer Prize winner, James Agee, would number among the children who were born in and loved the neighborhood of Fort Sanders. Agee acquainted the reader with this special place and time in his autobiographical novel *A Death in the Family*. The beautiful final narrative of the book describes a walk "westward up the steep hill to Fort Sanders," where little Rufus, the main character, and his uncle Andrew pause at the edge of the old fort and look out "across the waste of briars and embanked clay" (Agee 1957:275, 278).

Residents of West Knoxville touted their new town, saying that some of the "finest residences ever built" were located there. By 1922, Fort Sanders Manor, an apartment building, had been completed on the remains of the truncated northeast bastion for those who might want to enjoy the ambiance of the neighborhood without the complications that sometimes come with owning a home (*Knoxville News Sentinel* 1922).

Three huge houses, which would require lots of maintenance and housekeeping, were built after West Knoxville was annexed by the city. These well-preserved structures stand on the site of the fort on the north side of the 1700 block of Clinch Avenue. The Pickle house, probably one of the largest and most expensive ever built in the neighborhood, stood until recently at the east end of the fort location at 1633 Clinch Avenue; the remaining brick walls of the George Pickle house were torn down in 2016 after a fire severely damaged it in 2003 (Neely 2015).

Dr. William Waller Carson's two-story brick house (now the Ronald McDonald House, 1705 Clinch) anchors the east end of the 1700 block of Clinch; and the Briscoe house (now known as "White Columns"), located at 1733 Clinch, anchors the west end of the block. Across the street on the northwest corner of 18th and Clinch is the James Patrick Roddy house (1803 Clinch).

In 1980, the Fort Sanders Historic District was placed on the National Register of Historic Places in recognition of its classic Victorian architecture and important place in Knoxville's history (Cook 2013). A year later, a helpful guide, *Historic Fort Sanders: A Walking Tour of the Neighborhood,* was published by Knoxville Heritage (now Knox Heritage) for those interested in learning more about the amazing variety of architecture that can be seen in the neighborhood (Knox Heritage, Inc. 1981).

THE GEORGE W. PICKLE HOUSE

The Pickle mansion was one of the first houses to be constructed on the actual fort site (see figures 44a and b). The lot was purchased by George W. and Minnie Pickle in 1892, but the house was not completed until 1899 (Knox County Warranty Deed 1898). Several recent histories of the house erroneously say it was built in 1889. This architectural gem in the Richardsonian Romanesque style had curved porches, a two-story domed roof, a decorative stone frieze, and an upstairs ballroom (Knox Heritage, Inc. n.d.). Minnie Pickle, George's wife, recalled that it was the "scene of many fine gaieties" (*Knoxville Sentinel* 1917).

When he was 16 years old, G. W. Pickle joined the Confederate army as a private, but he was soon captured and placed in a Union prison camp. After the war, he became a prominent lawyer in the Knoxville firm of Pickle, Turner, Kennerly, and Cates, and during that time he was often called General Pickle. Some mistakenly took this to mean that George had been a general in the Confederate army. In fact, he received this title when he was appointed to the position of attorney general of Tennessee (Green 1947; *Knoxville Sentinel* 1917).

In the 1920s, the mansion, which had been called Confederate Hall and Fort Sanders Hall during its earlier years, became a fraternity house, and by the 1940s the house had been divided into apartments and was called the Westover Apartments. Although it was home to professional people at this time, most residents by the 1970s were UT students. A fire gutted the interior and destroyed the roof in 2003. Preserved brick walls stood for several years as preservationists fought to keep it from being razed, but it was finally torn down in 2016 (Neely 2003, 2015).

WILLIAM WALLER CARSON HOUSE

The Carson house, now the home of Knoxville's Ronald McDonald House, is located at the northwest corner of Clinch Avenue and 17th Street. According to a newspaper article, Civil War trenches had to be filled in before construction began (Aston-Wash 1983; Siegel 1975). This lovely brick home, built in 1903 by William Carson and his wife, Rachel Finnie, is in the asymmetrical Colonial Revival style, or free classic Queen Ann style. It had a hipped roof, two-story bay windows and a decorative sunburst detail added above the third-floor dormer windows. The house was greatly admired at that time because every one of its many bedrooms had a bathroom.

Born in Mississippi in 1845 to Dr. James G. Carson, a cotton planter, William W. Carson grew up in Louisiana on the plantation and enlisted at 18 as a private in the Confederate army in the 4th Louisiana Cavalry. After the war he entered Washington College (now Washington and Lee University), where he studied under Robert E. Lee. By 1869, he had received both his undergraduate and master's degrees in civil engineering. He taught at the University of Tennessee from 1883 to 1916 (*Knoxville Journal* 1930).

After his death, members of the family continued to live there until the late 1930s, when the house was converted into apartments. In the 1940s, it was the home of area professionals who worked at the University of Tennessee and Oak Ridge. At one time, the entire apartment house was rented to scientists who worked on the Manhattan Project in Oak Ridge "to keep them close and prevent security leaks" (Siegel 1975).

William and Rachel's daughter Katherine, who was born in 1881, was interviewed in 1975 for a *Knoxville Journal* article and asked about her most vivid memory of the place. "We had a very large attic," she replied. "Once when my sister had scarlet fever, she and my mother stayed up in the attic until the infection was over. We would put food at the steps and mother would come down and get it" (ibid.).

On March 8, 1985, the doors of the Carson family home were opened by the new staff of the Ronald McDonald House, and other families have been welcomed for the last 30 years to stay in this "home away from home" while their children are hospitalized at the nearby East Tennessee Children's Hospital (Hughs 2005).

WHITE COLUMNS

Built in the Greek Revival or Southern Colonial style with four Ionic-style columns, this elegant house has never received the same amount of attention as the other three historic houses described here. The lot was purchased in 1893 from the White heirs by E. G. Buckwell, who sold it in turn to Benjamin and Hattie Briscoe in 1902. The Briscoes did not build White Columns on this lot on the northeast corner of 18th and Clinch until 1911, probably because the lot was located on the west wall of the fort, an area that needed to be leveled before construction could begin (Basehart 1992). The house sits on a rise, and stone walls adjoining the sidewalk retain visible remnants of the fort.

Like so many of the houses in the Fort Sanders neighborhood, White Column's 23 rooms were eventually converted into student apartments. After this transformation in 1971, the house became so run down that it was in imminent danger of being razed. However, in 1982, it was purchased by two preservationists who restored the house to its original design, and it is now listed on the National Register of Historic Places (Knox Heritage 1981).

JAMES PATRICK RODDY HOUSE

In 1917, James Patrick Roddy Sr. purchased the lot at the northwest corner of Clinch Avenue and 18th Street and built his house in the Colonial Revival style with hipped roof, decorative arched-door surrounds, and accentuated entryway (ibid.). Like White Columns, the Roddy house sits on the remnants of the west wall, and hand-hewn limestone walls hold back what remains of that wall. Patrick Roddy Jr. described the family's move to the new house in his history of the Coca-Cola Company in Knoxville: "Construction of our new home having been completed in January 1918, our family moved from East Church Avenue to 1803 West Clinch. Clinch Avenue dead-ended at 18th Street. . . . We were at the end of the line" (Roddy 1983:49; see figure 48).

After tasting a new product called Coca-Cola, Patrick Roddy Sr. wisely decided to invest in the soft drink and partnered with W. H. Goodman to purchase one of the first franchises in Knoxville. He also became vice president and general manager of the Roddy Manufacturing Company. A generous philanthropist, he and his wife, Kate Collins Roddy, lived out the duration of their lives in the house. It was vacant in the 1970s but was restored to provide office space for accountants, attorneys, and real estate agents (ibid.). It is presently a private residence.

16

THE 1913 EXPOSITION AND IMPORTANT POSTWAR PHOTOGRAPHS

In 1913 Knoxville hosted a National Conservation Fair in Chilhowie Park. During the two months between September 1 through November 1, approximately a million people attended the fair, which focused on conserving the natural resources of the southern states. Hundreds of aged survivors of the war, many in their 80s, traveled by train from northern and eastern states to attend a G.A.R. encampment in Chattanooga, and many stopped in Knoxville on their way home from Chattanooga to visit the fair.

Those who had occupied Knoxville during the war "were prone to make rigid inquiries about the progress made . . . since they were here in the stirring days of the national conflict during the 60's." Plans had been made by two G.A.R. posts, the Fred Ault camp, and the United Confederate Veterans to see to the "comfort and convenience of the visitors" and for resident veterans to accompany them "to Fort Sanders and other points of interest around Knoxville" (*Knoxville Journal and Tribune* 1913). At that time, there was enough of the old fort left to make a carriage or trolley ride west worthwhile. Photographs taken in 1901 may show some remnants of the fort that were still present in 1913.

THE PHOTOGRAPHS OF WILLIAM BROWNLOW PATRICK

William Brownlow Patrick was the grandson of Parson Brownlow. He was 16 years old when he took the four photographs described below.

Fig. 47a. William Brownlow Patrick's 1901 photograph of the remains of the southwest bastion and the south wall. The pine trees seen behind the small remnant of the bastion are the same ones seen between the reunion tent and the southwest bastion in figure 46.

In late November 2017, while final revisions were being made to this book, the authors received these photographs. The images were taken in the summer or early fall of 1901, using glass plates that later had been donated to the McClung Collection, whose staff remembered seeing "Fort Sanders" labels on some of the plates and quickly scanned and emailed them to us. None of these photographs were known to exist prior to this discovery (Cotham 2017). Careful study of the photographs allowed us to determine exactly what remnants of the fort had been recorded by Patrick. One can pinpoint the location in each photograph by comparing it to the 1890 Blue-Gray Reunion panoramic view of the fort (see figure 46).

The first photograph (figure 47a), a view of the truncated southwest bastion, was difficult to interpret. The pine trees seen behind this section of the bastion are the same ones seen between the reunion tent

Fig. 47b. Patrick's west wall profile. A) Parapet; B) scarp; C) trench; D) counterscarp; E) glacis; F) future location of Roddy house; G) future location of White Columns

and southwest bastion in the 1890 photo. It appears that a road (future Clinch Avenue) was cut behind this remnant, creating the profile of the west wall in figure 47b. To the right of this bastion remnant, one can see part of the south wall exterior with shrubbery growing on it.

In figure 47b, the pine trees are again a key in deciphering which wall of the fort is seen here. They are growing just northwest of the southwest bastion close to the trench of the west wall. A perfect dissection of that wall appears in the photograph and shows the glacis (E), scarp (B), trench (C), counterscarp (D), and possibly the top of the parapet (A) and interior earth wall, minus the original wooden revetment that retained the soil. It appears that a road was cut behind the southwest bastion remnant, creating this perfect profile of the west wall. The layer of cobbles seen in the cut at the base of the profile is believed to be the cherty cobble that was encountered in Foss' auger test in the front yard of the Roddy house.

Fig. 47c. Patrick's view of the interior of the south wall.

Figure 47c presents a view of the interior of the south wall. The shrubbery in this photograph made it easy to determine that Patrick was standing inside the flat interior of the fort, looking south, when he shot this photograph. Note that the same shrubbery seen outside the south wall in figure 47a is visible on the inside of the wall in this figure. The treeless fort interior was later used for star gazing by residents of the neighborhood.

Figure 47d presents a view of the northeast bastion. Newly planted trees stand in front of the bastion to the left of the house. In the twelve years since the trees were planted in 1889, they had grown much larger, but the bastion can still be seen behind them.

The locations of the Harrison and Pickle houses in relation to each other can be seen in this photograph. The Harrison house faces an unseen Grove Street (Laurel Avenue), and the back of the Pickle house faces Grove. String lines to the right of the bastion indicate the future route of 17th Street (9th Street). One wonders why Patrick did not photograph either the northwest or southeast bastions, but it is possible that other photographs taken in 1901 may not have survived. The

Fig. 47d. Patrick's view of the northeast bastion, from the west side of future 17th Street. A) Graded area for 17th Street extension northward; B) string line indicating the west side of street extension; C) remains of the northeast bastion; D) Harrison house facing Laurel; E) rear of Pickle house facing Laurel (front faces Clinch).

northwest bastion had most likely been totally removed by 1901. There are well-used paths up the slope to 18th Street in the 1922 Thompson aerial (see figure 48).

This aerial reveals that only the trench of the bastion can be clearly identified as a part of that feature. It runs to the northwest corner of the Roddy property; the trench and the remaining defilade, rife pits, and sinkhole are clear indicators of the location of that bastion. One can reasonably conclude that the relatively undisturbed battleground was still revered. The west part of the northeast bastion was partially destroyed by 17th (9th) Street, but according to our research, there should have been easily identifiable remnants of the southeast bastion until Fort Sanders Manor was built in 1922.

The Patrick photograph of the northeast bastion shows that part of that feature remained in 1901, and a 1917 Sanborn map shows a large vacant area where remnants probably still existed and were intimidating enough to prevent construction of houses. There were definitely remains of the southeast bastion to be seen, as Fort Sanders Manor was completed nine years after the Conservation Exposition in 1913. Another decade on, there would be little left to see, but what Robin Thompson was able to record of the battleground from a biplane in the early 1920s was of critical importance to us in determining the location of Fort Sanders.

THOMPSON AERIAL PHOTOGRAPH

James (Jim) and Robin Thompson were the premier photographers in Knoxville from the 1920s through the 1940s. Their body of work is still appreciated as art and treasured for the visual history it provides of Knoxville and surrounding areas during that time period. Jim was a successful businessman who is better remembered than Robin because of his contributions as a conservationist, founder of the Smoky Mountain Hiking Club, work with the Rotary Club, and photographic input to the committee members who designated the Great Smoky Mountains as a National Park. It was, however, his brother Robin who took a key photograph from a biplane in the early 1920s, proving that the location of the west wall of Fort Sanders was on or near 18th Street and that the northwest bastion was located at the corner of 18th Street and Laurel Avenue (see figure 48).

It is said that this image, now contained in the McClung Collection, is one of the earliest aerial photographs taken in Knoxville. It is certainly one of the most important, for not only does it prove the fort location identified in this book, but it also records a Civil War battleground that was almost 60 years old. It documents an area that still contained evidence of the line of rifle pits laid out by Orlando Poe, the worrisome defilade that provided cover to Confederate soldiers as they attacked, part of the trench of the northwest bastion, and even the sinkhole that Porter Alexander described. Robin Thompson may have simply wanted to photograph Knoxville's new hospital and construction in that area, but he provided a picture of a landscape that will reveal for all time precious details about the battle of Fort Sanders.

Fort Sanders Hospital was chartered in 1919, and construction soon followed on part of the site of the Civil War battlefield. This first hospital was built in the 1900 block of West Clinch Avenue. Local historian Betsy Creekmore wrote that the present hospital "now occupies the slope up which General Longstreet's Confederate forces charged." As the 1920s hospital was being built, workmen discovered Civil War ordnance buried on the site (Creekmore 1976:305).

This photograph shows (A) the first Fort Sanders Hospital; (B) Highland Avenue; (C) West Clinch Avenue; (D) 19th Street to the intersection with Clinch, the connecting link to Cumberland under construction; (E) 18th Street; (F) the intersection of Laurel Avenue at 18th Street (note that there is no extension of Laurel Avenue beyond 18th Street); and (G) Roddy house on the northwest corner of Clinch and 18th Street.

Features that relate to the battle and Fort Sanders are as follows. The rock outcrop near Highland Avenue (H) can also be seen in the Buchtel engraving of the battle along the defilade that was used by Longstreet's attacking force for cover as they came up from the railroad cut (see figure 30a). The defilade along its entire length is clearly visible in figure 48, from the railroad (I) below Forest Avenue (J) to the site of the fort, just south of the remnants of the northwest bastion (K).

The defilade can still be seen today in the large parking lot behind the hospital, curving up toward 18th Street from below Highland Avenue. The remnants of the northwest bastion are still being removed on the west side of 18th Street. The sinkhole (L) observed by Porter Alexander in 1863 is located in the trees behind the Victorian-style houses (M) facing Highland Avenue. The Roddy house is located on what remains of the west wall. The bastion was cut through by 18th Street, which terminated at Clinch Avenue.

One of the most interesting features in this photograph is the dark outline of the trench (N) and an arc of dark circular disturbances in the plowed field between 18th and 19th streets (O). These are approximately 36 feet from the west wall of the fort and are believed to be the filled rifle pits dug by the Union defenders 30 feet from the western curtain

I
J
B
H
J
J
A
C

Fig. 48. 1922 Robin Thompson aerial photograph of the remains of the 1863 battlefield and surrounding residential development. Courtesy of the Calvin M. McClung Historical Collection. A) Fort Sanders Hospital; B) Highland Avenue; C) Clinch Avenue; D) 19th Street; E) 18th Street; F) Laurel Avenue; G) Roddy house; H) remains of rock outcrop seen in Buchtel engraving; I) railroad J) defilade; K) remains of northwest bastion; L) trees growing in sinkhole behind a Victorian house; M) Victorian houses; N) partial remains of the northwest bastion trench; O) remains of Union rifle pits; P) deposit for residential construction.

wall that was captured by the Confederates the night of November 28. These features form an arc around the northwest bastion, which can be seen on Poe's map of the battlefield (see figure 21). Three large rifle pits located east to west along the deepest part of the defilade can also be seen on Poe's map. Professional archaeologists can distinguish most human-made disturbances (features) in the soil by comparing the difference in the color and texture of the soil in the feature to the matrix, or surrounding undisturbed soil. In this case, these differences in the soils can be clearly seen in Robin Thompson's aerial photograph. Filled postholes dug in 1864 by Union soldiers for a stockade along the westernmost defensive trench can also be easily identified in an 1880s photograph of the back of the Cowan house (see figure 42b). The clump of trees (L) just north of a future alley are growing in the sinkhole located behind the Victorian houses. The sinkhole or "limestone sink," which artillerist Porter Alexander said would hold over 200 sharpshooters, was completely filled in in 2019 and the leveled lot now serves as a staging area: plans to expand a nearby parking garage are underway.

17

MONUMENTS AND MEMORIAL WINDOWS

In contrast to the careful and extensive documentation of the battleground prepared for the dedication of the Chickamauga battlefield in 1895, it was over five decades after the war before a Civil War monument or any markers at all were placed on either the site of the fort or the battleground to commemorate the battle of Fort Sanders. Perhaps this was because of lingering grief over the terrible loss of life in the battle or, conversely, that traumatic memories of the war years began to fade from memory or were thought to be "best forgotten." Those interested in documenting the site may have believed that any effort to do so was futile because the few physical remnants left of the fort were in imminent danger of destruction due to the rapid development of the area. That fact, in addition to the difficulty of access to the area because of street construction, may have discouraged any attempts to document the location of Fort Sanders.

THE 1914 UNITED DAUGHTERS OF THE CONFEDERACY MONUMENT

On November 28, 1914, the Knoxville Chapter of the United Daughters of the Confederacy unveiled an eight-foot-high monument of Tennessee pink marble to honor the memory of Confederate soldiers who lost their lives in the battle (figure 49). A bas-relief of a Confederate battle flag is draped over the top of this monument located on the west side of 17th Street between Clinch and Laurel Avenues. Beneath the flag is a Maltese cross containing a wreath, and beneath this cross, on a smooth, raised rectangular panel, the following words are chiseled:

To the memory of the Confederate soldiers who fell
in the Assault on Fort Sanders
November 29, 1863
Nor wreck, nor change, nor winter's blight
Nor life's remorseless doom
Shall dim the ray of glory light
That gilds your glorious tomb
Erected by Knoxville Chapter No 89
United Daughters of the Confederacy
Nov. 28, 1914

The *Sentinel* reporter who described the dedication of the monument wrote in the poetic style common in the late 19th century. Of the veterans attending, the reporter wrote, "some who were there fifty-one years ago as beardless youths were present Saturday their heads frosted by many winters. Gathered around the hallowed spot where their comrades fell, tears come into the eyes of those who wore the gray and those who wore the blue" (*Knoxville Sentinel* 1914a) The reporter may simply have added the "hallowed spot" phrase for dramatic effect.

Veterans of the battle who attended the ceremony could not have been younger than their late 60s or early 70s, and some may not have remembered the actual location of the attack. Perhaps the monument could not be placed in the correct location due to street work. Eighteenth Street was not completed to Clinch Avenue until 1915. Maybe the monument was placed on 17th Street because more people would see it. By 1914 this street had become a major thoroughfare. The second and much shorter *Sentinel* article that appeared on November 29 reporting the Saturday dedication is more specific, stating that the marker was installed at "the practical pivotal point around which was centered the bloody charge upon the fort" (*Knoxville Sentinel* 1914b). Whatever the reason for the present location of the monument, this marker and the two *Sentinel* articles over time became the "proof" of the location for the attack on Fort Sanders.

Fig. 49. United Daughters of the Confederacy monument on 17th Street between Clinch and Laurel Avenues. Photo by the authors.

The authors believe that Digby Seymour, in his work, based his location for the fort on a map published in Dr. Harold S. Fink's 15-page booklet entitled "The Battle of Knoxville in 1863." The text of the booklet, prepared for the Knoxville–Knox County Civil War Centennial Commission, was based on a scholarly article published by Professor Fink in 1957. To the best of the authors' knowledge, this booklet featured the first map ever published of the Union and Confederate works (based on Poe's map) superimposed over a Knoxville street map. Fink placed the northwest bastion at 17th and Laurel and the southwest bastion at 17th and Clinch, and he represented the southwest bastion as the "salient" (the bastion projecting farthest to the west) rather than the northwest bastion. Fink did not place the route of the defilade on his map as Seymour did. Seymour placed the location of the defilade between 20th and 16th Streets a half a block above the northwest bastion, north of the fort (Seymour 1963:189). The Daughters of the Confederacy monument and the 1914 *Sentinel* articles describing the commemorative event probably were determining factors in Fink's placement of the fort.

It is also possible that both Fink and Seymour might have believed that the fort was located on the topographical crest of the ridge instead of the military crest. We believe these three "archival sources" unintentionally discouraged further research on the actual location of Fort Sanders. Our research has made clear that the site of the attack on Fort Sanders took place a block farther west, near the corner of what is now 18th Street and Laurel Avenue.

THE 79TH NEW YORK HIGHLANDERS MONUMENT

In November 1917, the New York Monument Commission presented a request to the City of Knoxville for permission to erect a monument to the 79th New York Highlanders Regiment, 1st Division, Army of the Ohio, in the park on West Clinch Avenue (Knoxville City Council 1897–1917). This monument, also made of pink marble, was installed the following year at the intersection of 16th Street and Clinch Avenue. At the top of the monument is an engraving of a Union and a Confederate soldier shaking hands. The script below, written by an Irish immigrant, reads:

> The hands that once were raised in strife
> now clasp a brother's hand,
> and long as flows the tide of life—
> we shall as brothers stand,
> one heart, one soul, for our free land
> J. I. C. Clarke

After coming to America, Joseph Ignatius Constantine Clarke (1846–1925) became a well-known newspaperman, poet, and playwright (*New York Times* 1925).

The 79th New York Highlanders were represented nearly three decades earlier by 32 veterans who traveled as a group to Knoxville for the Blue-Gray Reunion. After arriving at the railroad station, they formed ranks and marched up Gay Street to their lodgings. The popular Highlanders had helped man the northwest bastion and were honored at several receptions. They were also entertained with a carriage ride to Bleak House (now Confederate Memorial Hall), where hostess Mrs. Robert H. Armstrong showed them several places the house had been damaged during the siege. At the end of their tour, the 79th raised a toast and gave three cheers to General Longstreet, who had made his headquarters at the house and also gave three cheers to Mrs. Armstrong (Conklin 2005:106).

MEMORIAL WINDOWS AT FORT SANDERS PRESBYTERIAN CHURCH

Another event honoring the men who fought at Fort Sanders took place when Fort Sanders Presbyterian Church was dedicated. The church was organized in May 1895, and members met in the Highland Avenue school building until their church was completed at the corner of 8th (now 16th) Street and Laurel Avenue (*Knoxville Journal* 1898a). On December 19, 1898, the new brick church of the youngest Presbyterian congregation in the city was dedicated in a service led by Dr. E. A. Elmore and local Presbyterian ministers (*Knoxville Journal* 1898b, 1898c). Dr. J. M. P. Otts, pastor of the Third Presbyterian Church, spoke about the beautiful stained-glass window that had been created to honor soldiers who died at Fort Sanders (ibid.). The window was installed in the west wall of the church sanctuary, where it was illuminated on sunny afternoons until severely damaged by fire in 1982. A column in the December 5, 1898, *Knoxville Journal* described the window and those responsible for its placement:

> A feature in the new Fort Sanders Presbyterian church will be the beautiful memorial window, which has been donated to the church by a large number of soldiers of various regiments that were encamped in the city during the past few months. The beautiful window is especially designed as a memorial to the brave defenders of the flag who fell on historic Fort Sanders in the sixties. The fact that the church is located upon this historic ground, and that it is named Fort Sanders Presbyterian church, and further that the window was donated by volunteer soldiers of the last American war [Spanish-American War], makes it eminently appropriate. This window will receive special attention upon the dedication of the new house of worship, which will be within a few short weeks. (*Knoxville Journal* 1898a)

In his address Dr. Otts credited members of a regiment in training in Knoxville for the Spanish-American War who donated the money for the window. The soldiers, who were stationed at Camp Poland, wanted to honor the "memory of the soldiers of the blue and the gray who fell on the outside of and inside Fort Sanders in '63." He further believed that "this was the first monument to piety and the fallen of both sides of the civil war ever erected in the broad world" (ibid.).

Although the Spanish-American War lasted only three months (April 25–August 12, 1898), thousands of men had volunteered to fight. They were sent to numerous training camps throughout the country, including Knoxville. Three army camps were established in Knoxville in the summer of 1898. Camps Wilder and Bob Taylor were near Chilhowee Park and Magnolia Avenue. Camp Poland was named for General John S. Poland, first commanding officer of the 2nd Division of the 1st Corps. Regiments of Camp Poland were located in three parts of town: the first brigade was near Camp Wilder; the second brigade was south of Lincoln Park; and the third brigade was at Lonsdale, north of the railroad shops. Their stay in Knoxville from the summer of 1898 to January of 1899 was short lived, like the war (Greguras 2005).

Sadly, a fire in the church in August 1982 damaged the west window so badly that it could not be repaired. It was removed and replaced with a clear glass window. The beautiful stained-glass window remaining on the east wall, dedicated to Reverend S. A. Coile, first pastor of the church, was undamaged by the fire. The church is now a well-known and respected performance center and the home of Jubilee Community Arts. The building is listed on the National Register of Historic Places.

18

THE FUTURE OF THE FORT SANDERS NEIGHBORHOOD

THE CIVIL WAR BORROW PIT IS DEVELOPED

The Civil War–era borrow pit, which was last called the "Rose Hole" by the older residents of the Fort Sanders neighborhood, has almost disappeared, but there is an excellent place to view the modified remains of the northwest corner of this site. The "Hole" is easily identified by standing at the southeast corner of 16th Street at Laurel Avenue behind the New York Highlander Memorial and looking east down the slope into the grassy area adjacent to the Knox Place Apartments. Most of the leveled area at the bottom of the pit is now occupied by apartments and the Scottish Rite Temple. The original excavation during the war covered much of the block between White and Clinch Avenues and 15th and 16th Streets.

How the borrow pit came to be called the "Rose Hole" is an interesting story that involves the transformation of this historic manmade feature of the landscape from a Civil War–era "earth mine" to an amphitheater for the 1890 reunion, later to a neighborhood park called the "Commons," and then the "Rose Hole." The final designation for this unique topographical area became simply the dug-out area behind the Scottish Rite Temple.

The shape of the "Rose Hole" was initially determined by the shape of the excavation that soldiers were digging in 1864, not an irregular hole as one might expect but a large rectangular pit. Such a careful excavation was required since only the softer topsoil layer was desired for making repairs and completing the four-bastioned fortification.

An early description of the amphitheater created from the Civil War excavation is found in the October 6, 1890, edition of the *Knoxville Daily Journal.* The reporter documented the construction of a "monster amphitheater for people to witness the gorgeous fireworks display" that took place on the last evening of the reunion (*Knoxville Daily Journal* 1890f). The drawing of this excavated area in the 1886 Bird's Eye View of Knoxville shows a rectangular stadium-like pit with three relatively straight-sided walls (see figure 45). There is no wall on the south side of the pit, as a sloping path was needed there for wagons to enter and exit the excavation.

A 1949 postcard, which features a colored aerial photograph of a portion of the University of Tennessee campus, also captures the north side of the park with its tiered, grass-covered earthen seating created for the 1890 reunion event. A concrete staircase provided access for visitors into the park from Clinch Avenue. The same staircase can also be seen in a 1920s Thompson photograph of this area of the neighborhood. This method of creating permanent seating for outdoor events is still used today. After the earthen seating was removed, the staircase remained for a number of years, terminating in mid-air from the edge of a vertical bank above the "dug out area."

In a 1948 *Knoxville News Sentinel* article, a longtime Fort Sanders resident was interviewed about early 20th century life in that neighborhood. It appears that no one knew the origin of the sunken area, as this resident told the reporter that it was thought to be "a natural amphitheater." It was called the "Commons" then and was used as "a picnic ground for schools, churches, and private groups" (*Knoxville News Sentinel* 1948).

The exact date when the "Commons" name for this area was replaced by the "Rose Hole" is not known. However, an article mentioning the park was published in the October 16, 2011, issue of the *Knoxville News Sentinel* stating that the monument to the 79th New York Highlanders was placed "in the park on west Clinch Avenue."

Fig. 50. 1920s Thompson photograph of a peaceful, snow-covered Clinch Avenue with mature trees and less ostentatious houses. Courtesy of the Calvin M. McClung Historical Collection. Notice the remains of the amphitheater/park.

Don K. Ferguson, the author, described his investigation into the origin of the name, "the Rose Hole." He interviewed older members of the Scottish Rite Masonic Temple, which was built in 1953, and they helped to unravel the mystery. Ferguson's elderly informants described the site on which the temple was constructed as a large flat area resembling an arena, surrounded by banks covered with rose bushes. Members transplanted some of these roses to an area in front of the Temple (Ferguson 2011).

This level area was popular with UT students in the first half of the 20th century and used for athletic games between fraternities and sororities, pep rallies, and bonfires. The area east of Ramsey's Cafeteria and the Temple was a parking lot, and one could see the vertical cut that was made when the earthen steps were removed from the north side of the Rose Hole.

ADDITIONAL IMPACTS ON THE FORT SANDERS NEIGHBORHOOD

About 5,000 students attended the university in the 1950s, and the small campus occupied only "The Hill." During the 1970s, the student population increased to almost 30,000 students. The campus began to expand westward in the 1960s, engulfing South 16th Street (now called Volunteer Boulevard) with new academic buildings and student housing, and the McClung Museum and Communications/Student Services buildings on Circle Hill Drive. In the ten years between 1957 and 1967, approximately $73 million in construction contracts were awarded, and the elegant homes built during the late 19th and early to mid-20th centuries by Knoxville's wealthy elite in this section of early West Knoxville were razed (Wheeler 2005).

Decorative Victorian trim, bannisters, doors, and various other architectural elements were salvaged by Professor Kermit Ewing, chair of the Art Department in the mid-1960s, and he created sculptural art works that honored the workmanship and beauty of these dusty bits and pieces of history. These unique works were exhibited for a time in the art gallery of the Frank H. McClung Museum.

An article by Mary Anna Towler published in November 1962, entitled "Apartments Rise in U-T Section, Once an area of Proud Homes," tells the story of encroachment into this historic neighborhood best. In the UT section there were "tall, ornamented houses with towers, which now are strange looking to all but the oldest residents." In these elegant mansions "dwelt some of the wealthier people of the community. One man was so concerned about the happiness of his guests that he had Kingston Pike paved—just so mud wouldn't spatter on visitors' carriages." Towler documented the loss of housing between Neyland Drive and Forest Avenue: "A quick drive through the area showed 14 'new' apartment buildings (built within the last two or three years). Three more were well under way. Signs indicated that houses would be razed for two more. Newspaper stories have announced that still more razings are planned" (Towler 1962).

In reaction to the continuing destruction of historic buildings, a 105-acre area of Fort Sanders was designated "The Fort Sanders Historic District," and listed in 1980 on the National Register of Historic Places. The majority of the approximately 400 structures included in the district were houses of Craftsman/Bungalow or Victorian design. Several churches and commercial buildings were included (Akchin and Akchin 1980).

Residents formed the "Historic Fort Sanders Neighborhood Association" in 1998, and members continue the fight to preserve historic structures, not only in the Historic District but other areas of the neighborhood as well. However, there have been significant losses. The proximity of the university and a revitalized downtown Knoxville near the Fort Sanders community has driven the market for new housing and development in this area, while continued expansion of the Fort Sanders Regional Medical Center and consequent demand for additional parking also threaten the stability of the neighborhood.

In 1999, the Knoxville City Council rezoned an area of Fort Sanders between 18th and 19th Streets and Highland and Grand Avenues from a residential to a high-density zone, enabling Texas-based JPI Construction to demolish houses in that area so that a large apartment complex could be built. Soon the University Walk Apartments were added to the west of the JPI Crown Pointe complex (Howard 1999; Flory 2013).

The Standard Apartments were recently completed between 17th and 18th Street on White Avenue near the Knox and Knoxville Place Apartments, which cover almost two blocks between James Agee Street (formerly 15th) and 16th Street between Laurel and White Avenues, the location of the "Rose Hole." In May 2013, the Tennessee State Building Commission gave approval for UT to purchase and demolish three Queen Anne–style Victorian houses on the southern boundary of the Historic District. In 2015 the university paid $1.1 million for the 1896 Victorian home at 1302 White Avenue (Locker 2015). In turn, on February 24, 2015, it was purchased from UT by a local preservationist who had it moved to a lot at 1201 Clinch Avenue on July 24, 2015 (Slaby 2015). The two other houses were razed so that a $100 million science building could be built. This expands the university facilities north of Cumberland Avenue into an area protected by a historic overlay.

Presently the official word of UT administrators is that new campus construction will go skyward: additional stories will be added to older existing campus buildings. As the future unfolds, it may be that unless the historically significant neighborhood of Fort Sanders located on White's Ridge is appropriately honored, the preserved remains of Fort Sanders may well be destroyed, and the neighborhood that bears its name will itself not survive 21st-century "progress."

19

BURIED HISTORY

ARCHAEOLOGICAL EXCAVATION AT FORT SANDERS

Until we began archival research in 2006 on the construction and history of Civil War Fort Sanders, no one, to our knowledge, had identified or written about existing, distinguishable remains of the fort located on the two blocks between Clinch and Laurel Avenues and 16th and 18th Streets, nor had anyone conducted scientific archaeological or geological surveys in this area. Although it was difficult to prove that there are existing remnants of the fortification because of extensive alterations of the topography in these two blocks—including the construction of roads, sidewalks, and houses—it seemed odd that no one in recent history had made the effort to confirm the exact location of Fort Sanders, as it is one of the most important historic sites in Knoxville. Why had there been no scholarly archival or archaeological research conducted to determine whether remnants of the fort still existed above or below ground that would tell the story of Fort Sanders? The reasons for this lapse in historical and archaeological inquiry, we came to believe, are explained in part, in the preceding section on the United Daughters of the Confederacy monument.

Regarding the absence of archaeological investigations in the area of the fort, it has only been within the past six decades that American historians began to seriously consider the importance of archaeological research in their study of the nation's brief history. In 1969, the eminent historical archaeologist Ivor Noel Hume wrote, "The professional historical archaeologist has realized from the beginning his need of the historian, but the historian has been slow to reciprocate. His attitude has been that all he needs to know is to be found in his documents and that if it is not there, it is irreparably lost. He is only now beginning to recognize his mistake and to see that excavation properly undertaken *can* fill in details missing from the written record and may even correct previous interpretations of it" (Noel Hume 1969:18–19).

It was not until the mid-1960s that professional anthropological archaeologists in the United States began to consider the historic archaeology of Euro-Americans, African Americans, and Asian Americans as equal in importance to the study of Native Americans. It was in the 1980s that the University of Tennessee's Department of Anthropology, building on a firm foundation of outstanding research focused on prehistoric Native American sites in Tennessee by the Works Progress Administration and University of Tennessee archaeologists in the 1930s, initiated a program of historical archaeology of East Tennessee under Charles Faulkner's direction. The department now features a modern historic laboratory, library, and a historic artifact-type collection; and its M.A. and Ph.D. graduates are conducting contract historical archaeology and teaching historical archaeology at colleges and universities across the country. Publications on historic archaeological projects completed in the area of Knox County under the auspices of the Department of Anthropology and the McClung Museum can be found in Patrick Garrow's chapter in *Archaeology of Southern Urban Landscapes,* edited by Amy L. Young (Garrow 2000).

Archaeology is a science that employs precise and testable research designs to collect data from the earth in a systematic manner so that the cultural past can be accurately reconstructed. Such buried data is usually preserved and recoverable on most Civil War sites. In an article about Civil War archaeological sites, Steven D. Smith pointed out that "the public and scholarly communities' interest in and intensity of feelings about the [Civil War] clearly imply that every bit of information, from whatever source, is precious, needed, and welcome. A subject of such demonstrated importance to understanding America must be studied from every possible viewpoint. No source can be overlooked, including material remains hidden beneath the American landscape. To ignore the archaeological remains is to exercise a partiality researchers cannot afford" (Smith 1994:8).

The importance of archaeological research in helping to complete the local historical record of the Civil War was demonstrated during the recent excavations of two important Civil War sites in Knoxville. These projects were completed and documented in publications by archaeologists in the UT Department of Anthropology. The Sevierville Hill site, a Union encampment excavated in 1991, was located in South Knoxville (Bentz and Kim 1993); the Morgan Hill site excavated in 2001 was one of General Longstreet's major artillery positions (Angst 2012). The latter site was located on University of Tennessee property at the southeast corner of Kingston Pike and Neyland Drive. Each of these sites was in imminent danger of destruction; however, artifacts and features were excavated prior to any disturbance using what is called rescue, salvage, or contract archaeology. This kind of archaeology can be funded by the agency, organization, or business responsible for the destruction of a site or with grants, but there is usually a limited time frame in which the archaeological data must be scientifically collected. The information obtained from each of these sites, both of which are now destroyed, has significantly supplemented the archival knowledge of the siege and battle for Knoxville as described earlier in this volume.

We believe the second reason the location of Fort Sanders and the history of its construction and destruction have not been researched is due to a belief, frequently repeated by those interested in the Civil War in Knoxville, that "only the memory remains" of Fort Sanders. While most of the above-ground traces of the fort have been destroyed or modified in the past 150 years by construction of houses, apartments, streets and so on, a careful study of past and present topography combined with historical photographs reveal remnants of features of the completed fortification that can still be identified today. Only scientifically conducted archaeology can verify the age and function of these remains and help to reconstruct the story of the life of Fort Sanders. The scientific archaeology method requires three steps in the field: survey, testing, and unit or block excavation.

What follows is the description and results of our archaeological research on the Fort Sanders site. Readers unfamiliar with scientific archaeology may well find some of the expository prose confusing and even boring, but we are following a mandate that research on an archaeological site must be clearly described and recorded, because any subsequent disturbance of the site will permanently destroy the data that has been protected by its final encapsulation in the soil. The information recorded here also provides a scientific foundation for any further archaeological study of the site.

PEDESTRIAN SURVEYS

Preliminary archaeological surveys consist of pedestrian coverage of the grounds of a site to locate any existing topographical features and material remains resulting from human activity. This preliminary survey includes verification of topographical features identified in earlier surface-level photographs, aerial and global positioning satellite photographs, and remote sensing data recovered from the site. None of these methods employed alone can exactly locate where buried features exist or indicate why and how they were created. Eroded areas, exposed surfaces, and disturbances produced by farming and modern construction may provide clues during the pedestrian survey as to where features and artifacts might be located.

In addition to a pedestrian survey, photographs of an area being investigated, if available, can provide key information. In the case of our research, a number of photographs of the fort and surrounding area taken in the last 150 years helped to determine the exact location of the fort and areas where archaeological remains might likely be found. In addition to photographs, archival materials—including maps, historical engravings, letters, autobiographical accounts, and newspaper articles—are important sources that should supplement archaeological research; all these various sources were implemented in this study.

The most significant natural feature discovered in the pedestrian survey of the fort area was the presence of a large sinkhole located in the rear half of lots number 5 and 6, which face Highland Avenue on the north. The east boundary of lot 6 borders 18th Street. The sinkhole (or limestone sink) was partially covered by a Fort Sanders Hospital parking garage on the west side. Three Victorian houses facing Highland Avenue bordered the sinkhole on its north side, and an empty brick grocery store sat on the sinkhole facing 18th Street (see figure 26).

This sinkhole can be seen on Poe's hachure map (see figure 23) and Poe's contour map (see figure 21) and was described by Confederate artillery officer Porter Alexander, an eyewitness who wrote, "within a stone's throw of the parapet there was a big limestone sink, making a dead space in which several hundred men could stand . . . & the edge of it be lined with sharpshooters" (Alexander 1989:325). The edge and bottom of this sinkhole can also be seen in the 1864 photograph of Captain Poe and Colonel Babcock in front of the northwest bastion (see figure 25). This sinkhole was the only existing natural topographic feature that existed at the time of the battle, and for this reason it was a landmark of exceptional significance in determining the exact geographical location of the fort. The property on which the sinkhole was situated should have been preserved for posterity since this landmark was the sole surviving feature of the battlefield. The three historic houses on this property were moved and will remain within the boundaries of the Fort Sanders Historic District overlay.

Another feature of the landscape observed during the pedestrian survey was a manmade cut that created an embankment extending north-south along the property line between the Carson/Ronald McDonald House property and the Monday property immediately to the west (1705 Clinch Avenue). Elevations taken on the 1705 lot at the bottom of the embankment on the east property line indicate it is about 27 inches lower than the ground surface of the adjacent Carson/Ronald McDonald property. The height of the cut varies as it extends northward to the south edge of Laurel Avenue. It continues on the north side on that street to the alley between Laurel and Highland, where it reaches a maximum height of around four feet. The cut and the perfected leveling of most of the area west of the embankment to 18th Street for construction of houses could have been accomplished with mechanical earth-moving equipment around 1920. We know that part of this area was previously leveled for a parade ground near the west wall prior to the battle. Additional work to level the interior of the fort would probably have been completed for the 1890 reunion. Houses built soon after 1920 still stand on both sides of Laurel between 17th and 18th Streets, and apartments were built on the property adjacent to the Carson/Ronald McDonald House parking lot. The Roddy house (1918) is located on the northwest corner of this intersection and White Columns (1910) on the northeast corner. Both houses were built on the remains of the south end of the west wall of Fort Sanders (see figure 47b).

SOILS

Because of the presence of lawns and landscaped areas surrounding most of the houses and apartments in the area of the fort, we were only able to identify soil types that were revealed on bare ground and eroded places during our pedestrian surveys. What was usually seen in these exposed areas is a cherty (gravelly) red clay, which is characteristic for the red clay subsoil (C horizon) that appears to underlie the entire fort area. This soil type can be identified in the 1864 photographs of the walls and bastions, where fragments of the light-colored residual chert are highly visible. The builders of the fort extensively used this clay for the walls and bastions because it could be tamped down to create a hard surface; only by archaeological testing would it be possible to determine whether this soil is undisturbed subsoil or the cherty subsoil that was removed elsewhere and used for fill in these areas.

Continued monitoring by foot and car of the fort area for construction sites that might reveal critical information was another aspect of our pedestrian surveys, which have been ongoing since the beginning of our work in 2009. In December of that year, construction began on a new house at 1644 West Clinch Avenue on the southeast corner lot at Clinch and 17th Street. A house built in the early 20th century had been torn down, and a basement for a new house was dug into the slope between Clinch and White avenues. Redeposited fill from the southeast bastion, which was located in this area, could not be positively identified in the profiles of this excavation. There was evidence of fill on the east side of the original house foundation, which consisted of subsoil red clay and darker humus-bearing soil. The former could have come from the fort area, but this could not be substantiated. It is probable that soil from the southeast bastion in this area of the fort was not used extensively to level the south edge of Clinch for the construction of houses. It is believed that soil from the southeast bastion may have been used to fill fort ditches and in the construction of Clinch Avenue after 1900.

In October 2011, a second striking and very important soil profile was exposed on a property at 509 18th Street. A deep trench was being dug underneath the front porch of a 1925 two-story brick home belonging to Rebecca Scarlett in order to repair and waterproof the house foundation. Ms. Scarlett allowed us to closely examine the walls of the trench, which had been hand-dug to a depth of about four feet. We believed that this trench was close to, or even on, the remains of the west wall of the fort.

We troweled the side walls of the trench to create vertical profiles, recorded the stratigraphy, and took photographs and soil samples. We discovered that the east wall of the trench had been disturbed by earlier backhoe trenching and a live gas line exposed in the wall prevented cleaning and interpretation of that profile. However, after careful troweling of the west-wall profile of the soil beneath the porch, we exposed stratigraphy dominated by a one-to-two-foot-thick, whitish deposit of soil. Retired UT geologist Dr. John Foss initially identified the whitish deposit in the profile as silt/loam or possibly loess (wind-blown silt). Later analysis by Dr. Robert Hatcher revealed that the deposit was silica sand.

SOIL TESTING

Determining the sites in the fort area where auger testing should be done was based on information derived from early photographs, analysis of soils from our surveys, and continuing examination of stratigraphic cuts created by construction in the fort area. This information was compared to the details of the fort seen in the 1890 photograph (see figure 46) taken during the Blue-Gray Reunion, and then a decision was made as to which areas would be most likely to produce archaeological remains of the fort by auger testing. The Harrison house, located at 1630 Laurel Avenue, dominates the right side of the photograph. Below the house and to the right of where 17th Street would later be constructed are the remains of the southeast bastion with three easily identified embrasures.

When Clinch Avenue was improved in the early 20th century, the entire south side of the bastion was cut away. The high embankment of the remaining part of the southeast bastion was later truncated when Fort Sanders Manor was built; however, part of the embankment of that bastion remains and is held in place by the rough-cut, limestone block wall built adjacent to the sidewalk there. Exposed earth on the slope of this remnant bastion is the same type of cherty red clay fill dirt described above. Remains of the fort's south wall west of 17th Street run parallel to Clinch, the front of the Carson/Ronald McDonald House and adjoining parking lot, and are also held in place by a limestone block wall. This high embankment above the wall disappears immediately west of the property line where the north–south cut was made, and this area was leveled to build the Monday Apartments at 1705 Clinch.

We decided that the most expedient method to geologically test the fort area was to use a bucket auger to expose and examine soil formations in what appeared to be the most undisturbed areas of the old fort. The pedestrian survey determined that such deposits were most likely to be found in the yards of houses along Clinch Avenue and 18th Street where the south wall, west wall, and southwest and northwest bastions had been located. These sites included the front yards of the Carson/Ronald McDonald House, the Roddy house, and the Scarlett property on 18th Street.

The most extensive open space that appeared to be undisturbed was a linear area 228 feet long on the Carson/Ronald McDonald property; it varied in width beginning at the east edge of the front yard, continuing past the front of the house and ending at the southwest corner of the side yard adjacent to the cut on the west side of the property. This area was auger-tested by Dr. John Foss on April 7 and May 23, 2011. Three auger borings were taken down a little over 3 feet in the front yard, at which depth all borings hit sterile, pure red clay (limestone residuum).

At a depth of 2.78–3.11 feet, possible surface horizons of clay/loam were encountered in Auger Test #1. Auger Test #2 was aligned with the southwest corner of the house and placed 57 feet west of Test #1. The stratigraphy of the soil horizons was very similar to that seen in Test #1, with two buried clay loam surfaces: one at 2.13–3.11 feet below surface and another, deeper one at 3.11 to 3.77 feet. Auger Test #3 was placed 106 feet west of Test #2 in an overgrown area of small trees, brush, and weeds in the southwest corner of the side yard. This auger test revealed a similar clay loam stratum buried 2.46–2.78 feet below the ground surface (Foss 2012).

The three auger tests at the Carson/Ronald McDonald House exposed old land surfaces characterized by buried clay loam horizons containing organic content approximately 2–4 feet beneath the modern land surface. These earlier ground surfaces were located beneath clay soils that appeared to be mixed, suggesting that these soils had possibly been "loaded" from another area and deposited as fill on top of earlier ground surfaces. This mixed-clay fill varied in thickness, indicating that it could have been originally deposited at this location during the construction and destruction phases of the fort (ibid.).

Another auger test was placed in the front yard of the Roddy house on May 23 in an area believed to be remnants of the southwest bastion. Foss's evaluation of that area was that "the entire section was disturbed sediments with subsoil dominating from 25–120 cm indicating mixing of subsoils with surface horizons" (ibid.). Foss was unable to auger beyond a depth of 120 cm because of a dense concentration of cherty gravel and cobbles. The disturbed sediments with subsoil and surface horizons described by Foss are similar to the mixture of humus and red clay that would be created by excavating for fill dirt, and the fill resembles fort walls seen in the 1864 and 1901 photographs.

UNIT EXCAVATION

Details of the interior of the fort are virtually unknown except for the Orth map. Fortunately, Private John Orth, a Union soldier stationed in the fort in early 1864, took an interest in his surroundings and made a record of important details within the walls that had helped secure the victory over the Confederates. The drawing he made of the fort and the surrounding terrain is priceless. Although he idealizes Fort Sanders, rendering it as a square star shape, he includes details about the interior that are not found in any other document. Orth shows the location of two cisterns and the bombproof. Although he does not indicate that there was a parade ground, we discovered a source revealing that a parade ground was created near the west wall.

Sources, however, contain very little information about living conditions in the fort. Those that exist focus on the deep muddy clay within the interior, which must have made it difficult to move about in these cramped quarters. Some soldiers related that they ate where they were posted by their commanders; some noted that they slept where they were posted. Those in the open trenches often curled up into holes they dug in the trench walls in order to stay warm. They probably obtained drinking water from the cisterns Orth shows in his drawing. If there were latrines in the fort, we did not find mention of them in the sources used for this book. In any case, from November 1863 through early 1864, the fort was certainly a horrible place to be, during one of the coldest winters on record.

In addition to providing information about features within the fort, Orth also added the locations of cannon emplacements and the U.S. flag raised by Union troops on the western wall on November 18, 1863. Unfortunately, because Orth drew a completed, idealized, star-shaped fort instead of the uncompleted quadrilateral rectangular fortification that existed in late November 1863, he placed the interior features symmetrically within an equal-sided structure. Because of this fact and the subsequent natural and human modifications that have altered the modern topography, one cannot definitely pinpoint the exact locations where Orth's features might have left an archaeological footprint. Nevertheless, by using the description and dimensions of the fort recorded by Poe in the *Official Records* and placing the fort at the correct location with the west wall at present-day 18th Street, we could with some accuracy determine areas that might produce archaeological remains of the features recorded on the Orth map and perhaps distinguish the original ground surface of the fort. Based on our archival research, the information produced by auger testing, and the study of exposed profiles, we chose to begin a systematic unit excavation at the southwest corner of the rear side yard of the Carson/Ronald McDonald House. Ms. Sue Beverly, director of the Ronald McDonald House, and its board of trustees granted permission to conduct an archaeological excavation in this area.

On April 25, 2012, we began the project by placing an iron bolt capped with a PVC pipe as a principal datum point from which the location of grid points, features, and artifacts could be mapped. We began the excavation on the site previously recorded in the State Archaeology Survey in Nashville as 40KN333, on April 25, 2012, and completed this work on July 3, 2012. Two sweltering weeks in June were among the hottest and driest on record.

Excavation units or blocks usually are larger square or rectangular areas that can be accurately mapped to the datum using corner pins (or stakes) and are dug in levels to progressively expose buried surfaces and features, allowing for larger numbers of artifacts to be collected for study. The units can be laid out in various sizes, depending on such factors as research design, soils, number of features encountered, and the depth of the archaeological deposits. We focused our excavation on two areas of the ground surface in the southwest corner of the side yard: the highest part of the level ground surface, and the top of the slope which began at the south edge of the level area. This slope continued down to the top of the limestone block retaining wall adjoining the sidewalk along the north side of Clinch Avenue. Seventeen units were excavated, ranging in size from 3 × 3 feet to 1 × 1 feet. These units were designated by letters of the alphabet from A–O and FA and FB. The units covered an area of 91.25 square feet.

Excavation was primarily done using trowels and other small tools, and excavated soil was screened through ¼-inch screens. The units were laid out spatially with a transit and the corners marked with 6-inch

Fig. 51. Excavation Unit C. Photo by the authors. A) Location from datum; b) modern humus; C) clay lens; D) late buried A; E) mottled clay fill of south fort wall; F) brick from Carson house; G) gully in late buried A.

gutter spikes, the southwest corner being the (spatial) designator from the datum tying the units to the grid system. Distance below the datum point (arbitrary 100 feet) was determined by using the transit to measure depth of artifacts and features below the surface. All measurements were made in feet and tenths of feet.

STRATA

Soil was removed by natural/cultural strata. These are soils that were laid down by human activity and/or natural environmental transformations. These strata were from latest to earliest in time: Modern Humus; Clay Lens; Late Buried A; Clay Fill (ranging from dark red clay to mottled clay); Clay/Loam Silt; Old Buried A; and Clay Subsoil.

The Modern Humus was a very dark, organic, rich clay loam 0.1–0.2 feet thick, which contained modern artifacts such as plastic and dating from the 20th century. This was underlain in the units closest to the parking lot by a largely sterile Clay Lens 0.05–0.10 feet thick, representing spoil earth from the grading of the parking lot in 1990. Below this was the Late Buried A, containing artifacts dating from the Civil War to the early 20th century. This soil was a lighter-colored clay loam that had formed on top of a red clay fill. It contained artifacts on the surface and inclusive features at the base of the stratum. The base was a very hard packed and eroded clay surface; gullies cut through that surface, originating on the level area and running down the south slope of the excavation area. This surface had obviously been an open area for several years, and the red clay surface had been baked and trampled until very hard. Our initial interpretation was that this surface was the compacted floor of the fort, which had been exposed to the elements for a long period of time. However, as features were uncovered, it became obvious that this was a post-fort land surface.

On the first of June, we began to dig what is called a sondage, a small test unit that penetrates deeply below a larger excavated surface so that any deeper stratigraphy exposed in that unit can be quickly examined. We hoped to reach a depth in the sondage that would reveal what had been identified as a deeper buried A in the auger testing. The buried A soil was now believed to be the original ground surface of the fort. This test began as a 2.5 × 1.5–foot excavation in Unit F through a deposit of subsoil clay fill, ranging from a dense red clay through a mottled red clay fill to a level of silt/loam about 1.5 feet below the surface, which sloped to the east. From that point, the sondage narrowed

Fig. 52. Sondage in excavated Unit F. A) Clay fill mottled with weathered silica sand; B) grayish clay area with mottled silica sand; C) posthole from pulled post; D) area excavated to set the post filled with silica sand; E) author's blue jeans.

to a 1.0 × 1.5–foot excavation, which terminated in a 0.5-foot square 2.5 feet below the surface exposing another buried surface. The surfaces exposed corresponded to the buried A surfaces found in Auger Tests 2 and 3. The upper surface probably formed after the fort was abandoned; a feature of major importance, a posthole, was identified 2 feet below the surface at the 1 × 1–foot depth of the sondage (figure 52).

FEATURES

Features are any disturbance, construction, or artifact concentration resulting from human activity or natural processes on a site. Features can be the result of a single or short-term episode or event in the history of a site and can often date these events and the activity that caused them. Twelve features were recorded in the excavation; the feature that revealed the most important information was Feature 12, a large, deeply buried posthole 2 feet below surface in the sondage. Feature 12 was 0.6 feet in diameter and filled with a very loose mixture of red clay and what had been previously designated as silt/loam; this deposit was indistinguishable from the whitish soil found much earlier under Rebecca Scarlett's porch which was mistakenly identified as loess. The whitish soil in the setting hole, measuring 1.60 square feet, was sampled by Dr. Robert Hatcher and identified as silica sand. The loose fill in the posthole indicated that the post had been pulled. The context suggested that the feature was associated with the fort and was likely a structural part of a cannon embrasure. The discovery of this posthole proves that intact, undisturbed features of the fort still exist under an overburden of clay fill soil that is 2–3 feet thick at this location. The remaining 11 features were identified as later occupation features, including a gully containing Civil War period artifacts; three small, shallow stake holes or postholes; four fired shallow basins; a large slightly fired surface; and two planting basins.

A shallow gully (Feature 1) extended from Unit A on the crest of the slope 4 feet down the slope to Unit C. The gully contained a small, tin meat can that was apparently opened with a knife or bayonet, part of a camp stove, a bone underwear button, and two early railroad spikes. Several other late shallow gullies were recorded running north–south in the hard-packed base of the units, but they were not given feature numbers.

Three small shallow stake holes or postholes were found in units A, F, and G in the level surface of the excavation area. The term stake hole is added here because the holes looked like they had been created by driving a stake or small post into the hard clay; no dug, setting hole could be distinguished around them. The posthole (F 2) in Unit A was 0.5 feet square and had been plugged with a machine-made brick identical to those in the Carson house, and it was also wedged with small chert rocks. Feature 3 was a possible posthole in Unit F chinked with red clay. Stake hole/posthole Feature 4 (0.4 × 0.4 feet) in Unit G contained a large square chert rock. These three features were in a slight southwest–northeast alignment with the street and 4 feet apart. These features might possibly be stake holes from the small tents that were erected in the fort during the 1890 Reunion.

Four fired/heated shallow basins grouped together were found at the top of the slope. They ranged in size from 1.5 × 1.7 feet to 2 × 2 feet. They were filled with small pieces of coal (pea or nut sized), cinders, and burned limestone. Only one basin showed evidence of having been heated sufficiently to harden the surrounding clay soil and change it to a reddish color. This indicates that these features were the result of only one event on the site. An associated surface area 2 × 3 feet in size covered the Buried A horizon in Unit O. These features contained only a few artifacts, most of these dated from the late 19th to early 20th century. The lack of heavy burning suggests that the coal/cinders were discarded from camp stoves during the 1890 Reunion or perhaps originated later in the Carson house fireplaces.

Two planting basins (Features 5 and 6) occurred on the level area of excavation. They measured 1.5 × 1.5 feet and 1.0 × .80 feet in diameter and were filled with a very fine humus. The point of origin appeared to be in the Modern Humus, and Feature 6 contained a broken, fully machine-made bottle indicating a post-1900 date.

ARTIFACTS

No artifacts were found in the clay fill or silica sand strata encountered in the excavation. Artifacts were present in the Modern Humus, but these are not relevant to the earlier history of the fort. The artifacts recovered in the Late Buried A are relevant to the earlier post-fort occupation of the site, and a sample of dateable and functionally identifiable artifacts are described below.

Forty-seven artifacts are in the sample from the Late Buried A in units A, C, F, and M in the excavation area. The types, size, and scattered nature of these artifacts indicate the Late Buried A was formed by what is called a sheet midden, which, by definition, refers to objects accumulated over a relatively long period of time, unlike a sealed midden where household trash is dumped and then covered quickly. Artifact classes include a wrought (handmade) nail (1); cut nail (1); wire nail (1); window glass (1); lamp chimney glass (1); early railroad spikes (2); iron wire (1); ceramics (3); melted glass (1); and bottle/jar glass (35). The glass containers indicate a date for this assemblage from ca. 1880 to ca. 1915 (Jones and Sullivan 1985). The percentage and size of the glass sherds (fragments) in this collection was unusual and for that reason, were of particular interest.

Of the 10 artifact classes in the sample, bottle/jar glass makes up 70 percent of the artifact assemblage. This is a very high percentage, especially when the bottle/jar glass frequency at other late-19th-to-early-20th-century archaeological sites in the Knoxville area is compared to the Fort Sanders sample. Using sites that were studied during the 1984 archaeological survey of the Pellissippi Parkway, the container glass from sheet midden context was compared to the other artifacts in the site assemblage. In the 10 sites used in the sample, glass ranged from a low of 9 percent to a high of 53 percent with an average percentage of all sites at 22 percent (Roberts and Faulkner 1984). Why was there such a high percentage (70 percent) of container glass found at Fort Sanders?

Examination of the container glass revealed an interesting fact. In a well-known study of container glass on historic archaeological sites, archaeologists William Rathje and Michael Schiffer, using what is called the McKellar hypothesis, found that small artifacts less than 4 inches in length + width + height will be left behind in a midden that is "cleaned up," or to use a military term "policed" (Rathje and Schiffer 1982; Moore n.d.). The largest of the 35 container glass sherds in the Fort Sanders site sample were 2 inches (23%); 23 (66%) were 1 inch, and 4 (11%) were 0.5 inches. The area was obviously deliberately kept clean.

What do these artifacts tell us about the formation of this midden? The rarity of ceramics and architectural artifacts such as nails suggests that the artifacts here did not originate around a dwelling. Because most of the artifacts were remains of vessels used to hold liquids, it is likely these were from beverage bottles brought to the site by picnickers, veterans who camped there, and visitors who attended the 1890 reunion. Larger sherds of glass would have been picked up for public safety.

ARCHAEOLOGICAL INTERPRETATIONS OF CULTURAL AND NATURAL TRANSFORMATIONS THROUGH TIME

What can the archaeological remains found on this one small area of the fort site reveal about the construction, abandonment, and reuse of the site during the later 19th and early 20th centuries? While open to a range of interpretations, this limited archaeological view through a narrow window of time indicates rapidly changing vignettes of human activity and a dynamically changing landscape.

Evidence of human activity discovered in our archaeological study was first identified in the strata exposed by construction on the Rebecca Scarlett property, in the auger tests, and in the unit excavation at the Carson/Ronald McDonald House. The Buried A horizon in the auger tests at the latter site is believed to be the surface of the interior of the fort, and it correlates with the Silt/Loam and Old Buried A in the unit excavation at the Carson/Ronald McDonald House; unfortunately these important strata could only be identified in the sondage because of the dry and hardened red-clay fill found above these two strata. A larger area could have been opened but only with tools such as mattocks and shovels, and this method of digging would have undoubtedly resulted in destruction of significant data. We chose to end the excavation at this point because the fort remains in this area are presently protected and can be studied at a more appropriate time when the soils are malleable and a larger crew is available to do the necessarily careful handwork.

The silt/loam soil present in the profile at the Scarlett property was initially identified in the field as possibly Ice Age loess. Loess dates to the end of the last glacial age and appears to be a rare soil in East Tennessee. Although some loess has been found on Chestnut Ridge in East Tennessee, it is much more common in the middle and especially the western portions of the state (Crownover et al. 1994). However, based on their study of the photographs of the west soil profile at the Scarlett house site, two other experts on eastern North American soils did not believe that this soil was Ice Age loess. They recommended that this significant soil warranted further study in the laboratory.

To determine the mineral composition of the silt/loess, samples of this soil were collected by Dr. Robert D. Hatcher, geologist in the Science Alliance at the University of Tennessee. A sample was taken from the deposit of this soil in the west profile on the Scarlett property and the silt/loam lens over the Old Buried A in Unit F at the Carson/Ronald McDonald House (Hatcher 2012a). Dr. Hatcher subjected the samples to X-ray diffraction (XRD Analysis) and found the samples to be identical. This soil contained zero clay minerals, which is unusual for the soils in the Fort Sanders area, indicating that the soil probably did not come from parent rock in this location and was transported to the site. X-ray diffraction found it to be fine grained and angular, and composed of 98 percent angular quartz (Sio2) (Hatcher 2012b). The fort soil differs from loess in that grains of loess are smooth and rounded because they are tumbled about as they are transported by the wind, and therefore are not angular. The mineral composition of loess is also different from the fort sample, being approximately 60–70 percent quartz, 10–20 percent feldspar and mica, 5–35 percent carbonates, and 2–5 percent heavy minerals—for example, apatite (*Encyclopedia Britannica* 2015). Since the mineralogical test also suggests that this is not loess, what is it, then, and why is it found in two areas of the fort site? One natural geological material that is almost 100 percent quartz is silica sand, a fine-grained, sandy silt that is used in making glass, among other industrial purposes. The only known source of silica sand in East Tennessee is still being mined at Bean's Station on the Holston River, and sand from this site could have easily been shipped by flatboat to Knoxville in the mid-19th century (Crownover et al. 1994:1739).

Over a decade before the Civil War, a glass factory was built in the summer of 1849 at the location where the South Knoxville bridge crosses the Tennessee River. By October of that year, plate glass was being produced and sold by this factory. Albert Miller Lea leased the property in 1851 and manufactured glass there until he went bankrupt in June 1853, when he then sold the property to John S. Van Gilder. The sale included all materials connected with glassmaking, including sand. Van Gilder is listed as a glass manufacturer in Knoxville as late as 1860, but after that date there is no evidence he manufactured glass at the Holston glassworks (Wells n.d.). That the glass factory was still standing as late as 1863 is documented by Union army engineers who used it as a landmark when illustrating their defensive lines on the Fort Sanders battlefield. It seems likely that any stockpiled silica sand would have still been on the property. It is hypothesized here that the silt/loam/loess strata on the fort site is actually silica sand from the glass factory site that was either shoveled into sandbags at the site or in Fort Sanders. This hypothesis is strengthened by the presence of this silica sand in two areas of the fort where cannon embrasures were located. The fort at the time of the battle had embrasures in the west, south, and north walls and northwest and southwest bastions. The most important supporting evidence of this hypothesis is found in the photograph of the northwest bastion and the west wall; what appears to be white sand can be seen spilling out of an embrasure down the slope to the bottom of the ditch (see figure 54).

In the same excavation unit (Unit F) where evidence of sandbags was found, a feature was identified that was probably associated with the construction of the fort. This is Feature 12, a large posthole having a point of origin in the same buried surface that, at this location, is covered with a thin lens of silica sand. The posthole indicates a round post, probably a small tree cut near the site, which was 6 inches in diameter and set at least 3 feet into the ground. The soft fill of the posthole indicates it was pulled after the abandonment of the fort and the hole naturally filled up with a mixture of clay and silica sand. Posts were used to secure the horizontal planks lining the sides of the embrasures which had been cut into the earthen wall, and for the revetments. Sandbags were usually added adjacent to the side walls of cannon embrasures to prevent damage to the walls from the concussive vibrations created by cannon fire (Swain 2013). The upper part of a wooden revetment can be seen in an 1864 photo of the bastion (see figure 25). Similar-sized posts can be seen in an engraving of the breastworks at Camp Butler, Newport News, Virginia. The fact that the post was pulled indicates that it was probably scavenged by local civilians in need of timber for rebuilding the town after the fort was abandoned.

Clay fill rested on top of the Early Buried A/Silica Sand strata. In the north profile of Unit F, the fill was about 1 foot in thickness on the west side; it then dipped down to about 2 feet in thickness on the east side of the unit. This might indicate that there was a subsidence in the Early Buried A surface that was filled in with clay. This subsidence of the clay fill may have been due to the softer soil within an embrasure at this location in the wall. The clay fill ranged from a very dark red, compact clay to a mottled clay, probably representing loading, to one mottled with silica sand above the posthole and the possible gun embrasure. This stratum undoubtedly represents the clay fill that formed the south wall; after the war, when the revetment was removed, the fill eroded down the slope because of rain and sheet wash to form a clay colluvium on the fort floor. The formation of this clay fill is believed to date from ca. 1866 to ca. 1890.

Although the Late Buried A stratum was excavated in all of the units and contained the majority of features found and artifacts recovered, it was the most difficult stratum to interpret. Associated artifacts indicated that it dated from ca. 1890 to 1915+. The base of this stratum had an extremely hard-packed surface, suggesting that it had been baked by the sun and the bare ground tramped on for many years. It contained well-defined gullies that had been etched into the hard-packed clay by runoff down the slope. Early in the excavation, the presence of a mixture of Civil War and late 19th century artifacts in the gullies at the bottom of this stratum suggested that it had been an open and exposed clay surface that may have dated to as early as the occupation of the fort. Later in the excavation, it became clear that this surface and stratum dated later in the 19th century and was exposed when the Carson/Ronald McDonald House was built. This was evident since broken bricks and roofing slate used in the 1903 construction of this house were found in this stratum. The activities taking place here during those two to three decades are still unclear. The size of the container-glass sherds certainly means that the area was cleaned up periodically, and the fact that many of these sherds were from bottles suggests that bottled beverages were drunk outdoors. The cinders and coal may have been remains from small camp stoves, and areas of fired clay earth may have resulted from small fires made on the ground surface. Small portable camp stoves were probably available, and the evidence of fire building for warmth or for cooking, combined with the numerous sherds of container glass and the line of shallow post holes (possibly tent stakes), suggests that this area could have been the location of the campsites of veterans who attended the 1890 Blue-Gray Reunion. The Late Buried A Stratum may also relate to the time periods of the 1895 Reunion and even the 1913 Conservation Fair. The old fort was still a featured tourist attraction during these two events.

Newspaper articles published during the reunion tell us that many of the veterans camped out at the fort in spite of the rainy weather. They surely used tents but also devised shelters similar to ones used during the Civil War, called shebangs. There are several definitions of a shebang, a word thought to be of Irish derivation and introduced during the war by Confederate soldiers from the South. To the Civil War soldier, a shebang meant a temporary, improvised, usually crude shelter created by various materials that might be available to them, including boards, logs, brush, or pieces of canvas (*Merriam Webster Dictionary* 2017).

One type of makeshift shebang was a shelter built against the interior revetment of the wall/parapet. These canvas shelters can be seen in numerous Civil War photographs and were made utilizing the parapet as a back wall. One side of a piece of canvas or a tent was attached to the revetment/parapet, then stretched forward into the fortification, creating a "roof" supported by poles or stakes driven into the ground. Veterans who attended the reunion and "camped out" probably used this method to prepare crude shelters to protect themselves from the rain. In that regard, the newspapers reported that on the afternoon of October 6, "a heavy rain storm hit the city." The next day, the "downpour had turned to a drizzling rain, making the footpaths in and around the fort quite treacherous" (Conklin 2005).

Fig. 53. Photograph of the north side bastion showing embrasures lined with sandbags, probably filled with silica sand from the old glass factory located at the south end of the Union's easternmost defensive trench on the Holston River. A) Trench; B) expanded ditch; C) berm; D) sandbags which have fallen out of the cannon embrasure; E) soldier; F) revetment on the south wall of the northwest bastion.

For a short period of time after this, the area of excavation may have been the location of a flower garden since planting holes intruded into the top of the Late Buried A stratum. What appear to be late-19th-to-early-20th-century flowerpot sherds were found in some units. This would make it likely that "policing" of the area continued during this time, which would be expected in a well-cared-for garden. Later in time, the area was neglected and became covered with shrubs and weeds; and the rich, black, modern humus formed that characterizes the surface soil today. This perhaps occurred after the last Carson family members moved in the late 1930s, and the house became a rental property.

It is unfortunate that we were not able to collect more data from the deeply buried archaeological remains on the fort site. However, we

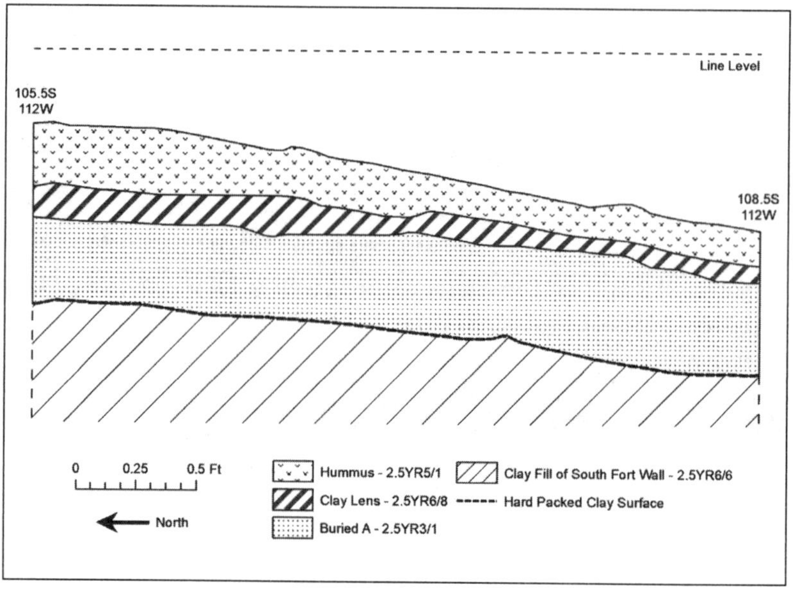

Fig. 54. Stratigraphy of east profile, Excavation Unit C.

now know that Civil War archaeological features are still preserved in the interior of the fort, and we know the depth of the fort floor in the area of the Carson/Ronald McDonald House and that the silica sand lens located in the area of the west and south walls indicates the probable location of cannon embrasures. The ground work has been laid, and we hope that this initial phase of scientific investigation will inspire further professional archaeological research in the future.

CONCLUSION

The initial objectives of our research were (1) to identify the correct location of Civil War Fort Sanders within the neighborhood that inherited its name, (2) to determine why that particular site on White's Hill was chosen by General Danville Leadbetter to begin constructing a fortification during the Confederate occupation of Knoxville, and (3) to discover why, after Federal troops occupied the town, Captain Orlando Poe chose to improve upon little more than the foundation of a misplaced bastion and an almost imperceptible west wall left by the Confederates to create the primary defensive position for Knoxville. Finally, we wanted to fully document for the first time the many contributions of General Davis Tillson, who was chosen to complete construction of this enormous fortification that secured Knoxville and East Tennessee for the Union.

It would have been impossible to write a history of Civil War Fort Sanders without first placing the construction of the fort in context; thus it was necessary to include a general history of the Civil War as it unfolded in the western theater, with an emphasis on East Tennessee and Knoxville. For this effort we relied upon detailed accounts of local historians and civilians who had lived through the war. We focused on including information from period newspapers and the personal memoirs, journals, and letters of both Union and Confederate soldiers who either fought in the battle of Fort Sanders and/or occupied Knoxville during the war years.

After extensive research revealed the answers to our initial questions, we decided to continue our studies so that we could perhaps discover how and why the massive earthen fortification completed in 1865 by General Tillson had been almost totally destroyed in the decades after the war, and which was, by the 21st century, considered to be "only a memory." The most straightforward way to achieve this goal was to use the method of historical ecology and a timeline to document the cultural and environmental impacts on Fort Sanders and the area surrounding it during the war and the years following the conflict until it was virtually destroyed during the 20th century. With information discovered during our eight years of scientific research, we have been able to identify locations where human interactions with the landscape altered the larger topographical area of White's Hill from the beginning of the construction of Fort Sanders in 1863 through the war years, to final abandonment and almost complete destruction of the fort. The time periods when alterations took place have been determined, and impacted locations that are still preserved and visible are described, as well as the areas where buried cultural remains may still exist.

When our research began, we were aware of the long-held belief of local Civil War experts that "only the memory" of Fort Sanders remained. We initially thought that this was true. In addition to the commonly held belief that there were no physical remains left of the fort, local historians were convinced that the west end of the fort was located at 17th Street and that the northwest bastion where the attack took place was located at the corner of 17th Street and Laurel Avenue. Confidence in these locations was based on the maps that appear in Digby Seymour's otherwise excellent book *Divided Loyalties*, first published in 1963. Maps in the second and third editions, the last being published in 2002, all show the location of the fort as it existed at the time of the battle with the west wall at 17th Street and the northwest bastion at the corner of 17th and Laurel Avenue. To our knowledge, no archival research or geological or archaeological testing was undertaken to either confirm or disprove these locations after the publication of any of the three editions, nor had any efforts been made to examine the topography in the area of the earthwork to determine whether there were visible remnants of the fort that could help establish the actual location of the fort.

We believe that the recent Geographic Information System (GIS) analysis that overlaid the historic map of the Fort on top of the modern street grid has inaccurately placed the west wall and northwest bastion at 17th Street. Attempts to use GIS to determine the precise location of the Fort must be tested with ground-truthing methods in archaeological or related fields. Beginning in 2011, we directed archaeological and geological investigations to prove or disprove the initial GIS results. Our conclusions are presented in this book, which clarifies the actual footprint of the fort and illustrates how it differs from Seymour's and Dr. Harold Fink's initial placement of the fort.

We present in this book the evidence that absolutely establishes the location, and we also explain why we think that Seymour believed his location was correct. We met with Dr. Seymour before his death in 2017 to discuss his placement of the west end of the fort on 17th Street, but he was able to say only that he placed it according to the "best information" he had at the time.

An earlier map showing the incorrect fort location, one that Seymour was surely familiar with, was produced by Dr. Harold Fink in his 1957 article, "The East Tennessee Campaign and the Battle of Knoxville in 1863," published in the *East Tennessee Historical Society's Publications*. Fink misplaced the west wall of the fort at 17th Street between Clinch and Laurel avenues, and Seymour's map duplicates this placement. An often-quoted but misleading *Knoxville Sentinel* article describing the 1914 dedication of the United Daughters of the Confederacy memorial on 17th Street may have influenced both Fink's and Seymour's location. This 103-year-old article is still routinely used today as sufficient justification for placing the fort between 17th and 16th Streets on the topographical crest of White's Hill.

The original objective of our research was to identify the correct location of the fort as it appeared in 1863 on Poe's and Tillson's maps. Results of archival research, newly discovered surface remnants of the fort, scientific archeological testing in the area, and information revealed in the 1890 Blue-Gray Reunion and Patrick photographs have enabled us to make a more accurate map illustrating the completed fort at the correct location on the military crest of the ridge.

The singularly most important discovery, and personally exciting moment, which rapidly propelled our research forward, happened in the summer of 2008. We had been confused about the shape of the southwest bastion seen in the 1890 photograph because of the wide cut, created for the 1890 reunion, that dissected it. We acquired a digital photograph that could be enlarged enough to show minute details and saw to our amazement a buggy entering the cut. It was then that we realized that the cut had been made 25 years *after* the war, to allow reunion visitors easier access up the steep slope into the western part of the fort.

Comparing the location of the cut in a 1922 Thompson photograph of that area to current KGIS street maps revealed that this steep cut would ordinarily have been made into an extension of 18th Street south to White Avenue, but instead had been eliminated from the KGIS city street grid, leaving a block-length gap in 18th Street. The level, horizontal east–west path at the base of the cut can be seen today as the asphalt alley between Clinch and White avenues, 18th and 17th Streets and the western section of the alley between 17th and 16th Streets. These features of the landscape, so perplexing early in our research, seem perfectly obvious now.

The south wall of Fort Sanders and the location where 17th Street would eventually be built at its east end were more easily identified in the 1890 photograph. The lone house on the ridge proved to be final and definitive proof that the location of 17th Street was at the east end of the fort's south wall. After checking the 1917 Sanborn Fire Insurance map of that area, we found that the house had been completed by J. B. Harrison in 1889 on Laurel Avenue (formerly Grove) east of 17th Street. The back of the Harrison house can be seen again in a 1901 Patrick photograph (see figure 47d) with the northeast bastion extending east of the route of 17th Street, which is staked out in the photograph. The rear of the Pickle house, completed in 1899, which is often mistaken for the Harrison house in the 1890 reunion photograph, is also seen in front of the Harrison house facing Clinch.

Considerably more proof of the fort location was discovered in the years to come, but verification of major significance for the newly identified location was found in the 1899 memoirs of Confederate artillerist Colonel Porter Alexander who described the parapet [of the fort] as a stone's throw from a limestone sink, large enough to hold several hundred standing men. The parapet Alexander referred to in his memoirs was part of the northwest bastion at the intersection of 18th Street and Laurel Avenue. From 1863 until 2019 when the remains of the sinkhole were destroyed by construction, this feature endured as the only visible original topography left in the area of the fort from the time of the battle. One could clearly observe this "limestone sink" by walking on the west sidewalk on 18th Street between Laurel and Highland Avenues and looking west after passing an abandoned grocery store. The 1920's Thompson aerial photo shows rifle pits in this sinkhole that match Poe's placement of Union pits closest to the northwest bastion on his 1863 map of Knoxville's defenses.

Leadbetter, Poe, and Tillson had attended the U.S. Military Academy at West Point and undoubtedly studied under Dennis Hart Mahan, who had begun teaching at West Point even before he graduated in 1824. These officers most likely had a copy close at hand of Mahan's *A Treatise on Field Fortifications*. This 1848 treatise contains explicit instructions and detailed illustrations for constructing fortifications in the field. Mahan advised in the foreword that his book was "not for study alone" but for the officer also to "take with him into the camp, and consult at any moment" (Mahan 1862: V).

During the summer months of 1863, General Danville Leadbetter, a West Point graduate and an engineer in the Confederate army, chose a location on the military crest of White's Hill and oversaw the initial construction of a fortification that was first called Fort Loudon by the Confederates. Leadbetter had apparently followed Mahan's advice that "a bastioned fort satisfies more fully the conditions of a defense more than any other work" (ibid.). There are no photographs or drawings of Leadbetter's unfinished Confederate works, but there are eyewitness accounts of Union occupiers, including Captain Orlando Poe, that describe the earthwork as the beginnings of a bastioned fortification.

Union troops under General Ambrose Burnside entered Knoxville on September 1, 1863. Because of the distinct possibility of a Confederate effort to retake the town, Poe was directed to quickly complete his defensive plan for Knoxville and supervise improvements to Leadbetter's earthwork even though the northwest bastion was considered to be vulnerable to attack because it was a salient in the defensive line.

As a West Point graduate well-educated in geometry and mathematics, Poe exactly described the fort on White's Hill as an unfinished irregular quadrilateral rectangle with bastions at the corners of the west wall. The 125-yard length of both the north and south walls conformed to Mahan's recommendations; the difference in the lengths of the west wall (95 yards) and the east wall (85 yards) was necessitated by the topography, and Poe added the word "irregular" to accurately describe the shape of the fort. Three huge lunettes served in the place of a bastion at the northeast corner of the north wall and allowed a wider space for maneuvering the guns; a small demi-bastion was built at the east corner of the south wall. Poe added many of the defensive obstacles in front of the west wall of the fort described in Mahan's *Treatise.* Some of the details of Poe's rendering of the fort are not consistent with the observations of a reporter who saw the fort shortly after the battle. He wrote, "No part of the fort is complete," and noted that only the northwest bastion and west wall were up (*Nashville Daily Union* 1864). Poe left Knoxville shortly after the battle, leaving the fort much as it appeared immediately after the attack. He returned in March 1864 and was photographed during his visit with Babcock standing north of the northwest bastion. The edge of the sinkhole described by Confederate artillerist Porter Alexander can be seen to their right.

Following General Davis Tillson's appointment to oversee the defenses of Knoxville in early December 1863, an enormous cut though the north wall and into the slope of the ridge was made; strangely, there is no mention of the Herculean effort made by Union troops during the coldest winter on record to accomplish this task and the assignment to repair and add defensive improvements in less than four months. It is likely that the enormous cut in the north wall seen in the 1864 Poe-Babcock photograph was used to bring heavy material into the fort.

Other official photographs taken in March 1864 show that construction of a stockade and a gate was underway as well as the southeast bastion. The southwest bastion and south wall were also being improved. General Tillson received high praise for his work from the inspector general, who reported that he had "evinced much skill in laying out the defensive lines, and an uncommon energy in their execution" (*OR* 1897:pt. 2, 251).

To our knowledge, the only illustration of the interior of the fort was drawn by John G. Orth, and he represented it as a square star fort, a type of fortification Mahan did not recommend because the number of men needed to defend it could not function well in the limited space afforded by the shape (Mahan 1862). The Orth map includes the structures inside the fort and also the landscape surrounding it. The location of the Union flag, two cisterns, the powder magazine, and the stockade with a gate are shown. Our research revealed that a parade ground was also added within the fort near the west wall. Even Tillson in his official drawings for the earthwork illustrated Fort Sanders as a square star fort, as did the artists who drew it for the Bird's Eye View of Knoxville in 1872 and 1888.

Several other important additional discoveries were made during our research. Thanks to digitized photographs of the Civil War landscape, the location of a large, deep rectangular borrow pit south of Clinch Avenue between 15th and 16th streets was finally identified as to its origin, and its postwar history was brought to light. The earth from that pit was carried up the slope to the fort in wagons and used in constructing the southeast bastion. Artists' attempts to draw this dug-out area three-dimensionally in the Bird's Eye Views were so poorly rendered that the borrow pit looks like a huge rectangular pan sitting on the surface of the ground. For this reason some historians have identified this feature as an above-ground reservoir. This huge scar on the landscape was transformed in 1890 into an amphitheater, where visitors to the Blue-Gray Reunion gathered to watch fireworks. In the early 20th century, it was used as a neighborhood park; and finally, it was planted with roses and known for years as the "Rose Hole." UT students often used it for various sports, as did local residents. We heard the question many times during our research: "Did you find out why the land is so deeply dug out behind the Masonic Temple and Ramsey's Cafeteria?" We are able to say that this decades-old mystery has now been solved.

Another enormous modification to the ridge, a second borrow pit, was recently identified in Mark Barnes's newly discovered photograph taken from the south side of the river by Barnard in 1864 (see figure 39). This borrow pit was located at the east end of White's Hill in the area north of Highland Avenue between 13th and 15th Streets. Dirt from this excavation was probably used to build the northeast bastion. The presence of that borrow pit may have been the reason that 14th Street was dead-ended on Highland Avenue between 15th and 14th Streets. The KGIS soils map shows a type of soil in this area that is found in only one other small area of Fort Sanders. The soil type is labeled "DyC" and is described in the Knox County Soil Survey as "urban land soil," which is redeposited mixed soil brought in from other areas for fill. This type of soil is also found on each side of Cumberland Avenue beginning west of the "Hill" and extending almost to 17th Street. Between 16th and 17th Streets, the deposit expands northward and covers the area where the pond seen in Barnard's photograph was located. It appears that soil was brought in, maybe at the same time the West Knoxville Council was filling in the excavation to raise and improve Cumberland Avenue in the low area existing at that time. This low area can also be identified in Barnard's 1864 photograph.

Excavating that area between 1863 and 1865 and then refilling the excavation before 1895 posed a huge challenge, as horse- or mule-drawn wagons and manpower would have been required to do the work. This undertaking was accomplished before the completion of the 1895 Ogden Brothers map, which shows platted house lots in that area and a dead-ended 14th Street at Highland Avenue.

An extremely significant and unexpected discovery was made on January 1, 2019, when Howard Cyr, Director of GeoArch Solutions, LLC, and Manager of the Laboratory of Environmental Archaeology at the University of Tennessee's McClung Museum of Natural History and Culture used remote sensing to determine if a prominent subsidence in an alley located in the area of the west wall and the northwest bastion could be the location of a defensive trench associated with the northwest bastion. The ground penetrating radar results show a man-made feature beneath the alley located on the west side of 18th Street between Laurel and Clinch Avenues which almost matches exactly the dimensions of Fort Sanders's defensive trenches described by Captain Orlando Poe (Poe 1888). This area must be ground-truthed to determine if the GPR data is correct. If this feature is found to be a section of the trench which surrounded the northwest bastion then it is additional proof that the placement of Fort Sanders on the military crest is correct.

Union general Davis Tillson oversaw the excavation of this second borrow pit, the successful completion of Fort Sanders, and the defense of the region in which it was located—a significant achievement that would safeguard Knoxville and East Tennessee for the Union until the end of the war. Tillson believed that African Americans could help win the war, and his determination to organize, train, and lead the first African American military unit in Knoxville, the 1st Regiment, United States Colored Heavy Artillery, helped to promote stability in the area. These men helped defend Knoxville from the summer of 1864 to the end of the war, and they were the last to leave the town in 1866 after President Johnson's formal declaration that the rebellion was ended. It is incomprehensible that the military service of African Americans has been virtually ignored in the Civil War history of East Tennessee. More information will be forthcoming about their contributions, however, as a daybook discovered in Washington, D.C., archives is presently being transcribed. The material will be preserved and curated by the staff of the Beck Cultural Center in Knoxville.

General Davis Tillson's exemplary service after the war's end as an assistant director of the Freedmen's Bureau has been almost totally ignored by historians. Hopefully, this book will create interest in Tillson, an honorable and capable man, who has not received proper recognition for his numerous achievements both during and after the Civil War.

Except for curious boys playing in the trenches and digging for artifacts, there appears to have been little interest in Fort Sanders for nearly two decades after the war ended in 1865. Knoxvillians were still grieving over the loss of loved ones, suffering the miseries of deprivation and destruction of property, and adjusting to the changes in their lives caused by war injuries. Worrying about the condition and future of Fort Sanders was low on their priority list. The apathy regarding the state of the fort seems to have been shared by Ambrose Burnside; during a Knoxville stay in 1874, he did not visit the fort where he had achieved a notable Civil War victory.

Why was Knoxville's Fort Sanders ignored during the last two decades of the 19th century while during that same period an enthusiastic effort was gathering momentum in Chattanooga to preserve the battlefields of Chickamauga and Chattanooga? The U.S. Congress was persuaded to provide funding to purchase the 5,300-acre battlefield of Chickamauga in addition to important sites on Missionary Ridge and Lookout Mountain. The vast Chickamauga battlefield was probably preserved because it was located on open farmland away from the town of Chattanooga. The southern outcrops of the Appalachian Mountains at Missionary Ridge, and Lookout Mountain offered cleaner air and more beautiful views of the countryside below, and were destined to become prime real estate for developers. Expensive houses now share the landscape with Civil War monuments and plaques (Hardy 2007).

The value of land also increased in Knoxville, especially in the west and north of town as wealthy citizens began to think that life might be healthier and safer away from the smoke, taverns and sewage-filled streets of Knoxville. Urban sprawl began to spread from Second Creek up the eastern slope of a ridge much less daunting than Missionary Ridge in Chattanooga, and that development relentlessly proceeded westward toward the crest of White's Hill. Knoxvillians suddenly realized that Fort Sanders was in imminent danger. The 1886 Bird's Eye View of Knoxville shows development approaching 17th Street and the location of the fort. A tug of war began between citizens who wanted to save the fort and those who wanted to ignore the historic significance of the fort and build houses on the land it occupied.

Possibly inspired by the success of the Chickamauga park organizers, some concerned private citizens submitted a proposal in 1890 to the federal government that land at the fort should be purchased for a military park, but this effort at preservation was rejected. The lack of interest shown by the government in funding the proposal could have been due to the fact that lots for homes had been sold near and even on the site of the fort, or perhaps because a large financial commitment had already been made by the federal government to preserve the Chickamauga battlefield.

As the death knell for the fort was sounding in the last decade of the 19th century, a group of distinguished Knoxvillians, including men who had fought in the war, preservationists who wanted to protect the site, and merchants eager to make money, took action. These influential leaders made a plan; they would generate interest in preserving the old fort by hosting a Civil War reunion of Confederate and Union veterans who had fought in Knoxville. The 1890 Blue-Gray Reunion was a tremendous success; the second Knoxville reunion effort in 1895 attracted travelers attending the dedication of the Chattanooga National Parks but did not fare as well as the 1890 reunion.

The town of West Knoxville was incorporated in 1888, two years before the Blue-Gray Reunion. Reading the minutes of the West Knoxville City Council from that year until 1897, when the town was annexed by the City of Knoxville, is edifying. The fort is often mentioned, but the comments are hardly sentimental, relaying only factual information about difficulties with road building, additional and high costs of earth removal, problems with steep grades, and the need for retaining walls. Large numbers of houses were being built on the north side of the ridge as witnessed in the Thompson aerial photograph taken in 1922.

Four photographs taken by W. B. Patrick recorded the condition of parts of the fortification that remained in 1901. There is little left of the southwest bastion, but it appears that much of the west wall remains. It is exciting to see the only clean profile cut through that wall known to exist; though eroded, one can see the counterscarp, trench, scarp, and part of the parapet (see figures 47a–d). A photo showing the interior of the fort is very important, as it is the only one known to also show a part of the south wall at any time in the history of that earthwork. The photograph of the northeast bastion and the tract of future 17th Street is significant additional proof as to the correct location of the fort.The 1920s through the early 1930s were the halcyon years for residents of the Fort Sanders neighborhood. The old fort was used for star gazing;

baseball games were played and butterflies collected in the old 1890 amphitheater; and children survived sled rides down 17th Street when there was snow.

After World War II, things changed as veterans entered UT on the GI Bill. Many lived on the Hill in trailers, and houses in Fort Sanders became homes for an increased student population. Expansion of the University of Tennessee campus to the north side of Cumberland Avenue soon followed and began to significantly alter the neighborhood. Many of the original houses were torn down for new buildings, including the White sisters' historic frame house. Others were razed for parking lots and new apartments. Among these were iconic remnants of Knoxville's architectural past. Several houses have been saved by moving them to different locations; many others have lost their exterior architectural integrity through alterations and additions. The interiors of large houses have been modified to create individual apartments for students.

Most UT students who have lived in the Fort Sanders neighborhood are probably somewhat familiar with the Civil War history of this region before they graduate. However, most will leave the university knowing very little about the Civil War in Knoxville and the historic area in which they lived while here. Those who walk the streets of Fort Sanders now are likely to be aware of only two of the three memorials dedicated to soldiers who fought and died here. These two historic markers are located on popular pedestrian and vehicular routes. The United Daughters of the Confederacy memorial, dedicated in 1914, was installed in a grassy area on 17th Street between Laurel and Clinch Avenues. The more noticeable 79th New York Highlanders' monument has stood guard since 1919 in a small, sunny plaza at the intersection of 16th Street and Clinch Avenue. Few people are aware that a beautiful stained-glass window was installed in the Presbyterian Church on Laurel in honor of both Union and Confederate veterans who fought in the battle of Fort Sanders.

We met many older residents and students during the year we lived in Fort Sanders, and many more during the ten years we sang Old Harp shape-note music at the Presbyterian Church on Laurel. After the church burned in 1982, we helped members and supporters of the

Laurel Theater clean the charred wooden trim in the sanctuary. During these times, we had no idea that there had actually been a Civil War fort in the area or that soldiers serving in the war had walked where we walked. Thirty years later, as we examined, measured, excavated, and photographed in the area of Fort Sanders, numerous curious 21st-century residents, young and old, temporary and permanent, asked what we were studying; when told, most were surprised. A few said they had heard that there might have been some kind of old fort and a battle in the neighborhood. Popular knowledge about the fort, or its importance to the Union victory and the ultimate reunification of this country, has not increased much since we lived in the neighborhood in 1965.

For many years there has been a constant refrain that "only the memory remains" of the old fort. Our study confirms that physical remnants of the fort are preserved and visible, and our testing and archival research verify that there are archaeological remnants of the fort, preserved but hidden, beneath the streets, alleys, and yards of 20th-century homes built in the immediate area of the newly-discovered location of Fort Sanders. Twenty-first-century residents and city and county leaders must realize that it is imperative to preserve and honor both the visible and hidden remains of Fort Sanders.

This was a task that late-19th-century Knoxvillians attempted but could not achieve. There is a completed design for a walking tour, prepared by the East Tennessee Community Design Center, which documents the location of the fort, the battle, major players, the soldiers, and the weaponry used. It is past time to honor the four Union soldiers who received Medals of Honor for their service here in 1863. And it is time to honor General Burnside and others who helped win the Battle of Fort Sanders and to mark the actual area where dedicated men fought and died for their beliefs on that freezing November morning in 1863. It is our sincere hope that this book will inspire and motivate those who read it to continue the effort to see that the site and the remnants of Fort Sanders are preserved and properly commemorated for future generations.

REFERENCES CITED

★★★★

Agee, James

1957 *A Death in the Family*. McDowell, Obolenski, New York.

Agnes, Michael (editor)

2003 *Webster's New World Dictionary*. 4th ed. Wiley Publishing, New York.

Akchin, Don and Lisa Akchin

1980 Nomination Form for Fort Sanders Historic District, National Register of Historic Places, National Park Service 4 March. Listed September 16, 1980. National Register #80003839.

Alexander, E. Porter

1962 *Military Memoirs of a Confederate*. Civil War Centennial Series. Indiana University Press, Bloomington.

1989 *Fighting for the Confederacy: The Personal Recollections of General Edward Porter Alexander,* edited by Gary W. Gallagher. University of North Carolina Press, Chapel Hill.

Anderson, Rebecca, Charles H. Faulkner, Richard A. Holt, and Jennifer Luedke

2009 The Lones/Dowell Farm: An Archaeological, Architectural, and Ethnohistorical Study. *Journal of East Tennessee History* 81: 42–57.

Angst, Michael

2012 Report: Archaeological Investigations at Morgan Hill, Site 40KN298, University of Tennessee, Knoxville. Archaeological Research Laboratory, University of Tennessee, Department of Anthropology, Knoxville.

Armour, Robert

1898 The Attack Upon, and Defense of Fort Sanders, Knoxville, Tennessee, November 29, 1863. Paper read before the Military Order of the Loyal Legion of the United States. Commandery of the District of Columbia, War Papers 30.

Army Mailbag

1864 *Army Mailbag* 30 May–6 October 1864. Knoxville, Tennessee.

Aston-Wash, Barbara

1983 Ronald McDonald Haven to Be in 1906 Structure. *Knoxville News-Sentinel* 30 October.

Augustus, Gerald L.

2000 *The Loudon County Area of East Tennessee in the War 1861–1865*. Turner Publishing, Paducah, Kentucky.

2013 *The Battle of Campbell's Station, 16 November 1863*. Cherohala Press, Cleveland, Tennessee.

Avery, Paul G.

2000 *1999 Archaeological Excavations at the Cowan House, 40KN229: Final Report*. Department of Anthropology, University of Tennessee, Knoxville.

Ballard, Michael B.

1997 *A Long Shadow: Jefferson Davis and the Final Days of the Confederacy*. University of Georgia Press, Athens.

Basehart, David

1992 The History of White Columns. Research paper, Department of Anthropology, University of Tennessee, Knoxville.

Bearss, Edwin C.

2006 *Fields of Honor: Pivotal Battles of the Civil War*. National Geographic Society, Washington, D.C.

Beck and Paul

1886 Balloon Map of Knoxville, Tenn. Norris, Wellge, Milwaukee, Wisconsin.

Benjamin, Samuel N.

N.d. Handwritten notes entitled "Fort Sanders." Benjamin Papers, United States Military Academy Library, West Point, New York.

Bentz, Charles and Yong W. Kim, editors.

1993 *The Sevierville Hill Site: A Civil War Union Encampment on the Southern Heights of* Knoxville, *Tennessee*. Tennessee Anthropological Association, Miscellaneous Paper No. 17. Knoxville.

Beyer, Walter F. and Oscar Keydel, editors

1901 *Deeds of Valor: How America's Civil War Heroes Won the Congressional Medal of Honor*. Perrien-Keydel, Detroit, Michigan.

Bible, C. Donahue

2005 The Hanging of the Greene County Bridge Burners. *Tennessee Ancestors* 21(2): 130–38.

2011 Captain Alfred J. "Jim" Lane—Civil War Recruiter and "Pilot." *Tennessee Ancestors* 27(1): 15–26.

Bilby, Joseph

2005 *Civil War Firearms: The Historical Background and Tactical Use.* Da Capo Press, Cambridge, Massachusetts.

Billings, John S.

1870 *A Report on Barracks and Hospitals, with Descriptions of Military Posts.* Government Printing Office, Washington, D.C.

Boatner, Mark M., III

1959 *The Civil War Dictionary.* David McKay, New York.

Booker, Robert

2011 One of the First African Americans to Join the Union Army. *Knoxville News-Sentinel* 2 August.

2015a Gay Street Bridge has Pontoon Roots. *Knoxville News-Sentinel* 27 January.

2015b Knox Took in Rascal Wounded in 1864. *Knoxville News-Sentinel* 26 May.

2017 *An Encyclopedia of Black People in Knoxville, TN 1844–1974.* Russell Printing Options, Knoxville, Tennessee.

Bourasaw, Noel V.

2004 Russell A. Alger, Logging Capitalist, Michigan Governor, Secretary of War. *Skagit River Journal of History & Folklore.* Skagit River Historical Society, La Conner, Washington.

Boyd, James P.

1885 *Military and Civil Life of Gen. Ulysses S. Grant.* P. W. Ziegler, Philadelphia.

Brearley, William H.

1871 *Recollections of the East Tennessee Campaign: Battle of Campbell's Station, 16th November 1863, Siege of Knoxville, 17th November–5th December, 1863.* Tribune Book and Job Office, Detroit, Michigan.

Brennan, Matthew

2005 The Civil War Diet. Master's thesis, Virginia Tech University, Blacksburg, Virginia.

Brewer, Alberta and Carson Brewer

1975 *Valley So Wild: A Folk History.* East Tennessee Historical Society, Knoxville.

Broadwell, Henry J.

1913 Service in the Old Signal Corps. *Knoxville Journal and Tribune* 16 September.

Brown, J. Willard

1974 [1896] *The Signal Corps, U.S.A., in the War of the Rebellion.* United States Veteran Signal Corps Association. Reprint, Arno Press, New York.

Burrage, Henry S.

1866 Retreat from Lenoir's and the Siege of Knoxville. *Atlantic Monthly* 18(105): 21–32.

1884 *History of the Thirty-Sixth Regiment, Massachusetts Volunteers, 1862–1865.* Rockwell and Churchill, Boston.

Burruss, Edward M.

1863 Letter to his father, Rev. John C. Burruss. Burruss Family Papers, Louisiana State University, Baton Rouge.

Carnes, Linda F.

1982 Archaeological and Historical Investigations of the North and South Cisterns, Old City Hall Complex, Knoxville, Tennessee. Department of Anthropology, University of Tennessee, Knoxville.

Carruth, Sumner

1884 *History of the Thirty-Fifth Regiment, Massachusetts Volunteers.* Mills, Knight, Boston.

Carter, William R.

1901 *The History of the First Regiment of the Tennessee Volunteer Cavalry in the Great War of the Rebellion.* Gaut-Ogden, Knoxville, Tennessee.

Catton, Bruce

1969 *Grant Takes Command.* Little, Brown, Boston.

1953 *A Stillness at Appomattox.* Pocket Books, New York.

Cederwald, Major A. A.

1928 The Remount Service Past and Present. *Quartermaster Review* November–December.

Chapman, Charles

1863 Letter to his parents, 28 December.

Charles Waring & Company

1873 Invoice for Excavating Dirt from White's Addition. McClung Collection, Knox County Public Library, Knoxville, Tennessee.

Chattanooga Times

1872 Chattanoogan Taking Notes. 4 June.

Cimbala, Paul A.

2005 *The Freedmen's Bureau: Reconstructing the American South after the Civil War.* Krieger Publishing, Malabar, Florida.

Civil War Journeys

N.d. Civil War Forts. Electronic document at website, http://civil-war-journeys.org/civil_war_forts.htm.

Civil War Trust

2018 Electronic document at website http://www.civilwar.org/learn/articles/civilwar-facts.

Cocroft, Horace E., Jr.

2007 Introduction. *The Art of War* by Antoine Henri de Jomini. Arc Manor, Rockville, Maryland.

Conklin, Forest

2005 East Tennessee Blue and Gray Reunion: Knoxville, 1890. *Tennessee Ancestors* 21(2): 110–16.

Conroy, Sara B.

1954 Old Homes on Forest Suit Residents Well. *Knoxville News Sentinel* 28 March.

Cook, Hollie

2013 Fort Sanders Historic Houses. Knox Heritage files, Knoxville, Tennessee.

Costello, Darcy and Justin Sayers

2017 Confederate Statues in Lexington Removed Tuesday Night in Quick Move. *Louisville Courier Journal* 16 October.

Cotham, Steve

2017 Personal communication.

Coulter, E. Merton

1999 [1937] *William G. Brownlow: Fighting Parson of the Southern Highlands.* University of North Carolina Press, Chapel Hill. Reprint, University of Tennessee Press, Knoxville.

Cox, Karen L.

2003 *Dixie's Daughters: The United Daughters of the Confederacy and the Preservation of Confederate Culture.* University Press of Florida, Gainesville.

Cozzens, Peter

1992 *This Terrible Sound: The Battle of Chickamauga.* University of Illinois Press, Urbana.

1994 *Shipwreck of Their Hopes: The Battle for Chattanooga.* University of Illinois Press, Urbana.

Creekmore, Betsy B.

1976 *Knoxville.* University of Tennessee Press, Knoxville.

Crownover, S. H., M. E. Collins, and D. A. Lietzke

1994 Parent Materials and Stratigraphy of a Doline in the Valley and Ridge Province. *Soil Science Society American Journal* 58: 1738–46.

Crozier

1897 *Crozier's Map of Knoxville, Tennessee and Suburbs.*

Crumley, Carole L. and William H. Marquart, editors

1987 Historical Ecology. *Regional Dynamics: Burgundian Landscapes in Historical Perspective*, 237–64. Academic Press, New York.

Cullum, George W.

1899 A Biographical Register of the Officers and Graduates of the U.S. Military Academy at West Point, N.Y. Supplement, Vol. 4 1890–1900. Edward S. Holden, editor. Riverside Press, Cambridge, Massachusetts. (Commonly known as "Cullum's Register.")

Cutcheon, Byron M.

1904 *The Story of the Twentieth Michigan Infantry: July 15th, 1862, to May 30th, 1865.* Robert Smith Printing, Lansing, Michigan.

1993 [1902] Recollections of Burnside's East Tennessee Campaign of 1863. In *War Papers: Being Papers Read Before the Commandery of the District of Columbia, Military Order of the Loyal Legion of the United States*, vol. 2, paper no. 39, pp. 283–99. Reprint, Broadfoot Publishing, Wilmington, North Carolina.

Dana, Charles A.

1996 [1902] *Recollections of the Civil War.* D. Appleton, New York. Reprint, University of Nebraska Press, Lincoln.

Davidson, James F.

1963 Michigan and the Defense of Knoxville. *East Tennessee Historical Society Publications* 35: 21–53.

Davis, Keith F.

1990 *George N. Barnard, Photographer of Sherman's Campaign.* University of New Mexico Press, Albuquerque.

Davis, Lee

1934 Fort Sanders Guns Boomed 71 Years Ago. *Knoxville News Sentinel* 25 November.

Deadrick, Lucille, editor

1976 *Heart of the Valley.* East Tennessee Historical Society, Knoxville.

Dickert, D. Augustus

1990 [1899] *History of Kershaw's Brigade.* Elbert H. Aull, Newberry, South Carolina. Reprint, Broadfoot Publishing, Wilmington, North Carolina.

Dodge, Russ

2000 General Davis Tillson. *Find a Grave,* Lehi, Utah. http://sites.rootsweb.com/~obituary.

2001 Joseph S. Manning. *Find a Grave,* Lehi, Utah. http://sites.rootsweb.com/~obituary.

Dowell, Mary

1986 Personal communication.

Dryden, Drury F.

1989 Civil War Letters from Tennessee: Drury F. Dryden, 19th Independent Battery, Ohio Light Artillery, U.S.A. *Tennessee Ancestors* 5(1): 5–10.

Duke, Basil W.

1960 *A History of Morgan's Cavalry.* Indiana University Press, Bloomington.

Dykeman, Wilma

1965 [1955] *The French Broad.* Rinehart, New York. Reprint, University of Tennessee Press, Knoxville.

Edwards, Lawrence

1976 *Bits of Memory.* Times Printing, Montevallo, Alabama.

Eicher, John H. and David J. Eicher

2001 *Civil War High Commands.* Stanford University Press, Stanford, California.

Ellis, Daniel

1867 *Thrilling Adventures of the Great Union Guide of East Tennessee.* New York.

Encyclopedia Britannica

2015 Loess. Electronic document, accessed athttp://www.britannica.com/EBchecked/topic/346022/loess/4270/Origin-and-age.

Erskine, Albert R

1918 *History of the Studebaker Corporation.* South Bend, Indiana.

Faulkner, Charles H.

N.d. Audio recording: Field notes a probable brick bake oven exposed by construction at the Duncan Law School building, May 29, 1992.

2017 Slavery in Knoxville, Tennessee: In but Not Entirely of the South. In *Slavery in the City: Architecture and Landscapes of Urban Slavery in North America,* edited by Clifton Ellis and Rebecca Ginsburg, pp. 123–39. University of Virginia Press, Charlottesville.

Faulkner, Terry

1992 A Brief History of Kingston Pike and One of Its Early Historical Farms—The Prater Place. *Tennessee Ancestors* 8(2):

Fenneman, Nevin M.

1938 *Physiography of the Eastern United States.* McGraw-Hill, New York.

Ferguson, Don K.

2011 Masonic Temple Built Atop Field Known as the "Rose Hole." *Knoxville News-Sentinel* 16 October.

Field, Ron

2005 *American Civil War Fortifications* 2. Osprey Publishing, Oxford, U.K.

Fink, Harold S.

1957 The East Tennessee Campaign and the Battle of Knoxville in 1863. *East Tennessee Historical Society Publications* 29: 79–117.

1965 *The Battle of Knoxville*. The Knoxville-Knox County Civil War Centennial Committee.

Flory, Josh

2013 Campus Renovation. *Knoxville News Sentinel* 12 March.

Foote, Shelby

1958 *The Civil War, A Narrative: Fort Sumter to Perryville*. Random House, New York.

Foss, John E.

2012 Preliminary Soils Investigation of the Fort Sanders Area, Knoxville, Tennessee. Draft copy.

Foster, Gaines M.

1987 *Ghosts of the Confederacy: Defeat, the Lost Cause, and the Emergence of the New South, 1865–1913*. Oxford University Press, New York.

Foster, John W.

1863 Letter to his family, 2 September 1863. (In Temple 1899, pp. 478–480).

Fox, Wells B.

1892 *What I Remember About the Great Rebellion*. Darius Thorpe, Lansing, Michigan.

Gallagher, Gary W.

2001 When Lee Was Mortal. In *With My Face to the Enemy: Perspectives on the Civil War*, edited by Robert Cowley, pp. 245–60. Berkley Books, New York.

Gallagher, Gary W., editor

1999 *Three Days at Gettysburg*. Kent State University, Kent, Ohio.

Gallagher, Gary W. and Alan T. Noble, editors

2000 *The Myth of the Lost Cause and Civil War History*. Indiana University Press, Bloomington.

Garrow, Patrick H.

2000 Urban Archaeology in Tennessee: Exploring the Cities of the Old

South. In *Archaeology of Southern Landscapes,* Amy L. Young, editor. pp. 192–216. University of Alabama Press, Tuscaloosa.

Goodspeed Publishing Company

1974 *Goodspeed's History of Hamilton, Knox and Shelby Counties of Tennessee.* Reprinted from *Goodspeed's History,* 1887. Charles and Randy Elder Booksellers, Nashville.

Gordon, John B.

1904 *Reminiscences of the Civil War.* Charles Scribner's Sons, New York.

Granberry, J. A. H.

1910 The Assault on Fort Sanders. *Confederate Veteran* 18:24–25.

Grant, Ulysses S.

1886 *Personal Memoirs.* 2 volumes. Charles L. Webster, New York.

Green, John W.

1947 *Bench and Bar of Knox County, Tennessee.* Archer and Smith, Knoxville.

Greene, William

1858 *Being a Treatise on Rifles, Cannons, and Sporting Arms, explaining the Principles of Gunnery and describing the newest Improvements in Firearms.* Elder and Company, London.

Greguras, Fred

2005 *Spanish-American War Camps 1898–1899 Period.* Los Altos, California.

Groce, W. Todd

1999 *Mountain Rebels: East Tennessee Rebels and the Civil War, 1860–1870.* University of Tennessee Press, Knoxville.

Groom, Winston

2012 Sherman's Folly at Shiloh. *MHQ: The Quarterly Journal of Military History* February 2012. Electronic document, accessed at *History Net* http://www.historynet.com/shermans-folly-at-shiloh.htm.

Gugliotta, Guy

2012 New Estimate Raises Civil War Death Toll. *New York Times* 12 April.

Hacker, J. David

2011 A Census-Based Count of the Civil War Dead. *Civil War History* 57(4): 307–48.

Hafendorfer, Kenneth A.

2001 *Mill Springs: Campaign and Battle of Mill Springs, Kentucky.* KH Press, Louisville, Kentucky.

Hallowed Ground

2013 Saving History for Generations: The Creation of the First Civil War Military Park. 14(3): 14–15.

Hardy, William E.

2007 *Historic Photos of Knoxville.* Turner Publishing, Nashville.

Harris, Gordon

2014 A Civil War Hero from Ipswich. In *Stories from Ipswich*, pp.1–4.

Hatcher, Robert

2012a Personal communication, 22 August.

2012b Personal communication, 21 September.

Hatfield, Edward A.

2018 "Freeman's Bureau." New Georgia Encyclopedia 24 September 2015.

Hathaway, Herman

1971 Clio's Southern Soldiers: The United Confederate Veterans and History. *Louisiana History* 12(3): 213–42.

Hayden, René, Anthony E. Kaye, Kate Masur, Steven F. Miller, Susan E. O'Donovan, Leslie S. Rowland, and Stephen A. West, editors

2013 *Land and Labor, 1866–1867.* Ser. 3, vol. 2, of *Freedom: A Documentary History of Emancipation, 1861–1867.* University of North Carolina Press, Chapel Hill.

Heck, Frank H.

1976 *Proud Kentuckian: John C. Breckinridge, 1821–1875.* University Press of Kentucky, Lexington.

Heidler, David S. and Jeanna T. Heidler, editors

2000 Edward Porter Alexander. In *Encyclopedia of the American Civil War: A Political, Social, and Military History.* W. W. Norton, New York.

2000 The War of the Rebellion (Official Records). In *Encyclopedia of the American Civil War: A Political, Social, and Military History.* W. W. Norton, New York.

Hess, Earl J.

2012 *The Knoxville Campaign: Burnside and Longstreet in East Tennessee.* University of Tennessee Press, Knoxville.

Holt, Edgar A.

1981 *Claiborne County.* Tennessee County History Series. Joy Bailey Dunn, editor. Memphis State University Press, Memphis, Tennessee.

Hoobler, Dorothy and Thomas Hoobler

1977 *Photographing History: The Career of Matthew Brady.* Putnam, New York.

Hoobler, James

1986 T. M. Schleier, Photographer. *Tennessee Historical Quarterly* 45(3): 230–43.

Hood, Robert N.

1890 Letter and memorandum from Robert N. Hood to Leonidas Houk, 25 January.

Horn, Stanley

1906 *Battles and Sketches of the Army of Tennessee.* Missouri Printing and Publishing, Mexico, Missouri.

Houck, Michael

1864 The Diary of Michael Houck, Nineteenth Ohio Battery, Second Division, Twenty-Third Army Corps. Typed copy.

Howard, Beau

1999 City Council Votes for Renovation. *Daily Beacon* 12 February. Student newspaper, University of Tennessee, Knoxville.

Huddart, William A.

1863 Letter to his father, 13 December.

Hughs, Ina

2005 A Little Comfort in Crisis. *Knoxville News-Sentinel* 8 March.

Humes, Thomas William

1888 *The Loyal Mountaineers of Tennessee.* Ogden Brothers, Knoxville, Tennessee.

Jankoski, Paul

2014 *Verdun: The Longest Battle of the Great War.* Oxford University Press, Oxford, U.K.

Johnson, Robert U. and Clarence C. Buel, editors

1887 *Battles and Leaders of the Civil War.* Vol. 3. Century Company, New York.

Johnson, Swafford

2012 *Great Battles of the Civil War.* World Publications Group, East Bridgewater, Massachusetts.

Jomini, Baron Antoine-Henri de

2007 [1836] *The Art of War*, 3rd ed. Translated by G. H. Mendell and W. P. Craighill. Arc Manor, Rockville, Maryland. (Original French edition, 1836; first English translation, 1862).

Jones, Olive and Catherine Sullivan

1985 *The Parks Canada Glass Glossary.* Parks Canada, Ottawa.

Karnes, Steven and Ronald S. Coddington

N.d. *Headquarters for Pictures: The Life and Times of Tennessee Photographer Theodore M. Schleier.* McClung Collection, Knox County Public Library, Knoxville, Tennessee.

Kelly, Dorothy E.

2002 Sanders' Raid. *North and South* 6(1): 76–86.

2013 William Sanders: Union General Died to Buy Time for Knoxville Fortifications. *Knoxville News Sentinel* 24 November.

Klein, Maury

1971 The Knoxville Campaign. *Civil War Times Illustrated* November: 40–42.

Knight, Glenn B.

N.d. *Brief History of the Grand Army of the Republic.* Sons of Union Veterans of the Civil War, website. Electronic document accessed at http://www.suvcw.org.

Knox County Register of Deeds

1898 Warranty Deed 155, from M. C. White to George W. Pickell [*sic*]. Register of Deeds, Knox County Courthouse, Knoxville, Tennessee.

Knox Heritage, Inc.

N.d. Fort Sanders Historic Homes. Write-up for the neighborhood tour. Archival collection.

1981 *Historic Fort Sanders: A Walking Tour of the Neighborhood.* Knoxville City Council, Knoxville City-County, Knoxville, Tennessee.

Knoxville City Directories

1888–1922 City Directories of Knoxville, Tennessee.

Knoxville Daily Chronicle

1897–1917 Knoxville City-County Minutes, Knoxville City-County Building, Knoxville, Tennessee.

1873 15 June.

Knoxville Daily Journal

1889 In Fort Sanders. 18 September.

1890a 24 January.

1890b 5 October.

1890c 6 October.

1890d 7 October.

1890e 8 October.

1890f 9 October.

Knoxville Daily Journal and Tribune

1903 Only Traces Remain of Old Fort. 29 November.

1913 Recount Experiences of Civil War Days. 16 September.

Knoxville Daily Register

1862 12 December.

1863a March.

1863b 23 June.

Knoxville Daily Tribune

1892 West Knoxville. 24 December.

Knoxville Journal

1894 Michael Hoey Is Dead. Obituary. 11 September.

1895 14th Annual Encampment of the Sons of Veterans. 11–18 September.

1898a Pulpit Work in Brief. 5 December.

1898b New Church Ready. 18 December.

1898c New Fort Sanders Church Dedicated. 19 December.

1930 Hold Carson Rite Today. 7 February.

Knoxville News Sentinel

1922 28 November.

1934 Fort Sander's Guns Boomed 71 Years Ago. 25 November.

1948 Hack with Bells on It Once Provided Transportation for West Knoxville Folk. 12 December.

2012 Restless Giant in Local Affairs. 24 April.

2013 UT Gets OK to Buy, Demolish Historic Houses. 23 May.

Knoxville Press and Herald

1872 About Knoxville. 7 April.

Knoxville Sentinel

1898 New Fort Sanders Church. 28 November.

1914a Unveil Monument on Fort Sanders to Honor Memory of Fallen Confederates. 28 November.

1914b Battle of Fort Sanders. 29 November.

1917 Knoxville Bar Pays Tribute to the Memory of the Late General G. W. Pickle, Eminent Attorney. 24 April.

Knoxville Tribune

1887 Street Railway. 10 November.

1890a Blue-Gray Reunion. 6 October.

Knoxville Weekly Chronicle

1874 8 July.

Knoxville Whig and Rebel Ventilator

1861 14 September.

1864a Taking Churches and Houses. 9 January.

1864b Enlistment of Negroes. 9 January.

1864c Hanging a Spy. 9 January.

1864d 5 March.

1864e 2 October.

Langston, Phillip

2000 *Tennessee: A Political History*. Hillsboro Press, Franklin, Tennessee.

Lanning, Michael Lee

2007 *The Civil War 100*. Sourcebooks, Naperville, Illinois.

Lindsley, John B.

1886 *The Military Annals of Tennessee, Confederate*. J. M. Lindsley, Nashville.

Locker, Richard

2015 UT Buys White Avenue House for $1.1M. *Knoxville News Sentinel* 12 February.

Long, E. B.

1971 *The Civil War Day by Day: An Almanac, 1861–1865.* Doubleday, Garden City, New York.

Longstreet, James

1896 *From Manassas to Appomattox.* J. B. Lippincott, Philadelphia.

Longstreet, Stephen A.

1952 *A Century on Wheels: The Story of Studebaker; A History, 1852–1952.* Henry Holt, New York.

Luckett, William

1964 Cumberland Gap National Historical Park. *Tennessee Historical Quarterly* 23(4): 303–20.

Madden, David

1980–81 Union Resistance to Confederate Occupation: The Bridge Burners of East Tennessee. *East Tennessee Historical Society Publications* 52–53: 22–40.

Mahan, D. H.

1848 *Treatise on Field Fortification.* John Wiley, New York.

Marcot, Roy A.

1995 *Spencer Repeating Firearms.* Northwood Heritage Press, Irvine, California.

Marvel, William

1991 *Burnside.* University of North Carolina Press, Chapel Hill.

Mason, D.

2000 *Verdun.* Windrush Press, Moreton-in-Marsh, U.K.

Matthes, François

1939 Report of the Committee on Glaciers. *Transactions of the American Geophysical Union* 20: 513–23.

Maynard, W. Barksdale

2012 Civil War Fort at Jamestown Is Dug Up to Get at 1607 Site. *Washington Post* 7 May.

McCrary, Frank and Enoch Lloyd Branson

1889 *Souvenir—Knoxville, Tenn.* A. Witterman, Importer, New York.

McKenzie, Robert T.

2006 *Lincolnites and Rebels: A Divided Town in the American Civil War.* Oxford University Press, New York.

McNabb, William R.

1991 *Tradition, Innovation and Romantic Images: The Architecture of Historic Knoxville.* Frank A. McClung Museum, Knoxville, Tennessee.

McPherson, James M.

1991 *The Negro's Civil War.* Ballantine Books, New York.

2003 *Battle Cry of Freedom: The Civil War Era.* 2nd ed. Oxford University Press, New York.

McRary, Amy

2012a Makeshift Hospitals. *Knoxville News Sentinel* 1 April.

2012b Born a Slave, Cal Johnson Became a Wealthy Generous Businessman. *Knoxville News Sentinel* 30 December.

2012c Tributes to Sacrifice. *Knoxville News Sentinel* 1 April.

Merriam-Webster Dictionary

2017 Online edition, accessed at www.merriam-webster.com

Michigan Historical Commission

1924 *Michigan Biographies: Russell Alger.* Lansing, Michigan.

Military Times

2014 Hall of Valor: Awards and Citations. Electronic document, accessed at https://valor.militarytimes.com/

Miller, Ernest I.

1957 *The Valley of Tennessee in the Civil War.* Cincinnati Civil War Roundtable, Cincinnati, Ohio.

Miller, Francis T., editor

1957 *The Photographic History of the Civil War: The Cavalry.* Pt. 4. Castle Books, New York.

Miller, H. C.

1914 *First O.V.H.A., Company "M."* Toledo, Ohio.

Moore, Palmyra

N.d. How Clean is Clean? Testing the McKellar Hypothesis. Research paper, Department of Anthropology, University of Tennessee, Knoxville.

Mosier, John

2006 *Grant.* St. Martin's Press, New York.

Mussey, R. D.

1864 Report from R. D. Mussey, Colonel, 100th United States Colored Infantry to Major C. W. Foster, Assistant Adjutant-General, Chief of the Colored Bureau. Nashville, Tennessee. Electronic document, accessed at *Lest We Forget*. http://lestweforget.hamptonu.edu/page.cfm?

Myers, Robert P.

N.d. Diary of Assistant Surgeon Robert P. Myers, Eleanor S. Brockenbrough Library, The Museum of the Confederacy, Richmond, Virginia.

Nashville Daily Union

1864 13 December.

National Archives

1864 *Bread and Bread Making*. Washington, D.C.

National Park Service

N.d. *Civil War Defenses of Washington*. United States Department of the Interior, Washington, D.C.

Neely, Jack

1999 *The Marble City: A Photographic Tour of Knoxville's Graveyards*. University of Tennessee Press, Knoxville.

2003 One More Loss. *Metro Pulse* 10 July.

2015 Scruffy Citizen: General Pickle's "Fort Sanders Hill" Is Apparently Doomed. *Knoxville Mercury*, 21 October.

New England Press Association Album

N.d. Photographs taken ca. 1880 by New England Press Association members on a group tour to North Carolina, Tennessee, Virginia, and Maryland. ImageBase, Virginia Tech, Blacksburg, Virginia. Accessed at https://imagebase.lib.vt.edu/browse.php?folio_ID=/cw/new

New World Encyclopedia

2017 Online edition, accessed at www.newworldencyclopedia.org

New York Times

1925 Obituary of Jos. I. C. Clarke. 28 February.

Newman, Dean

1939 *Cavalcade*. Vol.27, August.

Noe, Kenneth W.

2001 *Perryville: This Grand Havoc of Battle*. University Press of Kentucky, Lexington.

Noe, Kenneth W., editor

1996 *A Southern Boy in Blue, The Memoirs of Marcus Woodcock, 9th Kentucky Infantry, USA*. University of Tennessee Press, Knoxville.

Noel Hume, Ivor

1969 *Historical Archaeology*. Alfred A. Knopf, New York.

Nolan, Jacqueline V. and Edward J. Redmond

2012 Civil War Cartography, Then and Now. *LCM: Library of Congress Magazine* November/December:12–13.

Norrell, Kelly

2017 Civil War Site Marked at Third Creek Greenway. *Bearden Shopper News* 8 March.

Norris, Robert

1982 Story Time: Legacy of Family, Home Preserved. *Knoxville News Sentinel* 19 January.

Nosworthy, Brent

2003 *The Bloody Crucible of Courage*. Carroll & Graf, New York.

2008 *Roll Call to Destiny*. Carroll & Graf, New York.

Osborne, William H.

1877 *The History of the Twenty-ninth Regiment of the Massachusetts Volunteer Infantry in the Late War of the Rebellion*. Albert J. Wright, Boston.

O'Steen, Neal

1994 *The Second 50 Years: 1844–1894*. University of Tennessee, Knoxville.

Paige, John C. and Jerome A. Greene

1983 *Administrative History of Chickamauga and Chattanooga National Military Park*. National Park Service, Denver, Colorado.

Parker, Ezra

1913 *Personal Narratives of Events in the War of the Rebellion*. Rhode Island Soldiers and Sailors Historical Society, Providence, Rhode Island.

Poe, Orlando M.

1888 The Defense of Knoxville. In *Battles and Leaders in the Civil War*. Vol. 3, pp. 731–45. Century Company, New York.

Pollard, Edward A.

1866 *The Lost Cause: A New History of the War of the Confederates.* E. B. Treat, New York.

1992 *Mathew Brady.* PG Press, East Bridgeport, Connecticut.

Poore, Ben Perley

1882 *The Life and Public Services of Ambrose E. Burnside, Soldier–Citizen–Statesman.* J. A. and R. A. Reid, Providence, Rhode Island.

Purcell, Aaron D.

2007 *University of Tennessee.* Campus History Series. Arcadia Publishing, Charleston, South Carolina.

Ramage, James A.

1986 *Rebel Raider: The Life of John Hunt Morgan.* University Press of Kentucky, Lexington.

Rathje, William L. and Michael B. Schiffer

1982 *Archaeology.* Harcourt College Publications, New York.

Revere, Ray

1960 A History of Fort Sanders, Wyoming. MA thesis, University of Wyoming, Laramie.

Richmond Whig

1864 Special Correspondent from Longstreet's Army, December 11, 1863, Near Rogersville, East Tenn. 5 January.

Robbins, William M.

2004 [1887] From Chattanooga to Knoxville with Longstreet's Corps. *Philadelphia Weekly Times* 18 December 1887. Reprinted in *The New Annals of the Civil War.* Peter Cozzens and Robert I. Girardi, eds., pp. 345–51. Stackpole Books, Mechanicsburg, Pennsylvania.

Roberts, Wayne D. and Charles H. Faulkner

1984 Resource Survey of the Proposed Pellissippi Parkway Extension, Knox and Blount Counties, Tennessee. Submitted to the Tennessee Department of Transportation. Department of Anthropology, University of Tennessee, Knoxville.

Robertson, James I.

1984 *Tenting Tonight: The Soldier's Life.* Time-Life Books, Alexandria, Virginia.

Roddy, Pat, Jr.

1983 *75 Years of Refreshment.* S. B. Newman Printing, Knoxville, Tennessee.

Roemer, Jacob

1897 *Reminiscences of the War of the Rebellion 1861–1865.* L. A. Turney, editor. Estate of Jacob Roemer, Flushing, New York.

Rogers, Joseph L.

1864 Letter from Joseph L. Rogers to his wife, 27 January 1864.

Rothrock, Mary U., editor

1946 *The French Broad–Holston Country.* East Tennessee Historical Society, Knoxville.

Rule, William

1900 *Standard History of Knoxville.* Lewis Publishing, Chicago.

Sanborn Insurance Company

1917 *Map of Knoxville, Tennessee.*

Schmid, Cindy.

2017 George N. Barnard. In Georgia. *New Georgia Encyclopedia,* (last edited January 9, 2017). Electronic document, accessed at http://www.georgiaencyclopedia.org/articles/history-archaeology/george-n-barnard-georgia

Sealy, John, Dot Kelly, and Jim Tumblin

N.d. The Fairgrounds. Unpublished research paper.

Seymour, Digby

1963 *Divided Loyalties: Fort Sanders and the War in East Tennessee.* University of Tennessee Press, Knoxville.

2008 Personal communication.

Shaver, Lewellyn A.

N.d. History of the Sixteenth Alabama Regiment, Gracie's Alabama Brigade.

Sheridan, Phillip H.

1888 *Personal Memoirs of P. H. Sheridan.* 2 vols. Charles L. Webster, New York.

Sherman, William T.

1875 *Memoirs of William T. Sherman.* 2 vols. D. Appleton, New York.

Sidlo, Sid

2008 *The Sharpshooter and His Weapon.* Cleveland Civil War Roundtable, Cleveland, Ohio.

Siegel, Mark

1975 A House on the Hill at the Turn of the Century; Miss Katherine Carson Tells Her Story. *Longstreet Journal* 29 November.

Slaby, M. J.

2015 Moving Day at Last. *Knoxville News Sentinel* 25 July 2015.

Smith, David C.

1999 *Campaign to Nowhere: The Results of General Longstreet's Move into Upper East Tennessee.* Strawberry Plains Press, Strawberry Plains, Tennessee.

Smith, Samuel D. and Benjamin C. Nance

2003 *A Survey of Civil War Era Military Sites in Tennessee.* Research Series No. 14. Tennessee Division of Archaeology, Nashville.

Smith, Steven D.

1994 Archaeological Perspectives on the Civil War: The Challenge to Archive Relevance. In *Look to the Earth: Historical Archaeology and the American Civil War.* Clarence R. Geier Jr. and Susan W. Winter editors. pp. 3–20. University of Tennessee Press, Knoxville.

Smith, Wendy

2015 Confederate Cemetery Nominated to Historic Register. *Bearden Shopper News* 28 January.

Sorrel, G. Moxley

1905 *Recollections of a Confederate Staff Officer.* Neale Publishing, New York.

Stamper, James C.

2007 *Felix K. Zollicoffer: Tennessee Editor, Politician, and Soldier.* Wayne County Museum, Monticello, Kentucky.

Steely, Mike

2017 Third Creek Civil War Fort Dedicated. *Knoxville Focus Connections* 13 March.

Stern, Philip Van Doren

1961 [1886] *Soldier Life in the Union and Confederate Armies.* J. H. Brown, New York. Indiana University Press, Bloomington.

Stocker, Jeffry D. (editor)

1996 *From Huntsville to Appomattox: R. T. Coles's History of the 4th Regiment Alabama Volunteer Infantry, C.S.A., Army of Northern Virginia.* University of Tennessee Press, Knoxville.

Streip, Drew

2009 Thompson Photos Helped Sway Congress. *Knoxville News Sentinel* 26 April.

Sutherland, Daniel E., editor

1996 *A Very Violent Rebel: The Civil War Diary of Ellen Renshaw House.* University of Tennessee Press, Knoxville.

Swain, Craig

2013 Sandbagging on Morris Island . . . 46,175 sandbags to be exact. *To the Sound of the Guns* 26 July. Electronic journal article (blog), accessed at https://markerhunter.wordpress.com/2013/07/26/sandbag-morris-island/

Swift, Fredrick W.

1863 The Diary of Fredrick William Swift, January 31, 1831–January 30, 1916. Transcribed by Nancy Platt.

Tarrant, Sergeant Eastham

1894 *The Wild Riders of the First Kentucky Cavalry: A History of the Regiment, in the Great War of the Rebellion, 1861–1865.* Published by a Committee of the Regiment. Press of R. H. Carothers, Louisville, Kentucky.

Taylor, Paul

2009 *Orlando M. Poe: Civil War General and Great Lakes Engineer.* Kent State University, Kent, Ohio.

Temple, Oliver P.

1899 *East Tennessee and the Civil War.* Robert Clarke, Cincinnati, Ohio.

Templeton, Lucy

1949 Onetime Palatial West Knoxville Homes Have Been Converted into Apartments. *Knoxville News Sentinel* 16 January.

Thomas, Edison H.

2014 *John Hunt Morgan and His Raiders.* University Press of Kentucky, Lexington.

Thomas, Emory M.

1995 *Robert E. Lee: A Biography.* W. W. Norton, New York.

Thompson, B. F.

1885 *History of the 112th Regiment of the Illinois Volunteer Infantry in the Great War of the Rebellion, 1862–1865.* Stark County News Office, Toulon, Illinois.

Todd, William

1886 *The Seventy-ninth Highlanders New York Volunteers in the War of the Rebellion.* Barnlow, Barton, Albany, New York.

Towler, Mary Anna

1962 Apartments Rise in the U-T Section, Once an Area of Proud Homes. *Knoxville News Sentinel* 25 November.

Troll, Carl

2007 The Geographic Landscape and Its Investigation. In *Foundation Papers in Landscape Ecology.* John A. Wiens, Michael R. Moss, Monica Turner, and David J. Mladenoff, editors. pp. 71–101. Columbia University Press, New York.

Trudeau, Noah A.

1993 *The Last Citadel: Petersburg, June 1864–April 1865.* Louisiana University Press, Baton Rouge, Louisiana.

Tumblin, Jim

2012 Tragedy at Melrose Estate. *Bearden Shopper News* 13 February.

2013a A Tale of Two Monuments. *Bearden Shopper News* 14 January.

2013b Longstreet's Long Battle. *Bearden Shopper News* 9 September.

2013c Burnside's Journey to Knoxville. *Bearden Shopper News* 14 October.

United States War Department

1880–1901 *The War of the Rebellion: A Compilation of the Official Records of the Union and Confederate Armies, 1880–1901.* 128 vols. (Abbreviated as *OR* for in-text references within the main body of this book. Individual volumes cited there are listed below, series 1 unless otherwise noted.)

1882 Vol.4, Chap. 12. Operations in Kentucky and Tennessee. July 1–November 19, 1861.

1882 Vol. 7, Chap. 17. Operations in Kentucky, Tennessee, North Alabama, and Southwest Virginia. November 19, 1861–March 4, 1862.

1886 Vol. 16, in Two Parts. Operations in Kentucky, Middle and East Tennessee, North Alabama, and Southwest Virginia. June 10–October 31, 1862.

1889 Vol. 23, Chap. 35, in Two Parts. Operations in Kentucky, Middle and East Tennessee, Northern Alabama, Southwest Virginia. January 21–August 10, 1863.

1890 Vol. 31, Chap. 43, in Three Parts. Operations in Kentucky, Southwest Virginia, Tennessee, Mississippi, Northern Alabama, North Georgia. October 20–December 31, 1863.

1891 Vol. 32, Chap. 44, in Three Parts. Operations in Kentucky, Southwest Virginia, Tennessee, Mississippi, Alabama, North Georgia. January 1–April 30, 1864.

1892 Vol. 39, Chap. 51, in Three Parts. Operations in Kentucky, Southwest Virginia, Tennessee, Mississippi, Alabama, and North Georgia (the Atlanta Campaign excepted). May 1–November 13, 1864.

1894 Vol. 45, Chap. 57, in Two Parts. Operations in Kentucky, Southwest Virginia, Tennessee, Mississippi, Alabama, and North Georgia. November 14, 1864–January 22, 1865.

1897 Vol. 49, Chap. 61, in Two Parts. Operations in Kentucky, Southwest Virginia, Tennessee, Northern and Central Georgia, Mississippi, Alabama, and West Florida, January, 1–June 30, 1865.

1898 Vol. 52, Chap. 64, in Two Parts. January 1861–June, 1865. Supplement Operations in Southwest Virginia, Tennessee, Mississippi, Alabama, West Florida, and North Georgia. January 1, 1861–June 30, 1865.

1900 Series 3, Vol. 4. January 1, 1864–April 30, 1865.

Van Horne, Thomas B.

1875 *History of the Army of the Cumberland.* 2 vols. Robert Clarke, Cincinnati, Ohio.

Varon, E.

2018 Dictionary of Virginia Biography. Joseph T. Wilson (1837–1890). Retrieved from: http://www.EncyclopediaVirginia.org/Wilson_Joseph_T_1837-1890

2018 Joseph T. Wilson (1837–1890). *Dictionary of Virginia Biography, EncyclopediaVirginia.* Accessed at http://www.EncyclopediaVirginia.org/Wilson_Joseph_T_1837-1890

Veal, Jennie Frankenberg

2013 Sacred Ground: History Lives on at Crawford Springs in Chickamauga, Georgia. *Nooga.com.* Electronic document, accessed at http://nooga.com/163473/sacred-ground-history-lives-on-at-crawfish-springs-in-chickamauga-ga/

Walcott, Charles F.

1882 *History of the Twenty-first Regiment, Massachusetts Volunteers.* Houghton, Mifflin, Boston.

Walker, Bill

2002 *Find a Grave, Rootsweb.com.* Accessed at http://www.findagrave.com

Watkins, John

1863a Letter to Sara Probert, 15 December 1863.

1863b Letter to Sara Probert, 18 September 1863.

1895 Letter to his wife, 19 September 1895.

Wells, Kendall G.

N.d. Albert Miller Lea and the Holston Glass Factory. Research paper, Department of Anthropology, University of Tennessee, Knoxville.

Werner, Craig R.

2006 *A Change Is Gonna Come: Music, Race, and the Soul of America.* Rev. ed. University of Michigan Press, Ann Arbor.

Welsh, Danette

2013 African American Soldiers Buried in the Knoxville National Cemetery. *Tennessee Ancestors* 29(2):

Wert, Jeffrey

1993 *General James Longstreet: The Confederacy's Most Controversial Soldier; A Biography.* Simon and Schuster, New York.

West Knoxville, City of

1889 Charter of West Knoxville, and the Compilation of Ordinances. Ogden Brothers, Knoxville.

1888–97 City Council Minutes. 3 vols.: 1888–1889, 1890–1895, 1895–1897.

Wheeler, William B.

2005 *Knoxville, Tennessee: A Mountain City in the New South.* 2nd ed. University of Tennessee Press, Knoxville.

White, Chloe

2009 Life in the Trenches. *Knoxville News Sentinel* 5 September.

Wicklund, Doug and Michael Williams

2017 Sureshot: Confederate Sharpshooters Left No Doubt the Whitworth Was Their Weapon of Choice – When Available. *American Civil War Magazine* November

Williams, George W.

1882 *The History of the Negro Race in America, 1619–1880.* J. B. Putnam and Sons, New York.

1888 *History of the Negro Troops in the War of the Rebellion, 1861–1865.* Harper and Brothers, Franklin Square, New York.

Wilson, James G. and John Fiske, editors

1889 *Cyclopedia of American Biography.* Vol. 6. D. Appleton, New York.

Wilson, Joseph T.

1888 *The Black Phalanx: A History of the Negro Soldiers of the United States in the Wars of 1775–1812, 1861–1865.* American Publishing, Hartford, Connecticut.

Winik, Jay

2001 *April 1865: The Month That Saved America.* HarperCollins, New York.

Woodbury, Augustus

1867 *Major General Ambrose E. Burnside and the Ninth Army Corps.* S. Rider and Bros., Providence, Rhode Island.

Woodhead, Edward

1996 *Arms and Equipment of the Union.* Borders Press, Ann Arbor, Michigan.

Worsham, W. J.

1902 *The Old Nineteenth Tennessee Regiment*. Paragon Printing, Knoxville.

Yoe, Della

1949 Among Residents of West Knoxville Author Washington Irwin's Godchild. *Knoxville Sentinel* January.

INDEX

★★★★

Page numbers in **boldface** refer to photographs; *italics* refer to maps.